Film

World

Talking Images Series

edited by Yann Perreau

Series ISSN 1744-9901

Previously published in this series

Cinema: The Archaeology of Film & the Memory of a Century Jean-Luc Godard
&
Youssef Ishaghpour

Visions of England: Class & Culture in Contemporary Cinema Paul Dave

Film Fables Jacques Rancière

The Hollywood Interviews Cahiers du cinéma

Film
World

*Interviews With
Cinema's Leading
Directors*

Michel Ciment

Translated by
Julie Rose

Oxford • New York

First published in France, 2003, by Editions Stock as *Petite planète cinématographique*

English Edition
Berg
Editorial offices:
1st Floor, Angel Court, 81 St Clements Street, Oxford, OX4 1AW, UK
175 Fifth Avenue, New York, NY 10010, USA

Ouvrage publié avec le soutien du Centre nationale du livre – ministère français chargé de la culture.
This work is published with the support of the Centre nationale du livre – the French Ministry of Culture

This book is supported by the French Ministry of Foreign Affairs, as part of the Burgess programme run by the Cultural Department of the French Embassy in London (www.frenchbooknews.com)

Liberté • Égalité • Fraternité
RÉPUBLIQUE FRANÇAISE

Berg is the imprint of Oxford International Publishers Ltd.

Library of Congress Cataloguing-in-Publication Data

Petite planète cinématographique. English
  Film world : interviews with cinema's leading directors / Michel Ciment ;
translated by Julie Rose.—English ed.
      p. cm.—(Talking images series)
    Includes bibliographical references and index.
    ISBN-13: 978-1-84520-458-7 (pbk. : alk. paper)
    ISBN-10: 1-84520-458-1 (pbk. : alk. paper)
    ISBN-13: 978-1-84520-457-0 (cloth : alk. paper)
    ISBN-10: 1-84520-457-3 (cloth : alk. paper)
  1. Motion picture producers and directors—Interviews. I. Ciment, Michel,
1938- II. Rose, Julie. III. Title.
  PN1998.2.P4913 2009
  791.4302'33'0922—dc22

                                                                    2009011737

British Library Cataloguing-in-Publication Data

A catalogue record for this book is available from the British Library.

ISBN 978 184520 457 0 (Cloth)
ISBN 978 184520 458 7 (Paper)

Typeset by JS Typesetting Ltd, Porthcawl, Mid Glamorgan
Printed by the MPG Books Group in the UK

www.bergpublishers.com

For my sister

CONTENTS

INTRODUCTION

When I dived off the deep end into film criticism for the first time in the early 1960s, I had the feeling I was living a unique moment in time, one where the ebbing tide of the great classic filmmakers and the rising tide of the independent *auteurs* of modernity came together. This made that decade the richest in the history of cinema, along with the 1920s, when anything daring was already par for the course, from the German expressionist films of Lang and Murnau to those of the Soviet School, from the French avant-garde to the Scandinavian directors, via Stroheim and Keaton. Then, a narrative model epitomised mainly by Hollywood, one that produced countless masterpieces, shot to the fore and dominated the entire world for nearly thirty years. Only Italian neo-realism came to ruffle this consensual aesthetic – but what an exception to the rule that was! In the aftermath of the Second World War, it served as a model to a number of aspiring filmmakers, for, though it was only an isolated example, it was a true lesson in expression, and so imposed itself as a reference for all the new waves of cinema that flourished here, there and everywhere throughout the world fifteen years on.

I was lucky enough to be there at that period of great renewal and to be able to bear witness to it by joining the editorial team of *Positif* in 1963, at the age of twenty-five. In a single decade, *Positif* had firmed up its position as a review of reference, ardently defending the innovators of its day, from Wadja to Bergman, from Antonioni to Kurosawa, from Buñuel to Aldrich. Doors opened to its contributors and so I was able to meet those of my contemporaries I loved most – Bertolucci and Skolimowski, Jancsó and Makavejev, Glauber Rocha and Tarkovsky. This book is a chronicle of those years and of the years that followed up to the present day, detailing my discoveries, my passions, through fifty interviews (of which twenty-five are presented here) with filmmakers from thirty different countries, a maximum of three per country to better reflect the extraordinary diversity of international output. But I had to sacrifice nearly as many major film directors among those I was also lucky enough to get to interview, especially in France and the United States, the only two countries whose film industries have been in continuous production. It was a hard call, taking out Woody Allen, Robert Altman, Tim Burton, Michael Cimino, Ethan and Joel Coen, Francis Ford Coppola, Clint Eastwood, Terry Gilliam, George Lucas, David Lynch, Arthur Penn, Steven Soderbergh and Quentin Tarantino, among others, to mention only American cinema. I have in the past devoted a book to a few of those I've left out here: Stanley Kubrick and Jerry Schatzberg, Francesco Rosi and Roman Polanski, Milos Forman and Wim Wenders, in a work 'in several voices', *Passport for Hollywood*. But there are still others I couldn't feature here, to my great regret, for the simple reason that I never managed to meet them: Chris Marker, Rainer Werner Fassbinder, Victor Erice and Pedro Almodovar.

Only four directors that appear in this anthology made their first feature film before 1960: Robert Bresson, Manoel de Oliveira, Federico Fellini and Satyajit Ray. I've chosen to include these four not only because they have been harbingers of modern cinema, serving, in their intransigence, as role models for directors to come, but also because most of the films they've made have come out in the period I've witnessed.

Unlike certain movie buffs of my generation, I've never felt nostalgia for a golden age that would never return. Having grown up on the great Hollywood cinema, that of Walsh, Hawks, Ford, Minnelli and Preminger, I watched it fade from the horizon with a feeling of melancholy, but the sudden emergence of new talents kept up my faith in cinema. Curiously, in my memory, those great 'ancients' are connected to fresh discoveries I made at the same time. I remember Luis Buñuel receiving me in his house in Mexico in front of a map of the Paris Metro, before taking me around the studios of Churubusco; Fritz Lang at the Venice Festival in his suite at the Excelsior Hotel, teasing his biographer, Lotte Eisner, who couldn't come up with a definition of expressionism that satisfied him; Jean Renoir heatedly and volubly answering questions about *La Bête humaine* and *La Marseillaise* in the course of two encounters; Raoul Walsh, in 1972, wearing his young wife out crawling the art galleries of Saint-Germain-des-Prés so that she'd had to go and lie down; Josef von Sternberg receiving me and Robert Benayoun in his room at the Crillon, refusing to give a formal interview, while insisting that every word he spoke was immediately reported;

John Ford at the Montreal Festival in 1967, where I kept him company for a day and watched him throw out the window a copy of *The Valley of the Dolls* that the festival organisers had thought a good idea to send up to his room, or cursing under his breath while lighting his cigar as the credits for Dusan Makavejev's *The Switchboard Operator* rolled by, full of licentious engravings – I'd been keen for him to see the film (now, there's a happy meeting of the old and the new for you!); Frank Capra in a café at the Trocadero, savouring the tribute the Cinémathèque française paid him when his autobiography came out, thereby regilding a halo that had become a bit tarnished by that time; meeting William Wellman with Bernard Tavernier in his hotel in the rue de Rivoli, where he'd made up his mind to vote for George McGovern, as opposed to Richard Nixon, despite having a reputation as a die-hard conservative; Howard Hawkes yet again telling anecdotes in front of me that were sometimes made up but that he still managed to weave, little by little, into the stuff of legend. For each of these I'd have needed a separate volume at least as thick as the one of my conversations with Huston, Mankiewicz and Wilder, *Passport for Hollywood,* or as the books of interviews I devoted to Elia Kazan and Joseph Losey, which are like two journeys through the century.

While putting this book together, I was struck how the atlas of world cinema is constantly changing. In the 1960s, the Eastern bloc countries were hubs of creativity. Today the ex-satellites of the Soviet Union and Russia itself are in artistic limbo, a fact that can at least be explained: stopping state aid has led to a collapse in production, in the face of the invasion of Hollywood films. This is the reverse of the cinemas of Asia: for Western observers in the early 1960s, these were limited to Japan, and, in India, Satyajit Ray alone, but over the past twenty years Hong Kong, Taiwan, China, South Korea, Japan and Iran have all become objects of great expectations. Such collective infatuations have, of course, something to do with fashion, but they are also based on indisputable realities and we need to constantly redraw the map of cinema with its zones of great prosperity and others in the process of desertification. Rampant liberalism in economically weak countries and state totalitarianism have the same result in the sphere of art: they strangle production. When measures of support are taken, as in France at the end of the 1950s or recently in South Korea, we see independent filmmaking blossom and prosper. Similarly, even relative liberalisation of authoritarian regimes entails the emergence of talented artists.

It is what happened in Hungary, Poland, Yugoslavia, Czechoslovakia and the USSR in the 1960s, after the big thaw of the Khrushchev era, in China in the twenty years following the end of the Cultural Revolution, in Taiwan and South Korea when the soldiers packed up and left, and in Iran over the same period when society saw the conservatives and the reformers go head to head within the Islamist regime. For me, cinema is never isolated from the great seismic shocks that shake the world; it is, on the contrary, often the means of measuring the shock waves. I've always been sensitive to what André Breton once said in an essay on André Masson that appeared in an issue of the *Minotaure* in 1939: 'The problem is no longer as it once was of knowing whether a painting holds up in, say, a wheat field, but whether it holds up alongside the diary of everyday life, which is a jungle, open or shut.'

That was where I was most comfortable, in the intellectual community formed by the contributors of *Positif*. Some of us were part of the surrealist set (Ado Kyrou, Robert Benayoun, Gérard Legrand), others came from overseas (Petr Král from Czechoslovakia, Goffredo Fofi from Italy, Paulo Antonio Paranagua from Brazil). All of us were involved in political struggles, from the crushing of the revolts in Hungary and then Czechoslovakia by the Soviet troops, to the wars of Algeria and Vietnam, and we felt ourselves to be in step with the May '68 movement. 'Change your life', 'change the world', the war cries of Rimbaud and Marx, found an echo in us. I found the same political quest in a number of filmmakers – Francesco Rosi to start with, moving on to Jancsó, Rocha, Makavejev, Pintilie, Angelopoulos, Oshima, Imamura, Arcand and later Hou Hsiao-hsien, Edward Yang, Zhang Yimou and Jia Zhang-ke. In the artists I have most admired there has always been this libertarian spirit that refuses to believe in political ideologies (and we know what tyranny they can exercise!), in progress, in systems, in propaganda. Critics should follow their lead and reject the discourse of the leaders and the logic of theories and doctrines.

But surrealism also taught me to reject aesthetic hierarchies that privilege Great Art as opposed to popular art. At *Positif*, too, we were interested in all forms of art (painting, poetry, literature and even jazz and comics) in relation to cinema, in Resnais and Antonioni, but also in sci-fi, musical comedy and the western. Among my passions the reader will no doubt not be surprised to find Takeshi Kitano and his *yakuza*, David Cronenberg and his variations on horror and, in a different vein, the sophisticated performances, enhanced by painting and literature, of the likes of Manoel de Oliveira and Peter Greenaway.

There was a time when a few rare critics, thanks to their notoriety, travelled the globe, acting as scouts. Georges Sadoul, Robert Benayoun and Louis Marcorelles spring to mind. These days, thanks to the proliferation of information sources and the ease of transport, it is festival programmers who unearth the films; after that, it's up to the critics to make their choices from among their bountiful harvests. You will see in these pages what a major role Berlin, Cannes and Venice play – and also, to a lesser degree, events such as Nantes and Locarno – in the defence and display of a *cinéma d'auteur*. Though the festivals were long subject to the official choices of participating countries, they are freer today when it comes to the rules of diplomacy and they can compile their own menus more easily. This involves trial and error, naturally, and they do make mistakes, but, as Billy Wilder told us in closing a debate and one of his films: nobody's perfect.

This is one way of saying that I'm well aware to what extent this panorama, broad as it is, is partial and biased. If it has any merit – apart from refuting the death of cinema trumpeted for so long now – it lies in expressing a personal choice dictated by a love of invention, of singularity, of beauty and of aesthetic and moral courage.

1 BERNARDO BERTOLUCCI

(1941–)

Bernardo Bertolucci appeared when Italian cinema was still in its golden age. Along with Marco Bellocchio, he was the most gifted of the new generation. A protégé of Pier Paolo Pasolini, whose assistant he was and who wrote the script of his first film with him, *The Grim Reaper (La Commare Secca)*, this very young filmmaker (he was twenty-one at the time) confirmed his talent with *Before the Revolution (Prima della Rivoluzione)* (1964), a seminal work at the crossroads of several influences. The son of a poet and himself a poet, a cinephile *à la française* first recognised during the International Critics' Week at Cannes and not in his own country, a man of culture divided between old and new, Bertolucci was to enjoy a chequered career, which does not make his relations any easier with the critics who have followed him for forty years. I remember having confessed to him once my immense disappointment with *Partner*, presented at the Venice Festival in 1968 and in which the influence of Godard sat uncomfortably with his own sensibility. His subsequent films, adapted from Borges (*The Spider's Stratagem*) and Moravia (*The Conformist*), are among the most accomplished he has made, with worldwide acclaim greeting *Last Tango in Paris*. Over this last film, we may well prefer more reserved works like *Luna*, where he bounces opera off melodrama, or *Tragedy of a Ridiculous Man*, a black farce that has a complex relationship with Italian comedy. After the shattering failure of this film, Bertolucci embarked on an international career with *The Last Emperor*, *The Sheltering Sky* and *Little Buddha*, the first in particular enjoying considerable success. And yet, parodying Feydeau, one could advise him to 'see to Emilia', his native province which has inspired his best films. The return to his native soil with *Stealing Beauty* and *Besieged* attests to the uncertainty of a loveable and captivating man who feels torn when it comes to making choices, has long been in analysis and is always on the lookout for a guiding direction.

ON *TRAGEDY OF A RIDICULOUS MAN*

ROME, MAY 1981

When Primo (Ugo Tognazzi) asks Barbara (Anouk Aimée) why she married him, she answers: 'Because you made me laugh and you had a job.'

That's two social classes looking at each other. Barbara, as Anouk's allure implies, comes from the upper French bourgeoisie. At twenty, she studied artwork restoration in Parma, which explains her ties with painting, her fake Pissarro, etc. And she met this ex-peasant who'd made it. She's from a family of the idle rich and she's fascinated by his materialism. For the whole length of the film there's a confrontation between these two classes. Primo regards Barbara with admiration and rage because of her class. (As Selznick used to say, 'There are two kinds of class, first class and no class.') And she envies his energy and vitality. The choice of Anouk Aimée is obviously dialectical in relation to Tognazzi. This sort of echoes *1900*, since it's basically about the fascination social classes have for each other. She's someone who wasn't able to work and who's seduced by the positive side of her husband and also by a certain poetry, a certain nobility emanating from his vulgarity.

The film ends in a ballroom just as Luna *ended in a theatre performance. Here the father finds his son again. There the son finds his father again. In the two situations there is a show and music.*

The same as at the end of *Last Tango (Ultimo tango a Parigi)* and of *The Conformist (Il conformista)*. I suppose I've always needed a moment of music to wind up. In a ball, in a show, I may well feel that I can allow myself to take a few liberties with my characters. Anything can happen then. And in this precise case, there's the resurrection of Giovanni, the son.

How did the idea come to you of doing this film after other more 'cosmopolitan' films like Last Tango, 1900 *and* Luna?

I wanted to get back to the Italian language. It was a sort of wager. The hardest thing to do and generally the thing done least well in Italian films is the dialogue. Scriptwriters – and I count myself among them – have a tendency to write dialogue that's too literary. I wanted to see if it was possible to rid the language of its tawdry rags, to strip it and even to invent a film language. I'm happy enough with the result, which is due primarily to Tognazzi, who comes from the region the film's set in, the Po Valley. He's a man with a lot of common sense who, for quite a long while, trod the boards in the music hall – real theatre, according to Brecht. That experience of Ugo's was a great boon to me: his spoken language caused the written text to shed any literary heaviness it might have had. As soon as I'd finished writing the script, which I did in about forty days, I cut out a lot of the dialogue and kept only the essential.

To what extent was Tognazzi's work here different from what he's been able to do in certain comedies, themselves inspired by populism?

He made such a big investment in this film that it almost frightened me. Firstly, he identified with the character, then he understood the idea contained in the story, this utopia that Primo is living in. I didn't want him to perform in the register of Italian comedy. At bottom, my relationship with him was a bit the same as with Brando in *Last Tango in Paris*. What interested me was his personality, what he could bring of his personal experience. Tognazzi sometimes changed his lines during the shoot. To start with I'd written the film in the first person, there was a voice 'off' that you won't find the slightest trace of now.[1] It was to be a film viewed through Tognazzi's eyes, the eyes of this voyeur who's looking through binoculars when you first see him. He was a sort of guru–mogul–monolith in the middle of the story and all the other characters were moving around him. Tognazzi is a monster in the Jean Gabin mould. Between takes, he's quite capable of going and preparing a *risotto à éjaculation* as he calls it, where he puts a bottle of champagne in the centre of a plate of rice, then puts some sugar in the champagne and the champagne spills over into the rice. With him, there was no solution of continuity between the shot, the recipe and the following shot. In a way, we didn't really need to work together or even talk to each other for there to be a real collaboration.

It's interesting that the film had been written in the first person while, thanks to your age, you yourself are between two generations. Primo could be your father and Giovanni your son. In other words, how did the idea for the film come to you?

I was rather depressed in Los Angeles a year ago because I'd wanted to produce a musical comedy in Brazil where I would have handed over the direction to

Gianni Amico and the music to Gaetano Veloso and Chico Buarque. Everything was signed with Fox but after a change in the company management, the film was bumped. I was desperate because I believed very strongly in the film. Once again I found myself confronted by the narrow mentality of producers. Various films were offered to me in Los Angeles, but I couldn't get a 'feel' for any of the material. On the other hand, I felt the need to do a film in Italy, so I went home and my wife, Clare Peploe, was reading the paper and spotted a human interest story that had happened in Apulia. The son of a local political leader from the Christian Democrats had been kidnapped and killed. And the father had set about finding the money to save him. I changed the place and the nature of the character, who I saw as expressing a rejection of the very negative logic of violence in Italy with its use of sons, mothers and fathers as merchandise. With Primo there's a utopian strength that makes me think of *1900*. *Tragedy of a Ridiculous Man*, even though it's not trying to be overtly political, is in a way the third act of *1900*. Primo hits back at the cynicism of contemporary Italy. Even out of an event as tragic as the kidnapping of his son, he's going to get something positive, he's going to try and save the dairy from bankruptcy and, so, help the workers. And there's also the utopian ideal of the young people, Laura and Adelfo.

That said, I just started out writing in the first person like an idiot because I was bored writing in the third. I didn't really know where I was going with it, but what motivated me was doing a film entirely in Italian again, at home, in Parma, in Emilia: whence, perhaps, the need to identify and my recourse to the first person. I wrote the script a bit in a trance, at night, between eleven o'clock in the evening and five o'clock in the morning and in less than forty days. I'd met Tognazzi very briefly at the 1980 Cannes Festival, had told him the story in a few words and asked him if he was interested. As he was thrilled, I set to work straight away, but I always had him in mind for the main role. I didn't know him well, but I'd met him several times at the home of the film's producer, Giovanni Bertolucci, who is one of his mates and who produced, among other things, *The Bishop's Bedroom*. I saw in Ugo, in these society parties we went to, how lavish the pretence he had in him was and also a certain heaviness. And it's always interesting to go looking for the real 'me', the tortoise beneath the shell... Tognazzi's 'ego'. At the start of the shoot, he was exquisitely nice. He caught me unaware because I wasn't expecting that. In fact, I don't see many

Italian films but I'd seen Ugo in a few roles like in *Venga a prendere il caffè da noi*, where he's extraordinary. I found myself with an actor who had a depth, a stature, I wasn't expecting. I wanted to make a 'mean' film – stylistically and structurally speaking. I didn't want some beautiful calligraphy. I started writing at the end of May and I said we'd start filming on 29 September, which no one could believe. And yet everything turned out the way I said it would. We filmed for fourteen weeks with a few interruptions. We edited the film very quickly. It's a film that was made more at the speed of life than of the cinema.

It's your most 'provincial' film, along with Before the Revolution *and* The Spider's Stratagem.

It is, I think, closer to the second. That's partly due to the space 'off' that you don't see, to the aura of the place. The countryside where Primo's villa sits is Langhirano, where the best ham in the world comes from. That's also a common feature with *Before the Revolution*, this relationship with food, ham. But at the same time there's something in the film that hooks in with *The Conformist*: it's not an autobiographical film. I took a character who's older than I am and others who are younger. So there's no immediate identification.

What did the work of the director of photography, Carlo di Palma, bring you?

For the first time in eleven years, I changed cinematographers. With Vittorio Storaro I had the longest love affair of my life (nothing's ever lasted as long with any woman!). When Coppola came to Rome last year, we dined together, all three of us, to try and organise our filming schedules. But I still didn't know what film I'd be doing or when. By the time I'd made up my mind, it was too late; Storaro had already signed up with Coppola for *One From the Heart*. A camera head kept telling my producer that he really wanted to work with me. It turned out to be Carlo di Palma, who'd switched to directing after *Blow Up, Red Desert*, etc. The idea of taking on someone who was starting again from scratch, while having a huge amount of experience behind him, fascinated me. I met him and found him to be an artist like Vittorio, but I was about to ask him to do the exact opposite of what I got Vittorio to do. I wanted spotlighting, for the photography to be aggressive and to not use light in a theatrical way, I wanted the photography to be harder, close to hyperrealism. I was also looking for an interior–exterior connection. With Storaro, it's hard to set up because he always sticks projectors in whenever there's a window: he wants the light to come from natural sources (doors, windows, lampshades, etc.). So with Carlo I was able to use the villa's great big window, which opens onto the valley, and that is magic, I find. There's also the problem of nights: Vittorio cries when he has to film at night, especially in the country where there are no streetlights, for once again he needs a real starting point. I was able to ask Carlo to light up the night – like in the kidnap scene – according to the conventions of cinema where we don't know where the light's coming from and where it's not realist but hyperrealist, as we see can everything.

The contrast with Luna *is really striking as* Luna *is so lyrical, so close to melodrama and opera, with long camera movements. Here they're broken up, cut in the editing.*

Yes, *Tragedy* is close to film noir. I wanted to get back to that dialectical force that editing can have. Sometimes we get there. Sometimes we're so attached to the filmed shot we don't have the courage to cut. For example, Jean-Marie Straub doesn't touch any of his shots to cut them, to incorporate them into another shot. Brechtian and Marxist as he is, he rejects dialectics. In *Tragedy* I approached the editing as time for achieving a dialectic in relation to the filming. By breaking up a camera movement like this, you emphasise it perhaps even more than if you kept it in its integrality. When I see Rosi's *Three Brothers* or any of Angelopoulos's films, which I admire greatly, in spite of everything I sometimes feel like jumping on their shots, ripping into them, because there's something about them that's like overdone respect – especially with Angelopoulos – in relation to what's been filmed.

From Luna *to* Tragedy of a Ridiculous Man *we go from harmony to dissonance.*

But it's an unprogrammed dissonance. The structure of the script was linear and simple. But the shoot happened in such an atmosphere of delirium, such a mix of anxiety and happiness, that I almost never consulted the script. And I filmed in such a fashion that I could change the structure radically in the editing and that's what happened. For example, the search the *carabinieri* conduct at Primo's place occurred in the script towards the end whereas it now happens in the first part. The succession of episodes was thereby enormously transformed. Whence the inevitable impression of dissonance. It's a choice of structural freedom that allows the film to sail along like a 'work in progress'.

But even when they're floating, your central characters have a kind of solidity.

Ugo, this cheese maker, this *casaro*, produces the sort of milk that goes solid. He's a strange man, sitting on a throne in the centre of his fiefdom. I think it was Apollinaire who said: 'Our image is noble and tragic like the mask of a tyrant.' His peasant origins are noble, just as Barbara's education is noble. Primo is a bridge between a culture we want to destroy and the present. The wife has from the start an absolute confidence in the market economy of the bourgeoisie. You pay, she thinks, and our son will come back.

You have often filmed in the region, but for this film you chose other landscapes.

Normally I'd film in the Po plain, where the only landmarks are the top of a bell-tower or a poplar. This time I took to the hills for the first time. They're very close, only about twenty kilometres away. I even went as far as the mountains. The forest we filmed in is where I used to go every summer for holidays – *villeggiatura* – when I was a child. It's where I made my first film at sixteen – it was called *The Cable Car* and I shot it in 16 mm. It was a fifteen-minute film. In it, my brother, who was eight, along with a little cousin, was looking for a cable car he'd seen 'as a child'. The cables appeared from time to time through the greenery, but he got lost in the chestnut wood during the search. It was a summer afternoon's daydream. Twenty-five years later, then, I went back there and, being superstitious, I was a bit scared it'd be my last film, since it was exactly where I'd filmed the first one. Parma, and the province it's in, is, for me, a microcosm. And to go up to the heights was like an adventure, like exploring.

Tognazzi comes from Cremona. Is there a big difference between his region and the region of Parma?

No, the difference is above all cultural, the landscape is similar and so is people's physiognomy. But Parma has had the privilege of being occupied by the French, we pronounce our 'r's like the French do, we've had French architects, pastry cooks, cabinetmakers, while they have no idea what all that's about in Cremona. And we also eat better in Parma than they do in Cremona. But the dairy dating from the beginning of the industrial age and which I found for the film – the dairy, on the other hand, is in the province of Cremona. Ugo was truly the sovereign of this realm. All the people of Cremona came to pay homage to him. Ferreri caught this love of food Tognazzi has – his hedonistic side. He denied himself nothing. That's what he expresses when he kisses Laura and she says to him: 'You're brave' and he replies: 'I'm never frightened *before*.'

He also says a key phrase to her: 'What's important is not morality, it's sincerity.' That's a very romantic conception of life.

But Primo is a romantic. He was a partisan in the war and a member of the PCI, the Communist Party of Italy; he talks about 'the cause'. Lots of small-time industrialists in Emilia vote Communist and they show great creative imagination in their trade. They are true inventors with immense energy, and if the Italian economy is still on its legs it's no doubt thanks to them. Primo is the kind of industrialist who can't accept the rules of the game dictated by consumer society. While remaining completely within the economic logic of our system, he says – in a scene that's been cut – that, unlike manufacturers of televisions, cars or refrigerators, who work with dead matter, he, by contrast, was working with live matter, which is milk. Cheeses undergo fermentation, are alive right up to the moment we eat them: that was his industrial pride. There is also in him a feeling of shame attached to his social origins. And yet, when he talks about kolkhozes, Russian collective farms, he has a certain irony. He is a bit what Olmo from *1900* would have become if he'd followed the path our society laid out for him. He has identified with what was once the enemy for him in his youth. In that sense, the film really speaks of the mystery of Italy today, the endless baseness. In the looks the characters exchange, you can see the search for sincerity and at the same time the inevitability of betrayal.

But you avoid tackling politics, the problem of terrorism, head-on.

You can't treat everything. I was more interested in showing the vertigo that seizes each of the two generations when it finds itself face to face with the other.

Adelfo sums it up at the end of the film when he says to Primo: 'Did I lead you here or did you follow me?'

When they go to the dance hall together, we get the impression they're going to Mass, don't you think? In fact Primo doesn't understand anything about this generation, which, in any case, doesn't understand itself. For him, as he says, 'The sons that surround us are monsters. They can snicker but they don't know how to laugh. Either they have too much contempt for their fathers or too much indulgence. A person doesn't know how to interpret their silence: are they crying for help or do they want to shoot at us?' This last phrase is a variation on an article Pasolini wrote at the end of his life, which was published in the *Corriere della Sera*. *Salo* had just come out. I didn't like the film the first time I saw it because it was a few days after Pier Paolo's death, but now I find it extraordinary in the way it really deals with his relationship with young people. The truth of this work has nothing in fact to do with Sade or libertinism. It's much more an act of revenge against the young men who deceived him by losing their innocence.

The title of your film recalls Gogol's irony and Dostoyevsky's ambiguity; it suggests the atmosphere of a Russian novel with its opaque characters.

The Po Valley has something Russian about it for me with the snow in winter and its poplars, which are like the silver birches in Chekhov's short stories. Dostoyevsky also wrote a short story called *The Dream of A Ridiculous Man*. You have to interpret the title in the broad sense. I think that in Italy, at this moment, we are so tragic that we become ridiculous. And when you see how ridiculous you are, you become tragic all over again. There is a strict link between the two feelings and myself, when I look at myself in the mirror, I find myself ridiculous. That's why the film, in the end, is neither a satire nor a tragedy, but is situated in the give-and-take between the two terms.

It's not only the characters that are surrounded by obscurity, but the storyline itself. Is he alive, is he dead? We never stop asking ourselves the question.

In my view, Primo and the viewers must think that his son is dead. Only Barbara thinks he's alive. Adelfo learned that he was dead in the confessional. But the confusion reflects the state of political affairs in Italy. In Moro's case, as in Mattéi's, we know *nothing*, in reality, about their deaths. When I filmed *Before the Revolution*, I spoke of ambiguity, but that was more aesthetic, cultural; it was the malaise of an adolescent in his relationship to reality. Today ambiguity is our daily bread; there is no certainty anymore, including about the facts. When Primo, at the end of the film, watches Giovanni, Barbara, Adelfo and Laura dancing, we can clearly see he's scared and he goes off to get some champagne to escape from what he sees. He no longer understands a thing, he sees everything he's built crumble, he sees himself powerless, when he once thought he was omnipotent.

One could even be forgiven for thinking that the son 'arranges' his own kidnapping.

It's a possibility. There have been similar cases in Italy. An industrialist's son got himself kidnapped and died during the kidnapping. To get the family to believe he was kidnapped, they gave him ether but they overdid it, and he died. It was one of the most complex psychodramas in the Italian terrorist repertory. I took my cue from human interest stories I'd read in the papers without being literal at any stage since I didn't want to enter into the shabby details of terrorism.

Morricone's music is dealt with in a popular register.

Yes, it's inspired by popular waltzes, old tunes. He wrote it before the film based on certain airs of northern Italy and instruments like the accordion, the bandoleon. For the character of Barbara, in particular in the night scene where she meets Laura for the first time, we thought of a more cultured, a more 'French', piece of music with references to Satie and Ravel. I directed the film with the music in my head since it was already composed and that helped me with the filming, as usual. I listen to music a lot during shoots, of an evening and of a morning, whether it's Verdi, Prokofiev or Bernard Herrmann, it gives me ideas. This time, it was the two themes of the film that guided me directly, the one for the 'ridiculous man' and the one for Barbara.

What opera aria does he sing at the end?

It's 'Di provenza il mar, il suol', the aria sung by Germont, Alfredo's father in *La Traviata*. It's a quotation from Visconti's *Obsession*, where the husband sings it in the opera competition.

The film has a dark atmosphere that is almost dreamlike.

The film had a different ending. Primo woke up again after the open-air bar scene. That closes the loop before the office sequence at the beginning where he has a nightmare. The story was a dream, as though anticipating something that is about to happen. The atmosphere corresponded to the feeling of being bloated after a birthday party where you've drunk a lot. The film has kept this dream, this nightmare feel that was there at the start in the tone of the first-person narrative.

The more the character of Primo 'descends' and comes back to earth, the more the character of Barbara rises, becomes airy.

A psychodrama such as this kidnapping, in my view, drives those involved to reveal themselves in their most extreme truth. Barbara becomes airy, but also a sort of snowbound betrothed. When she's on the balcony, waiting, with her fur-trimmed cloak, she has the same binoculars as he had at the beginning; she stands out against a background of snow and sun. I then like the change of climate that goes with the sense of the film. We gradually go from the end of summer with the corn, to autumn in the woods and finally to winter.

All your films deal with the family, even Last Tango in Paris *where the father–daughter relationship is fundamental.*

I don't know whether I'm doomed to deal with the family or whether it's a deliberate choice. I clearly haven't settled all my personal scores. I've been in analysis for twelve years now, and all you have to do is look at my films to see the itinerary of my cure.

*In your previous films (*Tango, Luna*), the psychoanalysis was more explicit in one sense, as was politics in 1900. Here you can't see any trace of theory. Freudian symbols are never presented as such, they're part of the general opacity.*

There is a moment in analysis where you don't dream anymore, where you don't interpret your dreams anymore, where you seem to be talking about something else. It's a bit what happens in this film. That's why I said a moment ago that it's not as autobiographical as the others. It's as though I'd freed myself from certain cumbersome ideological, psychoanalytical and political ideas, as though I needed to see things outside those schemas, as though I were on a quest for the unpredictable. If there's less of a stance adopted at the start, everything then becomes more mysterious.

Where do your two young performers, Laura and Vittorio, come from?

Vittorio is an actor well known to a small circle of people. He works in the fringe theatre in Rome. He's the same generation as Benigni, who performs for students, intellectuals. It's very different from the 'pre-show' of thirty or forty years ago where Tognazzi and Sordi, for instance, got their training, but you find the same liberty and the same possibilities for promoting new talent. Laura started doing theatre two or three years ago. In the script, their characters were very vague as they were phantoms created by Primo. They only became clear during the filming. As I don't know much about young people, they themselves helped me to define them. I wanted them especially to represent the mystery of youth today. I don't think that all youth is mysterious. The youth of my generation, for example, wasn't. Maybe because they came after the war, they seemed sunny to me. Here, they're darker – both of them have black hair, a sombre look. Laura and Vittorio were anxious because they didn't know where they were going. And I myself couldn't help them except day by day, shot by shot. I told them I knew who they were when they came and stood in front of the camera, but that I may never know what they were as a whole. My relationship with them was the same as my relationship with the story: never knowing, not judging, not giving precise instructions – not even to the audience.

Do you have many non-professionals among your performers?

Yes, as in most of my films; the maid who dances rock and roll, for example, is a local woman. The loan sharks, too, come from the region. One of them was already in *1900*. The people dancing at the end aren't professionals, either. That's what's good about cinema: take something documentary and turn it into fiction. You get things with amateurs that would be unthinkable with actors.

In your shots you often have several levels. In town or on the road there are several horizontals along which the characters move.

I want to render the characters' interiority visually. The richness of the visual field should refer to people's contradictions. These contradictions fascinate me in life. With directors, too, what interests me is the sense of contradiction, hence of risk. That's what I'd like to say to certain of my *confrères* the same age as me who I really love, but who don't have the courage to take risks. They refuse to, claiming they want to remain true to themselves. On the contrary, I think you have to betray yourself.

What are the contradictions you see in yourself?

If you look at my first films, *Before the Revolution, Partner,* and the films I'm making now, it seems obvious to me. I was all for a cinema that talked about cinema. It was, let's say, a cinema in the spirit of Godard. It was at the same time very romantic, but I was enjoying myself, I was getting my kicks. Now I'm also getting my kicks, but in a way, I think, that's more generous. In the 1960s, we felt panic in the face of the public and we constructed elaborate theories to avoid confronting them. There was a need for love, which we deliberately deprived ourselves of. From that point of view, I think I've changed a lot.

NOTES

1   Since the film was screened at Cannes, Bertolucci has reintroduced the voice-over.

2 JOHN BOORMAN

(1933–)

For thirty years, John Boorman has made Ireland his adopted country and it is in the county of Wicklow, south of Dublin, that he lives nestled in the hills, among the trees, horses and streams. This is both home base and a haven where this adventurer of cinema can recharge his batteries, having filmed in the Amazon jungle (*The Emerald Forest*), on an atoll in the South Seas (*Hell in the Pacific*), among the torrents of the Appalachians (*Deliverance*), along the rivers of south-east Asia (*Beyond Rangoon*) and in the tropics of Central America (*The Tailor of Panama*).

The discovery in 1968 of *Point Blank*, his second feature film and his first American opus, was one of the most outstanding shocks of my life as a cinephile. Boorman's subsequent films, from *Leo The Last* to *The Heretic* and *Excalibur*, fuelled as they were by an intense energy, a feeling for nature and for action worthy of Walsh or Vidor, as well as a spiritual and moral quest, prompted me to write a book which came out in the mid 1980s. Since then, his oeuvre has taken on a more directly autobiographical cast, from the childhood memories of *Hope and Glory* to the self-portrait of *I Dreamt I Woke Up*, without for all that abandoning fiction firmly grounded in the political and social reality of his time.

John Boorman is much admired by his peers. When he was president of the jury at the Cannes Festival, Martin Scorsese gave him the director's prize for *The General* (which Coppola also publicly praised). Scorsese also featured him in the anthology he and Michael Wilson made into a monumental documentary, *A Personal Journey With Martin Scorsese Through American Movies*, as one of three of Scorsese's contemporaries, along with Kubrick and Clint Eastwood. Boorman's oeuvre, disconcertingly diverse and prolific, divides into equal parts between American films and British films. With *The General*, he has filmed an Irish story for the first time but his protagonist is the brother of his previous heroes, a rugged individualist, a social misfit, a dreamer in search of some impossible transcendence. As always with Boorman, the dynamic force of the direction and the vigorous depiction of the faces and landscapes accompany the main character's forward march.

ON *THE GENERAL*

LONDON, AUGUST 1998

You've been living in Ireland for twenty-five years now and, even though you've made films there, such as Zardoz *and* Excalibur, *you've never made any that have Ireland as their framework.*

I'd been toying for a while with the idea of making a film about contemporary Ireland, but I couldn't find a subject that really interested me. What dominates this country is, of course, the civil war in Northern Ireland and in any case most Irish films more or less deal with that. I'd known this character, Martin Cahill, for a long time and, in fact, I actually think he burgled my house one day! All the details of that theft truly bore his signature. They stole my gold gong that I won for *Deliverance* and I put that anecdote in the film. Cahill, when he was alive, was practically never sentenced for anything: none of the major offences he committed could be pinned on him because there was never any proof. So it was impossible to bring them up in a book or a film without being threatened with a defamation suit. It was only after his death that the journalist, Paul Williams, had the opportunity of publishing a very well-documented biography. That book really fascinated me and I wanted to buy the rights. I discovered, to my great dismay, that they'd been acquired by a young American producer, P. J. Pettite. I approached him and negotiations with him went on for months thanks to his paranoid behaviour, until I abandoned the project. He then turned to the BBC in Northern Ireland, which, in turn, gave up, probably for the same reasons, then to an Irish company, Little Bird, who finally decided to make their own version in a lighter vein. He then came back to me and sold me the rights, knowing that another film was going to be made regardless. He also started legal proceedings against Little Bird, which we inherited! In turn, Little Bird tried to stop us two weeks before the start of the shoot because they'd bought the rights to several articles that Paul Williams used for his biography. As I hadn't used those passages for my script, the court threw their case out. They still intended to film their version with Kevin Spacey under the title *Ordinary Decent Criminals*, which is an expression you'll find in the dialogue of *The General*.[1]

To what extent did your knowledge of Ireland allow you to understand the character?

What attracted me in him was that he seemed like an archetype of a certain category of Irishman that you meet with throughout the whole history of the country right up to the present day. You find him in the Celtic chieftains and, again, in Michael Collins. He's a rebel, opposed to all forms of authority, endowed with a lot of wit, cunning, crafty and fearless. In a way, to legitimise their status as rebels, these guys need to get killed. There is a real death wish in them. It comes from the fact that Ireland was colonised. Before conquest by the English, the country was divided into a host of small kingdoms always at war with each other – so much so that the violence is literally endemic. The other side of such behaviour is a tendency to make jokes, play pranks, do things out of mischievousness, ridicule the other person, which is yet another way of mocking authority.

What also interested me are the radical changes that have occurred in Ireland for at least the last ten years. On top of being colonised by the English, Ireland, even more significantly no doubt, has been colonised by the Catholic Church. Priests have ruled Ireland and kept it in their power; morality has been subject to an iron fist. This repression regularly caused irruptions of violence. Similarly, alcoholism has its source in that, as well. What's remarkable, on the other hand, in personalities like Michael Collins or Martin Cahill is that they don't drink, as though their rebelliousness expressed itself in action, not in alcohol. What's new with Cahill is that he didn't only oppose the police and the law, but also the Church. He considered it to be just as much of an oppressor. His lack of inhibition in the face of certain values like religion, his lack of respect for priests, for example, gave him a force and a freedom that other criminals didn't have. What fascinated me was seeing how his character cut across Irish society, in a sort of cross-section. For Cahill, Ireland was a corrupt country where there was no morality, only hypocrisy. In his view, it was the atmosphere of repression that covered up the corruption, from real estate speculation to fiscal fraud. All that is coming out now with a flourishing economy where the rich are getting richer and richer and the poor are getting poorer and poorer. The speed of this evolution carries many dangers for the country.

If the film is completely singular in the current cinematographic landscape, one could link it to the biopic genre as illustrated in Hollywood films like Public Enemy *with James Cagney, whose personality has points in common with Brendan Gleeson's performance.*

I certainly thought of that type of character, but what especially attracted me was Cahill's archetypal nature, which gave him a mythic dimension. That's the reason I wanted to shoot the film in black and white so that it would escape the quotidian. I wanted to suggest a parallel world rather than the real world. It seems to me that you can betray a project of this kind by using colours that are too familiar, that end up stopping viewers from seeing what you're showing them. Similarly, when we go out into the street, we end up not really *seeing* what's in front of us. I was trying for a kind of stylisation when I was shooting my other films so as not to treat colours in a naturalistic manner – whether it be *Leo The Last, Deliverance* or *Point Blank.* I've always thought that black and white films are closer to the realm of dreams, which we more often than not experience in black and white. That way I get closer to the unconscious. I've often had problems with colour, especially at the editing stage, where you jump from one shot to another and the colours tend to jump too. That's why I usually film each scene in a very narrow chromatic range so we're not too disoriented during the editing. It has to do with visual perception. Certain colours, like red, persist on the retina longer, so much so that, when you move on to the next sequence, the red is going to prolong its effect on you. Black and white allows you to focus your attention. I think that way it gets a face to say a lot more, as the work of the great black and white photographers proves.

But filmmakers have a lot more commercial pressure on them than photographers!

That's absolutely true, and there are certain of my films that I'd have preferred to shoot in black and white, but not all. I can't imagine *Excalibur* without colour. If I shot *The General* in black and white it's because the production was independent and there was no one there to stop me!

Did that pose further technical problems for you?

Actually, we filmed with colour stock, but that doesn't mean we can do a colour version since you use different lighting when you know a film will ultimately be developed in black and white. If you look at the history of cinema photography and the history of lighting, you'll notice that, when colour came on the scene, cinematographers continued using the same lighting techniques as when they filmed in black and white. Today that doesn't happen anymore. At the beginning of the 1960s, directors of photography like Geoffrey Unsworth started using soft, indirect lighting, reflected off polystyrene panels, relying on colour to delineate the shots. On the other hand, with black and white, you have to use more intense light to better define contours and shots. This modelling using lighting takes a lot more time. That's why, on *The General*, we adopted black and white lighting using more projectors.

This is the second film, after Hope and Glory, *which was itself autobiographical, that you've based on historical facts. How much freedom of imagination does the evocation of a past that was really lived leave you?*

There's an interesting balance to look for there because, of course, there's always a measure of invention. Clearly, his relationships with his wife and sister-in-law, and even with the members of his gang, are the product of my imagination. I'm relying on facts and events that really happened, only to then develop them using my own inventiveness. I had to start off with a very strong, very clear notion of the character, which I formed bit by bit, and the rest came really easily. Besides, most of these people are still alive. I wrote to his wife, I sent her the script and suggested she come and see the film before anybody else did, but she never replied. Which is only what I expected since her entourage, out of respect for his memory, don't want to have anything to do with the 'normal' world. I had lawyers by my side because, unlike Cahill, the two women are still around. I had to be very careful and not suggest in any way that they could be implicated in his crimes since they were perfectly capable of pursuing me for defamation. The fact that we know he was living with these two sisters, that he'd had children with each of them and that they lived together in harmony, allowed us to be a bit bolder in depicting their relationships. If we'd invented such a *ménage à trois* as pure fiction, we'd have had to explain it more and develop the situation! Since it was a matter of real fact, I was freer to dive in without any particular justification. Similarly, the scene where he gathers his gang together and dresses them all the same before sending them off in different directions to fool the authorities was told to me by his doctor. Every incident can be validated by some testimony, for, in Dublin, almost everyone has a story to tell about Martin Cahill!

The only contact we had with his family was with his elder son, Martin Cahill Jr and with Martin's sister. His son's an art student and he wrote me an intelligent letter during the shoot in which he told me how hard it was for him to make his life with that name and asked me not to give him his real name in the film. For her part, the sister turned up one day on the set: she was amazed at the physical resemblance between Brendan Gleeson and her brother, and she started talking about him and went on for two hours. After their conversation, Brendan told me how surprised he was to find that what I'd invented was true! I had a similar experience on *Hope and Glory* when my mother and my elder sister read the script and told me that what I thought I'd made up had in fact happened exactly the same way!

How did Brendan Gleeson prepare himself to play a character everybody knew?

Firstly, we talked to a lot of people who'd known Cahill. We also had access to an interview done with Cahill for television and that I stuck in The General practically word for word. I even asked the cameraman who'd filmed the original documentary to be in my film. We also studied some fragments of a report he appears in so that we'd get his behaviour right. And Brendan totally immersed himself in the character. That was a lot easier for his knowing the historic background. Before he became a professional actor eight years ago, he was a teacher in underprivileged areas and he'd hung around people like that. When I met him for a test, he wasn't all that good in the beginning, but bit by bit he managed practically to become the character in an almost disturbing way. I was sure there wouldn't be any false note. Every time we improvised or changed details of the script, he was still Cahill and a large part of the success of the film is due to his extraordinary performance. It had an effect on the whole cast. Whenever an actor turned up to play a bit part for a day or two and saw how high the bar Brendan set was, it incited him to surpass himself.

From that point of view, Jon Voight, who is the only non-Irish actor in the cast, slots into the whole perfectly.

There are good actors in Ireland and a certain number of them wind up in the film. I was looking for someone to play the police inspector who pursues Cahill. The actor doesn't have all that many scenes to get his character across in, and I needed someone capable of incarnating him with power and effectiveness. I thought of two or three Irish actors, like Ciarin Hinds who was in *Excalibur,* but none of them were available. So then I called Voight. For years he went through a religious phase and he hadn't appeared on screen. He'd converted to Judaism and turned down any role that wasn't up to the level of his highly ethical requirements, which practically eliminated everything coming out of Hollywood! Suddenly, he changed, and he accepted all sorts of propositions with a great deal of open-mindedness. When I contacted him to find out if he'd like to play an Irish policeman and if he could be in Dublin the following week, he immediately said yes, whereas I'd spent weeks trying to persuade him to feature in *Deliverance.* On the set, he was a bit intimidated being surrounded by all these people from the country who belonged to that scene. Luckily, I knew Gerry O'Carroll, one of the police inspectors who'd tracked Cahill down and who I'd engaged as a technical adviser on the film. I introduced him to Jon Voight, who was inspired by his personality in building his own character and he even borrowed his accent which is very particular, specific to the region between Cork and Kerry, where he came from. Jon did amazing work and got to the point where no one in Ireland could fault his accent. Moreover, he's the sort of person who never stops asking questions all through rehearsals, so he contributed to the film that way too. We also needed an actor of his calibre to counterbalance Brendan Gleeson's strong personality.

Being a policeman in Ireland must be a peculiarly complicated task.

A number of them are, in fact, sympathetic to the Republican movement, which is why Ireland has been a sort of haven for the IRA. Because of Cahill, who couldn't be caught even though he was being watched night and day by ninety men, the authorities ended up arming them and transforming them into a quasi-paramilitary force. I don't assert anything in the film but I leave open the possibility of police connivance in Cahill's assassination. Little by little the policemen charged with keeping him under surveillance were removed from their job, and, when he was no longer under any protection, the killer could execute him. What gave me the confidence to film the end scene (and the beginning) is the testimony of a deputy who was going past in the street just before the murder. He got a good look at the murderer, who had his weapon in a bag, then he went to the commissioner to make a statement concerning the physical appearance of the suspect – square face, light hair, small build, etc. After that, he left for overseas and when he got back two weeks later, he saw the description stuck on the walls: angular face, dark hair, beard! When he pointed this out to the authorities, he was told that that was what always happened with eyewitness photos!

Why did you decide to start the film with this final murder?

If you know the protagonist is going to die from the beginning, it creates a shadow that looms over the rest of the film and generates a certain sympathy for the character, even when he commits the most brutal acts. I was also hoping that it would give him a tragic dimension, as I never stopped saying to my collaborators, and to Brendan Gleeson in particular, that, without this tragic dimension, the film doesn't exist. The hardest thing was to find a balance in the portrait of the man, between the sympathetic traits and certain repulsive behaviours. His personality embraced those two extremes and Brendan's concern was not to give him a romantic aura. That's a worry I shared while not wanting him to be antipathetic, either. I think it's what makes the film disturbing. You feel attracted to the character and then suddenly he commits a violent act that disgusts you. There are viewers who are disconcerted by that. It's only normal that the people who are still alive who've suffered from his actions, can't accept that he's shown partly in a sympathetic light.

The difference between Cahill and the Irish or Italian gangsters of the 1920s and 1930s is that they were very conservative, very respectful of the political or religious order, whereas he is truly anti-establishment.

He's a true anarchist and that's what fascinated me about him. He's very representative of the state of mind of many Irish today, even if they don't have either the courage or the means to lead the kind of life he led.

In that, he closely resembles several of your previous protagonists, who tend to go beyond their limits and so bring about their own downfall or death.

I'm very attracted to the notion of someone's putting themselves somehow outside society, either because they feel rejected by it or because they don't accept the rules. Those sorts of people interest me.

Isn't his adventure like King Arthur's in negative, a proletarian version of a sovereign surrounded by his knights?

I've never thought of that but, when you put it like that, it's obvious. There is indeed something royal about him; he's lord of his realm. With his two women, he lives like a king and they have to feel barred from society to accept such a situation. In fact, he shared the younger sister's bed, but truth was stranger than fiction and I couldn't show that in the film! The two scenes I had the most trouble writing are precisely the ones where things get off the ground with the second sister. First, the scene where his wife realises he's attracted to her sister, and in a way approves of it, then the following scene. I told myself she was the kind of girl who, if she slept with a man, would ring her best friend the next day to tell her all about it. And that's the way I wrote it – with all the clichés it implies – except that her friend is her sister and the wife of the man she's just been making love to. In a way, that makes the situation normal.

His way of covering his face with his hand, as soon as he's in public, was that ever explained?

That was one of his contradictions. He had a large dose of exhibitionism in him. When he was asked to uncover his face as he came out of court, he took off his clothes but kept his hand over his face! He had a compulsion towards notoriety. Whenever he was under pressure, he'd give an interview. No doubt he thought that the fascination of the public for his person was important to his survival. The obvious paradox is the fact that hiding his face with his hand made him even more recognisable. It had to do with magic, a sort of ritual he'd worked out between himself and the outside world to signify that no one would ever know what was behind that hand.

Was he a pigeon fancier like Leo the Last?

He was actually passionate about pigeons and it was his only real contact with the world. He belonged to a club of pigeon fanciers, who he showed himself to be very generous to, and he went to England and France for related meetings. It's clearly a fascinating metaphor, since he started to get interested in it at the time that he lived in the slums of Hollyfield, as though it represented an escape towards freedom. At the same time, the pigeon always comes back. And it is significant that Cahill only trusted the people who came from around there. He didn't want to leave Hollyfield, whence his resistance to the bulldozers. When his women persuaded him to buy a house in a trendy suburb, he knew he was binding himself that way to regular, law-abiding society, whereas when he lived in Hollyfield surrounded by his people, he was sure they couldn't get him.

Your camera is very fluid and at the same time you resort more to close-ups than in most of your films.

The camera movements try to create a dynamic that you also find in the character. And I wanted to achieve a form of compression so that each moment was significant. Samuel Fuller used to say that a scene shouldn't evoke one single thing but several things at once. If you look at the action scenes such as the burglaries, you'll notice that they're filmed quite straightforwardly, in long shots, and that I hardly ever resort to the chopped-up editing that's in vogue today for this kind of sequence. I wanted them to be in the same style as the rest of the film, for them to have the same energy. I do in fact have more close-ups than usual since *The General* is first and foremost a 'portrait of a man' and it's on the faces that the story is told. It's a more intimate film than most of the ones I've made.

This is your first feature film with Seamus Deasy, your cinematographer.

Yes. He'd already done the photography on *I Dreamt I Woke Up* and *Two Nudes Bathing*. The latter was the first fiction film he shot. Before that he'd worked exclusively on documentaries. He's a wonderful collaborator. For the exteriors we used short focal lengths; for the interiors, since they lived in tiny rooms, I adopted long focal lengths to reproduce the impression of claustrophobia. The film was done with a local crew and in very tight budget conditions. My prop man, Derek Wallace, designed the sets, Seamus Deasy also took care of the frames, and the whole crew of technicians and actors was Irish. We did very little improvisation on the shoot but a lot during the six days of rehearsals, which allowed me to rework the script up until the last minute. When I hear the actors saying their lines, that often suggests changes to me and for me that was the most creative period. The editing was very quick, all the more so as I worked for the first time on an Avid. It's a process that can be pretty treacherous: traditional editing at the table allows you to reflect further because it's slower. The Avid can be useful for people who shoot at several different angles and use a lot of film, since it allows you to try out multiple possibilities. As I don't direct that way at all, and I have the film more or less in my head and don't do numerous takes, the Avid isn't much use to me.

How was the music selected?

I didn't want Irish music but an Irish sensibility. I really love jazz and I appreciate the work of Richie Buckley, a great Irish saxophonist who could, in what is his first score for the cinema, bring me two elements – jazz and an Irish touch. But the starting point was Van Morrison and in particular the song I use at the end of the film, *It Was Once My Life*, for Van Morrison's voice is the voice of my character; he's even a musical version of Martin Cahill.

Of all your films, it's certainly the one that's been prepared and made in the shortest space of time.

I started writing the script in the middle of the month of March 1997, and I finished the first draft in three weeks. At the beginning of May, I arrived at Cannes with my budget worked out. The longest part was finding the money; I even had to start filming at the start of August without having all the funds. In October, I started editing and I had a clean copy by March 1998, or exactly a year after getting the project off the ground, even if I'd done some research before that. I hadn't worked like that since *Catch Us If You Can!*

This film could actually be called Catch Me If You Can!

Maybe the speed with which I did it came from my frustration at not being able to finish my previous two projects. I'd worked for a year on an adaptation of *The Lion, the Witch and the Wardrobe,* based on C. S. Lewis's novel. It's a film that would have involved lots of special effects and we'd done more than 2,000 drawings and worked with Bill Henson's workshop to make imaginary animals. I also had an interesting collaboration with James Acheson, a wonderful costume designer who's received several Oscars and who worked with me on the visual design.

Sadly, the provisional budget reached eighty million dollars and Paramount abandoned it. If I'd made the film ten years ago, it would have cost infinitely less, but you're doomed to work in the context of the industry today. Now, the progress in computer-generated images is such that it involves prohibitive costs. It's a project dear to my heart as I've wanted to make a children's film for ages. I love fairytales and I've never stopped making them up for my children over two generations. That story, which is famous, is one I really love. During the Blitz, in the Second World War, a group of children leaves London and takes refuge in an old house. They find a wardrobe there, go in, and at the back they have access to a strange country where mythical creatures live, along with a wicked witch and a very nice lion. There's a mixture in there of Christian and pagan fancy and, in many ways, the book is like Tolkien's *The Hobbit*. I dreamed of adapting his *Lord of the Rings* once, in the 1970s. Curiously, C. S. Lewis and Tolkien were both professors at Oxford and each of them was very conscious of the other's work, with a mutual sense of rivalry. Tolkien was more inspired by Celtic mythology, while Lewis was inspired by the Greek legends.

After that, Paramount came back and offered me *Blood Simple*, a simple project in effect that could have been done quickly and that I liked. Five weeks before the shoot, Sherry Lansing, who runs the company, decided she needed a financial partner even though the film, in terms of American criteria, had a very modest budget of fifteen million dollars. Then, when she found one, she cancelled everything two weeks into the shoot, after having a fight with the executive producer, Scott Rudin, who works for the company a lot. He's someone I like but who has a reputation for being a difficult customer. When I was hired, there was already a script, but we reworked it in its entirety with Scott Smith, the author of the original novel. The action took place in a small town under snow in the north of the United States, with two brothers as protagonists. One of them is married to a woman who belongs to a higher social class than he does and the other is mentally deficient. They're both destitute until they find some booty on a plane that's crashed in the area. But the money they recover ends up destroying them. Billy Bob Thornton actually plays the retarded brother.

After The General, *you made a documentary on Lee Marvin, the first one you'd made since the one on Griffith,* The Great Director, *over thirty years ago.*

When Lee died, I encouraged Pam, his widow, to write her memoirs about him because she was so shaken up that I thought it might be a form of therapy. It took her several years and I helped her get the book into shape. I promised her I'd make a documentary after that to accompany the publication of the book. It's a very personal portrait of Lee. I introduce it, I'm the narrator and I did the interviews, in particular the one with the psychiatrist, Harry Wilmer, who knew Marvin well and specialises in the effects of war wounds on victims' psychology. What Lee went through in the Pacific had an enormous impact on him. No one has expressed violence like Lee and, in a way, he transformed his wartime experience by acting it out. He wanted to grasp the truth of that violence. It's a very affectionate portrait but, even though I knew Lee better than a lot of other people, I don't think I captured more than 10 per cent of his personality.

What are your projects now?

The story of Mary Wollstonecraft and her daughter Mary Shelley. The first was without a doubt the first feminist in history. She'd married Godwin, a philosopher who was influenced by the French Revolution and wanted to abolish all institutions, including marriage. When Shelley, who was nineteen, met Mary, he decided to live according to the principles of his father-in-law, who wasn't too impressed since his daughter was only sixteen! The second project, which I hope to make soon, is an adaptation of a book I've been offered – *Sadness at Leaving*, which is based on a true story. It's set in the 1960s, in New York, where a Russian man has been sent as a mole by the Soviet espionage department. His task is to assassinate his compatriots who carry secrets but who've gone over to the West. He fits into American society, marries a woman with whom he has a child, but keeps his activities secret until she tumbles to it. Parallel to this, he's driven to kill someone by mistake. This leads to a personal crisis, a conflict with his superiors, especially as they want to repatriate him on his own and they threaten his child. This notion of a double identity fascinates me, as does the period from 1961 to 1968, in which the action is set and which is a big moment in the history of the United States.

NOTES

1 The script of *The General* was published in English by Faber & Faber, with a preface by John Boorman.

3 ROBERT BRESSON

(1901–1999)

I was eighteen years old when I saw *A Man Escaped,* just after it was released in 1956, along with several other more or less contemporary films – Rossellini's *Voyage to Italy* (1953), Tati's *Monsieur Hulot's Holidays* (1953), Antonioni's *The Girlfriends* (1955) and Ophuls's *Lola Montès* (1955) – and it looked to me like confirmation that a new modern cinema had arrived. A former painter, Bresson shored up the notion of a *cinéma d'auteur,* surrounding the release of his works with a few lapidary comments like those of an artist accompanying the catalogue at the opening of a show. Bresson moved into film the way you enter a religious order or the way a writer at the turn of the nineteenth century once joined the *Nouvelle Revue Française,* with an exclusive passion for his art. In his *Notes On Cinematography* he urged: 'See your film as a combination of lines and volumes moving beyond what it portrays and means.'

This asceticism fascinated me. It irritated some, who were even more annoyed at Bresson's critical interpretation, entirely absorbed in Jansenism and the religious dimension of his films as it was. What I liked in Bresson, on the contrary, was his materiality, his attention to gesture and movement (of hands in particular), the beauty of the faces he filmed, his empathy with people's suffering, the infinite vibration that his sounds, his silences and his grey tones set resonating in the audience.

Bresson intimidated me. I only met him after his last film, *Money,* came out in 1983, a month after it was shown at the Cannes Festival. I wanted to do a portrait of him for *American Film,* the American Film Institute review. He was then the oldest of the great filmmakers still active but his art remained as vigorous and inventive as ever. He received me in the apartment on the Île Saint-Louis where he still lived, spoke with unfaltering elegance and precision, demanded to read the transcript of the interview and admitted to me in an aside that he had loved the ski scene, done with snow powder, in the latest James Bond, *For Your Eyes Only*. An admission that is not so surprising when you think that the presence of professional actors in his films or in the films of others was what most stopped him enjoying movies.

ON *MONEY*

PARIS, JUNE 1983

When people talk about your films they always evoke the asceticism. It has become a sort of cliché. What strikes me, on the contrary, is the vigour.

Vigour through precision. It comes down to the same thing since precision turns into vigour. When I'm not working well, I'm not precise. Precision can also be poetry.

Vigour … and speed. If you'd got any other filmmaker to do the script, there'd be a film two and a quarter hours long – not an hour and twenty-five minutes.

That's all to do with the composition. I say composition rather than structure. When I'm making them, I listen to my films the way a pianist listens to a sonata he's playing, and I tailor the image to the sound more than the sound to the image. All the transitions from one image to the next, from one sequence to the next, are like playing scales. Our eyes – our system of sight – occupies a very big place in our brains, maybe as much as two-thirds. And yet, our eyes' imagination is not as vast, not as varied, not as profound as the imagination of our ears. Surely we need to take this into account when we know the part played by the imagination in all creative work. Once, I never reflected at all between films. Then I started taking notes – I even put a little book together from them to get my ideas down on paper.[1] I asked myself the reasons why I worked the way I did. Well, they are absolutely innate. I don't have any preconceived ideas. I made my first film, *Affaires publiques*, in the 1930s. It's what we might call a 'burlesque' film, even though the term doesn't really fit. 'Burlesque' used to be applied more to certain American films of the time. Painters like me rushed to the movies practically every night because it *moved*; the leaves on the trees moved. The last part of *Affaires publiques* involved a boat launch. I'd got hold of images of the launch of the *Normandie* from Transat. The boat kept going down; it was sinking, and we still hadn't managed to smash the bottle. All of that was the result of chance and I believe very much in chance. In that film, there was a clown, Baby, who was the most incredible character imaginable. He didn't act at all. I let him do whatever he liked. That's when I realised that a film isn't put together by the performance of the actors, but by a series of inventions.

In my first feature film, *The Angels of Sin,* I felt like a bomb had gone off from the very first days of filming. I only had actresses on the set – they were playing nuns – and I told them straight away: 'If that's how it's going to be, I'll be off. There won't be any film.' What wasn't working for me was the superficial way they talked and their meaningless gestures. Every night, the producer would send me a telegram asking me to get them to act. And every night there'd be tears and gnashing of teeth. The ladies were lovely, anyway, and they managed to model themselves a little on what I wanted them to do. Already, my ear was more embarrassed than my eye. It was the intonations, the modulations of their voices more than their movements – which were easier to stop – that I didn't like.

Similarly, I realised very late in the day that phantom orchestra music was contrary to the spirit of a film. And it was also rather late in the day that I understood that sound was space. The voice heard as noise gives the screen its third dimension. When we sought some sort of relief, a spatial effect, in film, it wasn't at all interesting, we got it wrong. Because the relief was there. Suddenly, with sound, the screen hollows out, you feel like you can touch the people, pass behind them.

Is it because you work on the sound so much that you use depth of field so little in your films?

Maybe. But it's also because I only use a single lens while I'm shooting. I like getting up close to things and to people, to see them at the distance I'd stand in real life. That's why, in my films, the background is sometimes blurred. But it doesn't matter since, once again, it's the sound that provides distance and perspective.

To get back to my previous question, does Money *buck the trend, being so short? How do you explain why films just keep getting longer these days?*

It's because the movies are going to sleep. We'll soon see films three hours long because they have no idea, aren't looking for anything. It's time out, a holiday, sloppiness on the part of directors who are actually nearly always theatre directors. I'm surprised that those of them who can write – and often quite well – don't want to write themselves. But no, they hire a scriptwriter and I think I know why. If film really is an art, if you really do draw everything from out of yourself, you never stop feeling doubt and despair. So getting a pal to write the scenario completely removes your doubts and leaves you free to be a bit more laid-back in your work.

I'd really like to have a workshop and work with young filmmakers who have something to say. You know what Degas said: 'When you don't know, it's not hard.' So it's better to know as quickly as possible. On the other hand, when you're making a film, you have to forget what you know completely, be stripped bare and empty before your own will. That's what Cézanne said: 'I paint, I work, I don't think about a thing.' Cinema should evolve; let it evolve! It can even try something new with actors. I don't hold much store by that, though, because an art only finds its true strength when it sticks to being pure. I've noticed that certain directors take non-actors and just let them perform. You would have seen that in *Money*: no one performs. That's why it rolls along so fast: what matters is not what they're saying. At times, it was hard for me to get non-actors to work in a way that's satisfying to viewers' ears. This time, I think everything was 'said' properly, though with minute modulations. All the components of a film have to have something in common so there's an accord at each transition. This is as true for the image as for the sound. Non-actors have to have a certain way of talking, even if it's their own, that doesn't differ too much from the way the others talk. If we were to chart speech in film actors, there'd be huge differences in intensity whereas, with me, it's more even. All this just to be able to bring everything together without too much effort. The same goes for the image. I once said that I flatten images as though taking to them with an iron. I don't remove their significance, but I do tone them down so they don't have too much of a life of their own. The same goes for actors. In film, in general, actors seek to have a life of their own; the actor says, 'I am me', when the truth is that this 'me' is invented, willed – not their real 'me' at all.

According to you, the force of a sound should not correspond to the force of an image at the same time.

It's true that when sound and image go hand in hand, you get blandness, a loss of vitality. But things are more complicated than that. What enters through your eyes when you film comes out through two machines that are supposed to be perfect copiers but are nothing like it. One of them, the camera, gives us a false impression of people and things; the other, the tape recorder, reconstructs the very matter of sound as it is. To give a film some sort of real coherence, you'd have to get the camera to take from the tape recorder a bit of the reality that it has too much of. Think of all the things an audience could savour at the movies instead of just going along to see how good an actor is or to hear the modulations of a voice. At the end of *Money*, what I try to get is the force in the air before a storm. It's not something you can describe, but I do it by thinking of nothing. It's possible to calculate it, but it's not something you can know. You have to work with your sensitivity and nothing else. I've been labelled an intellectual, but I'm not an intellectual by any stretch of the imagination. When I write, it's painful, but I do it because I have to get everything out. Similarly, to call me a Jansenist or a Calvinist is madness: I'm the opposite of a Jansenist, I'm after impressions. I'll give you an example relating to *Money*. When I'm on the grand boulevards, out and about town, the first thing I ask myself is: 'What impression do they make on me?' Well, the impression I get is of a jumble of legs and feet making a crisp noise on the pavement. I've tried to render that impression through image and sound. So then I'm attacked for framing the bottom of people's trousers. Talk about stupid! I was attacked for the same sort of thing over horses' legs – in *Lancelot of the Lake*. I'd showed the legs of horses without showing their riders, so as to draw attention to the muscle-power of the horses' hindquarters when they brace themselves for the start of a tournament. I'm not going to show the rider because, if I did, then everything would be all muddled, something else would come into play, you'd be watching the rider, you'd be wondering what he was about to do. But, in ordinary life, we often look at the ground when we're walking along, or just a bit higher, but we don't necessarily look people straight in the face, except if a woman's pretty and we want to see her face. I know why people want movies to show the whole person. It's one more thing that derives from theatre, where you see everything.

You no longer choose your 'models' for their moral resemblance to your characters.

As long as nothing in their physical appearance, in their voice or their way of expressing themselves goes against them, I make my decision very swiftly. There are so many contradictions and eccentricities in people. Dostoyevsky practically turned such contradictions and eccentricities into a system. I love working with unknowns and for them to surprise me. I'm never disappointed in my models. I always find something in them that's new that I could never have imagined and that serves my purposes. And then again, I believe in accidents, in happy accidents. Lucien, the photographer's sidekick, like Yvon, the hero of the film, is a combination of happy accidents and my intuition.

You've never got a writer to help you with your dialogues, except in your first two films, and they weren't just any old writers: Giraudoux and Cocteau!

I owe those two a lot. After that, I was able to craft my films on my own, from writing them down on paper to the final form on screen. But, in the beginning, I was forced to or I wouldn't have been able to work. Giraudoux collaborated with me and I was absolutely full of admiration for that – like a schoolboy. I'd say to him: 'You need to sort of do this, you need to be brief, long, etc.' And he complied with a speed that was frightening. For *The Ladies of the Bois de Boulogne*, I'd written three-quarters of the dialogue with difficulty when I called on Cocteau, after trying in vain to work with Paul Morand, Nimier, Supervieille – it had never worked. Meanwhile, I was writing my own dialogues because I was convinced I had to do everything myself. And, finally, Cocteau solved my problems in his apartment, on the edge of a tablecloth, in one and a half hours.

Do you make a distinction between the films where you draw your inspiration very freely – from Bernanos, Dostoyevsky, Tolstoy – and those that are completely original like Au hasard, Balthazar *and* The Devil Probably?

There's not much of a distinction, it seems to me. With *Money*, what I took from Tolstoy's *The Forged Coupon* was his starting point and the idea of how evil spreads, and I let myself run with my daydreams right till the end, where I slip in the idea of the hero's rehabilitation and of redemption, which isn't in the same place in the novel. After a while, I let go of everything, like with a horse when you let go of the reins, and I go wherever my imagination takes me. The narrative is not the same as in Tolstoy. *The Forged Coupon* is a magnificent novel but, as soon as the first murder occurs, Tolstoy starts talking about God, the Scriptures. I didn't want to go down that track because the film is made to combat the unconscious indifference of people today who think only of themselves and their families. I'd made *The Devil Probably* to combat that indifference, too, but here it's in relation to what was happening in the world. At the time, you'll recall, there were quite a few suicides where young people set themselves on fire. That no longer happens. The younger generations don't even think of it, which is very curious. In fact, they find it normal, they've been born into a world people habitually abuse and it doesn't shock them. For *The Devil Probably,* I was told about a boy who set himself on fire in the playground of his high school in a village in the north of France. I wrote to his parents to ask them for his diary. I didn't use any of it; I just wanted to see what state of mind the boy was in. He wasn't very good at expressing himself, but he was completely panic-stricken about what was happening in the world.

What happens, while you're reading a story, to trigger your desire to turn it into a film?

With *The Forged Coupon,* it was immediate. I saw the film right away because it corresponded with my desire to make a film about a chain reaction that ends in some horrible catastrophe. A banknote that winds up killing a whole heap of people. Why does someone commit murder? Why did Julien Sorel kill Madame de Rénal? Did he know he was going to, five minutes beforehand? Surely not. What happens at that moment? It's a kind of unleashing of the forces of revolt, of hate you've compressed inside you. That interested me more in Tolstoy than the religious aspect, which is still absolutely fascinating, but it's just not the way we'd talk about it these days.

Tolstoy's short story had a very complex structure and you've fused several characters into a single one.

I simplified a lot by subtraction on paper and a lot more still during the shoot, because I didn't want to overload the images, make them opaque, which perhaps provides the film's consistency – something Edgar Allan Poe talks about in *Eureka*. The poetry, if there is any – not 'poetic' poetry, but cinematic poetry

– comes from this condensation. It stems from the simplification, which is nothing more than a more direct view of people and things.

In Notes on Cinematography, *you write in capital letters: 'A RESPECTABLE DISTANCE FROM ORDER AND DISORDER.' Which corresponds perfectly to your work, where meticulous preparation sits beside acceptance of chance.*

'You have to shake the tree,' as Chaplin used to say. But not too much, I think. Because you need a bit of real disorder. Curiously, some of my films that look really well prepared weren't at all. Like *Pickpocket,* which was written in three months and filmed in the midst of teeming hordes in no time at all. I also filmed *Trial of Joan of Arc* very fast, but that was easier because I had unity of place and characters. With *Money,* I was worried about the frequent changes of place, of human groupings, worried about losing the thread. But I managed to hop from one sequence to the next using shifts in sound – I'd like to say musical shifts. Once, people used to go in for dissolves, but sound shifts are so much more beautiful… But no one does it. I'm now accused of dragging things out at the end of a scene compared to current films where, as soon as the dialogue ends, you either have to have music or you have to move on to another set of dialogue. Otherwise, there's thought to be a hole!

It's hard to believe, watching your films, that improvisation has played such a large role.

In *Money,* and the film before it, I never tried to know in advance what I was doing, or how I'd do it. There has to be a shock in the very instant, you need to show what's new in people and things, to create surprises and throw them onto the reel. That's what happened with the sequence on the boulevards that I was telling you about. I felt the footsteps, I was interested in the hero's legs, and that allowed me to get him where he was going, through all those passing people. That's what the boulevards mean to me, all this movement… Otherwise, you're left with a postcard. What struck me in the films I saw when I still went to the movies was that everything was planned in advance, worked out down to the very last detail. The actors studied their roles, etc. A painter doesn't know in advance how his painting will turn out, a sculptor how his sculpture will turn out, a poet his poem…

How do your film titles spring to mind? For example, Money?

To me, it was obvious. Immediately: *Money.* I didn't think for a second. If anyone had told me I couldn't use that title because it was already taken, I'd have said: too bad… Whether we're talking about governments or people, money's the only thing that counts. Today the value of a human being or an object is reduced to two questions: Is he rich? Is it worth a lot of money? I was stunned to see an ad in the Metro recently that said: 'The most sold oven in France.' Always this notion of the best-seller. The film that sells the most tickets is the best. You see where we've landed. That's money talking. For *Au hasard, Balthazar,* I was looking for a biblical title. One of the three kings was called Balthazar. The word 'hasard' – 'chance' in French – came to me easily and I liked the rhyme. The title, *The Devil Probably,* is one I hit on early in the piece, while I was busy jotting things down on paper.

In The Devil Probably, *there is the same loop between predestination, inevitability and, at the same time, the freedom each and every one of us enjoys deep down.*

I believe in that more and more. More and more, I have the impression that the role we assign to movie actors is to explain what is psychologically inexplicable in them. A non-actor can't explain himself at all because he doesn't know himself. If he did, he'd be an extraordinary genius and we'd use him for something else. For me he has this total mystery which is to be found in every person I meet. It's interesting, when you want to get to know someone, to imagine what's behind those cheeks, that forehead, those eyes. The most fascinating thing in life is curiosity. I want people to want to know, to want to explore the endless mystery that is life. It's life, but we can't recreate it, only imagine it.

Your work is made up of a respect for fragments of reality, but those fragments are assembled in a certain order.

They are fragments of reality, but it's the relationships between the fragments and the way they're put together that are expressive – not the miming and intonations of actors' voices as in theatre. In a film, sound and image move in parallel fashion; they anticipate each other, back away, find themselves coming together and then push off again hand in hand. What interests me on screen is counterpoint.

You are always against theatre. On the other hand, you – a painter, someone born to paint – think that cinema in no way competes with the fine arts.

I love the theatre, but I don't think cinema gains anything by being theatre photographed or by being a synthesis of the other arts. I like to quote young people this phrase of Stendhal's: 'It's the other arts that have taught me the art of writing.' You have to turn yourself into an eye, an ear.

With you, the image is visual but never makes a 'picture'. Weren't you ever worried that painting would contaminate your films?

No. If I think of painting, it is to get away. I mean to get away from the colour postcard. But that's not why I don't construct my images with the eye of a painter. Note, in *Money*, the continual close-ups whose only *raison d'être* is the feeling they evoke. When the pianist drops the glass, his daughter is in the kitchen. She has the dustpan and the sponge all ready. I don't get her to come into the room, but I go immediately to a close-up that I love – the wet floor with the noise of the sponge. That's what the music is, the rhythms, the feelings. I'm not going to show a man walking into a room, like you get in theatre or the movies, but the knob of a door turning. Note also how the hero is not described straight away – at first you see only his legs, then his back, then you see three-quarters of him, then, all of a sudden, he reveals himself, walking completely on his own.

There are a lot of camera movements in your films, contrary to what people often think, but they are always subtle. There are never any tracking shots or showy pans.

Because that is phoney, totally phoney. You never see lamps or tables move by themselves, yet that's the effect you get with sudden camera movements. What I'm looking for is not a description but a view of things. Movement stems from a series of views and the way they're linked. But that can't be described. For, more and more, what I'm trying to do – and this was almost a method with *Money* – is to convey the impression I feel. It's the impression of the thing and not the thing itself that counts. Reality is what we make of it. Every individual has his or her own. There is a real reality, but it isn't ours. When I first started out, in *The Ladies of the Bois de Boulogne*, that wasn't what I was after: I was aiming for a certain coherence; that was all. But, today, I show the basket of potatoes of the little old lady who gathers them, and not her face. It's not worth the trouble because we see her shortly after in a much more important action, which is when she comes back up and is about to go off. That's also the only time the boy helps her.

You've worked with five different cinematographers: Agostini, Burel, Lhomme, Cloquet and De Santis. Did this mean a change for you, every time?

No, not really. We've always managed to get on well. I've never been influenced by their way of doing things. They've always found it easy to do what I told them to do, what I knew they could do. I love De Santis because we see people and things visually the same way. If I do *La Genèse,* which I hope to do, it will surely be with him. He manages to get something I love: he renders people in all their roundness, their convexity.

Do you talk things over with him before the shoot?

I explain to him roughly what I hope to get, the global vision I have of the film. Details fall into place as a surprise, but don't change anything of what we've agreed beforehand. Ideas for the lighting often occur in a flash. For instance, when Lucien is in front of the ATM, I'd put, in the script, that he'd be aided by the light coming from the streetlight. But as soon as I started filming, I found that the neon sign with its intense colours would be far preferable.

In Money, *you take a very tough view of this bourgeois world, the framers, the parents of the high school boy, Norbert. The sympathetic characters are Yvon, the man who delivers oil and the old woman who is exploited.*

Naturally, because that's the way I think. But it's not an anti-bourgeois film. It's not about the bourgeois world but about specific cases. I am, myself, bourgeois. I've simply observed people like that. That's what appealed to me in Tolstoy's novel. But there are people from other social classes who can do the same thing through love of their children. What they do is not evil in itself, but in the consequences that ensue.

What is pungent is the contemporary feel of Tolstoy's story – the high school kids, the photograph frames.

I was keen to keep the initial viewpoint because it's accurate. I've made it French, made it Parisian and contemporary. I've also kept the photographer so there's a darkroom and he hides in it.

Do you sample a lot of sounds with a view to mixing them?

I take as many direct samples as I can. If I hear a sound I like, I record it – a water noise, the fluttering of wings. The trouble with shooting outdoors is avoiding noise. When I'm not too tired, I take samples in the evening or at night. The water noises in *Money* were harvested that way.

What's lovely in the murder scene in Money *is that the emotion comes from the crying of the dog.*

Lots of animals have an exquisite sensitivity that we don't make enough of an effort to understand. I'd like to use that more often. It's like a doubling of our sensitivity, an extension of our joys and our suffering.

Among all the doors in Money, *the last one stays open, and the prisoner goes through it.*

If I feel like it, why wouldn't I stick ten times the number of doors in my films? Doors that open, that shut, that lead to the mystery that hasn't yet been solved are really beautiful. Why not doors? It's a musical rhythm. It's amazing how habit can kill people! It may well be too symbolic, but I really like these gaping onlookers staring into the void. Everything was there, now there's nothing.

You call yourself a 'happy pessimist' but your last films are darker compared to Pickpocket *or* A Man Escaped, *where there was a sort of final jubilation.*

I'm sorry that in *Money* I wasn't able to dwell on Yvon's rehabilitation, on the idea of redemption, but the rhythm of the film, at that point, wouldn't allow it. I probably do see the dark side of the world more than I used to. It's not at all deliberate, but something like that is going on.

You have rarely used film musicians, preferring, on the contrary, the great composers such as Mozart, Lully, Monteverdi, Schubert or Bach.

It doesn't matter any more since I've completely eliminated music as a support or accompaniment in my films for the last few years. I only realised very late in the piece what a bad effect music had, even when – *especially* when – it's glorious. The images are immediately flattened, whereas at the slightest sound, they dig in, go deeper, take on a third dimension.

Why did you choose Bach's Chromatic Fantasia for Money?

Because I didn't want my pianist to play sentimental music. That's exactly what you don't want, when the storm's brewing. Now it's still too sentimental even though Bach isn't at all. I missed my mark…

But Schubert's Twentieth Sonata, which accompanies Au hasard, Balthazar, *is an emotionally stirring piece of music.*

Yes, alas! Apart from the braying and the noise of hooves, there were silences I didn't know how to fill. I took that piece as the donkey's sort of soul language that comes back every time as a leitmotif. But I'm not happy with myself, and that's the last time I've put ghost music in.

Which of your films give you the most satisfaction?

I don't know since I never see them again, or practically never. They've all given me joy making them. Some of them I made very smoothly and fast, like *Pickpocket*. I love how fast it is and the way the images fit together. In *Au hasard, Balthazar* there are some nice touches mixed in with the imperfections. Unbelievable, insane coincidences have to happen if you're going to bring off things that are really hard work. In *Four Nights of a Dreamer*, I liked the theme well enough: 'Love is merely an illusion, so let's keep at it!' That one's not pessimistic! But no film is ever perfect.

What is really lovely in Money *is the sudden shift to the country.*

That change of place is the one I was most afraid of. I feared it was too disparate and would cut the thread. That said, there is a reason behind it: prisons are very often on the edge of towns, almost in the countryside. Yvon goes for a jaunt round there, he doesn't know what to do and he goes into the first hotel he comes to. That's where everything begins. I know the house where the murder takes place and the laundry; they're close to my place in Epernon.

Yvon has a bit of the exterminating angel about him.

Society abandons him. The carnage he commits is like the expression of his despair. What I was interested in, in his relationship with the little old lady, was the meeting of acceptance and revolt, and what was going to happen afterwards. I want to be able to put my finger on our moral pulse – not just tell a story.

But all your films are made of these encounters: between predestination and freedom, between chance and necessity.

That's how we are. Chance prevails, nine times out of ten, in what happens to us. And will shades into predestination. In *The Life of St Ignatius*, which I nearly did a long time ago, there was already this notion of predestination. This bloke just popped up by chance; he hadn't done anything much himself, but he knew all the right people and he set up the Jesuit order.

In your profession, too, there is the meeting of your will and all the chance elements of a shoot.

My will failed at certain moments, found itself in a pretty sorry state; but, now, it's flying along. I sense that I'd like to do so many things that I won't really get off the ground. I'm in a hurry to get on with work. There's also another book I'd like to write.

'Money is God made visible,' one character says. And so it is a false god since what counts for you is the invisible.

It's an abominable false god! What I meant was that you can't get away from it today. But it's true that everything that really counts is invisible. What are we doing here? What do life and death mean? Where are we going? What's behind these miracles of animal and/or plant life? You know that people are putting these two things together a lot now. I wanted to get that into *La Genèse*.

Do you see your film before you make it?

Yes, and I go on seeing it – and hearing it – all through the filming and editing, where it takes on its final form bit by bit. I don't try to purify things, to achieve asceticism, as has been written. That's not it. The problem is that you can't see things if they're messy. In a tree, you can't make out one leaf in particular. To be receptive to something, you have to separate it mentally from all that's stopping it from being seen. If it's overloaded, one image can't follow the other. There has to be some notion of simplicity. But, you know, as I've already said, photos lie. Take someone under two different sets of lights, and you've got two different people. My hero in *Money* has three faces. At times, he's really good looking, at others, he looks like an eighteen-year-old boy. I stumbled on Christian Patey by chance. My wife had known him from the house she'd lived in previously. He was a neighbour and he came to ask her for a favour. And then she thought of him for the role. He's a one-off. He has to be strong and violent, but appear not to be. He has to not be from Paris.

You only started using colour very late.

It used to cost too much. As soon as I had the means, I was only too happy to use it. Colour is light; it is light itself. All day, I paint with my eyes; I look at volumes, forms, colours. The move to colour happened without any difficulty and didn't change my way of composing or looking at people in any way. Whatever they say, when you paint, the drawing is already more or less complete, the main lines anyway, and that's all down in black and white. At times, I need a strong colour to balance the persistently neutral colours.

Do you still paint?

No, never. I haven't painted now for a long time. I don't think we *can* paint anymore. Painting had nowhere else to go. I'm not talking about Picasso. I'm talking about Cézanne. Cézanne went as far as it is possible to go. Others can paint because they're not as old as I am, but I felt very early on that I shouldn't go on. When I stopped painting, I had a very hard time, and film for me was just a last resort to occupy my mind, at least to start with. I think I was right to make the switch, as film can go a lot further than painting. Unfortunately, with film, there are all these expectations on the part of the backers, and not working with my hands annoys me, too. But for anyone with something to say, cinema, or rather the cinematograph, is the painting or writing of the future, using two kinds of ink, one for the eyes, the other for the ears.

Do you like poets such as Francis Ponge? One can't help thinking of him, watching your films, of Parti pris de choses.

Yes. I don't see Ponge anymore, I'm sorry to say, since he lives down south. He wrote some remarkable letters to me about my films and about cinema in general. I love his love of objects, of inanimate things. Cocteau, in one of his plays, has one of his characters say: 'Objects follow us like cats.' Watching my films, you might also think of Le Clézio. He wrote me a wonderful letter about *Money*. And I've also heard from musicians, painters. They see what I see.

What is the stage you prefer: writing, editing or filming?

The hardest part for me is getting it down on paper. You find yourself stuck between four walls and there are the doubts I mentioned earlier and the difficulties I personally have writing. But now I work differently, I do it while I'm walking in the street or swimming in the sea, in summer. After that I make notes. With the filming, the problem is that you have to be quick. The crew are always amazed that I have to stop, to reflect, sometimes for ten minutes or a quarter of an hour at a time. Once, years ago, when I was in Italy – where, curiously, I've never managed to make a film – there were directors there, I remember, who could just say, 'I don't feel inspired today, I'm going.' And no one would bat an eyelid. That's wonderful. But if I go round in circles for a while, if I change tack, everyone's shocked. All because movies depend on pre-production. Everything's worked out in advance. You know what angle you're going to be filming from and what corner of the studio since, most of the time, you film in a studio. All that creates a terrible mess where it's hard to tell what's real and what isn't.

It's the editing that suddenly makes the film, when images and sound fit together. Life suddenly materialises. From beginning to end, then, a film is nothing but a series of births and resurrections.

What's dead on paper is reborn in the filming, and the dead image is reborn in the editing. So that's the reward for all our labours.

In your book, you talk about the 'eye's ability to ejaculate'.

It's the ability to create. The eye demolishes what it sees and then puts it back together again according to the idea it makes of it. If you're a painter, your eye puts it back together again according to your feel for, or your ideal of, beauty.

Aren't your characters driven by desire?

The desire to live. And willpower too. The desire to make what you love appear before your very eyes. My characters push themselves to the limit. I can't do it any other way; otherwise they'd be dead. If I were painting a flower, I wouldn't paint it as a bud, but in its most luscious maturity, at the heart of its mystery.

A Man Escaped, *with its doggedly determined hero, is like a new version of* Robinson Crusoe. *He figures out the technical problems in his cell: how to saw the bars, etc.*

He doesn't let himself sink into metaphysical despair, but tries to find the resources within himself to survive.

You'll find a lot more of that in *La Genèse,* which I'll be working on in a few months. Adam, too, will seem like a shipwreck setting off to find some unknown island. What is so beautiful in Genesis is when God asks Adam to name things and animals. I find that wonderful. And everything's ready when he turns up on this unknown island. I'm now thinking again about doing this project after abandoning it fifteen years ago. It'll take at least a year to prepare. There is the problem of the birds, the insects, the big animals, the tree, the period. It goes on forever. The script's already fairly advanced, but there are still holes. It's huge. I'm like the *Marseillais*: worn out in advance.

For you, where does Genesis stop?

At the Flood or else at the Tower of Babel, at the invention of tongues. It will be a very long film, made for television and spoken in ancient Hebrew, which is a beautiful language with its mix of Aramaean. Adam can't speak in French or English. He has to speak in a language that almost no one will understand.

So it will be an even more musical film than the rest?

Exactly. Imagine the noises of the animals, not only at the moment of Creation, but in the ark during the Flood. What a concert, what emotion, what silence at times! I'm so keen to do it, I'll just dive in the way you dive into the ocean, and we'll see what happens.

Where will you film?

I don't know yet. Not in Palestine or in any other country in the Middle East. I don't want to typecast the scenery and, anyway, it's never mattered much to me. Rather than seeing a camel on top of a sand dune I'd prefer to stick him on the top of the Puy-de-Dôme. I'd quite like to film in the Auvergne, which is where I come from, because it has such varied landscapes.

NOTES

1 *Notes on Cinematography* (New York: Urisen Books, 1977).

4 JANE CAMPION

(1954–)

My discovery of Jane Campion occurred in two stages corresponding to the two interviews that follow. The first, with the screening at the Cannes Festival in 1986 of a programme of shorts that Pierre Rissient, headhunter of the cinema of the future and also a great rediscoverer of the films of the past, had brought together from one of his exploratory expeditions to the antipodes. *Peel, Passionless Moments* and *A Girl's Own Story* revealed an amazingly sharp eye, a feel for ellipsis and a specifically feminine sensibility that till then only Agnès Varda had made me feel to such a degree in film. The second stage occurred three years later, again at the Cannes Festival, with the presentation of *Sweetie* in competition. The film was overlooked by the jury, presided over by Wim Wenders, who gave the Palme d'Or to another first feature, *Sex, Lies and Video* by Steven Soderbergh. *Sweetie* was doubtless too singular, too cutting, too bold in its subject matter and in its form to seduce the majority. It was deserted by part of the audience, then booed and applauded in equal measure by those who remained. I met Jane Campion once more after that, when she was still distressed by the reactions she'd provoked. In conversation she is every bit as cheeky, vivacious and charming as her films. She often accompanies what she says with a contagious fit of the giggles, for this filmmaker is fearless. She knows how to look at the world warmly but not without a distant and sometimes cruel humour. She has the feistiness, the poise and the bizarre imagination of a whole line of Anglo-Saxon women, from the Emilys (Brontë and Dickinson) to Flannery O'Connor and Virginia Woolf. *An Angel At My Table* was to confirm this rare talent before the crowning glory of *The Piano Lesson*, which won the first Palme d'Or ever given to a female filmmaker. Some began to shun her after that, so great is the desire of cinephiles to keep the object of worship to themselves and so reluctant are they to see them adulated by others. Yet *Portrait of a Lady* and *Holy Smoke*, though very different in style, both offer proof of the same evocative power, the same ability to portray young girls doggedly determined to find themselves. Jane Campion has lost nothing of her insolence and the young girl that dwells inside her has not dutifully settled down.

ON THE SHORT AND MEDIUM-LENGTH FILMS
PARIS, OCTOBER 1986

You were born in New Zealand. What was your family background?

My parents were in theatre and their families had been in New Zealand for several generations. My mother was an actress and my father was a director, and they'd both been trained in England. They set up a company in New Zealand, put on Shakespeare and settled in the capital, Wellington. That's where I grew up. After that, they turned to farming. They were sick of dealing with the problems associated with the theatre where they didn't make much money. From time to time they'd go back and tread the boards again. At home the conversation always centred around the classic plays they staged and actors' performances. I myself was passionately interested in theatre and I had a go at it in high school. My brother and sister and I competed for our parents' attention, but we were very close at that age. At sixteen I went to university. But I spent my whole adolescence both in town and in the country since the town's right next to the countryside in New Zealand.

Why didn't you go in for the theatre?

Little by little I became very critical of theatre. The actors I met seemed artificial to me, not natural. I decided to get stuck into something more serious and I wanted to go to university in Australia. That's the kind of decision you make at sixteen. I studied anthropology after trying psychology and education, which I didn't much like. My degree didn't really take me anywhere but we had a fantastic teacher, a Dutchman named Power. He'd studied with Lévi-Strauss and we'd talk about issues of structural anthropology and linguistics. What interested me in anthropology was being able to study 'officially' what I was curious about anyway: how our thoughts work, their mythical content, which has nothing to do with logic, human behaviour. I think I have an anthropologist's eye, anyway, a sense of observation. I liked anthropology for both the theory and the poetry.

Your shorts, though, are distinct from many Australian films that take stock of the presence of aborigines, the role of myths. You come closer to a behaviourist study of the characters.

Actually I don't think the great aboriginal myths are really a part of Australian culture. People talk about them but very superficially. I'm very interested in that, as I am in everything that touches on human beings, but it isn't part of my world. On the other hand, I think that man thinks he's a creature of reason but he isn't, he's ruled by something quite different. And that's what interests me. So I finished university and got my degree. But then I realised that if I went down that path, I'd wind up expressing myself in ways that only other anthropologists would understand. And I wanted the opposite. I wanted to communicate with people and find common symbols, and you can do that by telling stories. So that's when I decided to go to Europe. That's where my heritage lies, that's the history I'd learned in school. I was curious to see what it was really like. I also wanted to learn painting, which is what I did in London while I was working as an assistant on a film. But I didn't really like London. I stayed there for a year and then I went back to Australia because the art school enrolment fees and the cost of living in general in London were too high. Everyone wandered around looking a bit lost when I was studying art there, including the lecturers! My experience at Sydney College of the Arts, on the other hand, was wonderful. The teachers were young, they had a clear idea of what they wanted and they weren't lumbered with all the traditions that prevail in England. What interested me, actually, was the relationship between art and life, how you react visually to an experience.

What sort of painting did you do?

I wanted to paint what mattered to me and I ended up telling little stories on canvas. It was figurative. I also liked writing, so I gave my paintings captions. At the same time, I put on plays about love and disappointment. They were filmed on video and I played some of the roles. I thought they were terrible and I didn't think I was much chop as an actress. So I then decided to make Super 8 films myself, directing actors in roles I'd written for them. That was very ambitious on my part, as I didn't know anything about film: it all came from a manual. But I was very motivated since I was really keen to tell my stories. The result was pretty unsatisfactory, as Super 8 requires a lot of precision and I lacked experience. I made two films. One was called *Tissues* and ran for twenty minutes, the other was called *Eden*. I didn't really finish that one since I've never added sound. *Tissues* foreshadowed *A Girl's Own Story* a bit. People really liked it as I'd put quite a bit of energy into it but it was hideous visually, since I didn't really know what a shot was!

What films did you like?

I wasn't really a movie buff. I'd go and see a movie whenever I happened to feel like going. But I remember I was completely knocked out by Buñuel, I tried to see everything he'd ever made. I also liked people like Antonioni and Bertolucci. On the whole I was more drawn to European cinema or to people like Kurosawa than to the world of Hollywood.

What did you decide to do after art school?

I didn't know what the next stage would be. I didn't see how I could get make contact with the people in the film industry or with the people at the Australian Film Corporation. One day, they seem to believe in you and the next day they've lost faith… So I decided to get into the Australian Film, Television and Radio School and from day one, I tried to make as many shorts as I could over the three years I was there. I made *Peel* in first year, *Passionless Moments* in second and third year and *A Girl's Own Story* in third year.

What was the idea behind your first film, Peel?

I knew this incredibly weird family and I thought they'd be interesting to film. They were the kind of people who are more or less out of control. I'd suggest scenes to them and, since they were extremely honest, they'd see that the scenes showed them as they really were. It was a very short film, about nine minutes.

Passionless Moments *was a more elaborate film.*

It was the result of collaboration with one of my friends, Gerard Lee. He had the initial idea and we wrote it and directed it together. Once we had the outline of the film – a series of sketches – we tried to think up as many stories as we could and we'd then tell them with a certain ironic detachment. In the end we wrote ten of them. Gerard and I wanted to show ordinary, sweet people – people you rarely see on screen but who have more charm than lots of well-known artists. They also had a funny side that appealed to us. The film was shot in five days, two episodes a day. I was also in charge of the photography and I realised the benefits of film school, where I'd learned about lighting and the potential of the camera in two hours, once.

What all your short features have in common is a sense of observation, the use of moments, epiphanies that show the way people behave.

That's always interested me. I remember that at film school my mates wanted to tackle big subjects or spectacular scenes with car crashes. That was the last thing I wanted to do.

You are a fan of your compatriot, Katherine Mansfield, who was also interested in observing details.

Yes. I love her books. When I was a kid in New Zealand, I used to play near her memorial, which was in a park close to our house.

To what extent is A Girl's Own Story *inspired by your own childhood and adolescence?*

I wanted to pay tribute to that period of our lives where we feel lonely and lost. It's such a part of growing up. It's a curious stage in our development, when we feel adult emotions but we don't yet have any experience. With experience, it's easier to face your emotions. The smallest things seem like huge obstacles when you're very young. I'd been though lots of experiences that I'd never seen portrayed. For instance, at school everyone used to kiss each other and then, as soon as they were bigger, they stopped doing it. Everyone acted like it had never happened. I also wanted to talk about the Beatles, whose music really affected my generation – I was born in 1954. The incest episode wasn't a personal experience but I remember how a very young girl, who was a neighbour of ours, was made pregnant by a boy in the same class and the scandal that caused.

Did the actors bring various things to it or was everything written down from the outset?

Naturally the actors always contribute a little. But in this precise case, the teenage girls thought I was really weird and swore they'd never done anything like that. Actually, basically they stuck to their lines. I had trouble finding actresses. The first one I chose didn't feel comfortable with the incest. She was too immature and I had to get someone older who looked young for her age. Officially the shoot lasted ten days but I managed to 'steal' extra time. All the crew were students and we didn't have a lot of experience but the film got a good reception in Australia and even won a few prizes. When it was shown the reaction was really good, people laughed so much you could hardly hear the dialogue. I was really touched since my lecturers had never supported my work. They were very conservative types who felt this genre of film was too strange for me to ever get a job.

You made After Hours *just after you left the film school.*

Yes. On the strength of my shorts, the Women's Film Unit invited me to write and direct the film. I don't like *After Hours* much; I felt my reasons for doing it were mixed. There was a conflict inside me between the project and my conscience as an artist. The film was commissioned by the Women's Film Unit and it was supposed to be overtly feminist since it was dealing with the sexual abuse of women in the workplace. I wasn't all that comfortable, as I don't like films that tell you how you're supposed or not supposed to behave. I think the world's more complicated than that. I prefer watching people and studying how they behave without blaming them. I'd have preferred sticking the film in a cupboard but it went round the world! I like making films I'd like to see myself as a cinemagoer and that just isn't the case with *After Hours*, though it was important for me to do it.

You then directed an episode of Dancing Daze *for the ABC.*

That was a commission, light entertainment for television. I was in the middle of writing a script for a TV series on the New Zealand writer, Janet Frame, and I wanted to find out what it was like working for television. It was an interesting experience, even if I'm not all that keen on the film, since I got to meet Jan Chapman, who later produced *Two Friends*. I was forced to work fast and make a fifty-minute film in a week, song and dance routines included. It was a classic story about a group of young people who want to set up a dance company in 1986. I had to be visually inventive. I had a lot of fun and it gave me confidence in how I could fit into commercial cinema.

Shortly after that you made Two Friends.

We had to be quick about it, because the ABC had a crew available and a slot in its production schedule. The pre-production period was short. As I said, Helen Garner's script had been offered to me by the producer, Jan Chapman. We agreed on the objectives and we had a relationship based on trust. I also really loved the script even if this notion of telling a story by going back in time wasn't my preferred option. What I loved was how fresh the observations were and how true the situations were. I felt I could really do something with it. Helen Garner had been inspired by the experiences of her daughter and one of her friends. I went down to Melbourne to meet them. The schoolgirl who played her daughter had blond hair and we didn't think she looked serious enough. We gave her chestnut hair and had it cut like a boy's. I think, on the whole, it's not too hard working with teenagers, even if there are days when they get very confused emotionally.

To what extent do objects, which there are a lot of in your films, help the actors in their work?

I first like to watch how they normally act in real life and then remind them of that when we're filming so their performance is natural, comes from real life.

Do you take charge of the camera a lot?

I like looking through the viewfinder, as I'm very precise about the frames I want. When we were filming *Two Friends*, the camera crew resented me a bit because they weren't used to a director taking charge of that. My director of photography didn't really understand what I wanted and I had to really dig my heels in to impose my shots. I had a very good relationship, on the other hand, with Sally Bongers, a friend who'd been in film school with me and who did the photography on *Peel* and *A Girl's Own Story*. For *Two Friends*, on the other hand, I had to use the TV crew. They were extremely competent; they just had very different filming techniques.

Do you do many takes?

No. With *Two Friends,* for instance, we'd decided on a visual style, we knew there'd be virtually no close-ups, and as soon as the actors had done a scene and got the tone right, we'd move on to the next shot. I didn't 'cover' myself, so to speak. It was a very economical shoot overall.

Will you go on mining this intimate vein?

I hope there'll always be the same sense of observation in my films since I think that's a strength, but I'm not so sure my stories will stay as intimate. I'd really like to work on a broader scale with stronger stories, different material. At the moment I'm working on a project that's close in spirit and atmosphere to a Grimm fairytale. It's a love story set in New Zealand around 1850, in a pretty bleak climate.

Did you decide to portray young people in A Girl's Own Story *and* Two Friends *because you felt safer starting off dealing with themes you were familiar with?*

In the case of *A Girl's Own Story*, I did in fact want to talk about a world I knew well. I also really like young people. I find them to be free and generous with themselves. But it's not an obsession on my part! Naturally, every time someone writes a story with young girls in it now they think of me to direct it. But every generation interests me. I'd actually like to tell all sorts of different stories. At the moment I'm re-reading *Treasure Island* and I'm getting a great deal of pleasure out of it. I love its power, its audacity, but also its sense of observation. Anyhow, I think I'll always have a certain ironic outlook on life.

ON *SWEETIE*

CANNES, MAY 1989

What have you been doing in the three years between your short features and Sweetie?

After my films were presented at the Cannes Festival, I thought long and hard about what I was going to do given the way doors then opened for me. The first project I wanted to see through successfully was *Sweetie*, as it seemed to me to take the most modern and provocative stance. What's more, it was financially doable. I also thought it'd be hard to do *Sweetie* after a more 'serious' film! I know I've got a provocative streak and I really liked the idea of tackling the material. I started developing the story with my co-scriptwriter, Gerard Lee, the friend who'd already written *Passionless Moments* with me and who is extremely intelligent. He knew the material well, it belonged to both of us, and we were on the same wavelength. It took me three years to make *Sweetie* because I was also working on other projects at the time. Such as *The Piano*, which is a very romantic subject in Brontë Sisters mode that I'd like to make later, and also *Janet Frame*, which will be my next film. It's a portrait of a New Zealand writer who wrote several volumes of an autobiography that turns on what it's like growing up as well as the problems of being creative. I love the style in her autobiographical trilogy. *To the Island*, which deals with her childhood, is really fresh and it's the most appealing of the three. After that there's *An Angel At My Table* and *An Envoy To Mirror City*, in which many of the events are set in Europe. That's why I was location spotting all over your continent recently. I'll make it for television in three hour-long parts, with an option to do a movie version.

Did you have trouble financing Sweetie?

It wasn't hard finding the money for the three projects I mentioned. As for producing *Sweetie* itself, it all went pretty smoothly because the film was very low cost, less than a million dollars. The script was written from that perspective. It was inspired by people and events I was familiar with. That's how I always proceed. It makes me write more authoritatively and even if I later stray from those experiences, I've always got a foundation I can come back to. The character of Sweetie was inspired by a man but for family reasons we changed the sex. That was a disappointment at first, but I respected the wishes of my co-scriptwriter. What I loved in Sweetie was all that potential she had in her and the way it floundered. That happens to all of us. One day, we're exploring what we could be, but the day disappears and then it's too late. As a character, she's heartbreaking, hopeless.

In a sense, Kay is the main character. The others gradually join in her story, Louis first, then Sweetie, then her parents.

We called the film *Sweetie* because it's a nice title, not because she's the heroine of the story. Kay evolves, she feels braver. I also think you can't love without there being some basis in reality, otherwise you only love an illusion and it doesn't work. But most of us set up illusions around what we're doing to some extent. We have an idea in our heads of what our partner is like and it's hard to accept that they're different from the idea we have.

Did you always plan to start with the voice-over and what's going on in Kay's head?

No. I originally thought of kicking off with shots of trees. They were really beautiful shots but I thought they'd disorient the audience. There were too many things to bring together. At the same time, when I'm filming, I get the feeling I can do anything, that I'm completely free as long as it contributes to the story, that it makes sense. I like things to be fresh and startling. With Kay's voice-over we wanted to indicate right from the outset that we weren't just interested in what the characters do, but also in what they think and feel.

What part of Australia is the action set in?

Basically in Willoughby, a suburb on Sydney's North Shore. The scenes where they visit the mother were shot at Warren in north-west New South Wales, a fantastic town, a centre for cotton crops and sheep farming. I loved filming there. We tramped over the ground to give it that arid desert look certain regions of Australia have that we couldn't afford to film in.

In Kafka's Metamorphosis, *everything is seen from the 'abnormal' son's point of view. Here it's more through the family's eyes as they look on Sweetie's strangeness.*

I still felt that it'd be good from time to time to get a sense of what Sweetie's thinking or feeling, like the point where the family heads west and where we see from her reaction how much of a baby she is. Her father's a traitor and a bastard who gives her false hope. He knows that if he takes Sweetie he'll never be able to get his wife back. I remember that the actor who played Gordon had the same reactions as his character. He really felt like he was in a mess at that point!

Did you study psychiatric cases, read books on the subject?

No, not really. We had living examples all round us. And we talked a lot about people we knew who'd gone mad. We also sent Genevieve Lemon to a rehabilitation centre so she could observe the patients. We wanted her to feel the threat. She found the experience pretty unbearable. There was one patient in particular who kept threatening her with a razor blade. You couldn't say we did in-depth research but we did, on the other hand, borrow a lot from personal experience. It's a subject I'd been chewing over for about a year. I didn't want us to have to meet the usual narrative requirements; I wanted to deal more with states of mind and emotions. I wanted to talk about the difficulty of loving, while introducing more sombre hidden currents. That's when I hit on the idea of superstition. I also felt like using metaphors as I think people think in metaphors a lot more than they realise, yet you don't often see that on screen. It seemed to me to give the film extra dimensions.

Then I asked myself what kind of story we wanted to tell. That's when Gerard and I got some money together and went and spent a fortnight in a house at the beach, where we discussed everything and acted each of the different roles. We felt it was important to get the tone right in each scene, and the way the people were going to talk. The script developed organically. I didn't know that Sweetie was going to eat the china horses before we got to that point in the story, when I wondered what she could do. We never knew what the next step would be before we actually got there. So much so that we had trouble re-jigging the story. It was like a chain with links you couldn't move around.

Did you work on the dialogue with the actors?

Everything was written down but we did lots of rehearsing, which is especially useful for getting to know them and getting them to trust me, and also for working out how to help each other out. It's also an opportunity to explore all the possibilities of their roles. Every actor is different and I worked with their differences. Genevieve likes me to tell her exactly what she's supposed to do. I had to trick her, put her in situations where she'd find out for herself what we needed. Karen Colston was the opposite, she knows exactly who she is and what she needs at any given moment. My technique with her was to ask her what she thought Kay would do and think at this or that moment. The funny thing is that in real life, Genevieve is an incredibly strong, incredibly intelligent girl.

The material could have led to a miserabilist film. But you stylise ugliness and vulgarity.

The artistic director deliberately created sets that were drab and awful. We thought about the interiors, taking into account the fact that people bring their own furniture to the flats they move into, while keeping objects belonging to the previous tenants, to the point where there's a mix of styles. Something ugly can look elegant through the lighting or the framing. It's a token of sympathy. It's more poignant, for my money, than a 'pretty' set that offers far fewer possible contrasts.

Your framing is amazing. Do you work it out beforehand or are you inspired by the shoot?

I had nothing to lose. It was a low-budget film and we could be bold, take risks. We make films for our own pleasure. Lots of things were worked out in advance. Sally Bongers, my director of photography, thinks like I do. We talk together, drink tea, laugh, dream up shots, look around us and pinch things. We're both very visually oriented and our aesthetic sense is very close. Sally's also very matter-of-fact about scenes: she frames according to the drama of the situation to create a poignant emotion but she's also careful to see that it's not too distracting for the viewer. We made those kinds of mistakes, though. In certain scenes, you got the feeling the characters weren't talking to each other because they were so far out on the edge of the frame! We had to shoot those scenes again. Sally Bongers and I are very close friends although that doesn't stop us from arguing, but it's always about who wants to be in control. She's very pigheaded, very strong, and she sometimes wants certain things. And since I'm just like her and I sometimes have opposite ideas, conflict is inevitable! It's not that we disagree so much; it's more the result of the pressures a shoot entails.

Sally was largely responsible for the lighting, and she's very intuitive. But we'd discussed it beforehand and we wanted soft light on the faces, as that's how we felt about the characters. To start with I was scared my framing would seem pretentious, but I don't have that awful feeling anymore. What I wanted to do was to cross the line that allows framing to create the poignant nature of a situation – the way you get in photography, which is much more adventurous in that respect than film. There's a sensitivity, a sophistication in photography that I don't often see in film and I'd like to be able to go on with this visual exploration at the same time as developing the story.

Were the nature scenes, like the beach scene or the dance scene at night in the bush, filmed as planned?

I draw a storyboard, which helps me see what I need, but often we make changes depending on what happens. For instance, the shot where the two cowboys are teaching each other how to dance comes from what I saw between two actors, with one showing the other a dance step. I found that delightful and I decided to put it in the film. You have to be on the alert and seize details like that. They give the feel of things. But, of course, the big problem's time. We had plenty of other ideas but we couldn't fit them in over a forty-day shoot. Eight weeks isn't all that short according to the usual criteria, but the way we film it was pretty tight.

The scene with the clairvoyant, whose son is mentally retarded, foreshadows Sweetie's appearance.

Except that the son is really defective. I liked the notion that this old woman accepts her son's condition so easily. You often find that with clairvoyants. Contrary to what you might think, they're often very down to earth. Sweetie's parents behave very differently.

The cemetery scene at the end, with the tree in the wind, the travelling shot all the way along the incredibly even hedges, then the shot of the grave with the plant growing inside the hole – was that completely mapped out in advance?

It was different in the script. But when I saw the cemetery I liked the formal character of the place and I wanted to bring that out more. I also noticed the tree, which looked like it was breathing. But it was especially in the editing that the feeling that it's alive emerged to that extent. I spend a lot of time on the editing, twelve hours a day, six days a week. I love editing; it's a stage where you can still bring in so much, where original ideas still crop up. The first assembly was two and a half hours long, but I'd always meant the film to be no more than one and a half hours.

Where does the music come from?

They're an Australian group of thirty singers, Cafe at the Gates of Salvation, but they aren't religious. They're original compositions based on the White Gospel tradition. The singers are warm and wonderful and they have a great sense of orchestration, they get together for the sheer pleasure of being together and they don't work for money. They just get better and better and being in a room with them and hearing them sing is a very powerful experience. The last song isn't one of theirs; it comes from a book of Jewish prayers. We feared the songs would come across as religious but once we'd laid one over the scene in the car park where they're making love, our worries were over! I'm not systematically in favour of music in film but there are moments when it makes all the difference. Such as in the car park sequence with Kay and Louis, precisely, where it allows our ironic point of view to come across in relation to the two characters at that particular moment.

The danger with this kind of film is being patronising.

I felt that the characters, being so vulnerable, so exposed, would end up winning the viewer's sympathy. I wanted the audience to end up identifying with them. In real life, I think people are both funny and tragic and I don't feel embarrassed laughing when they find themselves in a tricky situation. Sometimes, they're grateful to you for that because you allow them to see that there are two sides to the coin. We take our lives too seriously. There ought to be a limit to that. Actually we only see certain events as tragic because of the way we think. I'm not in the least filled with respect over other people's misfortune but, at the same time, I'm very sensitive to it. I myself have a tendency to whinge a lot about what happens to me and other people find it irresistibly amusing and have a good laugh!

Are you conscious of any differences between your short features and Sweetie?

Not really. Except that *Sweetie* is the best thing I've done and the most powerful. It's a film I didn't have as much control over, that took me in a direction I didn't really know I was going in, and in that sense it was more of an adventure. In that sense, I'm satisfied.

Are there films where you felt a similar investigative impulse, a desire to describe states of mind?

It's something that's pretty topical in literature and I don't see why you wouldn't do it in film. You just have to want to do it, to feel like digging in, like David Lynch. You don't discover the truth just by developing a plot, but by exploring different levels. I don't just want to look at how people behave. I want to find out what they're thinking and how they feel, like in certain novels of Duras' or Flannery O'Connor's. I think O'Connor is exquisite, ruthless and honest at one and the same time. *A Good Man is Hard to Find* is an amazing book, both hilarious and horrible. I feel completely innocent compared to stories of that kind! I really liked the adaptation John Huston did of *Wise Blood*. I love John Huston's films in general, anyhow.

I think that people are very symbolic in their understanding of the world. Things are rarely what they seem; they're a metaphor for what might be. And that's every bit as valid for our inner torments. One day a friend came to stay at my place because she was in a real quandary. She couldn't choose between two men. I remember that the whole world became a metaphor for her personal dilemma. Whenever we went shopping together and she noticed over-the-top shoes, for her that meant she wanted to live with the more adventurous bloke, or, on the contrary, that her own adventurous spirit needed the more stable of the two blokes. Whenever we were out driving and she spotted a number plate beginning with J, that meant she should live with John. We all do that more or less.

Are you familiar with Emily Dickinson's poetry, with its blend of the concrete and the metaphysical?

No, but I like the combination!

There's a cosmic feel in your work, too, based on small material details, a tree root, for example, and you seem to point to a connection between mind and external matter.

That's how I feel things. I think my generation is attracted to the spiritual and is less keen to join in the world's commotion. I myself have been meditating for the last five years. It helps me stay calm. I'm more aware, too, of my real feelings. Very often we're driven to do things out of sheer excitement when they don't correspond to our real selves.

Your characters are all very lonely.

Sweetie isn't. She communicates a lot in her own way – even when she's dishonest, which she sometimes is! She promptly makes friends with the neighbours, takes

Louis to the beach. No one realises what a threat Sweetie represents except Kay, who's the most exposed. It's hard to know how retarded Sweetie is. For me, she's normal, or at least, she was. From infancy she's been pushed over the edge a bit at a time by her family and she's ended up losing her balance and her sense of responsibility. In other circumstances she could have been different.

Was Sweetie's barking inspired by a case you observed?

No, that's a total invention of mine. There were quite a few rehearsals for that scene. It took courage for Genevieve finally to scare everyone. It was a decisive moment in her performance. She really became the character when she felt her power over the others and that she was capable of scaring them.

Why did you dedicate the film to your sister?

Because I was very touched by what she did. While we were filming, my mother was very sick, she was dying, actually, and I had to decide whether to stop, or to let another director finish the film, or to keep going. My sister was in England but she went home to New Zealand to look after her and let me keep filming.

5 JOHN CASSAVETES

(1929–1989)

Early in 1961, a few months after its presentation outside the competition at the Venice Festival, John Cassavetes's first film, *Shadows*, was shown at the Pagode in Paris. For we French fans of America cinema, who thrilled to the latest gems from classic Hollywood (Preminger, Hitchcock, Hawks, Ford, Walsh, Minnelli), nothing had prepared us for this raw, direct, emotional film or its flawed form. Independent American movies were badly distributed and Cassavetes was an unknown. If he acknowledged his debt to Kazan, a Greek in origin like himself, that was more for Kazan's handling of actors, his famous Method, than for anything else. A film like *On the Waterfront*, though it marked a distance in relation to Hollywood, nonetheless stuck to a classic form in its structure and dialogues. It is to the actor, which he was himself, that Cassavetes devoted all his attention, dragging unique voices out of them and gathering together around him a faithful band that included Ben Gazzara, Peter Falk, Seymour Castle and Gena Rowlands, his wife. Cassavetes had the reputation of being a bear, with an anti-intellectual stance that pitted him violently against the critics – he once stole a coat belonging to Pauline Kael, the famous *New Yorker* film critic and, another time, he threw her shoes out the window of her car. I had more luck when Michael Wilson and I met him for this long interview on *Woman Under the Influence* and another time when I talked to him about *Opening Night,* which he was presenting at the Berlin Festival. But he was not a director who sought out conversation with cinephiles, he didn't like explaining his work even though he was capable, as we see here, of passionate commentary. When I discovered *Faces*, perhaps his masterpiece, in 1968 at the Venice Festival, he hadn't made the trip. He also didn't turn up at Venice in 1980 to pick up his Golden Lion, which the jury, which I was on, attributed *ex aequo* to his *Gloria* and to Louis Malle's

Atlantic City. Cassavetes had a fierce personality that could only adapt to life in the bosom of a group of friends whose stormy outbursts, drinking bouts and emotional relationships fuelled his films. The films seemed to be an extension of his life: that, at least, is the feeling you got after a few hours spent with him and his entourage.

ON *WOMAN UNDER THE INFLUENCE*

PARIS, OCTOBER 1975

You once said that Faces *was a lot longer than the version we are familiar with. Has* Woman Under the Influence *also been cut much?*

All my films are long. As you get older, you become more complex, you see more sides to reality. When you make your first film, everything is pure, you're enthusiastic, full of constructive and destructive impulses and you couldn't care less about the world. By the second film you realise that it's hard work. And by the third you have to hit on a method of working if you want what you have to say to mean anything in emotional terms. I don't show my films for anyone's enjoyment but so that viewers better understand what's human in the film, what relates to them and not just to me. For, of course, all films are personal. Marriages that fall apart, love as mutual betrayal, the trouble two people, two faces, have communicating even though they live together – those are the problems I've tackled and that concern me. But they also concern everyone else. Sometimes people find it too painful to accept, or judge my point of view mistaken or quite simply aren't interested in the difficulty there is in communicating with others. But that is what interests me. With my actors I try to explore all that and to convert it into terms that ring true to everyone's everyday life.

Financially Woman Under the Influence *must also have been quite an experience. How do you make a film for a million dollars outside the system?*

Each film finds a different economic solution. For *Faces* and *Shadows*, we all contributed to the film. For *Woman Under the Influence,* the cast worked for very small wages and it was agreed, without any contract, that if we made money, we'd give it to them. I work with friends, people I'm fond of, and we understand each other because we have the same aims. What we're looking for is how to express feelings, emotions. Many colleagues think of their career, their next project and can't imagine stopping for two or three years. That doesn't worry me. Of course, I think about it, too, but only once the film I'm on is over. With *A Woman Under the Influence,* Peter Falk, Gena and I invested our money in the film.

You work by blocks of very long sequences. The relationship between what you shoot and what you keep in the editing must be pretty crucial. Do you cut whole sequences or do you trim each sequence?

There are whole sequences that have been cut. For instance, in *A Woman Under the Influence*, there were several scenes where Gena and Peter were alone together. I really liked what happened between them. There was also a very lovely scene, in the morning, where they told each other the dreams they'd had that night and they were walking in the rain. Watching the film end to end I realised that maybe unconsciously I was giving the public what they wanted, that it doubtless also corresponded to a certain romantic desire, on my part and on the part of my actors, for their union to last, in romantic fiction fashion. But my film is not romantic. Marriage, in my view, isn't total 'romance'! The moments where you have the time to be romantic are very brief. In a word, the rapport between the two characters was so intimate that you could no longer believe in the fundamental problems they were dealing with elsewhere. So I gave up those scenes. The first edit was three hours and fifty minutes.

A Woman Under the Influence *is your simplest film from the point of view of the script. There are almost no new facts in the course of the film, everything is given at the outset and everything happens on an emotional level.*

Almost everyone has been married or in love. So, with this kind of material you start off with major acquired knowledge on the part of the viewer. Physicists today also work on the basis of accepted arguments. There's no point repeating in a film everything that everyone knows from experience: when a man goes off to work at nine o'clock in the morning and doesn't come home till seven o'clock at night, his wife is alone, she goes shopping, she looks after the kids, watches television, reads a book, plays cards with girlfriends. The sole thing that remains to be tackled is the relationship between this man and this woman who don't judge each other like most couples do, who live together in great mutual tolerance and yet suffer in their marriage and in their mutual betrayals.

And there's the suffering of this woman who lives under the influence of a man, which isn't right, but which happens. Love has an influence: if you love someone you want them to be proud of you, to take care of you, to love you; you demand so much of them that you're asking for the impossible. And suddenly everything collapses because each person forgets the other, since they're absolutely certain they'll find them again, right where they left them. They don't worry about the other's problems until, suddenly, they're made dramatically aware of them.

We get the impression that, for you, making a film is more like creating an event than reproducing it. What part does improvisation play in your work?

I'm so good you don't even realise it, but everything is written down! [*Laughter*] Anyway, it'd all be the same even if there was improvisation. We deal with thoughts and feelings and my hope is that the actors don't feel like the material is written down. That way they don't think about their lines, they take their time and the words seem to belong to them. Sometimes, of course, an actor comes to see me and says: 'My character would never do that.' So then I tell them not to do it. There's no obligation on their part. Very often, then, lines of dialogue get dropped. I've never seen an actor forget his lines or feel obliged to say them: I always leave it up to them. In *Shadows* and in *Husbands,* there was a lot of improvisation, but everything was written down beforehand for *Faces, Minnie and Moskowitz* and *A Woman Under The Influence.* For me, the result is the same.

Do you alter the script at rehearsal stage?

Very often, if it isn't working. If you have a good actor and at a certain point he can't go on acting, it's because your script is lame, the writing doesn't work or the scene's intentions aren't clear. I don't think I'm perfect, not from any standpoint. Every morning I wake up and I tell myself that I'm not sure enough about my own life to be able to talk about other people's marriages! During rehearsals we talk together and sometimes we rewrite the whole sequence. In most films, the actors don't even meet. It's happened that I've acted in a film and discovered afterwards that such and such an actor was also in it. In my films, we come together for several weeks, every evening, for instance, and we read the script together. We like each other, we know each other and we've worked together for a long time. The actors turn up with suggestions and I ask them to write them down since sometimes I don't understand what they want to say. Gena, for instance, reads the finished script and says to me: 'I hate this woman. What does she do, what kind of clothes does she wear?' I tell her that at this stage I couldn't care less what she wears. But for her it's important and she's right, I'm the one who made the superficial remark. So, before starting the film, I visited about fifty working-class couples' homes. I knew what I'd see and I knew I wouldn't like it: furniture covered in plastic, a lovely kitchen, a lovely car, a clean façade but very few things inside, huge sloppiness, almost no art, not much interest in music. And, for entertainment, a family outing to MacDonalds at the end of the week to eat a hamburger. I'm an artist and I don't live like that. So I have to convert it into terms I find acceptable but that continue to be for the people I'm talking about. The set designer found a great big house, whereas working-class houses are not big usually. So we decided that the house had been given to Nick by his parents. We were able to change reality without justifying the changes at every turn since the house was a gift. After that we decorated it in keeping with the characters: sporting trophies, photos of kids. Everyone brings their own ideas. For example, is the house painted? So we paint the front, but the back of the house, well, given that he's in the building trade he could have had it painted by mates in exchange for a few beers, but he's left it as it is. He's too busy with his family life. With these elements that we bring to the actors, they get more and more interested in the clothes they're going to wear, in the effect of money on them, in the lives of their children, why they sleep downstairs, etc. Everything was discussed, nothing comes just from me.

Why did you choose an Italian milieu?

In America in the building trade, the workers are black or Mexican on the west coast and Italian, Portuguese or Irish on the east coast. But I think that the man could be something else entirely.

But it's important in the film.

Yes, in terms of the conflicts. She's of Swedish origin. But I know no more about Sweden than Americans do who have Swedish roots going back two or three generations. They know two or three words and eat smørbrød once a week as they retell old stories. We're fantasising when we represent the American 'melting pot' as the sum of European civilisations. American Italians go to Italy and are happy there but they're actually happier in America because that's where they have their Little Italy, where Venetians, Neapolitans and Sicilians feel united, whereas in Italy they wouldn't understand each other.

In your childhood, were you very conscious of belonging to the Greek community?

No, not really. I was proud of my historic origins, as I would have been of any other origins. My parents spoke Greek, still speak Greek; I also speak Greek, but badly! I was born in New York, but my parents took us to Greece and I didn't come back to America until I was eight years old. They tell me that at that point I couldn't speak English, I only knew Greek. For me language is just written symbols. The language barrier makes no sense to me. People's emotions are basically the same everywhere.

You often show the petite bourgeoisie in your films or even, in A Woman under the Influence, *the working class, which is fairly rare in American cinema. What are your reasons for exploring this milieu?*

Those classes don't interest me any more than any others. Maybe that has to do with world politics but not with my personal life. It doesn't matter to me whether someone works with his hands or is an international financier. For me, they are above all the people I meet. I'm pigheaded more than anything else. Now, there's an idea that's very widespread in my country in particular, which is that the public aren't interested in people who aren't rich. And the working class itself, it would appear, has no interest in seeing itself on the screen. Maybe that's true. But it doesn't concern me in this film. In my material, the woman has to look after the children herself and if she were rich that wouldn't pose any problem for her. In the working class, the woman is closer to her home. That's why I chose this milieu; it creates more emotional bonds with her children. When you're in a closed circle, you're closer to your family; you have more problems with them. If you're richer, you have other problems.

This is the first of your films where one of your characters shows signs of having mental problems. Did that pose particular problems for you in describing it?

Listen: I myself am half-crazy. And I think that everybody's on the edge of madness but no one wants to admit it – we all claim it's the other person who's wrong, that we hold the truth. I firmly believe that every woman who loves her husband and who's been married for a while doesn't know what to do with her emotions and that this can drive her to madness. Certain women find outlets; they decide to be more independent, for instance. This particular woman believes wholeheartedly that when you're a good wife, there's something reciprocal that should happen, but she doesn't know what. She's not really mad, just frustrated beyond belief. She doesn't know what to do and she's particularly inept emotionally and in her social relations. Everything she does is an expression of her individuality but she doesn't know how to behave with other people. In that sense she's like all of us.

Don't you think that stems from the fact that she has to play so many roles: the good wife, the good mother and so on, and that she finally cracks?

I don't think she ever changes. She's always been lucid. She's very direct, as women are – much more direct than men, in fact, which greatly shocks the latter. The husband has made himself ridiculous by coming home and getting indignant that the children are naked. He's the one whose behaviour isn't normal. Based on previous experiences, he draws the conclusion that something happened whereas nothing happened in actual fact. She tried to entertain a neighbour, took the children into the garden and played them *Swan Lake* and in the face of her guest's embarrassment she started acting crazy to distract him. But there's no harm in her conduct.

Their relationship is in fact the same I see all the time between a man and a woman. One day I tell myself it's the best life I've ever had and a minute later I want to kill myself or she wants to kill me! For me, life is hard and full of the mystery of what is going to happen or what I'm going to feel in a moment. Half of life is made up of unpredictable moods.

In the first scene where they find themselves together, they communicate together by means of a whole code of incredible gestures. It seems like a crisis point, an exceptional scene and at the same time you get the impression that they often 'talk' to each other like this. There must be a high degree of improvisation on the part of the actors here?

Yes. Everything in the film has to take its inspiration from the moment. Of course, the scene was written. The words are there, but two very good actors want to express more about their love relationship than simply saying lines.

As performers, they make choices: to love and to wait for something or not to wait for anything at all, to find an epic quality or not, to make demands or not. That's how they manage to believe in their characters and express them. This man is embarrassed by his wife's weird behaviour and at the same time he likes it. But he doesn't want her to expose herself to others like that and yet he invites them over at seven in the morning when she's going to behave like that… Their relations are a series of contradictions.

The fact that you have such huge emotional shifts must cause you problems as a director, on the set, in articulating the moments between them?

For me, anyone can be an actor. From childhood we know we can put on an act. I would never tell an actor that he's putting on an act, that what he's doing doesn't correspond to my interpretation. I count more on the actor giving me his interpretation. Of course, if he's lazy or doesn't take his role seriously, then I get out the knife, my revolver or my fist, and I kill him. I think I have a gift as a director, and that is to create an atmosphere where people can behave naturally in any given situation. I don't try and control the set, which is often noisy, anarchic, with the actors sometimes joining in against me. On the other hand, I like to shoot a film in continuity. The last scene, for example, would have been difficult to shoot as the first scene in the work schedule! That's the reason I don't want to work with a big company anymore because, for budget reasons, they chop the script up into chunks without taking any account of the chronology.

How many cameras do you have?

Basically one camera. Sometimes two for exteriors.

Do you think you'd go back to 16 mm if you had to?

I can't work in 16 mm anymore. My sights have been lowered. Moreover for me there's no difference except that it's easier to edit in 35 mm. The camera movements are the same; it doesn't change anything to do with the filming.

But in 35 mm you get the grainy quality of the 16 mm photo.

I suppose that's true. I've never liked metallic colours, 'hard' photography, not even in the days when it was fashionable: it leaves nothing to the imagination, there's no secret. When we did *Shadows*, we used long focal lengths as we didn't have a dolly to follow the actors. The sound in Hollywood films was of crystal-line purity. In *Shadows* we filmed in the street, the sound was bad, you could hear all kinds of noises and people were shocked by it. But I personally didn't know how to get 'pure' sound. I remember all the time we spent in the editing room trying to take out wonderful noises! And then it became fashionable!

Do you do many takes?

It's very variable. Sometimes very few. There are scenes where the actors don't trust you because they've been let down so many times by directors who've made them change their performance to adapt it to the story. What's difficult is to get people to trust you: you can then let them be what they are, reveal themselves.

How did you adapt your camera movements to the actors' displacements? To what extent were they worked out in advance? The film seems more controlled from that point of view than your other films.

I think it's a very simple story. I didn't want to do too many cuts as I don't think you believe in emotions stimulated by technical ideas. We lit the whole room and left the camera very receptive to the actors by using the whole set in the shot. If you see something convincing, it doesn't matter how you see it. It's the quality of what you see that counts. If it's good, then the scene's good, even if the framing is not good. A different director would shoot the scene differently. What I try to do is to anticipate the movement in the scene, to leave the actors as free as possible in the space. I can't ask actors to adapt to pre-established camera movements. They could only do that with rehearsals but it's tiring, it's boring, and the technical crew becomes the audience. If they get bored, the actors feel they're no good. That's why I do what I can to see that everything happens fast and I use long focal lengths and a set that has depth. I hate the idea of a film's being made according to the frame or the camera. I've never seen a good scene that isn't good no matter what the camera angle. I've seen scenes taken from seven or eight different angles and they were always good if the scene was good, always bad if the scene was bad. For me what matters is convincing the audience and yourself that what's on screen is really happening. In certain cases I'd have preferred it if certain films weren't so well framed, weren't so brilliant technically, but that what was happening in them was better! I don't try to adjust the scenes to the camera but the camera to the scenes. The problem is: what's the best way of seeing the scene? Certain scenes are overexposed but that didn't matter to me because the scene was good and on top of that it gave an idea of the sterility of the atmosphere, of the weariness, the sadness.

In writing the role for Gena Rowlands, you gave her a very different character from her previous characters. Every film, besides, shows her to us with a different face.

To me, she's a very great actress. It's hard for me to say so because she's my wife, but I think she's capable of playing anything she wants to. She's a straightforward woman, not neurotic, extremely serious and she feels things deeply. It's wonderful to work with her.

Is it a situation that drives you to make a film or the desire to portray a certain character?

It's the theme that stimulates me. So I'm going to make a film with Gena about an actress, but I want the public to understand what an actress is. We're going to talk about it together before I write the scenario. I take all our conversations into account: we talk about who's going to play the psychiatrist but since that doesn't have any connection to her, I drop the subject. On the other hand, the actress who plays another female character – that concerns her directly, and I won't choose her without talking to Gena first, otherwise that would affect her ideas.

In your last film did you use the same mix of amateurs and professionals? What attracts you in this chemistry?

Gena and Peter are super-professionals and I think that performing with amateurs helps to keep them alive. The professional tends to forget real life, to believe that their problems cover everything. Amateurs, in small roles, attract attention to themselves and when they bring something off they stimulate the professional. For instance, Lynn Carlin, who played the woman in *Faces*, had never acted before. In that film the ratio of amateurs to professionals was 50:50. But actually, today, how can we say someone's an amateur except by defining them as someone who doesn't get paid?

You only play a major role yourself in Husbands. *Did that pose particular problems for you?*

I didn't feel at all worried when I was making the film. But watching it, I can see how difficult it is. It wasn't a problem when I wasn't in the same scene as Peter Falk and Ben Gazzara.

Have you ever thought of setting up a repertory company?

Yes, when I was younger. It was a dream. Now I no longer believe in it. You have to tackle one film after another and do your best.

In a sense your films seem to be made as a reaction against your career as an actor. What did that bring you, good and bad?

I was never considered a director, except for these last few years. And I myself didn't consider myself as such. Now I've directed quite a few films and it wouldn't ring true to say I'm not a filmmaker. It's ridiculous to deny that it's my bread and butter, that it's my job. But in the beginning I simply wanted to have fun doing what I did and to share it with others. The ultimate success of the film didn't matter. What mattered was that we loved doing it together. After that we asked ourselves whether we'd shown the emotions clearly enough to the audience for them to react or whether it was too hard. Most of my colleagues in California don't share this point of view. They want to make the best film possible. That's not really my ambition. What I want is to enjoy it, for it to challenge some of the feelings I have or that others have, for the actors to have good roles, for the characters to express themselves with a certain dignity, even if they show themselves in a bad light.

When you were working in Hollywood, what did you suffer from most?

For me, there are two kinds of performance. The professional way of working in Hollywood, in television or in Paris is to take a script and do your work as well as you can, to make things credible within the limits assigned to you. The other way is the creative interpretation that aims, without regard to career or profit, to make your life clearer by expressing feelings and exercising intelligence. So much so that it no longer bears any relation to cinema: it's finding yourself in the character. Too many actors lead a fashionable existence. They make millions of dollars without really knowing why and listen to the advice of consultants who tell them to go on paying for a prohibitively expensive house, and so they accept certain roles and are no longer artists but businessmen.

Certain Hollywood directors, like Bob Aldrich, are friends of mine and I esteem them for what they do within their trade, but I can't work with just any director anymore as an actor. I don't trust them, and even with a filmmaker I respect, I'm scared we'd be condescending to each other. Acting for other people – that's over. I'd only work for Kazan and I think he'd like that, too. He's a wonderful artist and I think we value each other as actors. But the rest of them think of me as a director and that creates a false situation.

All worthwhile actors are lunatics, impossible to live with; they fight each other over their lines. It's only right that that's how it is. When it comes to acting, you don't want someone who's polite, level-headed. You want someone who's outraged. They ring me at five in the morning to insult me, and that's normal. If someone's outraged with me, I'm not going to tell myself that I won't use them again on the pretext that they cause me too much trouble. Life is made, on the contrary, to live through problems, to take part in them, don't you think? I sometimes take a completely wrong turn and the actor follows me blindly and the more fool he. But I have no right to make him bad. It's hard to admit that it's my fault but at the same time I can't give someone the impression of failure. Faced with a crew of fifty people, I'm always in the position of the one who's right and it's easy to incriminate the actor and to look devastated. But then all I do is destroy him, turn him into an enemy and destroy his dreams – but also my own. By defending myself, I finish myself off. And I've never liked directors because I always have the feeling that that's the attitude they adopt. All the actors I've known have problems. Once in a while you meet directors who really love actors and make an effort to understand them. Very often on a professional film they take you aside, they powder your face, they do your hair, they dress you and when you find yourself on the set you don't know where you are or what to do. You feel like talking to the filmmaker but it's the assistant who comes over to you to tell you, 'Hang on to your seat, it's not your turn.' Then you're humiliated, your confidence evaporates, you start shaking, you're going to be appalling, you're dead. If you're an actor, you should never accept being put in such a situation… If you came to see me I'd never tell you that you were about to have a fantastic time. I wouldn't give you twenty pages of script to read, either: What would you do with it? At night you'd go mad trying to understand it. No, I'd tell you to come back the next day to do a scene but meanwhile I'd talk to you, I'd try and make a friend of you not so that you'd feel comfortable but to communicate with you the same as with a renowned actor. And I certainly wouldn't ask you how you pour a drink or how you drink a glass of orange juice because how could you 'make believe' after that? And I wouldn't give you instructions about all that, either, showing you myself what gestures to use. That's absurd; it's limiting. No, what's needed is some mutual understanding and some understanding of human problems. Anyone can sit down or drink a glass naturally, if you don't force them to do things they don't really feel.

6 DAVID CRONENBERG

(1943–)

Along with Peter Greenaway, David Cronenberg is without a doubt the filmmaker who is the best critical interpreter of his own work and he can dissect the very body of his film with great precision when he takes a scalpel to it. The metaphor is not gratuitous. Cronenberg's cinema annexes medicine and surgery; he is concerned with mutations, excrescences, infections, whether they be caused by disease or quite simply by fear and fantasy. His elective territory is the horror film of which he is the greatest contemporary master, along with David Lynch. If the latter more closely approximates the freedom of dream, of a flamboyant surrealism, Cronenberg is more adept at a rational, clinical approach. His great subject is the fragility and degradation of the body. Again like Greenaway – while, at the same time, being more or less his contemporary – Cronenberg started off with experimental films. He then launched himself deliberately into very commercial small budget films in the flourishing genre of body horror. His first films provoked disgust, sometimes controversy, but very few people noticed the profound intelligence he displayed and the modernity of his themes, science not being a popular subject in cinema.

Videodrome (1983) and *The Fly* (1986), a remake of an old Kurt Neuman film, to which he added the philosophical dimension of a fable, saw him take a qualitative leap and attested to his increased interest in his performers and in the humanity of his characters. *Dead Ringers* confirmed this new aesthetic maturity with Jeremy Irons's magisterial twin performance, his reflections on genetic manipulation, his fear of sexuality and a refined attention to the set. It was the occasion of a first meeting with Cronenberg. Whether later adapting Burroughs (*The Naked Lunch*) or Ballard (*Crash*) or directing *Mr Butterfly, eXistenZ* or *Spider,* the singularity of Cronenberg's world and his artistic risk-taking have remained constants in his creative output.

ON *DEAD RINGERS*

PARIS, JANUARY 1989

Dead Ringers *is fairly freely adapted from a novel:* Twins. *What led you to choose that book and what direction did the adaptation take?*

You have to go back to the beginning of the project. I read in a paper, early in the 1970s, that twin gynaecologists, absolutely identical, had been found dead in New York. It involved very prominent doctors who'd specialised in the treatment of sterility. I found the story so perfect and so bizarre that I immediately thought someone would make a film of it. Then I gradually realised that if I wanted to see this film one day, I'd better make it myself. That happened well before I worked with the producer, Mark Boyman, on *The Fly*. At the time, I'd met a woman producer in Los Angeles who wanted to meet me after seeing *Scanners*, which had just come out. My agent asked me to go to California so they could see who I was and this woman, Carol Baum, who worked for Lorimar, was my first contact with what was happening in Hollywood. She asked me if I had a project and when I told her about the story of the twins, she was the one who mentioned the book, *Twins*, which was dedicated to them. The upshot of that conversation was that she became the executive producer on *Dead Ringers*. I read the book but it really disappointed me. Even though the authors claimed that their novel had nothing to do with the Marcus twins and even though it was a fictionalised version, to say the least, of this human interest story in the paper, it seemed to me that the book showed how not to do it. It explored possibilities that I refused to envisage. For example, one of the twins was homosexual. On top of that, they had sex together. That felt psychologically wrong to me; it didn't ring true. I didn't believe in it. I could imagine two homosexual twins or two heterosexual twins, but not that distinction. And to add incest to boot – that was too much, it was sensationalism. I thought I'd have to invent my twins. For legal reasons, my producer still thought it was safer to take out an option on the book and that's what he did. But for all those reasons, you won't see too many connections between the book and the film.

Did you read medical and psychological books on twins in preparing your script?

Not really. The two works I read that homed in on the subject were *Freaks* by Leslie Fiedler on the presence of 'freaks' in American culture, in which he evokes the case of Siamese twins in particular. And another one called *The Two*. I'm very lazy when it comes to doing research and since, in any case, what I make up turns out to be true, I don't see the need for accumulating documentation. But as the project took a lot of time to mature – the first version of the script was written in 1981 – and as lots of people had heard about it, I did accumulate an enormous amount of information, whether I liked it or not, and this information often came from twins who wanted to confide in me.

Twins had never really interested me as film material before I stumbled across this combination of three things: twins, both gynaecologists, whose fate is to die together. Of course twins are disturbing, fascinating and weird – I knew some at school – but in cinema they're most often used in a degrading way, as monsters or saints. Once I decided to tell this story, I wondered what attracted to me to twins. As I'm particularly interested in the mind–body relationship, in the case of twins you have a very peculiar example of two absolutely similar bodies and two different brains. I can imagine a world in which identical twins couldn't exist, just as there are no absolutely identical triplets.

Twinship also strikes me as a perfect metaphor for all couple relationships, man and wife, parent and child, that are both so intense and so claustrophobic at the same time. They exalt you and suffocate you. That's why *Dead Ringers* isn't just about twins.

The evolution of the brothers is interesting. In the beginning Beverly is introverted and weak, unlike Elliot, but, by the end, their relationship is reversed.

I think Elliot's strength is just an illusion; it's superficial. He's more ambitious and adapts more easily to society, but in fact they're both incredibly synchronous. On a deep level, Elliot is just as vulnerable as his brother though he manages to hoodwink you on the surface.

The character played by Geneviève Bujold also evolves. She asks for help in the beginning, then she becomes distant and finally protective before withdrawing.

I wanted her to be an actress, for her craft is to change identity and become other people. But we know all about that. We're different according to the different periods of our lives and, at the same time, we feel there is a central core, a continuity. We'd have to discuss in detail the changes that manifest themselves in Claire Niveau, but I think they're psychologically right. At the end of the film, anyhow, she knows she can't save him.

Did you have trouble getting financial backing for the film?

A lot. Not to exaggerate, Mark Boyman and I knocked on over forty doors. We even went back to see the studios that had turned down the project after they changed directors, which now happens every six months in Hollywood. People often asked us if they had to be gynaecologists. Couldn't they be lawyers? Couldn't one of them survive in the end? And so on. Those were classic commentaries made to us in all frankness. We contacted the big companies before *The Fly* and then after the great commercial success of that film, but that changed nothing. Lots of people in Hollywood claim that if you make a lot of money with a film you can then do whatever you want, but that's not true. There would have been no problems if I'd wanted to make *The Fly II*! That's why we decided to produce the film ourselves and so you see my name on the credits again, as with my very first films, *Stereo* and *Crimes of the Future*!

Similarly I had a heap of problems finding the lead role. I met maybe twenty-five of the best actors in American and they all said no for various reasons. Two stood out, though. As you know, most American actors are disciples of the Method used by The Actors' Studio, which is a very popular technique and I think that for them playing twins is terrifying. According to The Actors' Studio, you in fact identify with your role, you sit down and you enter into a relationship with the person opposite you. In the case of twins, there is no one opposite you, you perform opposite yourself and you have to let yourself be invaded by a kind of schizophrenia. And this is very hard to accept for a former practitioner of the Method. Some of them told me it drove them mad. The other main reason for the rejections I came in for is that my characters were gynaecologists. American actors are often very macho. They don't mind playing drug pushers or Mafia hit men, but incarnating gynaecologists disturbed them. And when you think about it, there aren't many gynaecologists on screen, not even in comedies!

It's interesting that you went and sought out a British actor, Jeremy Irons, as the British tradition of performance is the opposite of the Method, it's closer to Diderot's performer's paradox. Alec Guinness and Peter Sellers and even Laurence Olivier love playing very different roles, including in the same film. But Jeremy Irons does something even more complicated: he plays two roles that are almost identical.

He didn't of course have to worry about resemblance, since that went without saying. The question was knowing at what point they'd be different, and how that would be consistent. I didn't want them to be too different. Jeremy had to find all these nuances in himself. All I had to do was guide him, correct him slightly. He used tricks. For example, he asked me at the outset if he could have two dressing rooms, one for Beverly and one for Elliot. But I told him we couldn't afford it! Then he did his hair and makeup a little bit differently. When he was playing Elliot, he'd stand up on his heels, which made him a bit taller. To interpret Beverly, he'd stand on the balls of his feet, which made him look more defeated, less aggressive. He had to do this toing and froing ten to twenty times a day, since we never filmed a character with any continuity. To change like that every ten minutes is remarkable and he brought it off because of his talent and those little physical details that trigger different emotions. He was a bit nervous in the beginning as he didn't know me and he'd only seen maybe one of my films. He told me the script could lend itself to a great deal of vulgarity. I have to tell you that when I write a script, I don't indicate either the camera movements or the angles. So, for instance, in the sequence where he examines Geneviève Bujold, I hadn't written where the camera was, and that was a detail that worried him! Now, as you've noticed, even though we're dealing with gynaecology, you practically never see a woman's body. With Jeremy Irons we discussed what the film would be about. Another of his concerns was that he wasn't sure he could tackle the role to the end. He wanted to know what it would be like playing opposite a double who would not be him, then hearing his own voice in an earpiece so that he could give himself his lines. Technically, these were strange things for an actor! So he came to Toronto, we did some video tests and he realised he could carry it off.

What problems did Lee Wilson's special effects pose for the direction?

They were no different in kind – though they were more extreme in their extent – than those posed generally by the technology that goes with each shoot. Even before loading the camera with film, that was a problem posed every morning. For the choreography of a scene for example: you tell the actor to go to the window, to say his lines, then turn round. If you have two actors working together, that facilitates the exchange. But if you have Jeremy Irons's double, you don't care what he's thinking, he's just a body, you couldn't care less if he wants to move about the room or not. Which means that Jeremy Irons, even during rehearsals, had to keep toing and froing. He also asked me if I couldn't light each of the two brothers differently. I told him that wasn't possible since when they move in the space we couldn't change the lights to follow them, it would be too conspicuous, too artificial. Certain sequences, of course, were easier to film than others, but I'd decided at all events that the technology was not to take over the film.

I felt the only way to be convincing, after watching so many films with twins, was to avoid these long shots that directors draw out so we can all admire their special effects, which have cost so much money, when what we want is to see the faces in close-up. It's because I didn't want my film to be altered by technology that there are numerous scenes where the twins are together and where you don't see them in the same shot. I wanted that to come naturally.

The special effects technicians wanted there to be a storyboard so they'd know which shots the twins would be together in. I scrapped that idea, as I never work with a storyboard. I think it's an illusion, since, when you find yourself on set with the actors, everything changes and the storyboard becomes a handicap instead of helping you. So much so that I decided to get in a computerised camera for a week, which we used for the different camera movements (for fixed shots we used a split screen), and to leave it in a corner. I'd shoot the scene as though I had two actors and when I reached the moment where normally I'd show both of them together, I'd bring in the computerised camera. I knew that if I planned this long shot two months in advance, I then couldn't change anything as the whole crew would be focused on that shot and the entire scene would be determined by it. With, as a result, a diminishing of the illusion instead of its enhancement. That was my way of minimising the technology but, of course, it was always there. When you do an over-the-shoulder shot of a double with a wig, for example, you have to always watch that they don't move their faces too much, so that the viewer continues to confuse them with Jeremy Irons. The computerised camera also poses a problem, since you have to shoot each shot twice. For instance, in the scene where the twins are sitting on the bed and the camera moves in on them, we had to do the same movement twice – once with one of the twins sitting in one spot, and again with the other twin sitting in another spot. In reality it's quite a bit more than twice, since you do several takes. Similarly when they're walking down the corridor, the frame follows Jeremy Irons and his double and the computer stores this movement in its memory. The camera can then redo it very precisely image by image, but this time with Jeremy Irons and his double changing places.

You were talking about the choreography that you'd devised for a sequence. What do you mean by that?

It seems only natural to me, even though all directors don't do it. In my view, when you've got good actors, you want them involved in your film, for them to participate in it, rather than having to tell them everything right down to the last detail. Even though I don't expect them to improvise their dialogue since I've spent some time writing it, it corresponds to what I want and unless they can't pronounce it or prove to me that there's something better, I don't make changes. A word, a phrase perhaps here and there, but no profound alteration of the sequence. On the other hand, when you arrive in the morning on a new set, I send the whole crew away except the continuity person and with the actors we discuss the movements, the position of bodies, what they'll do with their hands, etc. When I started directing, what I actually found the most difficult was to carve up the space into cubes, squares, rectangles, etc. The camera doesn't move around like our eyes. When we walk into a room, we approach everything pell-mell, we do a sort of visual editing. With the camera, you can't do all that.

To work the space with the actors, to perfect the movement and composition of the shots which, with me, are very intuitive solutions, to assimilate the drama, the actors' moving around, the dialogue, I count a lot on this preparatory choreography on the set. In fact, I start with the actors as if it was theatre and I gradually move towards cinema. So each element can modify another. And I trust my actors' instincts in offering me possibilities, since they're responsible for taking control, not of the film, but of their characters. And at the end of the shoot, they often know more about him or her than I do and can show me things that surprise me.

At the beginning of the film the twins talk about life and having sex underwater and it's all the more striking that the film is in marine colours. Blue and green dominate.

Yes, they're the colours in an aquarium and it's what I asked Peter Suschitzky, my brilliant cinematographer, for. But of course, before working with Peter, I collaborate with Carol Spier, my art director. In fact, we didn't know that Peter Suschitzky would be our director of photography, since the set was built a year before the shoot, when we were supposed to be produced by DEG, Dino de Laurentis's company. After he went bust, we had to wait and to stop the sets from being destroyed.

We started out with simple ideas. As always happens with the set designer, you ask yourself questions: do the characters read or not, do they have stereo equipment… Since the twins don't have a clearly defined identity, our idea was that they would have asked an interior decorator to give them whatever was best, to make them a beautiful apartment. But this apartment, not being the expression of their tastes, would be cold, impersonal. As though they were living in someone else's place. The marine colours come from this coldness. Geneviève is earthier, warmer, so the tones, the textures of her place are more complex and varied.

And the idea of red clothes for the operation sequence?

In the script, I only indicated that they would perform surgery. I had already filmed the scenes in the operating theatres. My designer showed me photos of several operating rooms and I was depressed because in North America the imagery for this type of place is very standardised. You see open-heart surgery on television, laser eye treatments, and they're always the same colours, not white anymore but green, blue with a few stronger touches scattered here and there to prettify it. I realised that if I treated the scene in a documentary realist style, I'd add nothing to the film; it would be a purely narrative sequence. So I decided to create my own operating theatre as well as the costumes. I embraced a certain expressionism. In fact, what Beverly accomplishes in this scene, is not only his work, but a sort of priestly ritual as though he were answering a religious vocation. That's where the idea sprang from for using colours that recall the purple of cardinals.

Since the film came out in Canada, the United States and England, have you noticed different reactions depending on whether the viewers are women or men?

It's interesting to observe that there aren't enormous differences. For many men, however, the first gynaecology sequences are hard to watch, as most men don't know what happens when a woman goes to a gynaecologist. For women, on the contrary, it's perfectly routine. On the other hand, later when it gets weirder, women catch up with their fears in the face of the power gynaecologists have over them, while men further identify. So much so that at the end, people find themselves with the same overall reaction, whether they're men or women.

In several of your films, the man is pretty narcissistic; he's afraid of the outside world and of women in particular. This instability seems to interest you above all.

Certainly. Instability is interesting from a dramatic point of view. But people tend to confuse the director with his films or with his characters! Which is often way off the mark. For me the conflict is the basis of the drama. If everyone is happy and in good health, you don't have anything to film. But these twins are not only men, they're also monsters, my tropical fish, floating around in my aquarium. I'm not saying they represent humanity, but it's true that my male characters generally have trouble with the outside world. Take note, though, my female characters also have problems with men! You're well aware that Claire Niveau (Geneviève Bujold) has had a few problems with men, that she's given quite a few men a run for their money! That's why gynaecology was an important aspect of the film. It let us discuss sexual politics, surgical and clinical problems. These two men have a hermetically sealed life, they don't need anyone, they don't need other men any more than they need women. Their approach to sexuality is very rational, very cold. Once again, we're dealing with the mind–body duality Descartes explored. I love this process of thinking analysed by your philosopher, where each phase appears logical, reasonable, but when you get to the end, it seems crazy and you wonder how on earth you got there. Elliot and Beverly are very reasonable. They think that women are bizarre, different from them, that they're attracted to them and that by analysing them and dissecting them, by observing what makes them tick, they'll manage to control them better. But of course it doesn't work like that. For Beverly especially, a woman is like a mathematical problem, he'd almost prefer it if she wasn't around and this is why he isn't interested in pregnancy, childbirth, the husband... It's too complicated for him. He prefers theory.

From that point of view, there is Elliot's speech about the aesthetics of the inside of the body, about criteria of beauty concerning the spleen, the kidneys or the liver.

When I was promoting *The Fly,* it's what I used to say. Our first reaction, when faced with a fly, is to be disgusted, but if you start thinking of it as a magnificent creature, little by little it becomes beautiful. So I gave the same speech as Elliot's. After 50,000 years, we still haven't developed an aesthetics of the inside of our body. We know it's there, we can feel it, but we don't have any criteria for judging it, appreciating it. It seems that dolphins, who don't have any facial expression as their features don't change, can tell their emotional state using sonar, a kind of sound radar, by letting out little cries that bounce around inside their bodies. Through the disposition of the viscera of their opposite number, according to whether these are tense or relaxed, they can tell if they're happy or sad. So they have a much more intimate knowledge of the other's insides. Elliot delivers this speech with humour, but it's also the truth.

Your scientists are always authoritarian figures. What's your attitude in their regard? Do you share the point of view of the authors of the nineteenth century who seem to have developed the horror genre and the irrational as science became important?

I'd like to resist that stereotyped vision of the scientist. In fact, in *The Fly*, I show a man of science who is more human, more eccentric. My heroes are often tragic heroes, but they're archetypes of the powerful creator. I could just as well make them artists. For me, the best scientists are like artists. They're very creative, work a lot by instinct. Science today is not mechanistic like the science of the nineteenth century; it's organic. This is very obvious in the case of Einstein, who hesitated between science and the violin. I think that, actually, from this point of view, the horror film is the result of the conflict between the rational and the irrational. If we enjoyed the total freedom of the irrational, there wouldn't be any horror. What I seek to find out in my films is whether mind and body can be integrated. Rationally, we note that they can't exist without each other and yet we very often feel that they're separate.

Dead Ringers *presents itself as a tragedy. From the beginning we know that the characters are doomed.*

That was very deliberate and I'm happy that it's perceived that way. In the opening sequences, for instance, I don't show the parents of the twins when they were children, as I didn't want to enter into Freudian explanations of the kind that go: if their mother had only dressed them differently, none of this would have happened. I wanted to suggest that their fate was sealed from birth. External phenomena – including the parents – couldn't change anything.

Howard Shore's music accentuates the Liebestod *aspect.*

Yes. It's something romantic, post-Wagnerian, close to Mahler. Shore has composed the music of nearly all my films with the exception of *Dead Zone* because he wasn't available at the time. I really like working with the same collaborators all the time as we wind up knowing each other inside out. As soon as I have a first draft of the script, I send it to Howard Shore and he starts thinking about the music. In this precise instance, he sent me the theme on synthesiser which now takes up the credit roll sequence. Then, as usual, we started discussing the instruments, whether they'd be electronic or not, the size of the orchestra, the distribution of the strings and the woodwind. It's a very pragmatic approach, which starts off not worrying about references. Any conversation about music is weird since it's a non-verbal form of expression and the sound is even more subjective than the image. In fact, I have a lot more stormy discussions during the editing than on the set, for a sound suggests different associations for each person. Once the film is completely edited, I sit down with the composer and the editor and that's when we get very specific, when we place this particular musical chunk just after a character has said this specific sentence, right up to the end of a certain take. Even though we rarely discuss specific compositions, we often come back to Mahler, Stravinsky and Bernard Herrmann. My films seem connected to their music.

You were telling us how little difference there is between the art world and the world of science. You yourself hesitated between biology and literature when you were at university.

Arthur Koestler has shown that, fundamentally, artistic creation and scientific creation are similar. I studied science for a year at Toronto University as I wanted to be a biochemist, that is, to study the chemistry of bodies. But I didn't get far since, even though the material was fantastic, I found the teaching structures suffocating. I really didn't enjoy it and I decided to switch to arts, even though I like to think, not without arrogance perhaps, that I would have been a very good scientist. It seemed to me, though, that there were strict connections between art and science, that there was no difference between scientific research and reading and experiencing a brilliant story. I'd also been interested in nature and in animals since I was a child. To a certain extent, the twin children in the film are like me, except that I was never so weird and I never went as far as they do! I collected insects, for example. And the clothes they wear in the film are the same as those I had in those days in Toronto. But we shouldn't take the autobiographical elements too far...

You come from an artistic background.

My mother was a pianist and my father a writer. Those activities were natural for me, self-evident. Later on I realised that many children in my street didn't have books at home, or musical instruments. My mother taught me to play the piano when I was very young, and I played classical guitar at the age of eleven and up until I was twenty-two. I even thought of becoming a concert guitarist but I realised that it wasn't for me, that it wasn't fundamentally creative, that I was just a performer. Like lots of young people in the 1960s, I was attracted to Eastern music because it was different. You had a form in the beginning but then you improvised, you created the way you do in jazz. But in those days I was already committed to writing. I wanted to be a writer and in a sense that's also what I've become.

Was reading more of a pastime for you than watching films?

Going to the movies, that was what you did on weekends. At least before television took off. For kids like us there was nothing spectacular about it, it was part of the weekly routine to go to one of the three movie theatres nearby. In the suburb where I lived and where new immigrants came, the last wave was composed of Italians. And I remember that there was a cinema, the Studio, opposite the one that I usually went to as a kid, which only showed Italian films in the original version. I'd walk out of my movie house, where I'd just seen a western, and on the other side of the street men and women would be coming out of the Studio, sobbing. I was stunned that adults could react like that to a film so I crossed the street to find out what was going on. They were showing *La Strada*. I think that was the first time I discovered that cinema could exercise a hold over people's emotions.

And what were your literary tastes?

I was attracted to the underground writers published by Grove Press or who had things published in the *Evergreen Review*. And that lead me to William

Burroughs and Vladimir Nabokov, who were without a doubt my two greatest literary influences. I was also very interested in medieval literature – it was my speciality – Chaucer, translations of Boccaccio. The Middle Ages had a great influence on my imagination. The men of the time were obsessed by death and tackled it very explicitly. That fascinated me.

All your films, with the exception of Fast Company, *derive from the gothic. Now, what the gothic tackles is the problem of death.*

Yes, death is at the heart of the genre. And in a way the genre protects me. For example, in *The Fly*, two young people fall in love. The boy then contracts a horrible disease and starts gradually dying before his companion's very eyes and then he asks her to kill him. If you wanted to tell that story in Hollywood outside the gothic genre and you asked a company for ten million dollars, they'd think you were nuts. If, on the other hand, you made a horror film, they'd let you go to extremes that would be unthinkable elsewhere. If *Dead Ringers* had had more gothic or science fiction elements, I think I'd have had a lot less trouble finding the money.

When did you decide that cinema would be your future, that you were going to make films?

I can date that moment precisely. I'd seen a film made by a student at Toronto University, *Winter Kept Us Warm*. That was a real shock to the system because the idea of shooting a film in Toronto was as strange as the idea of making a car there. Hollywood was where you made films. Down there, since your father or your grandfather was in the industry, you thought that one day you, too, would join the trade. But not in Toronto. And there I am suddenly discovering that friends of mine were performing as actors in *Winter Kept Us Warm!* It was a pretty little film that was a real revelation to me, for suddenly I had the impression that it was possible, that I could make movies. Today of course it's totally different. Everyone's making films – my nephew, who is ten, has already shot ten films at school!

Have you always written your scripts yourself?

I used to write short stories, before. I thought I'd be a novelist one day. I won prizes at university for my stories, and even during the year when I was studying science. I took first prize for a short story when I first started doing science, even though I was up against fourth year students, the crème de la crème of the literature department. That was a story about a man stretched out on a bed, dying, with his sister at his side, and he remembered and imagined things. Other stories were closer to horror and gothic.

How did you start out in cinema?

I'm completely self-taught. At the time there were practically no film schools in the country in the English language, outside the London School of Film Technique and the University of California (UCLA). I used to consult the *Encyclopaedia of Film* where I'd read the entries on 'lenses', 'camera', film stock'. I also read a review called *American Cinematographer*, including the classifieds, to try and understand the mechanics, like, for instance, synchronisation of sound and image, which appeared mysterious to me. Then I'd hang around shops where you hired the equipment. There were operators there who shot advertising films and who'd come in for a glass of gin. I'd listen to them talking among themselves, then I'd ask them how, for instance, you stripped down an Arriflex. Once I'd familiarised myself with the technology, I went back to the same shop and hired an Auricon camera, which was very popular at the time for shooting current affairs films, and also a Nagra, a mike, and so on. With a script I'd written and friends who agreed to perform, I was able to shoot my first film. I then recorded the sound, did the editing and made every possible mistake. But that's how I learned. That was *Transfer*.

What stage do you prefer in the making of a film?

I feel comfortable at every stage! Of course the filming is the craziest part. Writing is hard. You can go mad sitting alone in a room scribbling away. It's all the harder when, like me, you stop for a while. For example, I haven't written anything for a year. But at the same time, writing is gratifying; it's a fundamental creative act, alone with yourself. I visualise the film to be made but only to a certain point. I can, for example, describe a character in detail knowing full well that the actor who will play it will be completely different. But I need to write my script as a story to feel the reality of the characters, whereas a professional scriptwriter would be happy just indicating that 'the man is thirty-five years old and a good-looking boy.' I write for myself – I've never written for anybody else, in fact – and I write what I need to write. It's a very literary exercise, pretty remote from directing. After a while, I feel the solitude weighing down on me and I need contact with people. The moment I start hating the writing is when pre-production on the film starts! That's very exciting, and I get feverishly impatient waiting for the shoot to begin. So each phase has a different rhythm. Filming is like a war; it's very hard and you don't get much sleep. And just when you're exhausted, everything stops and you move on to the editing. That phase is like the writing, with a few more people around you, but the atmosphere is calm and the approach more theoretical. Finally you get to mix the soundtrack, which is a lot more emotional, more agitated, more intense. This phase is often neglected but it's essential and the problems of communication are difficult, in particular with producers.

Was it different when you directed the only script that you didn't write – for Dead Zone?

Not really, because when I'm filming, I look at my script as though someone else had written it. It doesn't help me at all in directing. I have to say, too, that I did have a hand in the *Dead Zone* script. When I turned up for the project, there'd already been five scripts written, one of which was written by Stephen King, and I scrapped them all. I then worked with Jeffrey Boam and told him what kind of film I wanted to make, what I wanted to keep or chuck from the novel, what tone I wanted to adopt. We worked on the script like they do in Hollywood. He'd write five pages, I'd read them and we'd discuss it. So I was very much involved in getting *Dead Zone* ready and during the shoot I even wrote in two scenes I needed.

How did you move from the underground film to a more commercial kind of cinema?

My first feature films, *Stereo* and *Crimes of the Future*, were still typically underground. I did everything – the photography, the editing – and I filmed in natural sets. It was practically just me and my actors. But those were also my first trials in 35 mm. *Stereo* was financed by the Canada Council and various grants. For *Crimes of the Future*, I got the money from the Canada Film Development Corporation, which has since become Telefilm Canada. I was very influenced by the New York underground. This was in the 1960s and Jonas Mekas and his cohorts used to say: 'Cinema belongs to us. Do it if you want to. You don't need to be in Hollywood and work as an assistant for twenty years.' That's what I wanted to hear and it helped me a lot. We founded a cooperative in Toronto with Ivan Reitma and other friends. Then, in 1972, I went to live in the south of France for about a year, at Tourettes-sur-Loup. I made small films there with a Beaulieu that I'd bought. I remember that I drove down from this little isolated, quiet medieval village to go to the Cannes Festival. I felt like a mountain man who could hardly cross the street because of all the traffic. I was horrified by Cannes. On the façade of the Carlton Hotel there were banners five storeys high to launch a James Bond. And there was so much hoopla that I went straight back to Tourettes. But once I got there I began to reflect and I told myself that if I wanted to make films, I'd really have to learn to deal with all that: money, publicity, talks. I didn't want to keep making underground films. I had the impression I'd been there, done that. So I went back to Cannes and spent a few days there to see how it worked. If you approach the festival with a sense of humour, it's a lot of fun and I stopped being intimidated. I actually found it rather entertaining and since then I've gone back to sell my films – in the market, not in competition!

It's Shivers/The Parasite Murders (Frissons) *that, in this sense, marks your real debut.*

Yes, that's my first professional film to the extent that I was paid for my work and I had a crew around me who were also paid. I'd written a script that I'd sent to Cinépix, the only Canadian company at the time that was producing at a remotely steady rate – they specialised especially in soft porn. They hired Ivan Reitman as a producer, but the film took three years to get made because Cinépix didn't want me to direct it. They'd seen my underground films and they weren't sure I could go the distance and make a commercial film. I have to say that the constraints and pressures were enormous since the film was made in a fortnight! And I had to learn as I went along over those two weeks. But they wound up entrusting me with the direction and if they hadn't, they wouldn't have got the script!

The Parasite Murders *is the first in a series of films that talk about what happens to the body, its transformations, viruses and epidemics.*

I find it hard to explain this constant in my subjects. It comes naturally to me. If you study insects – one of the passions of my youth – metamorphosis is one of the primary features of their lives. Each insect goes through one or more mutations and some of them are striking, even incredible. That's also true for other animal species. It seems to me that that also happens to people, it's just not as visible. What I wanted was to make human metamorphoses more visible. I'm apparently giving a rational explanation here whereas it came spontaneously out of my typewriter when I started working on my scripts.

For example, I was just sick here in Paris for twenty-four hours and it's amazing what happens. I believe that the body is very unstable, that our equilibrium has something of the miraculous about it, that each cell is fragile and complex, and that if one of them is affected, it can have repercussions for our entire organism. This stability is an illusion we have to believe in to hang on to our mental health, but at the same time we have to try and understand what life is and what it isn't. You only have to be ill for a day for everything to change: you no longer know where you are, what time it is, you find yourself in a total blur. When you're sick, you finally become conscious of your body and of the relationship it maintains with your brain, of the influence it has on your mental state. Just as interesting and mysterious is the effect your psyche can have on your body, which also happens, naturally.

You've claimed that Chromosome 3 (The Brood) *was your most personal film. It was made at a turning point in your life, as you had just lost your father and divorced your first wife.*

The Brood was a real catharsis. It is, I think, the only film I've made where there were truly autobiographical elements. Scenes from my life wound up in the script and the dialogues almost as I lived them. When the man wants to hang on to his child at any cost, for example. Of course all art is autobiographical in the broadest sense of the term to the extent that you can only feed off your own experience, whether intellectual, physical or emotional. But it was different with *The Brood,* where I really represented moments from my life. The energy to make the film came from the divorce that I'd just gone through. I don't think, on the other hand, that *The Brood* was really connected with the death of my father. I'd made films on death well before the death of my parents. Today my mother is dead, too; I'm no longer anyone's son. There is no protective barrier between me and death. I'm next in line and I now play the role of my parents for my own children. And that's a whole education, this reversal of roles!

My father died of cancer while his mind remained completely lucid, and that only confirmed everything I'd thought. I was scandalised that the mind could be destroyed because the body was caving in. And for me it's a mystery that I still can't manage to fathom.

The names are important in defining your characters. Mantle for the brothers in Dead Ringers. *Claire Niveau for Geneviève Bujold. But also Bianca O'Blivion and Barry Convex in* Videodrome, *Darryl Revok and Arno Crostic in* Scanners, *Murray Cypher and Dan Keloid in* Rabid. *Those are strange inventions!*

My use of names is not exactly the same as Nabokov's as he was a lot more attracted to semantic games. I don't know what attracts me in a name, but when I write, I feel like I haven't found my characters until I know their names. It's totally intuitive. It's not a play on words, and I don't like it to be obvious or burlesque, either. If you go too far, you can kill your character. Sometimes a name feels good on paper but you can't really say it. For instance, we called our production company The Mantle Clinic. And people on the phone would say to us: 'The mental clinic?' Well, I hadn't thought of that.

Just why did you call your twins Mantle and the woman Claire Niveau?

It's not entirely symbolic. Beverly and Elliot Mantle sounded right together to me. It evokes things without being too explicit. As for Geneviève Bujold's name, it feels very appropriate to me. At the beginning you think the twins have themselves under control, that they're very organised and that Claire is very unstable. But little by little you discover that she's the strongest and that she's very 'clear' and very 'level'. The key to her behaviour is that she becomes aware of the danger they represent and she has a survival instinct. I don't think she's as in love with Beverly and she gradually withdraws as she can smell death in him. At the end she cries over the tragedy but she knows there's nothing she can do.

Your institutions, your hospitals also have curious names. The Institute for Neo-Venereal Disease, Oceanic Podiatry Group, Somafree Institute of Psychoplasmics… A lot of humour goes into them.

Definitely! Note that the word 'corporation', like the adjective 'incorporated' that we use in English in the world of business and industry, means to transform into a body. The Romans, I think, were the first to invent the idea of a group of men coming together to form another body, separate from each of them and subject to the same laws as any other body. In a sense a corporation is a strange thing, living and organic. Today when I see the names of certain companies, they seem so funny I feel like I've made them up.

One of your films, Fast Company, *stands alone. It doesn't belong to the world of science.*

That's a good little B-grade film. I don't think it has much connection to the others. It reflects my interest in racing cars. I still haven't managed – although I'm working on a project at the moment – to integrate this passion into my other cinematographic concerns.

Yet the interior of a car resembles the inside of a body and the mechanic is a surgeon.

I'm glad you said that! Opening up an engine is like being inside the brain of the person who designed it. Every engineer has to resolve the same problems, but their solutions are so fantastic, so different! A German's solution is so far from an Italian's. But you won't see that in *Fast Company,* which I'm fond of, but which is more of a western with fast cars. I still have to make *my* film on cars. I was on a project with Paramount on Grands Prix, but it didn't go anywhere. I wouldn't have wanted to make a novelistic documentary on racing circuits like we've seen so many of. But competition cars, that's really one of my passions and I collect them. I've had a Ferrari and a Cooper.

Going to English-speaking Canada, doesn't that, for an American or an Englishman, correspond to Freud's notion of disturbing strangeness? Everything seems familiar and yet everything is slightly different.

An American said that to me one day that, for him, seeing one of my films was like living in a dream: the streets of our towns are like those of his country, but at the same time you can't mistake them. Same for the accent. Toronto is halfway between Hollywood and Europe, and I think my films are subject to those two influences. I feel the need for those two sources. People send me all kinds of scripts, from *Top Gun* to *Beverly Hills Cop* and *Flash Dance*, and I tell myself as I read them that they're too American for me. Harlem, cops, drug trafficking – these subjects are fiction for me. I don't understand them intimately.

Have you seen Peter Greenaway's A Zed and Two Noughts? *Your sensibilities are very different but there are strange connections between his film and* Dead Ringers.

That's a very funny film and in a way the story is similar, with the two twin scientists who die at the end. But his concerns are different from mine. He's more interested in symmetry, for instance. Not only do I like his film a lot, but I showed it to my crew before filming *Dead Ringers*. It'd make a good double bill.

7 ATOM EGOYAN

(1960–)

In his early days, Egoyan showed all the signs of being a child prodigy and of being strong on themes. After several shorts, he signed his first feature film, *Next of Kin,* at the age of twenty-four, and followed it with *Family Viewing*, while continuing to work all the while on TV documentaries, in particular to do with music. As the titles of his first films indicate, the family is a theme that plays a central role for Egoyan. And to top it off, his wife, Arsinée Khanjian, is his favourite performer. Born in Cairo of Armenian descent, Egoyan went to Canada with his parents at the age of three. His background is also a subject of predilection for him: *Calendar* (1993) and *Ararat* (2002) are devoted to the land of his ancestors, *Ararat* being more especially a reflection on genocide but also on cinema and the relationship between reality and fiction. For Egoyan asks himself about the film process itself, the proliferation of images, the new technologies (which he occasionally uses) and voyeurism. His art is the art of mise en abyme and this goes against the dominant film narrative governed by identification. He explains himself on the score very conscientiously in the interview he did with Philippe Rouyer and myself after the screening of *Exotica* at the Cannes Festival. What is admirable is that Egoyan has been able to conduct this research for twenty years without any concessions to English-speaking Canada, which is more sensitive to the lure of Hollywood than any other country in the world. In that sense, his integrity is similar to that of David Cronenberg, who puts up the same resistance to the sirens of American cinema. Even if Egoyan's trajectory as an artist might appear to tend towards a more accessible narrative, with his adaptations of novels by Russell Banks (*The Sweet Hereafter*) and William Trevor (*Felicia's Journey*), Egoyan's cinema remains one of the most demanding in contemporary production, deploying labyrinthine plots, with their mix of passion and frustration, in an extremely sophisticated style.

ON *EXOTICA*

CANNES, MAY 1994

What was the genesis of Exotica?

There are two very different sources. The first is a photo I saw in a newspaper of a woman who'd been apprehended at customs while she was trying to get through with exotic birds' eggs strapped to her stomach. She had a very voluptuous body and this image was disturbing to me, with its mix of fertility and artifice. There was a contradiction between the eggs, whose function is to protect what's inside, and their presence outside. The other source is an incident that took place in Toronto. A young boy had disappeared and a group of people had set out to find him. One of my friends who was in this group had told me that he'd met a young woman there. There, too, two contradictory elements coexisted: the birth of a love story and the most morally ugly thing, the kidnapping of a child. I think that these two images, with the presence at once of hope and evil, stayed in my brain and started to develop. In the film, we see institutions that are designed to protect but that can be used to invade. For example, the entrance, that antechamber which Zoë's father has always said is made to protect and which, in reality, allows voyeurism to be practised. We never know where our place is or how things get used.

At the heart of the story, there is a tax inspector. There was already a tax man in The Adjuster.

I have a peculiar relationship with people who have an ordinary job, but one that allows them access to your private life, through various rites. I also had a financial controller, in the strangest way, working on the takings for *The Adjuster*! He never stopped asking me questions and the more questions he asked, the more interested he got in everything about the world of cinema. You could feel he was attracted by the glamour of the job. I wanted to have access to his life in turn; I wanted a form of exchange. I started imagining what he did at night, and so on.

How do the characters gradually come to light, get added on?

Based on an emotional connection to the basic material. It would be too easy to offer a rational explanation retrospectively. The process of writing is very intuitive for me, but, at the same time, what people represent for each other, and their role in the film, is very organic. There's a tight network of mutual needs and also a specific event that has resonances in the lives of each one of them. You could talk about dramatic necessities and why a particular character has to be there at a particular moment, but that feels like too clinical an approach to me and it goes against what I feel while I'm writing. It's hard to explain. For a time I'm in the grip of a thematic. I studied music and I'm most particularly influenced by baroque music, with its technique of counterpoint and its way of developing certain rhymes. Different melodic lines have different significance in themselves, but also a relationship to others that they maintain harmonic resonances with, as in Bach or Purcell. That's a very natural way for me to work, as much at the writing stage as at the editing. I start by writing a first draft, then I try and formulate what the central metaphors are and articulate them together. For this film, for example, the notion of protection and help, the idea of a sanctuary and of a perfect world, the idea of an exotic place and how you keep it that way, the concept of nature as the pastoral ideal but also as a real threat. I then had the idea of the club as an environment that's natural but stylised, made stronger. I thought of the Douanier Rousseau's paintings as an inspiration for decorating the walls. I thought of the use of eggshells. Each element leads naturally to the next to form a very tightly woven tapestry. Once the exotic set is seriously in place, you can use domestic animals in the nicest way. Like with the room where the aquariums aren't maintained and where the exotic fish get sick and die. What happens in that polluted water is grotesque and contrasts with the very clean place Thomas lives in. The film evolves through change: an egg is going to open, a child is going to grow like this child who doesn't want to babysit anymore. Beings change, nothing remains fixed, whereas ritual, to exist, has to remain rigid. That's a bit the theme of the film: we create rituals to manage our neuroses, but in doing so, we create additional problems for ourselves, our state gets worse. Speaking of that film, two separate questions need to be asked, failing which it risks remaining superficial. Why does she wear that uniform, and how did he meet her in that club? At the end we discover that Christina had a troubled past. When she saw the little girl's dead body, lying in the field, the same little girl she used to babysit of an evening, she suddenly projects all her fury at the world into an image. And so she, in turn, puts on a uniform to exorcise that image. When Francis comes into the club and sees

Christina, the girl he'd hired to mind his child, wearing the uniform, he has to make a decision: either to leave the club or to begin this ritual by means of which he maintains the memory of the deceased. I don't think his relationship with his daughter was incestuous, but the problem is that he keeps it going after her death in a sexualised context. Suddenly he has to confront not only the iconographic representation of his daughter but also the guilt that the context fuels in him. That's when the memory of his own daughter becomes exotic in his eyes. That's the sense of the word 'exotic' in the film. There are times when our experience of family, or our relationship to it, can become exotic for us. In Francis's case, this ordeal can become masochistic. I don't think there's anything erotic for him in the ritual and yet he's decided to keep indulging in it. And it's endless, for once he's opened Pandora's box, he has to re-evaluate his whole previous relationship with his daughter.

Was the nightclub inspired by a pre-existing place or is it a pure product of the imagination?

In Toronto, there's an activity that's very popular known as table dancing, but the architecture in the film is totally invented. When you consider the character of Zoë's mother, you can't help but think of her background in the Middle East and of a type of cabaret native to the region. There's a burlesque side to the decor, and if you look at the paintings on the wall, you get the feeling of another era.

How did you work with your set designers, Linda del Rosario and Richard Paris?

Everything was built. We worked with models and spent a lot of time discussing the architecture of the place. I wanted the place to be seductive, since people want to spend time there. When you walk into a real nightclub and you think about the decor in view of a film, you most often find them extremely ugly. I wanted the decor to be truly exotic, in the correct sense of the term, and for it to attract the visitor. We did a storyboard but only for the scenes in the club, since we had a very tight work schedule and the lighting problems were considerable. Setting up each shot took a lot of time and if we hadn't known which way we were headed, there would have been a real waste.

How did you approach the different scenes where Christina is dancing?

The dancing was very hard to get right as I felt strongly about using that particular song and it's not especially designed for any choreography. Table dancing is an extraordinary ritual in which public experience and private experience vie with each other. The woman gets paid five dollars a dance – that is, every four minutes, to keep up this very great intimacy that is unreciprocated on the part of the man watching her. Unlike prostitution, there is no consummation and there's also the public dimension. Whence a certain dose of masochism. You have to see the fantasy of the bacchanalia in there and of the harem, too. Every man has to know the parameters of his sexual behaviour and have safeguards that have to be respected. It's infinitely complex and fertile ground.

There is masochism in Francis and a manipulative streak in Eric.

There's also masochism in Eric. He continues to be romantically attached to Christina and yet he keeps on seeing her with other men. The only way for him to alleviate his suffering is to deconstruct her image. He tries to shatter the innocence of the little girl. When Zoë takes him aside and tells him he's making the customer uncomfortable, he replies that his job is to create a special feeling in each person. The same feeling he feels for Christina. It's as though he's living out his own fantasies himself.

When you imagined the character of Zoë, your wife Arsinée Khanjian, who plays her, was not pregnant. How did her condition affect the development of the film?

I was faced with a choice. Either I could do without her or I could make use of the situation. There's something extremely perverse and irresistible in the fact that a pregnant woman, who is the incarnation of a certain type of femininity, is the owner of the club. She was in a state of total confusion and was also going through a crisis. She's obsessed by her mother and dresses like her. Some people ask me why there's no video in the film. That's an absurd question since, in my other films, video plays the role of performance, whereas in *Exotica* everyone's already performing. Christina is decked out like a schoolgirl; Zoë wears her mother's clothes. Everyone is searching for their identity in the most theatrical way. Besides, the film's references are theatrical: the music hall, the opera, nightclubs. When I wrote the first draft of the script, I realised all the characters were in the middle of some sort of ritual, but I didn't know how it had started. It was important for me to show the start of this ritual and it's thanks to Thomas that I can do it. It happens accidentally when an opera ticket turns up in his car. And the system of exchange continues throughout the film by means of money. The characters are so invaded by the emotions tormenting them that their only way of controlling them is to practise exchange.

Music plays an essential role in these rituals.

I'm proud of the soundtrack. When the girl presses the button, the piano starts playing by itself. Suddenly, the theme she's playing invades the nightclub, then it goes back to being the score she's playing. The sound becomes a means of integrating the show and the screening. What is seen and what is presented merge. It's a bit like in *The Adjuster* where, during the projection, you hear the sound but you don't see the images. The viewer then puts his imagination to work. I love those moments where the audience is aware that people are at a show that's hidden from the audience itself. The more the subject's addressed to the viewer's subconscious, the happier I am. Sometimes people reject my films because there's no romantic notion of cinema, no possibility of escape with me. In my films, the images can carry you away, but only to the extent that you are aware of them. The audience has to know that they're covering this ground so they can get back to a form of identification.

The music was recorded in Bombay. Why?

My composer, Mychael Danna, is very meticulous. He absolutely had to have an Indian flute, a shenaï. He searched in vain not only in Toronto but in the whole of North America for someone who could play one. We were getting close to the editing stage and he suggested going and recording on the spot. I didn't have the money to pay his fare and he decided to take care of costs himself. He went off to India for four days, found a musician in a village somewhere and brought him back to Bombay to record him. The rest of the music was composed before the shoot, obviously, as you see it played in the film. When she plays the piano or when she dances.

At what stage in the development of the script did the shots of the characters walking in the fields appear?

At a certain point, I felt the need for an opening; the climate of the film was so claustrophobic. I wanted to offer the possibility of taking a breather in nature. But, of course, it was a deceptive feeling, since you can't breathe in this story. What I thought was a breather turns into the most horrifying moment in the film. There are several moments like that in the story, where your expectations are thwarted. Like the scene where Francis is in a car with a young woman who you think is a prostitute until he says to her, 'Say hello to your father.' I love those moments where the dramatic sense of a scene is reversed.

Did the film change in the editing?

Essentially only in relation to the character of Thomas, who appeared in a greater number of scenes. The whole ritual he's involved in, for instance, when he meets the people at the opera, plus the conversations after the show were a lot more developed. There's also a scene with the eggs that I cut out because I didn't think it was necessary. A man, who's in love with Thomas, steals the eggs and doesn't want to give them back because he knows that Thomas won't be interested in him afterwards.

How did you work on the visual concept of the film?

It's the product of collaboration between my two designers, Paul Sarossy, my cinematographer, and myself. It was important to have a very precise green, for example, in the background of the pet shop. We also worked a lot on the smoke and the light sources in the club. I was really lucky in the outdoor scenes, with that cloud and that soft even light in the fields. I work with tight budgets and I have to know in advance which days I'm going to shoot outside. In a Hollywood film, if the atmospheric conditions aren't right, you wait. Me, I can't afford to. For this film, as for *The Adjuster*, I had exactly the time I wanted! Nature was on my side, which was lucky with a budget of only eight million francs! I have to say that the film was shot very fast, in exactly twenty-five days.

Do you rehearse with the actors?

Generally, yes, but *Exotica* was a sort of challenge since I very quickly realised that Mia Kirshner, the young actress who plays Christina, was at her best in her immediate reactions. On the other hand, there are actors who need rehearsals. So I had to juggle those two contradictory demands: how to prepare one actor to the point where they're really ready, while preserving the other's spontaneity. That's why, for the first time, I abandoned rehearsals with the whole cast as I realised that certain performances weren't convincing. The important thing was that each actor fully understood the subtext of what they were saying. That's also why I often use actors I've already worked with: they understand me without my having to spell things out. The same goes for my technical crew: over the years, we've developed a telegraphic style. I like to hold emotion back, which is sometimes hard for an actor. For example, at the end, when Francis tells François what's happened, the natural tendency for an actor would then be to collapse emotionally. I went to great lengths, on the contrary, to stop Bruce Greenwood from doing that. It's often frustrating for an actor, and you have to convince them, get them to trust you.

What are your criteria in choosing your actors? Do you hire them because you feel they have character traits of the persona, for example?

That depends, really. I have to confess that for Francis, I really wanted someone seductive. Given the experiences he goes through and the lack of sympathy you feel for him in the beginning, he couldn't be physically unattractive, either. For the role of Christina, I had a shock. I'd hired Mia Kirshner, but, when she turned up on the set the first day, I felt very uncomfortable as I would never have thought she'd look so young dressed up like a schoolgirl! Yet she's twenty-one and she managed to transform herself remarkably well. I'd also noted in her eyes an ability to express anger, which suits the character. On the whole, all my actors had to be seductive since the film offers a melange of romanticism and cynicism.

How do you place yourself in relation to other filmmakers, such as Greenaway, who, like you, privilege the ritual and the visual?

I feel a strong emotion watching films where the characters are subjected to a series of ritual behaviours they don't really grasp the meaning of. That's why a film like *Drowning By Numbers* especially appeals to me. There's both something ineluctable in the impulses at work and a sadness in the face of the possibilities of change. That's a film about the frailty of human needs and about the desire to cling to things that are necessarily going to be transformed. I feel similar emotions when I see Cronenberg's *Dead Ringers,* where the twins have established a whole tangle of behaviours in their life and then they see it all unravelling before their very eyes. It's the same idea you find in *Calendar* when the character says, 'Everything that's made to protect us is doomed to disappear.' For me, that's the tragic essence of all ritual. We put a lot into a relationship that, by necessity, is going to evolve. Of course, the Lolita syndrome is the most explicit when it comes to this established fact, since Lolita, by definition, can't stay what she is. That's what makes the last scene of Kubrick's film so poignant, when Humbert Humbert tries desperately to hang on to an image that already no longer exists.

You have a most particular relationship to emotions which obviously fascinate you but which you mistrust.

I think my conception of the expression of emotions on screen has evolved since my previous film, *Calendar*. Before that, I was heavily influenced by Bresson, especially after seeing a retrospective of his work ten years ago, when I'd just started making features. It really impressed me a lot and I read his *Notes on Cinematography,* which became my bible, with his conception of the actor as a 'model' and his refusal to allow the tiniest trace of theatricality in a performance. Before going to Armenia to film *Calendar*, I stayed for a while in Paris, where they were showing several of Cassavetes's films. So I had the opportunity of seeing them again and that really marked me, especially *A Woman Under the Influence*. I realised that I felt ready to use emotion in a more direct way, whereas before that I'd felt a lot of mistrust towards anything emotional. The fact that *Calendar* was more spontaneous as a project allowed me to put that into practice and to give the actors more room. You know, this mistrust goes way back. My wife comes from Lebanon and I'm from Egypt, we're Armenian, so we come from a culture where emotions are expressed openly – as often as possible. That's what we grew up with in our families but at the same time it's very hard to take all these demonstrations all that seriously. It's impossible for us, for example, to watch a melodrama at the movies and, afterwards, to really take much notice of what it says. On the other hand, I completely accept Cassavetes. The difference between his films and melodramas is, I suppose, the lack of conventions and codes: with him, the emotional situations are never what you expect and the viewer finds themselves given real room to reflect on what they're seeing. I lay claim to the ritual of emotions as deliberate performance, as I practise it in my cinema, but the ritual of sobbing at funerals, as you see it practised in the Middle East, leaves me cold. One of the transformations that affect our society is that we always live with images of the deceased and so we don't have room to lament their absence. That's one of the themes of *Exotica*.

You are part of a trend in modern cinema that places huge importance on the visual while seeking new forms of narrative.

I'm very conscious of belonging to a tradition. For a long time I believed, as an English-speaking Canadian, that I could throw a bridge between the *cinéma d'auteur* and Hollywood. I realise more and more, particularly with *Exotica,* that that can't be done, that I'm in a different stream from classic American cinema. This observation has freed me. Talking to American distributors and producers, I'm aware that I don't come from that world and that I'll probably never get any closer to it. It's a relief for me to see so clearly, especially this year, at Cannes, how my cinema is the opposite of the reigning image industry. Ninety-five per cent of films today have the prospect of television in mind; on the small screen, images are supposedly taken at face value, they're totally literal and the public is meant to identify with them totally. That's not, obviously, what I'm looking for.

8 FEDERICO FELLINI

(1920–1993)

If, in the 1950s, *The Young and the Passionate (Il Vitellone)* and *The Swindle* (Il Bidone) seduced me, I found Fellini less compelling than certain of his contemporaries, such as Antonioni or Visconti. I didn't share the ardent enthusiasm surrounding, say, *La Strada*, or *The Nights of Cabiria*, original as they were. With *La Dolce Vita* and *8½*, he struck me as one of the masters of modernity in cinema. Curiously, after that, as the years wore on, Fellini had more and more detractors, as attested by the cool reception given to *Fellini Satyricon* at the Venice Film Festival or to *Roma* at Cannes. I, on the other hand, admired the freedom of a cinema that was perfectly inspired, as much in the great frescoes of *Casanova* or *City of Women* as in intimate films like *The Clowns* or *Interview*. Fellini had nonetheless turned into a myth I didn't feel I could approach. I discovered a man who was quite the reverse of the myth, extremely warm, doubtless sensitive to the admiration I felt for an oeuvre now suffering from the disaffection of the critics.

Every time I visited Rome, I had to submit to a telephone ritual which meant that at the other end of the line, the maestro – no doubt pinching his nose – would put on the voice of the Spanish maid to announce that the *signore* had gone out or gone off to the country. After the first fruitless attempt, an appointment was soon made to meet at his home in the via Marguta, or at 'Cesarina', his favourite restaurant, or on the set of his latest film. So, from my visit to the set of *And the Ship Sails On* and *Casanova*, I remember a generous Fellini who even made me the extravagant gift of a preliminary sketch. For this interview on *Orchestra Rehearsal*, he preferred the calm of his Cinecittà office where he was in pre-production on *City of Women*, chopping between French, English and Italian to make himself understood.

ON *ORCHESTRA REHEARSAL (PROVA D'ORCHESTRA)*
ROME, DECEMBER 1978

How did the idea of filming Orchestra Rehearsal *come about?*

I'd the idea for a long time. Whenever I sat in on the recording of the music for my films, I was always struck by a feeling of surprise and incredulity and I was also moved to see a miracle recurring each time. Individuals who were very different from each other would come into the recording studio with their various instruments but also with their personal problems, their bad moods, their illnesses, their transistor radios so they could listen to the sports results. And I was amazed to see how, in this context of disorder and approximation, with these rebellious schoolboys, by dint of repeated attempts, we'd manage to meld this heterogeneous mass into a single, even abstract, form, which is music. This operation of turning disorder into order stirred some great emotion in me. It seemed to me that this situation carried within it, in a way, in emblematic fashion, the image of life in society. In it, expression as a whole was compatible with the expression of each individual, each instrument remaining itself in its identity, in its vocation and at the same time melting into a harmonious discourse that involves everyone. That's all extremely banal but what I mean is that I wanted for a long time to make a small documentary that would inspire in the viewer the reassuring idea that it's possible to make something together and yet remain yourself while doing so. That is the ideology, the philosophy, the emotional side of my project. When I say documentary, I'm not thinking of the timely travail of a journalist, but of a lyrical documentary that would recreate the impressions I've just mentioned by choosing between 2,000 exemplary anecdotes picked up during orchestra rehearsals. So I offered to do this special show for Italian television and it turned into the expression of all the anguish, all the despair of any Italian living in this country today. Almost unconsciously the rehearsal presented itself to my imagination in a sinister and apocalyptic light.

You wrote, after The Clowns, *that you weren't happy with the film as a television film. How did you approach* Orchestra Rehearsal *after your previous experiences with the small screen?*

For me, television has nothing to do with cinema. It reduces, deadens films. Moreover, I don't think there is a television style, I don't think a true *auteur* can find a means of expression in television. For me, television is a household appliance; it can not reproduce the images of an authentic filmmaker. And there are several reasons for this: first, the viewer must be able to inhabit the imaginary of an artist and he can only do that in a movie theatre where he finds himself in a position of inferiority in relation to the size of the screen, in the ritual of choosing his film, going to the movies, sometimes in a group, stepping into the dark. Even if cinema has lost a great deal of its sacred character, it always sets off a series of processes and forces humility on the viewer. Faced with television, on the other hand, you're in a position of authority; you are the owner. The image doesn't drown you, you aren't obliged to look at it, with unconscious respect, you can turn it on or switch it off at will.

But even though I don't believe in a television style, I thought that *Orchestra Rehearsal* would be better adapted to television than *The Clowns*, for example, that it ran less of a risk of being betrayed, that it would be stronger on the small screen. The interview, the close-ups of artists talking, that auditorium, a unique place, and even the view of an orchestra as a whole, are images televiewers are used to. So I could play on that familiarity, which is even blown out of all proportion at times, as with the endless interviews pouring out absolute nonsense all the way through since everyone's just saying whatever pops into their heads.

I was surprised to read in several Italian newspapers that, with Orchestra Rehearsal, *Fellini was finally taking an interest in the society of his time, was making a political commentary. Those concerns have been constant in your work, from* La Dolce Vita *to* Roma. *How do you explain such reactions?*

They're a kind of intellectual limitation, a taste for mental categories. This film can be seen as a fable, so everyone says: Fellini is changing his world, his style, he's taking an interest in the world of today. Yet, when it comes down to it, you could say I was just talking about an orchestra and that the film has nothing to do with the political situation!

Why did you choose that place, a former crypt?

I wanted to recreate a mystical and archaeological ambiance. I needed a set that was both utterly convincing and utterly symbolic. So I thought of a deconsecrated church with the remains of a choir stall, which is completely acceptable since a good number of concerts are performed in former chapels or monasteries.

Are you a music lover?

My relationship to music is one of defence. I have to protect myself from it. I accept I have to listen to music when I'm working on a film, my collaboration with Nino Rota is then intense, our complicity total and I read the score note by note. But I'm not someone who goes to concerts or the opera. Music creates a sort of wariness in me. I'm afraid of being invaded, conditioned, and I close myself to it. On the other hand, when I'm working, I can confront it because work gives me the impression of being invulnerable. I then feel a lot stronger. I'm in my truth, in my most authentic state. That gives me a strength, a robustness, that protects me from music, fever, flu, taxes. Otherwise I'm almost pathologically sensitive to music. If I go to a restaurant or an apartment where there's a record playing, I'm forced to ask them to take it off. I don't understand how people can eat, drink, talk, drive, read, with music on. As for me, I have the sensation that music sets up some mysterious communication that will possess you totally. And so to assert my autonomy, I reject it. Well, I'm exaggerating a little, but I have to confess that in general, I prefer not listening to it. For the film, Nino Rota specially composed four pieces for me, *Twins in the Mirror, Little Melancholy Laughs, Short Wait* and *Full Gallop*.

What made you think of a German conductor?

First and foremost because the actor I'd chosen was a northerner. And that wasn't intentional. I have photographic archives composed of maybe 20,000 portraits of actors and actresses with their addresses, but also people I've met in the street. And every time I begin a film, I consult this catalogue. This man, who's Dutch but lives in Berlin, had sent me his photo, about two years ago. When I was getting ready for *Casanova*, I looked for him through a sort of Interpol. At that moment he was living the life of a hippie in Stockholm, since he was not a professional actor, even though he'd had small roles on Dutch television. I thought of him for the role of the Duke of Wurttemberg, but when I saw him I found his face too modern and I opted for an English actor instead. But when I was getting ready for *Orchestra Rehearsal,* I remembered this Balduin Baas and I had him come to Rome. I chose him because he's the least musical type in the world. He's totally immobile. If I'd opted for an olive tree in his place, it would have been more active. But his face had an extraordinary authority; it even had the obtuse look a calling gives you, that doomed innocence of certain artists who exercise a power and identify with a mission with all the neurotic distortions such fanaticism arouses.

The great difficulty was getting him to direct the musicians. I called in a real conductor to help me and I must tell you that he, too, identified mysteriously with his persona at the last moment and he performed with a sort of rage, violence and a great power of suggestion. He only spoke German or Dutch and I had to go through an interpreter. To be obliged every time to speak to this embodied fantasy, which a performer is, through the intermediary of someone else creates a psychological tension that's very positive. An actor is in effect the materialisation of a mental image. I've written scripts that are disembodied dreams. When you choose the actor who's going to interpret your dreams, he becomes a very mysterious creature, for he suddenly materialises an unreal side of yourself. If, on top of that, he doesn't speak your language, he finds himself confirmed in his nature as a foreigner. That sometimes creates a sort of wonderment and stupor in me. I preferred to make the extraordinary effort of communicating my feelings to the point of rage and insults via the mediator, which an interpreter is, for the distance always gave me the impression I was dealing with a real conductor, a character for me completely unknown because I know nothing about music. This foreignness forced me to remain in the viewer's position, which is the most appropriate vantage point for a creator – being inside and outside at the same time.

Was the film completely written before the filming began?

Before I wrote the film, I interviewed a lot of musicians, a hundred, maybe. I met the greatest Italian soloists. I took them out to lunch; I questioned them but without real conviction since I'm a very bad journalist. I don't know how to put a question and the answer doesn't interest me! Despite this major drawback, I managed to take from each of them a bit of this madness that stems from their identification with their instrument. With them, there is this very appealing side to Italians which is their love of their job. Though that's in danger of disappearing. And the first part shows this attachment to their instrument, which they talk about rhetorically, with amusement, ignorance and even madness. After doing the interviews, I started writing the film. In the beginning, I thought I'd use a real orchestra by choosing the musicians' faces from different orchestras based on a typology. But I was forced to abandon that idea because of the cost involved. To shoot a film over four weeks with two weeks' preparation hiring Italy's greatest musicians would have cost more than the moon landing. For that reason and also because I wanted as always to have expressive faces, I left for Naples and began looking for people who, naturally, had a certain familiarity with a musical instrument but were also well-defined types. I picked up sixty people that way and about fifteen of them are genuine small-time musicians. The others had to be taught every day how to hold an instrument.

Your attitude to the conductor is ambiguous. At a certain point we can believe that a conductor is needed to organise and direct, then you show how he aspires to oppress.

That's true. I show the necessity for order and the potential danger it holds at the same time. But ambiguity – that's life. I felt the need to not end the film with the consolation of a happy ending. You can't build something collectively without reflecting individually on the necessity of having an internal guide. If you hand over the responsibility for your own life to someone else, there's always the danger of falling back into an undifferentiated collectivity. And then the risk is that this collectivity will once again project the fantasy of an authoritarian father. In my view, you have to try to be your own father. It may well be cheap philosophy, but that's what I wanted to express. I reject the happy ending because it takes away all responsibility from the viewer. On the contrary, if I end with a question mark, it's up to the viewer to find a good ending for my story. In all my films, I've been faithful to those suspension points in conclusion and besides, I've never written the word END on the screen.

The film raised a number of controversies in Italy.

Usually – you know my legend – I try to forget a film as soon as I've finished it. This time, it's harder since *Orchestra Rehearsal* hasn't yet been released and already there's, not so much a polemic, but a lot of chat. Everyone's trying to hijack the film. For some, it's a film about historical compromise; for others, it's mystical; for still others, it's an extra-parliamentary film; for the rest it's a conservative, reactionary film, where the voice of Hitler at the end is not a threat but rather a hope. People honestly say the most unbelievable things. As far as possible, I've tried to avoid any political interpretation of the film because I think that's dangerous; it will devitalise the film, cause it to die. Politics means reducing the work, impoverishing it. Apart from political professionals – politicians, journalists, etc. – most people look on politics with suspicion, they feel it's something that doesn't concern them. Giving my film a political label means running the risk of putting people off. So, with all the strength I could muster, I tried to discourage anyone who wanted to slot it into such a category and I said it was just an orchestra rehearsal – that's all.

But you can't stop people interpreting it politically.

Yes, but in talking exclusively from a political point of view, you place a barrier between the film and the audience; you prevent any emotional, individual impact. Already the future audience knows that the orchestra is Italy; the conductor is authority; you start to uncover characters based on real people. The little clarinettist, they'll tell you, is Fanfani. And since the trade union rep has a Sardinian accent, well! It's got to be Berlinguer. Yet it was a completely innocent choice on my part. As you know, pure Italian doesn't exist, so I dubbed the characters in all the possible Italian dialects and I'd almost exhausted the list by the time I got to the union rep. I asked him where he came from and he told me Sardinia and as I'd recorded his voice, everyone now says he represents Berlinguer![1] This game that consists in reading into the film all the political currents, all the Italian predicaments, is going to kill the film's innocence. For me, it is an ethical fable, not a political one.

But elsewhere, we observe this in the world every day, too much disorder inevitably leads to conservatism, to even greater repression than before.

That's the truth. The President of the Republic, Pertini, who saw the film at the Quirinal, said the wisest and least biased thing: 'This film is neither progressive or reactionary, it's true!' And it was courageous for a president to talk that way about a film that presented such a disaster!

But showing the film as a preview at the Quirinal, was a red rag to the bull of political interpretation!

It was completely involuntary and I have to tell you how it happened. One night last summer, I was strolling about a square in Rome and I was stopped by Pertini, who was not yet President of the Republic. He wanted to congratulate me on *La Dolce Vita*, which he'd just seen again in Paris on television. And he told me he'd really like to see my next film. I told him I'd keep him posted. A few months later, the head of the presidential press office phoned me to remind me of my promise!

You made The Clowns *right after* Satyricon *and now* Orchestra Rehearsal *right after* Casanova. *Is it a break for you, a sort of breather after an immense fresco?*

I like making films without a break. What I hate is being forced to remain idle because the great machine of the cinema of co-production is slow and complex. What I'd really like is to work all the time, even taking photos for *Positif*! You know, I'd like to make small films more often, but if I suggest a very low-budget story to a producer, I see the lack of interest on his face, the humiliation. For him, Fellini must make a film costing ten million dollars. The film is the last thing that counts, what matters is to set up a business on my back, the Fellini business and, after that, to build a financial edifice of grandiose proportions. And there I am, rooted in my film, with all the problems it poses for me and, right next to me goes up this immense labyrinthine construction desired by the greedy producers, and those piranhas, the distributors, who hope to score the deal of a lifetime. I filmed *Orchestra Rehearsal* in sixteen days and I did the editing in two weeks, that is, in a week of real work. It's the dubbing that took me the longest, four weeks. As far as the dialogue went, what I wanted was to give the impression that the unexpected actually produces in daily life, but not like in *cinéma-vérité*, on the contrary, in a very organised way. I tried to create a phonetic chaos by mixing different languages, dialects, approximate expressions. You know that dialects are rubbished in the Italian media. There's a convention of dialects in cinema, on radio, on television. There's a vulgar side to a dialect that you hear on a show. So I wanted to get back to the truly pathological meaning of the expressions of each region and I looked for actors capable of giving the dialect back its meaning and its original feel. It was a huge effort because even the actors speaking dialect have forgotten where they come from, they speak Neapolitan, for instance, the way people from the north are prepared to hear it. I think the film has a real emotional impact or, at least, that's what I felt after one of the first screenings that I put on for the workers at Cinecittà. It's for that reason, I repeat, that I've tried to block the political generalisations that trash the meaning of the film. If you go and see the film with tinted ideological glasses, you won't see it. Now, what I want is to force each and every viewer to find an answer that can't be put off any longer. But an individual answer and not a general, abstract answer, which is meaningless. I haven't succeeded in blocking all that since, on the contrary, *Orchestra Rehearsal* is presented everywhere as Fellini's first political film. So...

NOTES

1 Since this interview, Fellini has dubbed the trade unionist with a different voice in order to avoid any possible allusion.

9 JEAN-LUC GODARD

(1930–)

Meeting François Truffaut one day in 1958, I expressed my regret that Jean-Luc Godard, in his essay on Nicholas Ray's *Bitter Victory* published in the *Cahiers du Cinéma*, hardly bothered talking about the actual film. He said I was wrong, for Godard was, in his view, the most gifted of them all. Truffaut was right. Along with Eric Rohmer, Godard was to build the most coherent oeuvre of the new wave filmmakers, both of them remaining faithful to a certain financial marginality and to a new aesthetic they have stuck to come hell or high water. When I joined *Positif* in 1963, it was still a Mecca, with Robert Benayoun and Louis Seguin at the helm, in the battle against Godard, and even if I allowed myself, not without impudence, to sing the praises of *A Married Woman*, when it was shown at Venice, I shared the editors' irritation with the provocative stance taken by the author of *Alphaville*. In the 1960s, I admired certain flashes of the artist in Godard rather than any coherent line. He seemed to me more of an instinctive filmmaker, with his acute sense of montage (his *'beau souci'*, or wonderful preoccupation), of colour and sound, and not so much a thinker of any great lucidity, even if *Week-End* or 'The Chinese' took on prophetic tones.

After the period in the wilderness of the 1970s and his deluded excursions into Maoism, Godard went back to making movies that were more like essays. As Truffaut had implied, Godard as a critic was already a filmmaker. Today the filmmaker doubles as a critic. Which is why I wanted to meet him in the company of a young collaborator from *Positif*, Stéphane Goudet, to talk with him about his monumental *History(s) of the Cinema*. In this interview we were prepared to get polemical if the occasion arose, for the unanimous adulation surrounding Godard for so long now is doubtless the worst favour you could do to this rebellious spirit whose brilliance no one any longer contests.

ON *HISTORY(S) OF THE CINEMA*

PARIS, NOVEMBER 1998

We'd like to focus this interview on History(s) of the Cinema *and on your re-lationship to images as a director and critic. You've always loved the transparent cinema of Hawks and Rossellini, yet have always made films involving a critical dimension. The eight episodes of* History(s) … *aren't they a sort of ending from this viewpoint?*

Not really. But I've always turned movies into hand-made books. I don't have any children and men, even more than women, always try to pass something on. I wanted to pass on those eight programmes, even if I know hardly anyone will see them. At the end of the day, if I'd been able to do without my royalties, I'd have loved not to sign the books, so that they remained like traces of the cinema. At one point, I even thought of doing a play from *History(s)*… It would be called *The Book of Cinema*. But that takes time; a person is too alone. It would have to be performed on a cathedral square, with equipment relayed by short actors who'd turn the pages of a great big book on which images would be projected while the text was recited.

You thought of not signing them, but the films and the books are, obviously, very personal.

I don't think so. They're photos and texts that were put together by an editor or a composer, who happens to be me. It's a souvenir book of the film. Others would have arranged things differently. There could be hundreds of *History(s)*… Instead of souvenir albums about the great Garbo for collectors. There are a lot of cinema books around today. There were very few when I started. For a long time I looked out for Eisenstein's *Film Form and Film Sense*, which hadn't yet been translated into French. I've got them now, but I never read them. As for histories of cinema, properly so called, I realised that I hadn't read any and that they didn't interest me, except for the very first, written by Bardèche and Brasillach. So I put a little poem of Brasillach's in the first programme, but people didn't recognise it; it's his will, written in prison. I'd read his book on André Chénier a long time ago as well as *Our Avant-Garde*, without knowing anything about politics, as *Positif* and Freddy Buache quite rightly noted.

The project goes back to the 1970s?

Yes, it's part of a project about Henri Langlois. Afterwards, I thought of doing a film based on Malraux, which would be called *The Metamorphosis of the Gods*. And little by little, it took that particular shape, with the title the same as the 1980 book, *Introduction à une véritable histoire du cinéma*. The idea of the book was that there would be as many images as text, that they'd be dealt with on an even footing, without any sense of which comes first. I respect the histories of Sadoul or Mitry, but that's something else. I was after a book that was critical, in its very matter, for instance. When the woman who heads the Belgian Cinématèque tells me I don't talk about American comedy, I have no comeback. There is effectively a certain pretentiousness in saying: there's only one way to write history and this is it. But cinema has this capacity, through its photographic material and through this lingering feeling that it has some sort of relation to reality, which is different from the copy that painters make. It also seemed to me the right moment to tackle it, for we've come to the end of a certain era in cinema and even in art in general, an era that lasted for about ten centuries.

You've claimed to have a fairly Hegelian vision of history. What do you mean by that?

I don't know Hegel. I quote a lot of people I've read three sentences of. Hegel talks about the 'end of history'. But he believes history exists, like Péguy when he wrote *Clio*. And I believe it does too.

What is striking in History(s) of the Cinema *is the astonishing complexity not only of the cutting between images, but of the relationship between image and sound and of the work done inside the very frame by superimpositions and inserts. Has editing always been for you, contrary to Bazin or Rohmer, the very basis of cinema?*

That certainly corresponded to something in me but it also stemmed from my contrariness. I can see that clearly, still, with certain of today's critics: the desire to take the opposite stance, like what happens between *Le Monde* and *Libération,* but, with me, they don't do that... In the beginning, I was very much a follower in relation to Rohmer, Rivette and Truffaut. I took a long time to find my feet. Yet we were all relatively in agreement in saying that form and content were basically the same. I didn't really know what Bazin and Rohmer were getting at with their theory of the sequence shot. I felt that in the shooting script, the shot/countershot business, there ought to be something other than the usual click... In my article, 'Montage, mon beau souci', which is written in a pretty pompous style, I cited a novel of Balzac's, *Les Chouans,* which we all liked a lot, to show that only editing could express certain things and that a sequence shot doesn't follow eye movement. That said, today, we don't know how to follow eye movement the way they did in the days of silent film.

Your predilection for editing is also found in the way you welcomed the advent of Hiroshima mon amour, *and in your admiration for Welles and Eisenstein.*

When we saw *Hiroshima* we were jealous: we were clearly behind. We hadn't seen it coming. Other people were saying good things about it and we immediately organised a roundtable, like Stalinists, to try to contain the enemy. Whereas I'd absolutely raved about *Le Chant du Styrène,* for instance, before... With Welles, it's different. His style depends largely on the trouble he had filming. If he begins *Touch of Evil* with a sequence shot, it's because he had a very short shoot and if a sequence shot is well set up, it can save you five or six days. But for *Confidential Report (Mr Arkadin),* which took him three or four years, he had to resort of necessity to montage when he had a shot filmed in Berlin in spring and the countershot in Spain in autumn. Yet, in Welles, there's a kind of fluidity with extremely short shots and a way of chopping up reality that's just incredible. His way of editing is very different from Eisenstein's. When Bazin, on the other hand, pitted Ford against Wyler, I just didn't get it. At the time, I didn't like either of them. Then, very slowly, I came round to Ford and today I find *The Best Years of Our Lives* magnificent, one of Wyler's best films and one of the greatest works on war.

Doesn't the editing correspond to your way of thinking and seeing things? You claim you never finish a book, you hop from one idea to the next...

I think editing is an ideal figure of cinema and thought, whose heir it should have been. But society was against its making this inheritance bear fruit. The old way of thinking, this one, two, three business, the idea that there isn't a single image, but that you have to take into account the one before and the one after – all that is obvious in film. It's the Koulechov experiment ... that no one ever saw and that was possibly made up by Poudovkine. The figure three is found in all studies on civilisation, in the three orders in Dumézil, in Duby, in Michelet, in dialectics, naturally... In *Woe Is Me*, I quoted the philosopher Léon Brunschvicg, who, in about 1900, said of the Christian divinity: 'The one is in the other, the other is in the one, and they are three.' Cinema was the secular trustee of this idea. It was its very matter. And anyone who makes films or produces criticism is in a position to account for this historic aspect of the world.

But for you the arrival of the talkies meant this bid to reveal the editing sort of lost the plot.

Yes, I think so. Because they re-established the omnipotence of the text, which is not the great text, but a political text, a text that tries to dominate the image sociologically, like with television or the press. I don't know what cinema might otherwise have become; it's impossible for us to know. But it was primed to become something else. In 1929, radio existed, the gramophone existed and cinema was silent, which is incredible. For a long time no one complained about that. The sudden commercial boom might have occurred in 1920. That's what the great historians study, historians like Braudel and Duby, who was in there at the start of *History(s) of the Cinema* with La Sept, as well as Koyré. They start with examples to study what happened to this or that theory or phenomenon. I said to Duby: 'Cinema is the end of the Middle Ages', which didn't end till the end of the nineteenth century. And he laughed, but he acknowledged that I was not wrong... The problem now is that this ontology no longer exists as it did in the days of Bazin or myself. We thought we were the first, but we were the last. You don't see shots anymore, you see words, 'pictures', from advertising; you almost never see the raw image of a woman crying, a beggar begging, a war causing slaughter, anymore. If I proceed by breaks, leaps, short-circuits, it's because we are the children of quantum mechanics. We are waves and corpuscles at once. You leap and you never know where you are. And all these discoveries date from the end of the nineteenth century, the same time as the first screenings. This is why I say in the film that the twentieth century didn't much exist in itself. That's a tad provocative, but our century didn't invent wars, or quantum mechanics, or cinema. Everything that caused it to exist, it owed to the previous century. And I don't have the impression that any of the other centuries were as dependent on the one that preceded them.

Someone like Rohmer has a way of thinking that is very different from yours. There's nothing discontinuous in, for example, his essay on music, De Mozart en Beethoven.

But he's not doing history. That's the text of a cultivated mind, it talks about art, but it's not interested in history. Personally, I believe in history. But I think other people don't believe in it and don't like it. Already they don't like it in themselves: the history of their bodies, their illnesses, their love affairs. And I'm the same as the rest. It took me years to get interested in my own history rather than other people's. One of the most hated men today, after all, is Freud. Or, rather, we don't so much hate him as we prefer to forget him or to say that he's outdated. When he died, a refugee in England, the British had written 'Enemy Alien' on his passport. They could have put 'Foreign Friend' but he'd come from Vienna and Austria had rallied to Germany... Yet, at the same time, they took him in, protected him...

In History(s) of the Cinema, *you opt to use only very short extracts. Why?*

There are so many of them, we couldn't get everything in. In 35 mm, the project would have been impossible to produce. With video, you can wipe the canvas and start again. By hand, by the feeling. At a given moment, you tell yourself: 'Right, we're away.' After that, if you put down a particular image, you wonder what needs to follow to hold the note. In fact, there are fewer images than people think, since a lot of them keep coming back, from Eisenstein, Rossellini, Hitchcock... When you know what you're doing and you like one or two things, they're enough, especially as you get older. What video lets you get, like in music, is the fluidity of superimpositions. The new wave had a hand in doing away with small banal superimpositions – someone leaves the room, superimposition, he goes downstairs, superimposition, we see him in the street. Personally, I really liked superimpositions, in particular in Stevens, who used very long ones in *A Place in the Sun.* When you turn them into the main material, they allow you to go from one place to another without forgetting the place you started out from, without yet knowing the one you'll get to, knowing that in the middle, or three-quarters in, the unexpected can suddenly crop up. That's why I mentioned music. Video lets you play two-handed or four-handed piano, while literature only works with one hand.

You describe the history told by cinema as 'the greatest history, because it can be projected', yet we now find it reduced to a television screen. How do you deal with that contradiction?

But cinema no longer exists. On television, it's not projected, it's broadcast. Yet we can still tell stories, anyway, and this one's an old-timer's story for his grandchildren: 'Once upon a time, there was something that was projected...' You see it broadcast now, but what it was like when it was shown on the big screen is impossible to know anymore. That's what I call the memory of a screenable story. And one day, when Anne-Marie's grandchildren hit thirty-five, they'll stumble across this story by their grandmother's friend. Given what cinema will be in their day, they won't understand a thing about it and they'll say: 'Right, so that's what Grandma called "cinema"?' And they'll suddenly realise that there was a time when people went to movie theatres.

Another film makes the connection between history and the history of cinema by questioning the concept of projection: Syberberg's Hitler, a Film From Germany.

Yes, that's an interesting film, not as methodical as mine, not as ample, but just as much about cinema, true. His style is a lot more that of a historian, in the good sense of the term, than Visconti's in *Ludwig,* which is a more classic film, magnificent to boot. *Ludwig* is closer to a history painting painted in his own manner or to *La Chanson de Roland,* whereas Syberberg's film is very influenced by the philosophers of history.

There are also aspects of Chris Marker's approach, up to Tombeau d'Alexandre (The Last Bolshevik), *that are like you: the importance of editing, the reflection on history, the relationship between image and commentary...*

There's more than that, but it's a bit the reverse of me. Chris was very literary. He headed a collection at du Seuil. He started out with the word and ended up with the image. I started out with the image and ended up with what I'd been taught in school, that is, the text. In a way, we met in the middle, but there's always a point of departure and Chris is, after all, more of a wordsmith and less of a painter.

Yet he is also a photographer.

Yes, but the photographs have always been very much bound up with the words. Underneath the photo there's a caption and its power is immense. In the 1920s, the surrealists, Duchamp included, decided to take an ashtray and call it *Portrait of a Young Girl Naked (Portrait d'une jeune fille nue).* The first time, it produced a shock, less so the second time, the third time, it did nothing. Today, everyone does it; it's become a new academism. There's a whole epistemological history there to tackle. But maybe cinema would have needed to develop differently for such research to be taken on. The main department of the Centre national de recherche scientifique, the CNRS, ought to be the film department. In my first essay on Rouch, perfectly naively and instinctively, I wrote of *I, A Negro*: 'A researcher at the Musée de l'Homme, what better definition of the filmmaker!' That was in the days when I was trying to find my way and even a voice, because I used to use Rohmer's and others' a bit when I talked. One of the essays that influenced him and Rivette every bit as much as me is Schérer's 'Le cinéma, art de l'espace', in *La Revue du cinéma,* where we discovered the theory of cinema put forward by Langlois before he went over to the Cinématèque. Rohmer marked a decisive new direction in relation to Bazin, which, curiously, I'm only just now discovering.

Even if it means taking the opposite view... You explain that the young Turks of Cahiers *established their hierarchies according to 'the works, not the authors'. Now, Bazin precisely blamed the 'politics' of the review for privileging the people over the films they made and occasionally falling into an 'aesthetic cult of personality'.*

That's what we used to think, but then later I gradually came to realise that it was wrong, that it was even the reverse. When anyone and everyone claims to be an *auteur*, I tell myself I prefer to refer to the work and reject the title of *auteur*. Besides, instinctively, I only rarely signed my films. For me, the new wave was the works, not their authors.

Truffaut nonetheless adopted Giraudoux's saying: 'There are no works, there are only authors.'

François, he was more into that, yes. He, more than me or anyone else, needed to carve out a niche for himself, to personalise his relationships, given his past.

He'd had a difficult relationship with his parents and he always looked for father figures: Renoir, Hitchcock... He was the first to enter into negotiations with authors like Becker, Joffé... And he was the only one to attack certain filmmakers by name. The rest of us attacked the works. That was a time when, in film, the author was the scriptwriter. Directors were considered producers, not authors. The great filmmakers like Hitchcock had their names well below the title or weren't even listed. There was a quarrel between *Cahiers* and *Positif,* but the two reviews were part of the same movement and both said, with perhaps more insistence in *Cahiers*, that the person who makes the film is the director.

You forget that 'film authors' were defended by La Revue du cinéma *as early as 1930. Vidor, Sternberg, Lubitsch, Lang were acknowledged as directors. In 1945, already, a journal as popular as* The Saturday Evening Post *defined the 'McCarey touch' as being halfway between the 'Lubitsch touch' and the 'Capra touch'...*

Yes, most of them were recognised as authors because they were their own producers. And look at the great authors: they were broken by the studios. Stroheim is the prime example. Chaplin, Lang were cultural celebrities, names, but I think it was celebrity itself that was recognised in them rather than the author. What we did was extend the notion to the unknowns. Jacques Daniel-Norman's *L'Ange rouge* (with Tilda Thamar), which François and I especially loved, became a film *d'auteur*. I'd like, for the pleasure of the duel, to concede that we said it badly. And I've said it again badly since, but there was something behind the politics of the *auteur* and that was the word 'politics'. For us, that was the important bit.

You get the impression a bit in seeing History(s) *that your tastes, your passions, crystallised in your days as a critic. You don't give much space to the generations that succeeded you or the most contemporary cinema, except for a film title of Kiarostami's, a shot here and there of Coppola's, Angelopoulos's or Garrel's. How do you explain that there are so few films later than 1960, apart from your own?*

What do you want? History is history, told here at a given moment. I don't claim to tell all. People also say I know nothing about contemporary painting, that I stopped at Picasso. But that's my history. I'm not stopping anyone else from telling theirs.

And how do you explain the West-centric nature of these History(s)*...?*

But cinema is a Western art, made by Europeans and Americans. That's all there is to it. Furthermore, America is reduced to the United States and there have only ever been three or four filmmaking nations in Europe: France, the USSR, Germany before the war, Italy.

Why deny the existence of British cinema?

I'm not saying there haven't been great British directors. Those I prefer come from the documentary school: Dickinson, Grierson... The others, Hitchcock, Chaplin, sought exile in the United States. I'm saying England is not a great nation for film. That's not so terrible. Any more than realising that we are not a great nation for music, and that Spain, which has had great painters, is not a great nation for painting, unlike Italy, Holland, for a time, or France. I think that England and Japan are not great nations for cinema. Because they haven't had a cinema history, an awareness of that history. I know very well that there have been a few great Japanese directors, but I don't think that's enough to make a great nation on a par with France.

What justifies thinking now of cinema history by nation and making this territorial allegiance a decisive factor in retaining this or that film?

It's a fact of history. It doesn't matter where we are today with the idea of what a nation is. In these four countries, there are so many filmmakers that in the end that has become what cinema is. On the other hand, for the rest of them, there could be a hundred good directors, but it won't amount to a cinema.

Aren't you struck by the fact that silent film, omnipresent in the History(s), *has been erased from our landscape and our memory? From that point of view, hasn't passing on been interrupted?*

In the days when we were critics, it already no longer existed. It existed for us, but not for anyone else.

You distinguish two epistemological breaks in the history of cinema, the arrival of the talkies and the existence of concentration camps.

I tell myself that the camps were foreseen, heralded by cinema, by *Grand Illusion* (*La Grande Illusion*), *The Rules of the Game* (*La Règle du jeu*), *The Great Dictator* (*Le Dictateur*)... Similarly, music before the First World War or at the end, with Wagner, in its way heralded the disasters that were looming. But, after the camps, cinema threw in the towel. Only the newsreels still serve to relate history. Cinema lost its documentary eye. At the Liberation, there was a kind of shame in Europe, and a resistance film saved honour in Italy.

But it was the liberation by the Americans that allowed Rossellini, a former maker of fascist propaganda films, to take on Rome, Open City.

Roberto's personal history, here, doesn't count. The fact that he made *The White Ship* beforehand doesn't change anything. He simply did work that was a little bit redeeming. The first time, there was some success. But from *Germany, Year Zero*, it was all over... The problem is that no real thinking went into what had happened. There were books but there were no resistance films, no matter how stupid, shot in London or Algiers. There were rolls of film, cameras, actors, directors. They didn't do it. If you tell me that in the Vercors, in France, in the snow, you couldn't make a fiction film like that, all right. But that wasn't where it ought to have been made. Afterwards, having not been made during the war, no one made the film, except the Poles. But Munk's *Passenger* is a film of atonement, which they had to make because of their anti-Semitism and because the camps were on their territory.

You yourself thought about making a film on the concentration camps?

Yes, but it was just hypothetical. I had no idea. I was too young. I couldn't get a feel for it. The only idea I had was a bit like what Mikhail Romm did in *Common Fascism*, which is very interesting, even if he stays in the German camp without going to have a look in the other one, the Soviet one. I would have made a film about the working of a camp, on the bureaucratic side, daily management, with secretaries, accountants, only showing the deportees here and there. It was a notion about form, if you like, as a way of getting to the bottom of it all. And then, I didn't get to it. I didn't feel up to it, or I forgot about it.

Do you now regret not having made it? Do you think it was essential?

Yes, but not made by me. By others, who should have made it.

In the first part of History(s)…, *you shift from the word 'German' to 'Jew', then from 'Jew' to 'Muslim', a name by which Jews who were nearing the end were known in the camps.*

That, I am the only person to have observed. It's a filmmaker's observation. I read about it and stuck it in *Here and Elsewhere*. Yet, twenty-five years later, it's still not talked about. And Lebanon and the so-called occupied territories; it's still a mess. No one, including any of the deportees, has said that it is after all weird that the Jews and the Muslims are fighting when, in the camps, the Germans called certain Jews 'Muslims'. But in *Here and Elsewhere* we had something to prove, we wanted to pit the good camp against the bad. We were more didactic.

You once said you were interested in the concentration camps 'because of your past, your social class, your guilt.' How do you mean?

I was in a family who were more collaborators and I read a lot of right-wing books, notably on the war. I felt guilty, even if unconsciously, because no one had told me about them. I got interested independently in the Resistance and in the camps, but I should have come across them sooner. The same way you discover your own history very late in the piece. When I saw *Night and Fog*, my interest in the subject was still theoretical. It came later, through the gang, in a back-to-front way. I often start things back-to-front, even when I read a detective story. I really delved into the issue by filming the Palestinians… Because in militating for Palestine, we started to think about Israel, and so on. And then it became more real, it made sense, it was the people we'd seen…

How do you view your Maoist period today?

I thought I was a Maoist, subscribing to *Pékin Informations*, etc. I've always been a bit marginal and liked marginality, I think. And it was a small group… In reality, it's not that we didn't want to know, but that it takes time depending on what place you're in. If you're caught in a rip, you have to get out of the rip to start with, to think that you can get out of it. We couldn't believe Simon Leys. But, you know, the main anti-Soviet and anti-fascist essays were published in the 1930s – those written by Boris Souvarine, André Gide, Panaït Istrati… Well, we didn't listen to them. Later, I got interested in history. Making amends, if that's possible. But no one knows much at all about the history of that particular period in France. And we were young. I feel like I'm only just beginning now to catch up after lagging so far behind in film: I started thinking about film between the ages of twenty and thirty and making films at thirty. In film terms, we were babies. Now I've got forty years of cinema and seventy years of life under my belt, the superimposition is beginning to take. Before, in my personal relations with people, I was, I think, better in film and not good at all at what we might call life. Which was a bit the case with everyone in the new wave, I think.

Religion is very much a part of History(s) of the Cinema, *with the themes of the apocalypse, paradise lost, original sin.*

Religion is part of history. And the Christian religion in particular has been very much bound up with the philosophy of the image, which was not the case with, I don't know … the Aztecs or the Chinese. I took up a great line of Wittgenstein's, replacing Christianity by cinema: 'You have a history, there, believe in it, no matter what.' And then again, cinema invented the happy ending and the Bible the happy beginning, no?

The authors you most often quote are Bernanos, Malraux, Sartre…

That comes from my adolescence and it's stuck. You know, I've never read *Don Quixote* or Montaigne. You have to keep a few of them in reserve. After the Liberation, I remember, the first book I liked was *Thomas the Obscure* by Blanchot. It's linked to German romanticism, which, as an adolescent, is what I liked best. Maybe that comes from my father, but only unconsciously. He never said to me, this is what you have to read, not that.

A sense of loss is one of the meeting points between German romanticism and Christianity.

In *Forever Mozart,* the director says this sentence Anne-Marie dug up for me: 'Cinema is wonderful for showing the world, but it's a shame that when you do that, you have to abandon what really matters.' That's almost ontological. There is in the image a sense of buying back, of merit, redemption, which was expressed by the Church fathers. After that, if something other than religion gets made of it… But it's true that if 120 people stare into the dark in the same direction at the same time…

The notion of cinema as an instrument of thought, which Deleuze also examines, seems close to your History(s) *project… It seems unachievable.*

Completely. That's not what we were after. But we're not after painting either. And music is tolerated, accepted and loved, but we don't ask it to think. As for Deleuze, the problem is that he wrote really badly, alas for him, like Levinas, especially if we compare them to Bergson.

In the last episode you break up Wellman's title Public Enemy *and transform it into 'The Public, The Enemy.' Why?*

It's a phrase that belongs to Jules Renard, who says of the critic that he 'deserts his camp and goes over to the enemy. What is the enemy? The public!' You know, often, the public, the audience, has the courage to live out wonderful adventures, but they don't have the courage to relate them. So, when we go to a show, we're in a state of abdication of responsibility. As a result, when a film is the opposite of a blockbuster, as we say, we can redeem ourselves; we have a sense of resisting. But, between going to see a good film by Straub or Cassavetes and a bad Bruce Willis or De Palma, even I prefer to buy myself an ice-cream cone, and see the Willis munching away, because I'm part of the public. Afterwards, you're ashamed of yourself…

How do you live with this extraordinary notoriety and quasi-unanimous critical acclaim that tends to transform you from an iconoclast into an icon?

Really badly. I try to get myself forgotten yet at the same time the only chance I have of making a film is to go and borrow a bit from the bank or from Canal Plus by assuring them: 'You see, I'm not forgotten.' It's a total contradiction. In fact, I'm the most famous of the forgotten. I still have to represent the possibility of saying: we can still make the film we want to, outside the usual confines, or we can make the film we can. What's hard is not coming up with the money, it's making the film you have to make, morally, in its own way.

How do you view the waning power of criticism?

Criticism belongs to the cultural pages. I notice that the books pages of *Libération* and *Le Monde* are infinitely more serious, in the classic sense of the term, than the cinema pages. At least they talk about books! The others don't talk about

films. Read the articles on Benigni or the so-called Ophulsian sequence shot in
Snake Eyes. The critics talk about a cinema that's part of Paris life, it's not the
same thing. And then, there are heaps of cliques, but, well… Me, I'd have liked
to see my books reviewed by Dagen, or someone, anyone who sees an art book
in a different light, Maggiori, say, in *Libération,* anyone but Gérard Lefort! In
Le Monde, same thing, anything but a review by Frodon, preferably a review by
Roger-Pol Droit, who does philosophy. But maybe those blokes wouldn't have
done it…

Let's go back to History(s). *You systematically liken the German occupation during
the Second World War to the 'American occupation' that, according to you, followed.
How do you justify this semantic and geographic slide of the nouns 'occupation',
'resistance' and 'annexation'?*

That's my point of view. Historically, it has been proved by films and by the visual.
American literature did not invade French literature; the press, not entirely. But
to the extent that we spend hours in front of the television and that practically
everything we see comes from the United States… On the other hand, there is
still *Le Figaro*… It could very easily have been replaced by the *New York Times* in
French. In this century, more Germans than anyone else emigrated to America.
Germany has historically been the country closest to the United States. It was
their only rival in cinema and in many other industries. They had to bring them
down a peg or two to have them in their power. The Americans have always
waited till they were killing each other in Europe before intervening. In the
end, they did after all choose one camp over another, between the two brawling
brats. But they turned up when everyone was worn out, never at the beginning,
neither in 1914 nor in 1940. All they wanted was to invade! And they still want
to invade, because they don't have a past. They need to invade countries that
do. Now, they're everywhere. They'll see in the future which is the past most
amenable to becoming an ancestor of their own. In *Germany Year 90* I'd taken
up something good old Giraudoux said, that went: 'The United States have
never waged war. They have only waged civil war.' And when they've waged
war against a country, they have done so to a country with the same faults as
their own. Normally you wage war against a country you reckon has qualities
different from yours, that you want to appropriate. With Saddam Hussein,
it's very clear. They're waging war against an American who happens to live

in Baghdad and who has exactly the same faults they do. And they can't stand anyone else having their faults. They have always waged civil war. Against the British, among themselves, then against the Germans.

But to make a connection between the destruction of European cinema by this American cinema that you've loved so much and the word 'Endlösung', 'The Final Solution', isn't that confusing the two issues?

Yes. But, since the link is made by something of which Blanchot says: 'The image is happiness' and that it is 'nothingness gazing upon us', it's a bit of both. And for my part, I can't believe in the mix-up. Or maybe it's a mix-up that muddies the waters. Hitchcock said: 'If you want to be sure of being understood, hit hard.' You don't hit hard with a hammer. You hit hard with an image, with a comparison, which is not hitting hard at all. I'm not the one saying *Endlösung* is hard. It's the Jewish people, the Germans, they're the ones saying it... In the business with the *sans-papiers,* last year, what really touched me was that it was filmmakers who said: you only have to read the texts. We use the same words today as under Vichy. We also say to them: you mustn't confuse the issue! But they're right to say: the words are the same, and that's all there is to it!

We might also wonder when you compare split-screen images of deportees in a concentration camp and images from a pornographic film. What do this form and this comparison set up by way of thinking?

It's what's happened to West German cinema.

So the comparison bears on the effect of national continuity, because the porn is German?

Yes, but people don't actually know that. Only I know it's German porn.

What the viewer reacts to is the common nakedness of bodies.

There is something obscene there. An obscenity we need to be able to talk about better, without anathema. But I agree, there's something that jars.

Something obscene in comparing the two images?

Yes, but we ought to see if there isn't something that allows us to make such a hard-hitting comparison. And to see, if need be, what the comparison is up against, what comes before and what comes after, so that it's not taken just like that, at face-value. It's not a matter of saying by way of comparison: the Russians killed eighty-five-million people and the Germans only killed fifteen million… At certain moments, you feel like putting two images of dead people together and saying: where's the one that…? The relationship between images allows us to approach these issues more calmly, to perhaps show the violence that there is in things.

So it is the violence of pornographic cinema that is supposedly 'revealed' by this confrontation?

Historically, the image of the camps we chose was an image from Munk's film. He actually re-enacted a scene where a dog eats a deportee, fights him. After, we can use the same image of the dog. If Munk hadn't used it, I could never have made it up.

To wrap up, let's go back over the issue of the way the work is viewed. How, in your opinion, can one view these History(s)? *Who are they addressed to?*

For me, the best way to look at these shows is to get into the images without having names or references in mind. The less you know about them, the better.

Do you really think so? When you follow Tous en scène *(Everyone on stage) immediately with* Faust, *we don't see the apparent connection if we don't know that the director in Minnelli's film is endeavouring to stage a modernised* Faust. *So the work is enriched by this outside knowledge and a knowledge of film. And it risks excluding those who haven't seen those films, no?*

I don't think so. But maybe, from that point of view, the books come off better, since you're not tempted, while you're reading them, to try and identify this or that extract at any cost. Obviously, I don't make any old connection…

Take the more precise example of your 'Introduction à la méthode d'Alfred Hitchcock'. In the mixing, Hitchcock's voice from an interview ends up dominating yours as you comment in a voice-over on what the viewer retains from seeing his films. Your voice is covered and we can't follow your written text, which is nonetheless particularly pertinent.

For that, you have the book.

That means the work doesn't exist in itself, that it has to be grasped scattered between different places and arts, between the book and the film?

Well, yes, that's right. But other things are enough. At times, you don't need to hear the voice. You heard it before and you hear it a bit later. I'm a good enough technician to know how to make what I want heard when I want.

No doubt. But the reflex action which consists in systematically casting back to the written text or to the works quoted to fill in the gaps and hollows in the film, reintroduces the book, the meaning, the caption, which you wanted, in principle, to get around.

Then it's a fault...

You can obviously play on loss, on the impossibility for the viewer of fully mastering what he sees, but why gloss over these rather lyrical sentences that, beyond Hitchcock, describe your very project?

I thought they'd be heard clearly. That's a fault I have, too. I'm a confused person and I sometimes hide my confusion behind a lyrical and musical side that isn't necessarily appropriate. This can be criticised. And a good critic would do it. Good criticism does not consist in saying: 'Godard is an idiot', or Godard is something else, but in saying, 'there, we should have heard this and not that.'

10 PETER GREENAWAY

(1942–)

Nothing prepared me for the discovery, at the Venice Festival of 1982, of *The Draughtsman's Contract*. Peter Greenaway's already consistent work had up till then remained almost invisible outside England. A painter and editor, for fifteen years Greenaway had directed a considerable number of experimental films before crowning this first phase of his career by *The Falls* (1980), an amazing three-hour feature film in which ninety-two characters appear, all with names starting with 'Fall'. I only later saw this bizarre kaleidoscope where you already encounter a love, similar to Georges Perec's, of mystification, numbers, games, false documents, series that was to fuel his future cinema. With *The Draughtsman's Contract*, where in the England of the end of the seventeenth century, a painter receives a commission to do twelve drawings for the wife of a rich landowner who is away on a trip, Greenaway adopted the cover of a refined thriller to celebrate a marriage between cinema and literature and the visual arts. He would not cease to experiment over the following two decades, resorting more and more to digital images in *Prospero's Books*, *The Pillow Book* and the gargantuan multimedia undertaking represented by his six-hour trilogy, *The Tulse Luper Suitcases*, the first part of which, *The Moab Story*, was presented at the Cannes Festival of 2003.

Peter Greenaway has fierce opponents not only among critics but also among his peers who scarcely exist in his eyes, contemporary cinema being reduced, according to him, to variations on outmoded forms inherited from the nineteenth century, except for Godard, Resnais, Antonioni and a few, rare others. He cultivates a splendid isolation, professing that 'I've often thought it was very arrogant to assume you could make a film for anyone other than yourself.' Greenaway belongs to a tradition of eccentric Britishers that goes from Beckford to Joyce via Edward Lear, Lewis Carroll and John Martin.

I won't forget my first meeting with him in the garden of the hotel Quattro Fontane on the Lido in Venice where Greenaway, talking like a book, delivered me a user's guide to his film. Many interviews would follow on *Z.O.O.*, *The Belly of the Architect*, *Drowning By Numbers*, *The Cook, the Thief, His Wife and Her Lover* and *The Baby of Macon* and the exegesis was every bit as brilliant as it was peremptory.

ON *THE DRAUGHTSMAN'S CONTRACT*

VENICE, SEPTEMBER 1982

To start with, you were a painter?

I did a course on mural painting. So I decorated large surfaces, ceilings, walls. My heroes were Tiepolo and Veronese; I loved vast baroque compositions. You find that in *The Draughtsman's Contract*, which talks about baroque painting. At the same time, I was interested in cinema, they were like two parallel passions and I couldn't find the middle way to take. In those days, the Royal Court of Art had set up a film school and I would have liked to go there, but there were several hundred candidates for a dozen places and I didn't get in. So then I concentrated on painting and my large-scale compositions got smaller and smaller until I was working on surfaces the size (almost) of a postage stamp! It was the graphic aspect that held my interest: book illustration, religious iconography, miniatures. I held several exhibitions around 1963. But at the same time I wanted to express the other side of my personality, which is a love of stories, anecdotes. So I started looking for odd jobs here and there to earn some money and I started making my own films.

Were your artworks figurative?

I was inspired by cartography, geometry, diagrams, equations. I was very marked at the time by people like Kitaj, Polozzi, the graphic artist, and Peter Blake, the pop painter. So my pictures were not really figurative, but I wouldn't describe them as abstract either. Lots of images were accompanied by texts. And some of my first films were happy just recording in a static way the pages of one of my illustrated books that someone turned with the text on one side and the image on the other.

What sort of books did you illustrate?

Mine. They were labyrinthine, cryptic books, a bit in the style of Mervyn Peake, of his *Titus Groan* and his *Gormenghast*. Those were the days, too, when I, and everybody else, discovered Borges and he fascinated me, and later Calvino. I wrote about eighteen books, but only three of them were ever published. One of the reasons I became a filmmaker is that I couldn't get my books published. The images I'd done for my books wound up in my films. And so *The Falls* contains several hundred illustrations for all these aborted projects that didn't find their way to the printers'. Another reason for going over to film was that I couldn't arrange enough exhibitions of my graphic work and film became the means of circulating the information. But it's so hard making films in England that if things don't work out the way I want, I'll go back to illustrating books!

You were also an editor?

I had to earn my living somehow, so I decided to go to an editing outfit to look for work. It wasn't a vocation, but rather the result of a series of accidents. I found myself at the Central Information Office, a sort of government propaganda organisation. I edited countless documentaries. It's a bit the same sort of training as John Grierson and Humphrey Jennings got when they worked for the Crown Film Unit during the war. Or rather it was a bastardised version, in peacetime, of the great days of British cinema. I spent eight years there and it was very good training for me, since the documentaries were so diverse that there was no particular method to apply. I was thereby able to learn the trade.

So you had an education that was both visual and rhythmic at once, practising draughting and editing.

For me the most important thing in film is the conception of the idea at the outset, and the long work at the editing table in conclusion. That's what I really love. The part in the middle, that is, the filming, doesn't interest me as much.

Is The Draughtsman's Contract *your first film with actors?*

It's my first film with such a large number of actors. I'd made documentaries with a few actors, as well as shorts, but it's the first time they have such a significant place. I was a bit apprehensive before filming as I didn't really know how it would work out with them. We made sure, in choosing the actors, that they'd had theatre experience. They needed to be able to say their lines over long takes. We also decided that the technical crew and the actors would go off together to the shoot location fifty kilometres from London, to that closed place, to get to know each other. In the beginning, there were a few misunderstandings as to our intentions, but after three or four days, everything was back in order and the shoot went very smoothly.

A certain number of your short features have names like Train, Trees, Windows, Water... *What are they like?*

I used to be very interested in land art; the concept was very popular at the end of the 1960s and the beginning of the 1970s. I did a lot of it. I used to go to the country; I'd paint trees. A certain number of my films played with structuralist ideas in relation to the landscape. One of them was called *Vertical Features Remake* and consisted of a series of 121 shots that presented different aspects of the landscape rearranged to form four different films. This film has certain visual links with *The Draughtsman's Contract,* with the way it's structured, returning to the same landscapes at different moments of the day to see how the light has changed the forms, the lines, the shadows and what sense they take on at these different moments. I'd say the background for such research was more symmetrical than structuralist; it had to do with the musical theories of Phil Glass, Steve Reich, John Cage and Robert Ashley, who interested me a lot. We've come full circle today as I now do portraits of those musicians for Channel 4.

Before The Falls *you also teamed up with the British Film Institute in 1978 for* A Walk Through H.

I was doing drawings based on maps. I've always been fascinated by cartography. For me maps represent the visual equivalent of research based on classifying chaos. They conjugate the three tenses of the past, the present and the future. You can see where you were, where you are, where you will be. That's something that fascinates me. So I created around 300 imaginary maps, of a country called H – H representing Heaven as well as Hell ... or Hammersmith! The idea was to look at maps as the terrain where the reincarnations of an ornithologist take place, for I was also attracted to that as a discipline. We imagined this artificial terrain that doesn't exist any more than the maps representing it do.

As in Borges's tale where, in the back of beyond in the Andes, you find, rolled around some trees, a gigantic map on a world scale. In the film there are lots of references to birds, which I got to know in my childhood because my father was, in actual fact, an ornithologist.

In 1980, you made The Falls.

That was an attempt to create a vast encyclopaedic film based on the notion that the history of the world ought to be the history of each one of its inhabitants. An impossible task, of course. So we chose ninety-two people whose names began with FALL (Anthior Fallwaste, Orchard Falla, and so on – whence the title, *The Falls)* to describe so many biographies for characters who shared a fear of flying and a love of birds. It's a bit like a continuation of the last shot in *The Birds*, where Hitchcock leaves us in suspense. The study of birds is a very British occupation. Every character also had a fictitious language, capistan, hartilus B, etc. It was for me a chance to play around with words and a heap of ideas I'd wanted to put in a film for a long time, and it's a bit like wrapping up a whole period of my work in its very scope. You'll recall that at the start of the 1970s the *Whole Earth Catalogue* was published in the United States, it was a great black book that catalogued the universe and every hippy had one. You could find everything in it; it was a sort of stacking of all of twentieth-century culture. *The Falls* was based a bit on the same idea.

Were the two films you made after that, Zandra Rhodes *and* Act of God, *in the same vein?*

Zandra Rhodes was just an essay on a fashion designer. It was my first attempt at biography. *Act of God* was much more interesting. I wanted to try and classify something that couldn't be classified. It was about people who've been struck by lightning. I looked for survivors throughout the country. I found about thirty. I suppose they might have been more numerous in Mexico or India. They told me terrifying tales, about their burns, about the scar a pen had left in their flesh. A young fourteen-year-old girl straddling her pony suddenly saw it reduced to a puddle of fat on the grasslands. I wanted to examine all the mythologies associated with lightning, this 'act of God', and to draw up a catalogue of circumstances, to compare them. It was a series of interviews. I was accused of behaving like Diane Arbus, of using witnesses against their will. I'd like to think that wasn't the case. What matters is that they were filmed against a background that was always revealing. I found ten Welsh football players who'd been struck at the same time. The eleventh died. He was called Peter Greenaway.

Those two films, where you had to face human beings, prepared you for The Draughtsman's Contract *where, for the first time, you use actors.*

Yes, I'd also made *cinéma-vérité* type documentaries with people in them, but never a film about people playing a role. With *The Draughtsman's Contract,* it all began in the summer of 1976. Everyone in England remembers it, since we had four months of splendid weather. I'd spent some time in Gloucestershire doing a series of drawings of the façade of a modest Victorian house in different lights. I'd get up at six in the morning and draw for two hours. Then I'd go back at ten when the shadows had moved slightly. I'd just finished reading Robbe-Grillet's *La Jalousie*, with its minute descriptions of shadows on walls. That had a big influence on me. Of course, there were interruptions, like a herd of sheep, the desire to eat, my children coming to see me. And I found those as interesting as the project itself. The script of the film came out of those two ideas.

So it was all imaginary. You weren't inspired by any historical chronicle or a work of fiction?

My problem was justifying the script. It wasn't very likely that someone in the twentieth century would commission an artist to do a series of drawings of his house. Today, you'd ask a photographer to do it, like David Hemmings in *Blow Up*. So I had to find a time before the invention of photography. At first I thought of an extraordinary character, William Beckford — actually I'm in the process of doing a show on him for BBC2 — the author of the first Gothic novel, *Vathek,* a brilliant book. I was living in a village, Wardour, near which there was a pile of ruins that was the Abbey of Fonthill, where Beckford lived, and I got into the habit of going there on foot. I'd written stories for children on Beckford. One of them involved Lord Nelson and his mistress, Lady Hamilton, who'd spent five days in his home. Beckford gave a great party in their honour. My initial idea was that Beckford would have commissioned the drawings to give them to Anna Hamilton who would have offered them to Nelson before he set off for the Battle of Trafalgar. But since the abbey had disappeared, I didn't have a central artefact, a direct 'hook', and I abandoned the idea. I then went back in time and cast my mind back to the period of George III, the eccentric monarch who created Kew Gardens, the botanical gardens in London. We then invented an artist, William Storridge, from whom the king would have commissioned drawings for his wife and the home would have been The Queen's House, a Dutch house located inside Kew Gardens. The problem was that it's still open to the public and we couldn't use it. So we ended up choosing an even earlier period, 1694, four years after the Battle of the Boyne, with all that that represents for English culture, when the Stuarts, who were Catholic sovereigns, lost their throne and were replaced by the Dutch Protestants, merchants who kick off modern history in England. It was a good era for me to play around with. It was also an era when women enjoyed much more freedom than in later times. It also corresponded to the Restoration period in theatre and in the art of conversation.

It's rare for an avant-garde filmmaker to launch themselves into a narrative tale of this kind. What drove you to it?

I'd been thinking that *The Falls*, in its encyclopaedic reach, was a bit like the end of the road for a whole research project. I could have continued like that. I had an enthusiastic, if limited, audience. But if I wanted to have more means at my disposal and create more interest, I had to broaden my audience. All that might seem set up in advance but chance played a great role. I was interested in this project, I contacted Peter Sainsbury from the British Film Institute and he asked me to write the script, which then went over very well and, before I knew it, the film was up and running. And I'm happy now to reach a larger number of viewers.

But your experimental films, with their algebraic, geometric elements, were a good preparation for The Draughtsman's Contract.

I'd like to think that there isn't much difference as far as my intention or sincerity go. My taste for symmetry is to be found in the film, the dissolves to black by way of opening and conclusion, the close-up that opens and ends it, the central scene filmed as far away as possible from the camera. Similarly the rigorous structure, emphasised by the finishing of each drawing.

The adventure this draughtsman goes through is a bit like a metaphor for your life as an artist. Like the experimental filmmaker, he starts off not wanting life to get into his creation but, little by little, human beings invade his frame. A bit like with you, the characters come and dissolve in the formal play.

I've never thought of that, but it's a perfectly legitimate interpretation. In a way I am the draughtsman without necessarily having that erotic experience. The drawings in the film are mine, naturally. If an art historian were to examine them, he'd note the mistakes. To start with I asked an architect to do them for the film. But I wasn't happy with them; they didn't have the truth that I felt was necessary. I got down to work and it took me a long time.

Were you inspired by Restoration theatre for the language of the characters?

What I'm going to say might seem arrogant. Outside my memories of the period from school and after checking a few dates, I didn't do much intensive research. I've always thought it limited you and railroaded your imagination, stuck you in a straightjacket. I first wrote the text, then I did some research to get exactly what I wanted. But as for imitating the style of Sheridan or Farquhar, I didn't dream of it. It's true that some people say I talk like that anyway!

Did you always have this web of multiple themes in mind: art, sex, society, the thriller? Or did you set off from a particular concern?

To start with there was just a draughtsman, plonked in the middle of a magnificent English landscape, doing drawings. Then I wondered what sort of relationship he might have with the owners of the place to justify his contract. I started writing fragments of dialogue, conversations that would take place at six o'clock in the morning behind a bush. I very soon had pages and pages of it, which I had to link up and so scenes ended up emerging. To go from scene A to scene C, I had to invent scene B and piece by piece the whole thing took shape, a bit the way you shift fragments around when you're editing a film. Initially most of the dialogue was written without having particular characters in mind. I had to invent them later to fit the words. So Mr Talman, the Dutch interloper, was only dreamed up quite late in the piece, and you can sense that – I find him too much of a caricature. I would have liked to make him more complex.

Are you interested in detective stories?

Only in their metaphysical dimension, as in Borges's stories. In fact, it's only in writing the scene between Mrs Talman and the draughtsman, where they discuss the truth, that I realised that the thriller was a perfect genre for my story. Sometimes I'm a bit disappointed because on that basis you know more or less how the film is going to unfold.

The genre works through codes and conventions, which in a way sits better with your formalist concerns than if the subject had been freer of all references.

It's a sort of tragedy in three acts: the first six drawings, the last six drawings, the dénouement and finally a coda. It's fairly faithful to the Elizabethan tradition: the death of the anti-hero is necessary at the end; he must appear to be a victim.

None of the characters is really sympathetic.

You know, no crime has been committed by Mr Neville. He has very much sinned, and so his punishment is based on considerations of an ethical order, not a criminal order. Some people would have liked him not to be killed and for him to sign another contract. His death seems to me, on the contrary, to be necessary. There's also a parallel with the assassination of Kennedy, then of Oswald by someone else, and so on.

Your film departs from the realist tradition of British film that critics and historians tend to favour in relation to people like Hitchcock, Michael Powell and Boorman, for whom the imaginary is essential.

You find the same attitude when it comes to television. A film like *Kes* (Ken Loach) is held up as an example to follow. And this tendency doesn't interest me much. It's a bit sad to want to restrict British cinema to that.

At the same time with you imagination and intellectual speculation have to have a very concrete, very real basis.

It's a bit the case with good science fiction. There's a relationship between the historic film and the science fiction film. You have to be very disciplined to be credible. I used a precise historical framework as a support but within that framework I'm free to manoeuvre.

It's a very literary film at a time when sophisticated language is disappearing from the screen; it's also a very erotic film with a minimum of nudity.

That's how I wanted it to be for hidden sex is much more troubling than anatomical details. The film was conceived and filmed that way. There are no 'daring' scenes that would have been cut in the editing. The only thing that was added to the shoot was Mrs Talman's masturbation scene to suggest that her husband was impotent, a motif for what was going to happen later.

Did you do rehearsals with your actors?

Only four days at the Old Vic. But the actors were so enthusiastic that they spent their spare time rehearsing. During the filming, we rehearsed an hour before each take. We had to do lots of takes since the scenes were very long and lots of post-synchronisation because of the difficulty of the dialogue and also the modern noises you could hear on the sound tape. The shoot took seven weeks, but I spent six months in the editing room. I wanted fixed shots that correspond to the impression of painting. In the first edit, there were about 200 shots, but I chopped a certain number of them up and in the final version there are 300. But the actors complained that there weren't enough close-ups!

All your actors had theatre experience.

Yes. Janet Suzman, who plays Madame Herbert, is a great Shakespearean actress, for instance. She has a role in Fellini's new film, *And the Ship Sails On.*

Your film is very different in its conception from Barry Lyndon*, but how did Kubrick's film influence you?*

I've always admired the book. I don't agree with the choice of the lead actor but I love the vision of history, cold, neutral, passionless, that Kubrick offers, and the sumptuous nature of his visuals. We discussed the photography with my head cameraman. We didn't want, for example, the candles to tremble like in *Barry Lyndon.* For we'd noticed that in this Jacobean pile there were no draughts. I must say, too, that since Kubrick's film, the emulsion is faster and lenses have been further perfected, which allows you to work with very weak natural light.

You have very few camera movements in this film.

It's a bit of a reaction to the St Vitus's dance of certain films, with their diarrhoea of travelling shots. It also stems from my admiration for the static qualities of landscape painting. A further advantage is that if the camera is static, the audience listens more closely to the dialogue. And it was necessary for each word to really be heard. It's time to give language back the place that is its due in films.

How did you design the costumes?

I had very set ideas. I wanted to exaggerate the way they looked, so the wigs are even bigger than in Largillière's portrait of Louis XIV. Before Mr Herbert's death, everyone's dressed in white, which corresponds to an image you have of the English countryside: cricket players, for instance, with the green of nature in the background. After the murder, everyone's in black. To start with I wanted everyone to be in red in the central scenes but it cost too much.

Had you already worked with your cinematographer before?

No. Curtis Clark is Texan. He was living in London, working in advertising films. This is his first feature-length film. We'd met before and we'd discussed the possibilities of Super 16 and promised ourselves to experiment with it together one day. That interested me since I could lower the cost of the film that way. He had one of the two Barinokinetal lenses in existence in the country, which no one had yet used and which allowed you to get an extraordinary depth of field with a very weak light. We were both very interested in the new technologies. We had long conversations together and we went off to see the pictures of Caravaggio, De La Tour and the later Raphael, all three associated with the 'tenebroso' style. We also studied proportion in the works of Poussin and Claude Lorrain, the 1 × 1.66 relationship they keep to. We were also very attentive to the problems of baroque painting and to the use of imaginary optical processes, 'grids', by painters like Dürer and Canaletto, who had their camera obscura. We invented our own grid, which you find throughout the film with the use of windows, verticals and horizontals and the elimination of diagonals. The grid the draughtsman looks through is very close to the eye of the camera.

The gardener is very intriguing as a character. In the middle of this rigorous formal play, he comes across as a whimsical element.

There was a historical precedent. I don't know if you know the diary of a famous English traveller, Celia Fiennes, who went on trips by horse, a bit like Defoe and Evelyn. She did commentaries on the gardens she visited. Landowners were in the habit of putting statues about the place that would surprise their guests. You'd go closer and get hosed. The other idea, one that we invented, this time, is that all these wealthy Englishmen who had stacks of money and very little culture – a bit like the Americans today – would go to Italy and bring back Roman statuary to stick in their gardens. Mr Herbert, not having enough of a personal fortune, asks his gardener to become a statue and to stand in the distance so that his guests can see him. The servant throws himself into the game and demonstrates a mad inventiveness.

The film is also a commentary on class. The artist takes revenge for his inferior position on the social ladder.

That's suggested when he talks about the Scottish monarchy and declares himself to also be of the Catholic religion. His father looked after an apple orchard, which indicates an inferior social situation. He's an 'outsider' who wants to make it into an upper-crust milieu and, as often happens, he's better dressed than his superiors, since he wants to ape them. Just as the German pretends to be an Englishman, the artist pretends to be an aristocrat. And, of course, he gets it wrong and, at the start, when everyone else is dressed in white, he's decked out in black. But later on, when the nobles are wearing mourning gear, he commits another faux pas and dresses in white. Of course, he speaks very refined English for he's had some success and has been in this social milieu for a long time. There's a certain innocence about him, which means he doesn't really follow what's going on. If he were more intelligent, he'd have been aware of being manipulated.

The film is associated with the spirit of the eighteenth century, whereas the action takes place in 1694.

Actually, the eighteenth century in England began with the coming of William and Mary to the throne. That's the beginning of the Whig oligarchy that remained in power thanks to Walpole up till 1740. Similarly, you could say that the eighteenth century ends not in 1800, but in 1789. I also wanted the film to have the cruelty, the nastiness of an earlier era, the one that corresponds to the Jacobean theatre, with plays like *The Duchess of Malfi*. I'm not afraid of anachronisms because an art historian could also attack me for anticipating the interest shown in landscape for itself, which doesn't really happen until after Constable, with the Lake poets. The allegory painted in the garden that goes by the name of *Tribute to the Optical* is the work of a German artist that dates from 1740: there, again, there's a discrepancy.

The blend of passion and reason is typical of the eighteenth century. Man wants to control everything, but he is the victim of deep-seated impulses.

But the films I made previously deal with that: the organisation of chaos. The height of this preoccupation no doubt occurs in England in the eighteenth century. I've been working for ten years with my composer, Michael Nyman, and we would really love to concretise a project set in 1610 at the start of the Catholic dynasty of the Stuarts, when James I succeeded Elizabeth I. It's a film about masks called *Jonson and Jones* as it deals with the relationship between the playwright, Ben Jonson, and the architect, Inigo Jones, who collaborated for over thirty years – a bit like Nyman and me, not to be too pretentious – though they never stopped squabbling the whole time. The subject of their debate was: what was more important, theatre or poetry in that Ben Johnson wanted to publish these masques that were intended for the stage. We'd like to create a very elaborate film, a sort of *42nd Street* of the eighteenth century, but that would obviously be very expensive. I think my next films will be more emotional.

I have another project about three women who murder their husbands, which would be set in the twentieth century and whose visual inspiration would be Bonnard and Vuillard. It will be called *Drowning By Numbers*. I'd like people to feel that I really enjoyed making a film, that it's a physical, sensual pleasure, and I hope people realise that while watching *The Draughtsman's Contract*.

There is also a lot of humour in the film.

Yes, I really love Sterne's wit in *Tristram Shandy*. As for film, I was marked by Godard's first films, Truffaut's *Jules and Jim* and *Last Year At Marienbad*. You can feel the joy of making cinema in that. There was also humour in my experimental films, which didn't fail to shock the groups who support this genre of cinema. It made me a bit anathema. I was always a bit of an outsider since irony seemed to me to be an essential ingredient. But, you know, when I was young, I wasn't really interested in cinema; I'd go and see commercial films like everyone else and that was it. One day when it was raining and I was supposed to go to a cricket match, a friend carted me off to see Bergman's *The Seventh Seal*. I was sixteen. I was knocked out and I went back six or seven times. That's when I realised the possibilities of cinema. Then I found a small job at The British Film Institute and I saw a whole heap of films there. After that I discovered the new wave, took a trip to Paris, then it was Antonioni. Little by little I deserted cinema as a cinemagoer and since 1970 I hardly ever go. Literature and painting interest me a lot more.

You were talking about Michael Nyman. How did you work with him on the music of the film?

We've done ten films together and we've always been very attentive to the relationship between music and image. We've never gone in for theories about it, but it's one of my constant concerns. Our most satisfying collaboration was no doubt *Vertical Feature Remake*, where we really shared the visual and musical ideas. For *The Draughtsman's Contract*, we wanted a score that both evoked the period and the structure. The initial idea was to write a dozen pieces of music that corresponded to the twelve drawings. We based ourselves on the music of Purcell. Michael Nyman is a musicologist and he'd written a book, ten years ago, on contemporary American music, people like Phil Glass, Steve Reich, who've revived certain concerns you find in Purcell, beyond romantic music. So he knew the period very well and he wrote a score that, we hope, is not a pastiche but resurrects the spirit of the time.

Do you still paint?

Yes. I have an exhibition project: *The Tulse Luper Suitcases*. I invented this character who's a sort of Buckminster Fuller or Marshall McLuhan. He knows everything and, in 1939, he fills a suitcase that then disappears. It turns up for five minutes in London, then in New York for just as short a time, then in Los Angeles. Everyone's amazed by this suitcase that has the exact proportions of the space created in the spacecraft sent into the cosmos and that is supposed to represent our civilisation in extraterrestrial worlds. It's like the secret chamber at the heart of the Pyramid of Cheops. The suitcase contains 4,001 objects. It is carefully emptied and there are layers of dust in it, like you find in archaeological digs, that correspond to different periods of the past. All the objects are examined for their meaning and are interpreted like any image for personal use. There are controversies between specialists. This could be material for a film, but in any case it will be an exhibition, at Riverside Studio, where I'll recreate the contents of the suitcase and present an imaginary catalogue of the 4,001 objects.

11 WERNER HERZOG

(1942–)

Now that he has slowly faded from the horizon of cinema in the 1980s and 1990s, it's hard to imagine the place Werner Herzog held in contemporary cinema for over a decade. Of the three great German filmmakers of his time – Herzog, Rainer Werner Fassbinder and Wim Wenders – Herzog was the one who represented his country's romantic tradition. He was also the most painterly. His images left an indelible trace right from his very first film, *Signs of Life*, which I came across in 1968 while selecting films for the International Critics' Week at the Cannes Festival (his producers preferred the Berlin Festival in the end). The seven years that followed were studded with outstanding works up to *The Enigma of Kaspar Hauser*, which was at last presented in competition at Cannes and lead to this initial encounter. The man, today remarkably mellow, due perhaps to his long exile in California, was not easily approachable and was deliberately trenchant and full of a sense of his own singularity as an artist. But you could expect no less from a creator in love with parables and metaphors, who peopled his world with dwarfs, halfwits, wolf children, deaf people, blind people and mad conquistadors, and revealed a fascination for extreme situations and grandiose sets: tumultuous rivers, deserts of torrid heat, snow-capped mountain peaks... Herzog's passion for the handicapped is tied to his personal philosophy: man, in general, is a suffering being, a victim of his dreams and his deficiencies. Whence the desire to force him to the wall to test his resistance. The visionary nature of Herzog's inspiration has its source in a quasi-documentary observation of reality. A great traveller, Herzog has roamed the world and, like the great romantics, has tried to explore all aspects of the world's fauna and flora. To fend off his native pessimism, he has always sought to transcend himself and this extreme tension has no doubt ended up getting the better of him. There remains a whole oeuvre to rediscover and *The Enigma of Kaspar Hauser* remains one of its highpoints.

ON *THE ENIGMA OF KASPAR HAUSER*

PARIS, FEBRUARY 1975

The Enigma of Kaspar Hauser (Jeder für sich und Gott gegen alle) *echoes all your previous films in a certain way. There is the dream of the Sahara from* Fata Morgana, *the Indian, Hombrecito, from* Aguirre, *the dwarf from* Even Dwarfs Started Small (Auch Zwerge haben kleine angefangen), *the evocation of Greece by a Northerner, Lord Stanhope, who makes reference to* Signs of Life (Lebenszeichen), *the blind man as in* Land of Silence and Darkness (Land des Schweigens und der Dunkelheit).

May I add other references, of a different order? The pianist is the same as the one in *Signs of Life*. And the skier I filmed in *The Great Ecstasy of Woodcarver Steiner (Die Grosse Ekstase des Bildschnizers Steiner)* is one of the drunks hypnotising the chicken. But we shouldn't get stuck on these references. All my films belong to a family and if a character turns up again in another film, that shouldn't carry too much meaning. Maybe it just means that the films are all related and that's why I like them being shown back to back. The decision to put a dwarf in the film came perfectly naturally, not arbitrarily. *Kaspar Hauser* isn't a synthesis, but in a certain way things were clarified for me after so many years of working in cinema; the film is a bit like a résumé of what I've done till now, like regrouping before going off down a different track. Whence the dream scenes, which are new images, a new perspective, a new way of seeing things, like climbing up the mountain or the caravan driven by a blind man. You could say that was already in *Signs of Life* with the windmill scene or in *Fata Morgana*, which is a film entirely 'seen through a window', but I think in *Kaspar Hauser* there's a stricter relationship with the story told.

What fascinates you about the desert?

It's like a landscape in a trance, and even more than a landscape, the dream of a landscape, its transformation into something that has never been seen before. Cinema allows you to see reality in a new way. The desert sequence lets me formulate what I've seen and show it to others. It's no longer just information, it forms part of a look at reality and this can slowly transform the way people look at things.

But dream and reality blur with you. The dream Kaspar has of a mountain that men and women climb is no different from the opening shots of Aguirre, *where a column of conquistadors advances on the jungle.*

Yes, it's the same clouds. Yes, it's all real. Similarly, ten thousand windmills in a valley, in *Signs of Life*, are real. For this dream I went to Ireland, as I knew that every year there was a procession of 60,000 pilgrims and this dreamlike vision is very real, there are no special effects, and yet you've never seen it before.

In the same way, there is no clear separation in your films between those that are fiction (Signs of Life, Aguirre) *and those that are closer to documentary* (Fata Morgana, Land of Silence and Darkness). Aguirre *is a bit like a documentary of a work of fiction, whereas* Fata Morgana, *which starts out like a documentary, becomes a fiction, a poem.*

But you don't know the origin of *Fata Morgana*, which had a story, at the start, close to science fiction and which spoke of a new planet, though we knew it was our own. The inhabitants of the comet Andromeda arrived here and discovered it. The first day of filming, I chucked the script and only kept the visions, this fresh perception of our world. And I don't agree with you about the documentary aspect of *Aguirre*. What intrigued me, fascinated me, was this fever that took hold of people and landscapes. And then details, like the boat hanging from the trees, indicated pretty clearly that there was no documentary intention.

Sure, but the maniacal care that you take in recreating the very conditions for this kind of expedition, the physical effort you demand of everyone, give the film the factual feel of a document. I think of Murnau taking German expressionism out of the studios and shooting Nosferatu *in real sets, thereby giving it a quite different tension, and making a documentary on vampires.*

Then I understand what you mean. *Nosferatu* is one of the very great films Germany has produced. And Murnau is for me, by far, the most important of our movie directors. This factual feel that you note in *Aguirre* comes from the life expressed by the landscapes, the people, the river, by their physical presence. That brings the film closer to documentary, but in fact it's a mile off. I can't stand live cinema, for instance. In film, there are several levels of truth and so-called *cinéma-vérité* represents the most basic and the most boring truth. If I could, I'd bury *cinéma-vérité*. In my documentaries I went against *cinéma-vérité*, inventing things that are not, not 'true', but of a different kind of truth, intensified. So in *Land of Silence and Darkness*, Fini Strauwinger, the deaf and blind woman, talks about her youth and the fascination she felt watching the ski jumpers' faces, their mouths open as though they were in ecstasy, as though they were crying out, while they're flying through the air. And she adds: 'I'd love you to see them yourself.' Then I cut and I insert the shot of a skier jumping. Now, all that is my invention. I asked her to say those lines even though she'd never seen a ski jump in her life. Yet, it's still a documentary. It's not a lie; it's an intensified truth. At the end of *Aguirre*, you no longer have the jungle, the trees; you have a dream of a jungle, arrows, feverish people. But it's true that, in *Aguirre*, there's a kind of authenticity. The danger is not created in a studio. The people you see in danger were in danger when they were shooting the film.

What was your starting point for The Enigma of Kaspar Hauser?

The case of Kaspar Hauser is unique in world culture. A man grows up in a dark cave without knowing anything about the outside world. He was attached to the ground by a belt, but he wasn't worried about that because he thought it was part of his anatomy. He never saw anyone, he didn't speak, he'd never seen a tree or a house. He had no conception of the world. From one day to the next he was thrown into society. And still, today, no one knows who he was, who shut him up, who killed him. The case didn't only excite the imagination of his first 'biographer', Anselm Ritter von Feuerbach. In 150 years, more than a thousand books and more than ten thousand essays were devoted to him. There's a play by Peter Handke, *Kaspar*, a novel by Jakob Wassermann, *Caspar Hauser oder die Trägheit des Herzens*, a poem by Verlaine, 'Je suis venu, calme orphelin'… But, apart from Feuerbach's book, I was especially inspired by a sort of autobiography about ten pages long written by Kaspar himself, as well as a poem that's very sad because he was trying to master language. It's one of the most fascinating cases and anyone who doesn't share this fascination has no culture. Culture doesn't mean going to the opera, it's feeling a vital excitement of the mind. The problem of Kaspar Hauser exists in all of us. It's anxiety, the difficulty of adapting to the world.

That's also a very modern problem since it shows that what we call 'human nature' does not exist, that man doesn't have a nature: we have a history.

I don't think in abstractions. I see things in terms of movement, people, scenes. All my films wonder about man. How the deaf and blind in *Land of Silence and Darkness* make themselves understood, how they are excluded from society. In *Even Dwarfs Started Small*, I force the viewer – and that's the reason for the controversies the film caused – to recognise that there's a dwarf in each of them. That's what makes it a desperate film. When you look at isolated dwarfs, they're very beautiful, very well proportioned and yet there's something different inside them. They're like a condensed version, an essence of what we are. At the end of the film, the dwarf's laugh, in a certain way, is *the* laugh, every kind of laugh summed up in a single laugh and that's really terrifying, really complex. It's the same phenomenon that happens with Kaspar Hauser.

In a certain way, at the beginning of the film, it's harder to establish a rapport with Kaspar than with the characters in your other films. There is no point of reference for the viewer. It's only bit by bit, when he learns to communicate, that the contact is established.

The first time you see him, he's less evolved than an animal. Then sympathy takes hold of us slowly. At the end we regret his death. That's what I loved about the film. The way it creates a feeling for a creature that you've first seen as coarse, repulsive. I didn't want my film to be compared to Truffaut's, but rather to films of passion like those of Dreyer. It's 'the Passion of Kaspar Hauser.' I saw *The Wild Child (L'Enfant sauvage)* and I said to myself: 'That bastard's done the film I'd have liked to do!' I think it's a good film but it could have been more than a good film. Victor doesn't have much to do with Kaspar, either. He's a child who, under the influence of the environment, came to resemble a wolf. The interesting question he poses is: what remains of the human, beyond his wolf-like characteristics? But Kaspar, himself, was not affected by anything: he wasn't influenced either by the light of day, or by animals, or by society. He was totally excluded. Furthermore, Truffaut is interested in pedagogy, in eighteenth-century ideas about education, which is not the case in my film. Anyway, comparisons detract from the meaning of the film, more than they help you understand it.

What did you decide to keep in or, on the contrary, to discard all the information you had on Kaspar Hauser?

I changed a lot and invented a lot. I also simplified a lot. Kaspar was handed on among four or five families for his education; in my film, he has just one teacher. Most of the details are mine: he was never exhibited in a circus, he never met a teacher of logic who wonders about his abilities in this domain, he never heard talk of the Sahara, etc.

We know he didn't like green, for instance, or nature. You don't talk about that in your film.

No, but I show how he didn't like church choirs. For him, it was a nauseating shriek. And that is a matter of record. But you know, I didn't read too much about him. This is the first time I've heard that he didn't like nature, for example.

How did the actor prepare to play a role like Kaspar?

We call him Bruno S. since he wants to remain anonymous. I discovered him in a documentary basically made about him by Lutz Eisholz, which I saw one night on television. He'd spent over twenty years in prisons, in correction houses and refuges. His mother, who was a prostitute, wanted to get rid of him by putting him in an institution for mentally ill children. He ran away. He was arrested. He ran away again and so on. He'd break into cars at night, just to sleep inside. And the police arrested him and put him in prison. I've never seen a human being so destroyed by society. He was sidelined like Kaspar. He didn't join in, in society. His whole life was a passion. In his private life, he's different from what he is in the film. For instance, he doesn't speak German; he speaks the Berlin dialect. And yet, in the film, he speaks German, but it's like a foreign language for him. He was fascinated by the film. He's a very sensitive man and he knew that it was also a film about him and about his life. His despair, his fragility, his lack of communication, his loneliness, his fear are all found in the film. At night, he refused to take off his clothes, to get into the bed in his hotel room. He slept on a divan. When he learns to walk, he got down on his knees, stuck a stick behind his legs and stayed like that until he could no longer feel anything. In the end, when we started filming, there was no longer any feeling in his feet, he couldn't walk, and he felt able to express the effort involved in trying to walk. He works as a labourer in a steelworks in Berlin. I didn't want him to quit his job and so we shot the film during his holidays. For six months, before the start of filming, we'd see each other and discuss the role. On weekends he plays the accordion, paints pictures and sings in people's courtyards so they'll throw money at him. He's a talented man, most fascinating.

Didn't you have a similar experience with Hombrecito, to whom Aguirre *is dedicated?*

He was mentally retarded. He played the flute at the markets in Cuzco and refused to film with us because he thought that if he left town, the people would die. Finally, he came with us. He didn't even know his name and people called him Hombrecito, little man. He was the only saint in the crew. He wore three shawls one on top of the other and I had trouble getting him to take them off during filming since he was supposed to wear a poncho. He was afraid they'd get stolen and he went off to hide them in the jungle. And at night, the whole crew was obliged to go and look for them because he never knew where he'd put them. After the shoot, I found him back in Cuzco in the market square. This time he was wearing three jackets that he'd bought with his wages. I asked him why he wore them on top of each other. He answered that it was to protect himself from the gringos' bad breath. I preferred him to the lot of them. He carried all the humiliation, all the oppression, all the despair of his race, on his shoulders. When you see him, you see all the disasters the Indians have had to live through at the hands of white men. That's why I wanted him to feature in *The Enigma of Kaspar Hauser*. He's part of my family; he represents my love for the Indians, who I got on very well with.

With all your films set in the past, are you very meticulous in the re-enactment?

No, I don't feel like I'm a bookkeeper of the past. For example, in *Aguirre*, there's Gonzalo Pizarro. Well, he died two years before the expedition. Father Gaspar de Carvajal never went with Aguirre, either. The bit from the chronicle that comments on the film is entirely my invention and in no way an authentic document, as many people think! But I'm very accurate in the physical details. I like getting involved in them. It's not just to recreate an era, but, for instance, for the allure the actors will have in their costumes. We had a sword and a dagger made especially for Klaus Kinski. In the beginning, in the script, Aguirre was to kill his own daughter, Flores, so that she doesn't see the shame of his demise. In the end I filmed differently. But my idea was that a man like Aguirre would not use a normal dagger, he'd have a dagger as fine as a needle so that, when he struck someone, you wouldn't see the blood. The person would die of an internal haemorrhage. It had to be a dangerous and vicious instrument. In the end you don't see the dagger in the film. I learned a lot from Kinski from this point of view. He has an extraordinary feel for costumes. In *The Enigma of Kaspar Hauser*, I had a garden planted six months before so that it'd be ready for the film. I had to think about the Biedermeyer period, about the animals found then, such as storks and bees, and also the plants. I'm just as demanding when it comes to sound. This film, like most of my other films, uses live sound. I had to quarantine half of Dinkelsbühl to avoid interference.

During the filming, I devote more time to the sound than to the image. Aguirre's monologue, where he threatens the people with imprisonment if they take more than their ration of corn and when he names himself 'The Wrath of God', is accompanied by a contrapuntal sound made up of birdsong. We spent weeks in the jungle collecting songs and sometimes, based on eight tapes, I recomposed the song of a bird. Nothing is accidental; everything is composed, as in music. That's why the jungle looks so alive, so strange, so dangerous. It's like a dialogue with nature. It's hard for me to explain my interest in it, like my interest in music, animals, landscapes, dream images, moments of dead time. The figure of the circle like the shot of Aguirre turning in circles on his raft. The dromedary, for instance, fascinates me. It's on its knees in an immobile position, stuck between standing and lying down. It's a desperate situation that might go on for a long while. Chickens frighten me, but what fascinates me is that you can hypnotise them, and that's what I show in my films. Monkeys, on the other hand, I really love and they're important in my work.

Aguirre *and* The Enigma of Kaspar Hauser, *like your first feature,* Signs of Life, *use classic narrative devices (an expedition, the education of a child, a military adventure in Greece) and subvert them from within, throwing the viewer off balance, operating a shift in interest, frustrating him.*

I'm not all that bothered about narrative forms. For instance, in *Aguirre*, I didn't intend to use a chronicle to accompany the film in order to create a rhythm. But editing at the Moviola, I felt the need for a more precise tempo, so I hit on this text. It creates the impression of time dragging on more and more until it actually seems to stand still. It also allows you to provide dates and to stress how time's running out. The rhythm of my films is very variable, but I like uncomfortable pauses that prelude danger, the explosion. They are moments of tension, like when there isn't the faintest hint of a breeze before an earthquake.

A characteristic sequence, for example, in The Enigma, *is the scene where Kaspar is in the middle of the square in Nuremberg: you alternate shots of a peasant with a pipe, a bourgeois couple, a cow next to a tree, the bell-tower, etc. Do you have an idea of the order of the shots before the editing?*

No, I don't have a precise view about it. Later, while editing at the Moviola, I look at the material and I see if it has a genuine inner life. That's when I get more involved in the script. The film material lives its own life on the editing table and you mustn't try and force it into a mould that wouldn't be appropriate.

How did you choose the music for The Enigma of Kaspar Hauser?

At the start and at the end I used an aria of Tamino's in Mozart's *The Magic Flute*. It's a curious recording. I heard it while I was out driving and I stopped the car because the sound was so bad. The recording dated from 1911 and Tamino was interpreted by the tenor, Heinrich Knotte, a contemporary of Caruso's and in my view the greatest tenor of the century. It was very important for me to have his voice. And the lines he sings also play a role in Kaspar's story, expressing the sympathy he so badly needed.[1] The start of the aria opens the film and the end accompanies the last shot. I also used bits of Pachelbel, Roland de Lassus (Orlando di Lasso) and Albinoni. I'm careful to see that the music is totally appropriate to the film. So Couperin's *La Leçon de ténèbres*, so desperate, so sad, was the perfect accompaniment, in *Fata Morgana*, to a long travelling shot in an abandoned military camp in Algeria. For *Aguirre*, the music was composed specially: I wanted a choir that was out of this world, like, when I was a child, I thought, while I was walking at night, that the stars were singing. I also believed that the soul was like a white handkerchief and that after you committed a sin, it went black. Then the black handkerchief flew away and on contact with the stars, it became clean again for a new life.

I'm very shaken up, very stirred by music, almost as much as by films. Sometimes, the true quality of an image can't be appreciated except through music.

One example would be the travelling shot over the sand dunes in *Fata Morgana*. After looking at it several times on the Moviola, I realised all of a sudden that it was a feminine landscape. So then I accompanied these landscapes with a women's choir taken from Mozart's 'Coronation' Mass and the viewers were then able to grasp the feminine quality with great clarity.

Fata Morgana, of all your films, is the one that poses formal problems the most radically.

Maybe, but not for me. I made it as though I was in a dream. I still can't explain how it happened. Every night, when I was sleeping in the desert, I didn't know if I'd be filming the next day. It was like a hallucination. Once the film was finished, I knew I'd made it, but I was flummoxed. During the filming I didn't ask myself any questions, I just let myself go; I didn't think of the structure, I opened my eyes and my ears. And I went on like that during the editing…

Yet the film is organised. It starts with static shots without human figures. Then there are panorama shots, travelling shots, and the landscape becomes inhabited.

I feel the same way you do, now, when I see the film. There is an order, a structure, but they weren't planned. It was the order or the disorder of my emotional state at that moment, of my despair at the time. It crops up in my films. I did it for my first feature as it took me four years to finance it and that creates a sort of distance. I had the feeling that the film was the end of my childhood and that all my childhood was to be found in it. I didn't have any years between nineteen and thirty-five: I never was twenty years old; I turned thirty-five straight away. I didn't do what you do between twenty and thirty-five. My friends went into business, studied, learned a profession, established themselves, had responsibilities. Me, I leapfrogged all those years and filmed *Signs of Life*, which was written when I was nineteen years old. In *Fata Morgana*, I filmed my first impressions, directly, I didn't wait a year, I filmed what happened to me. And now I don't have a private life anymore, though that doesn't mean I think my films are private, for all that.

Were the three parts of Fata Morgana: *Creation, Paradise, The Golden Age, planned in advance?*

No, it's only after seeing the images that I thought of that. From the first day of creation, there is a latent catastrophe, mistakes. The text for the first part is drawn from a sacred text of the sixteenth century, created by the Indians of Guatemala: *Popol Vuh*. I didn't change it much. The text for the other two parts is mine: it stemmed from my own queries, from my perplexity faced with the images I saw on the Moviola. It's a desperate film, like a vision of disaster. Seeing the images, we see debris, the waste, all we've stuffed up. These fragments of civilisation are simmering away, ridiculous, in the sun. When I see the film I tell myself how beautiful the world could be and how little it is in reality. And it's our fault. In a way, it's a utopia, and it's no accident if it was originally based on a science fiction story.

Where did the idea for the musician couple come from?

I was in the Canary Islands to film *Even Dwarfs Started Small* and I'd already shot the greater part of *Fata Morgana*. I was fascinated by the madam of a brothel who played piano and by the man, a pimp, who sang while he played drums. I gave him glasses and stuck black paper over his eyes so he couldn't see anymore, as he just kept slapping around any of the prostitutes who weren't being nice to the clients they were dancing with. Then we filmed this couple and I felt they formed part of *Fata Morgana*. 'Fata morgana' means 'mirage' in German. We shot a lot of film of them. For example people get out of a coach and seem to spill out everywhere like pencils and the coach seems to be sailing on water. Now there wasn't a trace of tyres around. Maybe, sixty kilometres away, there was a coach and the layers of hot air reflected this image we'd shot.

Several of your films are structured in a loop. As in Signs of Life, *the last shots of* Fata Morgana *evoke the first shots. These are views from a plane.*

At the end, we filmed a lake between Kenya and Tanzania at an altitude of 500 metres. It's a pink colour due to the millions of flamingos you find there. The planes were, first, shot at the airport in Munich, but you get the impression it's the desert. I'm fascinated by these shots. We began filming at five in the morning and we finished at two in the afternoon on a very hot day and each plane that took off was more blurry, more unreal, than the one before it because of the condensation. They were like birds in a dream. And I knew that that endless repetition of take-offs was going to cause viewers to walk out after only five minutes of film, but that was good because the ones who remained would know what the film was about and would stick it out right to the end. It was a signal for them.

I felt *Fata Morgana* was so fragile, so close to what I felt deep inside, that I wouldn't dare show it. I was afraid people would just laugh and that I'd feel hurt. I wanted to leave it with my best friends and I kept it a secret for a year and a half before it was torn from my hands for Directors' Fortnight at the Cannes Festival. And when I saw the reactions of the public I understood that films have to be shown. There's only one of my films that I've kept secret – for eleven years – and I'll never show it, but I'll pass it on. It's my second short, *Game in the Sand (Spiel im Sand)*, a problematic film about an unresolved problem. Like the film on the dwarfs, it would be too controversial; it's a desperate work, cruel and anarchistic. I shouldn't have made it.

Signs of Life *has a title that could serve as an epigraph for all your films.*

We're talking here first of all about the authentic life. And signs are signals, calls. Stroszek, the hero, is not so important as a private person. At the end of the film, he lays siege to a whole town with fireworks, he fights his friends and his foes and he becomes important to the community. But it's at that moment that I cease to show him as a private person, I look at him from afar, at a distance of three or four hundred metres, a bit like an ant. What interests me are the signals he sends. He repeats the signs of cruelty, of absurdity, of stalling for time that he's seen around him. They're explosive responses. He can no longer speak; all he can do is show signs. You find that in my films: in moments of profound despair, there is an exchange of signals. So in *Even Dwarfs Started Small*, it's not cruelty they display, it's not real damage that they cause; those are gestures of provocation and anarchy. Of course they destroy a fair bit but they could easily have burned the house down and killed the director.

At the end of that film, one of the dwarfs circles around in a car. At the end of Aguirre, *the camera circles the boat. The circle is a dominant figure in your films as in* Signs of Life *or the sun in* Fata Morgana.

For me the circle suggests both ritual and the inevitable at once. We find the ritual again in *Aguirre*, in the way the emperor is crowned, this sort of opera where gestures are repeated. There's also the ritual in *Dwarfs*. In *Last Words*

(Letzte Worte), which I filmed in Crete and which is the one I prefer of my shorts, there's this sort of ritual with people watching the camera. It's the story of an old musician who's mad, but only in the film. He lives on a desert island where there's a small village and a leprosarium; he thought he was king, but his family declared him mad and made him leave the island. Since then, he doesn't talk any more, he plays the violin and he sings in bars. It's a very strange film. At the end, he stares at the camera and tries to drive it off with his hands while repeating non-stop: 'I won't talk, I won't say anything, I'll keep quiet.'

You like static shots where the characters look at the camera.

In *Signs of Life,* there's a shot of a wedding. Everyone was in position; the camera was ready to roll. I then asked Peter Brogle, who was playing Stroszek, to run seven or eight kilometres with me until we were exhausted. He came back to take his place in the wedding shot and that makes the image very strange because he's getting his breath, his mouth is open and he looks haggard. In *Fata Morgana,* I got the waiter to stay in front of the camera in close-up and to show the fennec fox he was holding in his hand. I begged him not to move, not to bat an eyelid and I promised to pay him well if he stayed like that. He held the pose for ten minutes until he was exhausted and it was only then that I started to film a shot lasting about two minutes.

In your films there's a compassion for the victims that's devoid of any sentimentality: Aguirre's Indians, *Fata Morgana's shanty town Arabs, the deaf and blind of* Land of Silence and Darkness, *the retarded man of* The Enigma of Kaspar Hauser. *In contrast, in* Dwarfs *I don't sense that compassion. You show them as being cruel and reinforce the viewer in his feeling that they're beings who are different from him. You encourage his racism.*

I think there is the same compassion and the same love for them. When you torture a dog and you shut it in a cage, it ends up biting you. The cruelty of their revolt is not real cruelty: those are gestures towards cruelty. And when they act with real cruelty, when they kill the pig, for instance, they have bad consciences. It's not so much cruelty with them as violence, blasphemy, anarchy, which are so many cries for help. I looked for dwarfs who are beautiful, well proportioned. And all their actions are justified. When they put petrol in the flowerpots, you get the feeling they're right, that they're the first to do what should be done with flowerpots. But you know, *Even Dwarfs Started Small* provokes violent reactions: some love the film; others hate it.

Only two of your films don't have victims as protagonists. And in both cases (Signs of Life, Aguirre), *it's the story of a man who goes mad.*

They are closer to each other, it's true, but it's hard for me to put that into words. In the same way, *The Enigma of Kaspar Hauser* is closer to *Land of Silence and Darkness.*

Signs of Life *is adapted from a novel by Achim von Arnim,* Der tolle Invalide auf dem Fort Ratonneau (The Mad Invalid of Fort Ratonneau).

The starting point for the film was the site. I went to the island where my grandfather, who was an archaeologist, had worked. He died insane, and as I admired him a lot, I wanted to see what he'd done over there. I was struck by the places, which coincided more and more with the tale I wanted to tell. When I was studying history, I'd been very interested in the Seven Years War and the problems of military strategy. I'd discovered in a newspaper of 1807 a short article on an incident that had taken place in Marseilles during that war. And I later learned that Arnim had used the event to write his short story, which I read after that and which is wonderful.

How were you led to make Land of Silence and Darkness?

I ran into Fini Strauwinger at a gathering while I was on a shoot in Munich, making *Handicapped Future (Behinderte Zukunft)* about children who were victims of thalidomide and had no arms or legs. She was deaf and blind herself and she looked after the deaf and blind. I dug up her address, managed to communicate with her by learning her alphabet and decided to do a film with her. I made it with very little money. When she was nine, she'd had an accident. At thirteen, she went blind, and at eighteen, deaf. She was bedridden for thirty years. Only her mother could communicate with her and when her mother died, she remained without any assistance. She had to fight like mad to get out of all that, as much because she'd become hooked on opium, which alleviated her suffering. But she refuses to talk about her past in the film. There, too, it's a passion-film. I followed her around with the camera for five months trying to make up my mind whether to film or not. Sometimes I staged events: for her birthday, I hired a small plane and gave her her maiden flight as a present. I also knew that Fini wanted to go to the zoo and that the deaf and blind had never been there. So I decided to do that sequence after persuading the director of the zoo to free a chimpanzee.

Can you tell us about your background and your debut in cinema?

My mother's a Yugoslav. She's called Stipetic. I have a very complicated family. My father lives like a hobo. He married twice. I have lots of brothers and sisters, but some of them are half-brothers or quarter-brothers. Legally my name is Stipetic, but I took Herzog as a name. I was not brought up in the system. I'm a self-taught man and I've never been to any film school. While I was studying, I worked nights in a steelworks in Munich. For two whole years I was on the assembly line from eight o'clock at night to six o'clock in the morning. I earned enough money to make my first short in 35 mm. Before that, at eighteen, I'd gone on a trip to the Sudan. I didn't have a penny to my name and I became very sick. I spent five days in a barn, at death's door, with a high fever, and rats started biting me after they'd eaten through my clothes. They even bit my face – you can still see the marks.

I got a scholarship to go and study history in Pittsburgh, but I gave up the scholarship after three days. I had no money left and I was expelled from the United States. So then I spent six months in Mexico where, to earn a living, I did rodeos and ran guns and television sets between the United States and Mexico.

We don't know much about your short- or medium-length films.

It's not worth the trouble of talking about my first film, *Herakles*. I don't much like it. It was filmed in Germany and I used stock shots, car races in particular. *The Unprecedented Defence of the Fortress Deutschkreutz (Die beispiellose Verteidigung der Festung Deutschkreuz)* was made near the Hungarian border. It's a sort of prologue to *Signs of Life*. It's about four people who shut themselves up in a fortress and wait indefinitely for an enemy that will never show. At the end, they come out and storm a wheat field. *Precautions Against Fanatics (Massnahmen gegen Fanatiker)* is a very strange and very funny film. The people in it are VIPs like Mario Adof. I shot it on a racetrack in Munich. There's an old Bavarian who never stops leaping about all over the place trying to push the characters out of the frame. He wants to protect the horses from the fanatics, but you never see a single one of them!

The Flying Doctors of East Africa (Die fliegenden Ärzte von Ostafrika) was made for friends who work there. It's a documentary that shows how hard it is for medical aid in that region. They set up a truck with an operating theatre and an X-ray theatre costing tens of thousands of dollars. After sticking it in the middle of the Masai desert, they realise that the whole thing's pointless, since the Masai refuse to mount the five steps that lead to the interior of the truck. And I filmed how an African medical assistant drags them up the steps.

The Great Ecstasy of Woodcarver Steiner was made for German television. It's one of a series of films about extreme situations. Steiner is a Swiss, a world champion ski jumper, who's a wood sculptor by trade. He flies over 170 metres, but at each jump there's a critical point. He's so good that the drop areas are always in danger of being too short for him and he could die if he falls from an altitude of 110 metres onto hard ground. People always think he won't make the critical zone but, in Yugoslavia for instance, he defied all the experts' calculations and beat the world record of over 190 metres on ski jumps too small for such an exploit. He hit the ground very hard (and when they fall, a jumper carries on his shoulders six times his weight!), he lost his memory for half an hour, then he was supposed to start jumping again, even though he could hardly stand. It's a film about the anguish of death, the ecstasy of the body, and loneliness.

NOTES

1   Dies Bildnis ist bezaubernd schön,
   Wie noch kein Auge je gesehn?
   Ich fühl es, ich fühl es,
   Wie dies Götterbild
   mein Herz mit neuer Regung füllt.
   Dies etwas kann ich zwar nicht nennen,
   doch fühl ich's hier wie Feuer brennen;
   Soll die Empfindung Liebe sein?
   Ja, ja, die Liebe ist allein!

The picture is enchantingly beautiful,
No one has ever seen its like!
I feel, I feel
How that divine face
Is filling my heart with new emotion.
I can't say what it is,
But I feel a sort of flame right here.
Could this be love?
Yes, yes, it's only love.

12 HOU HSIAO-HSIEN

(1947–)

For certain filmmakers, the path to recognition is a long haul. That has been the case for Hou Hsiao-hsien, even though he is without a doubt the greatest director to have emerged on the international scene in the 1980s, along with Abbas Kiarostami. His name has imposed itself gradually, thanks in particular to the Nantes Festival of the Three Continents where, in 1984, his fourth film – and, to be honest, the first of any real importance – *The Boys From Fengkuei (Fengkui laide ren)*, won the Grand Prix. Then Berlin, Locarno and other film festivals led to the discovery of the chronicles about young adolescents, *A Summer At Grandpa's (Dong dong de jia)*, *A Time to Live, A Time to Die (Tong nien wang shi)*, and *Dust in the Wind (Lian lian feng chen)*, where the Taiwanese filmmaker really imposed his style. This involved rigorous framing that didn't rule out spontaneity on the part of actors who are often non-professionals, and long static shots that for some evoked Ozu. Hou films the movements of young people who are always between a rock and a hard place, along with their lost illusions, their melancholy, their loneliness. *A City of Sadness (Bei qing cheng shi)* in 1989 marked a decisive turning point. Firstly, thanks to the Golden Lion of Venice (the Venice Festival played a pioneering role in the 1950s in recognising the cinemas of the East, with Kurosawa, Mizoguchi, Satyajit Ray, who were all 'lionised'), then through history's grand entrance into Hou's movies. The first part of a trilogy about the island's past, *A City of Sadness* was to be followed by *The Puppetmaster*, then *Good Men, Good Women (Hao nan hao nui)*. *The Puppetmaster* and all Hou Hsiao-hsien's subsequent films were entered in the Cannes competition. An indefatigable inventor of forms, with *Goodbye South, Goodbye* (1996) and *Millennium Mambo* (2001), Hou was to forge ahead as a filmmaker in his quest for quasi-musical narrative structures, while homing back in on contemporary youth. *Flowers of Shanghai* (1998) demonstrated an art of modulation worthy of Sternberg. A director enthralled by concrete conversations, modest but determined, both cheery and grave, Hou Hsiao-hsien granted me this interview just before he received his Grand Prix at Venice and it was followed subsequently by quite a few more.

ON *A CITY OF SADNESS (BEI QING CHENG SHI)*
VENICE, SEPTEMBER 1989

In style and subject, A City of Sadness *is different from your previous films. It has a broader scope, a panoramic dimension. Why did you want to take it on, today?*

In all my films I've started out from my own experience. I've narrated things that happened to me personally or to my family, but at the same time I'd never been able to express an essential aspect of my temperament. I actually have a pretty foul personality, I'm hotheaded and on top of that I wanted to tell this particular tale, which has a lot to do with me and with my political views. There were quite concrete reasons for the sort of tranquillity, the apparent calmness in my films since I was working with amateur actors who are really scared of film. The cinematographic form we arrived at actually has a lot to do with the real conditions of production. To the extent that I couldn't ask them to do action scenes that were too difficult, there are a lot of things I couldn't envisage filming in my previous films. In a way, my approach to scripts in the past has always been unconscious. Working with amateurs for me meant taking charge of all they couldn't bring to the task.

With *A City of Sadness,* it's the first time there was a conscious process I went through to achieve a goal that flowed directly from my subject. I was a bit sick of working in the same conditions with non-professionals all the time and I was happy finally to be able to collaborate differently with my actors. Like, for instance, the big brother, Wen Heung, and the deaf mute, Lin Wen-ching, that is, Chen Songyong and Tony Leung, experienced actors who were able to hit on and control the tone of every scene. I mixed them in with television actors who played a number of the secondary roles, and also with amateurs. Li Tianlu, who plays the grandfather, is not an actor, he's the greatest puppeteer in Taiwan. He's already appeared in a number of my other films. To understand my method with the actors, you need to know that I tried to study how other directors

I'd been very interested in went about it. I could cite Fassbinder, for instance – he worked with a company he'd already used in the theatre. It's that kind of obvious, concrete relationship that I've always wanted to have with my actors.

In gearing up for *A City of Sadness*, I began contacting professional actors, but I was immediately disappointed, as I couldn't get them to understand what I wanted. Every time, they'd ask me what expression I wanted them to put on out of a catalogue of expressions they offered me. In the case of the deaf mute, Tony Leung, I was fairly satisfied, but I still had to drag him off to the rushes to show him the scenes he'd shot with Xin Shupen, who plays his wife, Hinomi, for him to see the difference in their performance. Xin Shupen is a semi-professional and she brought an element of truth. She was different in each scene, whereas Tony Leung, being a professional actor, revealed himself to be incapable of not reproducing the same movements, the same expressions every time. Well, that was the last thing I wanted. I still preferred the over-the-top performance of the big brother, Chen Songyong, to this tame, repetitive performance Tony Leung was giving me in the beginning, when he was still too rigid.

Is the idea for the script yours and how was the work distributed between you and your scriptwriters, Wu Nien-jen and Chu T'ien-wen?

The subject is very personal and it was dear to my heart. If I've waited this long to do it, that's because it's only now that the political conditions in Taiwan allow such a film to be made. We actually went through a period when censorship of information was more strongly exercised than it is today, when there are more opportunities for expression. As far as my relations with the scriptwriters go, you have to make a distinction with Chu T'ien-wen, who has been my fervent collaborator for a very long time. I spent three months with her looking for documents of the time and even reading the contemporary novels of the period. Once we'd digested all this material, we put it aside and devoted ourselves to imagining the characters and tried to map out the relationships between them. After we'd drawn up a diagram of their relationships, we tackled the third stage, which was a shooting script based on the diagram which Chu T'ien-wen wrote and which was the essential basis of the script. Wu Nien-jen's role began at that point: he went from Chu T'ien-wen's treatment to the scenario with dialogue. Obviously in the process of writing a few changes were made. In the beginning, each time we imagined a character, we were thinking of a particular actor, and that choice determined the writing. Today we joke about that, because if I'd really kept the actors I chose beforehand to play the roles of the big brother and Hinomi, the film would probably be a lot less interesting. They were extremely traditional actors, the man especially. He was the president of the actors' guild. Luckily they had too many commitments elsewhere and so we completely abandoned the idea of working with big stars.

What were the most delicate elements of the script that you wouldn't have been able to handle at an earlier time?

It's hard for me to be specific about the themes that I wouldn't have been able to take on to the extent that I would always have made the same film, knowing that, in any case, it would have been censored. And anyway, it's not out of the question that when it gets shown in Taiwan, there'll problems with the censors.[1] But what has changed today – even in relation to a very recent period – is that the voice of public opinion counts enormously and that the government is obliged to take it into account. To sum up the situation in Taiwan, if you like, the turning point between the two periods was the death of Chiang Ching-kuo, the son of Chiang Kai-shek. He's the one who wanted to muzzle the press and the media, and who wouldn't accept the existence of political parties, even if there was an opposition in Taiwan.

One of the most complex aspects of the film for a Westerner is the role played by the different languages and dialects – Mandarin, Hokkien, Shanghainese, Cantonese and Japanese.

You have to start off with one essential consideration: the national language of Taiwan up until 1945 was Japanese. After the end of the period of Japanese occupation, we were forced to learn another language that no one could speak – that is, Mandarin. People coming from the mainland each spoke their own dialect. And so there was a national language, artificially imposed, and living languages that each corresponded to a different group of the Taiwanese population.

Your film plays on the characters of the four brothers, one of whom is an absence, he is missing in action, another is an absence–presence, since he was tortured and left in a state of prostration, the third is deaf and dumb and finally, the eldest brother is a gang leader. How did you articulate these relationships?

Actually the relationship between the brothers, and especially the one between the eldest brother and the deaf mute, is fundamental to the whole script. On one side, the big brother represents local roots, whereas the other one incarnates utopianism and romanticism. But also, from the point of view of the internal dynamics of the story, the big brother commits acts that are very fast, very violent, and it's no accident if, on top of that, the character of Lin Wen-ching is deaf and dumb. Every time he appears, everything goes all quiet and his calm movements contrast with the permanent excitement of the other man.

You also introduce narrative elements that are literary and that shatter the classic narrative: on the one hand, the cartoons with ideograms written on them that express the conversations about and with Lin Wen-ching and, on the other, letters written by the young girl.

That was one way of avoiding the trap of traditional realism. I also wanted to provide a tone of objectivity. So the ideal solution was to have cartoons and also voices 'off' for Hinomi, who reads in a serene, calm manner, while occasionally saying things that are very hard and very violent. You also have to take into account the fact that, by shooting the whole film in real interiors, I managed to subvert the theatrical aspect of it. I didn't want to have camera movements and I couldn't get the dynamism any other way.

The songs also play a role as indirect commentary.

The choice of songs obviously results from my desire to represent the concrete nature of the different languages and cultures. First there are the Taiwanese songs that date from the period of Japanese domination. These are mainly love songs that, for instance, tell of the loneliness of a woman waiting for her lover who's gone off to war. They're in the style 'the flower awaits the morning dew to be able to open'. After that there's the importance that classical western music, like *Die Lorelei*, took on during the period of Japanese occupation. In fact, when Japan opened up to the West with the restoration of the Meiji, we were invaded by popular symphonic music from Europe. The third group of songs represents Japanese songs sung by native Japanese, for during the fifty-one years of occupation, a good many Japanese were born in Taiwan and they acquired a particular identity, living in a very odd relationship with their country of origin that they basically saw as a foreign land. The fourth musical group is the music of the mainland, with opera music in particular and more especially, the music of the Peking Opera that was known as 'the melody that comes to us from outside'. In fact, starting from 1945 and especially when the nationalists set themselves up in Taiwan, the latter tried to impose their most classical music and started singing it in restaurants like you see in the film. The fifth group is traditional local music, the ethnic music of Taiwan, the music of ceremonies and opera in dialect. This music, in the film, is always mixed with ambient noise, festivities. Think of the scene where the singing and dancing merges with the fireworks. I should also add the patriotic, anti-Japanese songs that correspond to the very late arrival of mainland revolutionary songs.

What is the role of music that you wanted from your Japanese composer Naoki Tachikawa in relation to these songs?

It was a pretty difficult collaboration, all the more so as I didn't want him to come up with a score that was descriptive of what you see in the film. I wanted the music to express my point of view about things and in a way a conception of the traditional worlds that you might sum up in the Chinese formula: 'An objective point of view of heaven's ways'. The music had to be detached in a way, but at the same time it brings in local elements to link the scenes together. But unfortunately that's something the Japanese composer didn't manage to do since he didn't belong to that culture.

I got him to listen to old Taiwanese songs, hoping he'd be able to use them as a starting point but this didn't produce the desired result. In any case, there aren't a lot of good composers of film music, and in Taiwan there aren't any. So this made me less embarrassed about wheeling in a foreign musician and, since it was clear that the first country the film would be sold to was Japan, there was a good commercial reason for choosing a composer from Japan!

Nature is used to magnificent effect in your film. What's your personal relationship with nature and how do you use it as an element within the overall rhythm of the film?

There's something important you should know about my conception of film. I never decide the structure in advance. So the rhythm can just come when we edit. All the nature shots are without people. I shot them after filming the interior sequences with the actors, but I knew that that might allow possibilities of expression in the editing. By working with professional actors, I couldn't ask them for an expression, a gesture, an action that I might then chop up into a certain number of very close shots. I had to keep working with long shots and a fixed camera and I needed shots of nature to create a dynamism. This principle of the long shot and the fixed camera suits me down to the ground since it allows me to build a red thread that runs through the whole film. I always try in fact to represent the real time and space of situations. So meals, washing clothes, all those domestic chores have their specific duration on screen. What I'm looking for – maybe this is very oriental – is to find the pace of daily life. Without that my films wouldn't perhaps make any sense. It's a very conscious process for me.

In what sense did you mean you can't fragment the performance of professional actors? Isn't it rather your own style – and not the type of actors you choose – that leads you to film shots in continuity?

It's true that that's my style. But a filmmaker's style is his personality. And if I want to film that way, that's because it corresponds to what I am. Style means understanding something – or not. Every time, I have to know what I have to film and what has to be in a shot. And based on those certainties the logical structure of the film, the succession of shots and sequences, is established. The construction of space, for instance, also comes when we're on the set, based on improvisations, inventions, just as much as in the editing. It's hard to express but in a way my emotions and my feelings are a reaction to what I called the ways of heaven a moment ago. As far as my work with the actors goes, and the problem posed by the fragmentation of performance, my response can only be extremely concrete. I have before me professionals, non-professionals, actors from Hong Kong, and it's very hard to match them. If I ask professionals to act, they are effectively going to 'act' – that is, to do it in a way that's too stilted. So to get what I'm looking for, I have to film in secret. I tell them it's just a rehearsal, they light up a cigarette, don't know I'm in the process of filming, and that's the shot I'll choose. At that particular moment it becomes impossible to cut into a shot. The only professional actor with whom I could discuss relations with non-professionals was Tony Leung. He was the only one who understood how he could blend in with them. With the others, I always had to trick them.

What is striking in your films in general is the presence places have, as though they underpinned the whole direction.

It's true that the places are a determining factor. I have been known to change an initial idea because of a place I've found. Locations are chosen going on memories I have of certain spots. If I think a place might be right for me, I decide to film the scene there. I also often have places in mind even before I write the first draft of the script. But all this was a long process of creation. At the outset I didn't think I'd ever be able to do without natural sets. Today I feel ready to film in a studio.

You work a lot with depth of field, as in the shot where the deaf mute is in the foreground while his brother is in the background eating incense sticks.

I started doing that as soon as I started making films. I've always liked having some action covering another action or better still, revealing another action. With a long-shot aesthetic, it's clear that you can't devote yourself to frontality alone, there has to be this depth and actions have to be dynamised at different levels of the depth of field. You have also always to connect the different spaces. But if, on the one hand, you have to hide parts of the frontal space to avoid excessive theatricalisation, you also have to highlight the space off to left and right since at a given moment the action might get extended without my having foreseen this development.

In that sense, what is the role of frontality and depth of field in the expression of the violence that is so strongly present in A City of Sadness, *but at the same time, kept at a distance?*

On the one hand, there's the fact that I didn't want the film to be too long, and on the other, the obvious fact that there are a lot of events and characters. If I'd decided to follow everything happening in the action scenes (some of which are violent) too closely, to bring out the details, the film would have been a lot longer. This way my shots remain 'clean'. It's also an ethical position. I don't find that the scenes of violence in most films correspond to the reality of violence. When you see a scene of violence taking place, you only feel a tone, an atmosphere, you don't perceive the details. That's why I want to stay very objective, not get any closer.

At the end of the film, we have a very strong feeling of waste, of lost illusions. The passage of time is also very perceptible.

To the extent that so many energies have been expended, the conclusion does effectively give you a feeling of exhaustion. You can express time a lot better with ellipses by juxtaposing the very concrete details of daily life and the signals that indicate its flowing by. So there are two speeds in the film: the very slowed down one, of works and days, and the accelerated one, of historical time. At the end of the film, for example, that's the way I solved the problem of the girl's pregnancy and the birth of the baby.

Did you anticipate that the film would be two hours and thirty-eight minutes long at the outset or were there many more elements that you had to sacrifice?

Originally, I had a very different project. There were eight hours of cinema, the whole story of the family over three different epochs that were perfectly distinct, three generations. But I decided to limit myself to the first part of the saga without knowing if the film would last two or three hours. What decided its length was the producer's directive not to exceed two and a quarter hours, since that way the film would be more saleable. Even then, I didn't really respect it! Since the film's actual duration is connected to the fact that with Liao Qingsong working on the editing, we couldn't cut any more.

Your direction is very elaborate. In the use of space that we were talking about, it recalls certain films of Mizoguchi or Welles's Magnificent Ambersons. *Do you go to the movies a lot?*

You may not believe me but I've never seen any of Mizoguchi's films or Orson Welles's *The Magnificent Ambersons*! When I'd finished *The Boys From Fengkuei (Fengkui laide ren)*, one of my assistants told me it reminded him of Ozu's films. He brought me in a cassette and one night I watched *End of Summer (Kohayagawa-ke no Aki)* and I fell alseep, I found it so boring. When I came to Europe for the first time, Marco Müller dragged me off to see *I Was Born, But... (Umarete wa Mita Keredo)*. That time I loved it and I felt my cinema had a lot to do with his! It's really good; it's really healthy that I didn't see all these films beforehand. Today I try to see as many classics as I can. But my relationship is different from what it might have been before; it's become a relationship between one director and another. Now I understand what they were saying, the goal they set themselves. That goes as much for Ozu as for Antonioni. When I saw *Blow Up* for the first time, I understood that the question he had put to himself, about what the truth actually is, shares something with my poetics. The same with Fassbinder. If you want to know what I like, I'd cite *Amarcord, Breathless, Oedipus the King* and *The Apu Trilogy* along with *Tokyo Story (Tokyo Monogatari)*. I appreciated *I Was Born, But...* straight away but I later realised the depth, the force and the irony of *Tokyo Story*, which dates from Ozu's mature period. Porno film also interested me a lot from a theoretical point of view. To ask yourself how you can shoot sex differently is an idea for a movie that excites me. I think I can say that if I were to make hard core porn, I'd do it very well!

NOTES

1   The film had its premiere in Taiwan after the Venice Festival. *A City of Sadness* was passed uncut and it is not out of the question that the Golden Lion awarded to Hou Hsaio-hsien by the jury of La Mostra contributed to this decision on the part of the censorship board. The film has since enjoyed huge public success in Taiwan.

13 WONG KAR-WAI

(1958–)

While King Hu, followed by Tsui Hark and John Woo have demonstrated all possible variations of traditional genres (swashbuckler films or gangster films) within the context of Hong Kong cinema, Wong Kar-wai has managed to directly impose a *cinema d'auteur*, as attested by his selection in the Critics' Week at Cannes in 1989 for his first film, *As Tears Go By (Wangjiao Kamen)*. His second film, *Days of Being Wild (A Fei Zhengzhuan)* (1990), a non-conformist portrait of Hong Kong influenced by Godard and Pasolini, miscast known actors and was a resounding commercial flop, barring the way to any release on French screens. It was only after that, in 1994, that I discovered *Chungking Express* at the Festival of Locarno, followed swiftly by *Ashes of Time (Dongxie Xidu)* at the Venice Festival, meeting for the first time on the lagoon a free and easy playboy in dark glasses who was as sophisticated as his cinema. The thriller and the sword film gave way successively in those two films to developments of a singular originality that confirmed Wong's taste for formal investigation. A virtuoso filmmaker, with the aid of the very talented Australian cinematographer, Christopher Doyle, he gave his shots a perfect fluidity that went with characters who are in perpetual motion. The same brio is found in *Happy Together*, a story about homosexual love, filmed in the antipodes, in Argentina, but haunted by the memory of Hong Kong. The vital boiling over of his characters masked an existential void and a difficulty in communicating. There is in Wong a disenchanted romanticism that was to flower in the elegiac film, *In the Mood For Love* (2000), his greatest success to date. If art for art's sake can become a trap that you risk getting caught in (as with the formal dead-end of *Fallen Angels* in 1996), mannerism in Wong is more often transcended in a proliferation of forms, colours and sounds that brilliantly express the rhythms and tonalities of the modern urban world.

ON THE FILMS UP TO *CHUNGKING EXPRESS (CHONGGING SENLIN)* AND *ASHES OF TIME (DONGXIE XIDU)*

VENICE, SEPTEMBER 1994

You were born in Shanghai in 1958 and at the age of five, you left for Hong Kong.

Yes, but it wasn't easy! We left in 1963, just before the Cultural Revolution. My father was the managing director of a hotel, and my mother was a housewife. I was the youngest of three children, and my mother took me with her to Hong Kong. The idea was that she would then go back to Shanghai and bring my brother and sister back. But, one month later, the Cultural Revolution broke out, the border was sealed even more tightly, and she couldn't go and get them. Everyone was frightened of going back to China and not being able to get out again.

What did you study?

After high school, I went to a polytechnic school for graphic arts since that was the only place where there was a course in photography, which really interested me as a discipline. Drawing, on the other hand, didn't interest me much. When I was very young, I remember my father was always buying books, especially Chinese literature, and I spent most of my childhood reading. Later on, the only way I could communicate with my brother and sister was by exchanging letters. In their letters they used to talk to me about French, English and Russian classics of the eighteenth and nineteenth centuries – you could still find old editions in China. To exchange ideas and impressions with them, I'd get myself the same books in Hong Kong. So, as an adolescent, I also read a lot.

Did you do much photography?

Yes, but in a non-professional way, even though I was quite good at it. In my second year at the polytechnic I dropped it to do a course in production at TVB, the Hong Kong Television station. TVB wanted to train directors and it was the first time they'd set up this kind of teaching. I was nineteen and I didn't go back to my graphic arts courses again. After that, for a year and a half, I was an assistant director in television before going freelance and writing film scripts.

What did those years of study give you?

I have to say I was not a model student. While I was at the polytechnic, I always had a camera on me and I often went off to take snaps. I also hung out in the library a lot – it had a large section on art and photography. It was a great opportunity for me to acquire different kinds of knowledge from what I'd learned in high school. My mother was mad about films. My father worked of a day, and when I came home from school at about one in the afternoon I was free and my mother would take me to the movies. I'd see two or three a day. She particularly loved westerns, the films of John Wayne, Errol Flynn, Clark Gable, but also Alain Delon! Later, at the graphic arts school, I discovered another cinema, the films of Bertolucci, Godard, Bresson, and the Japanese masters like Ozu and Kurosawa.

When you started writing scripts, did you already think you'd make films?

I think I've always had the feeling I'd become a filmmaker one day. Though the two activities seemed to me then, and still seem to me, to be totally different. When I write a script, I tend not to be specific about anything in the visual realm; I don't think people would understand. For me, words can't express a vision. So I stick to dialogue and the description of certain situations and actions. I often get scripts from young writers, full of visual directions. I always tell them it's pointless, that the pace and the images belong to the director.

How many scripts have you written?

About fifty, even if my name is only listed in the credits of about ten films. The rest was brainstorming. In Hong Kong, at the time, six or seven young scriptwriters would be brought together in one room and they'd chat away for days on end, throwing ideas around. And the eldest one would write the script… That's how I worked as a scriptwriter for seven years. There was a very experienced scriptwriter in there, too, Wong Ping-yan, who went by his English name, Barry Wong, and he was in a way my mentor. We worked in the same company, and, for me, he was responsible for 70 per cent of the important films made in Hong Kong in that period. Even though Barry was very fast at writing scripts, he was short of time and passed on a certain number to me. It's his name that was listed in the credits, but we shared the money. Our company was called

'Always Good' but it also subcontracted for big studios like Golden Harvest or Cinema City.

What kind of scripts did you write?

All kinds – comedies, action films, kung fu, even porno. In the beginning, I didn't see the directors I was writing for because I was very shy. I'd meet them, offer ideas, and when they agreed, I'd go home and write on my own. I was very slow and I remember that once I took a year to finish a script, which drove everyone mad. Later, when I had more confidence in myself, I'd have a meeting with the director every day and I'd write every scene with him.

Out of the ten films whose scripts are credited to you, what are the ones you like best?

They were all directed by different filmmakers. I particularly like *Final Victory* by Patrick Tam, about failed gangsters from very humble backgrounds. The hero has an affair with his big brother's wife and mistress. I think that Patrick, who isn't making films at this moment, was an important film director at that point, the most talented of Hong Kong's 'new wave'. He introduced me to the films of Rohmer, Antonioni and Godard. We became very close friends and later on I asked him to work on the editing of my second film, *Days of Being Wild*, as well as on *Ashes of Time*. We know each other backwards!

Did you become a filmmaker because you weren't happy with what people did with your scripts?

I don't think so. I have no desire for power and I wasn't jealous of the filmmakers I was writing for. I didn't have any particular reason to complain, either. On the other hand, I remember certain visits to a set where I felt like yelling 'Action!' because my ideas on the angles of shots were different and I wanted something different from what I was seeing. So much so that the day someone asked me if I was ready to direct, I said yes.

How did that happen?

Alan Tang, a famous actor from the 1960s with close to 200 roles to his credit, had become a producer. I'd worked with him on two scripts. He liked giving young directors their chance. After numerous discussions we'd had together, he decided, with all his experience as an actor, that my ideas about characters and plots were very convincing. For him, I could become a good filmmaker. That's how he gave me my break.

That was As Tears Go By *in 1988.*

The idea was that this first film would be part of a trilogy. The first part has – still – not been made. The third part is *Last Victory*, by Patrick Tam, when the gangster has reached thirty and he realises he hasn't made it. In *As Tears Go By*, the second part, he's twenty-something. In the first part, which was going to be called *Hero for A Day*, he'll be an teenager.

Your film is inspired by Mean Streets. *How do you see the connection between Scorsese and Hong Kong society?*

I think that the Italians have many points in common with the Chinese: their values, their sense of friendship, their Mafia, their pasta, their mothers. When I saw *Mean Streets* for the first time, it was a real shock because I had the impression that the story could just as well have happened in Hong Kong. In fact, I only borrowed the character played by Robert de Niro. The others stem from my own experience. When I was a scriptwriter, I had a close friend who was a stuntman on films and had been a bit of a gangster. We'd spend whole nights, till five in the morning, in the sleaziest bars in Hong Kong. I gleaned a whole host of details from that, which you find in *As Tears Go By*. We knew someone who didn't know a word of English, but who had a British girlfriend, a waitress in a bar: she kept running away from him and then coming back. They were an odd couple who didn't communicate at all. That inspired me with one of the characters in the film. So I spent three or four years of my youth drinking, fighting, driving fast cars.

How do you work with your head cameraman?

I've had a total of two cinematographers for my four films. Law Wai-keung, who shot *As Tears Go By*, had only done two films before. He also worked with the second crew on *Days of Being Wild* and *Ashes of Time*, and he did the lighting on the first part of *Chungking Express*. The other cinematographer is Christopher Doyle. Law Wai-keung is very energetic, the best at the hand-held camera. He knows everything and we communicate really well together. His only weak point is that he lacks finesse when it comes to really sensitive lighting. Today, he's become a director, but I think he can achieve real status as an artist. As for Doyle, he's a master of light and we get on well: even if we don't speak the same language, we have the same references, painting and film. He has a great aesthetic sense, but he's less technical in wielding the camera. He started out as a sailor. Then he went in for photography. That's what gave him the artistic qualities that appealed to Hu Hsiao-hsien and Edward Yang, who he worked with in Taiwan. I needed someone like him for *Ashes of Time*.

What's amazing is that there is no difference in the photography of Chungking Express *despite the use of two different cinematographers.*

I was the one who controlled the continuity and I told them we were going to work like in a jam session. Neither of them knew the story. I got hold of Doyle in Japan where he was working on post-production for another film. Three days later, he joined me in Hong Kong and finished the film in two weeks. We filmed like madmen. I told him that this time, we wouldn't have to set up so many lights (apart from in the apartment) as it would be filmed like a road movie, with no fixed point. We didn't have time to set up a tripod or use a dolly: I wanted it to be shot like a documentary, camera in hand. And Doyle took up the challenge, photographing very fast, while coming up with a high-quality image. But for *Ashes of Time* he took forever to polish the shots. Every day he'd say to me: 'It's death in Yuling,' after the name of the place in the north of China where we were filming!

Was it the success of As Tears Go By *that allowed you to have all those famous actors on* Days of Being Wild?

The film didn't go over so well in Hong Kong, but it was a triumph in Korea and Taiwan. Still, it got nine nominations for the Hong Kong 'Oscars', which is unusual for a first film. My producer then offered to let me make the second film with the actors I wanted. I'd made *As Tears Go By* at twenty-nine and I was thirty-one when I made *Days of Being Wild*. Hitting your thirties is major, you feel like you're getting old! In the second film I wanted to evoke things I was afraid I'd forget later on. When I was a child, not long after I arrived in Hong Kong, I felt very alone, because I didn't speak Cantonese. We, my mother and I, were in this little apartment of a day and we'd listen to the radio, and I couldn't understand a thing. The only theme I can still remember is for the BBC news bulletin. One evening, my parents went out dancing and I woke up in the middle of the night and I was frightened. I turned on the radio and I listened to the last BBC bulletin and felt reassured. This is the era I evoke in *Days of Being Wild*, which starts in 1960 and ends in 1966. I really love the story, but it took me two years to structure it. I show two families across the first post-war generation. One is Cantonese and originally from Hong Kong, the other, Leslie Cheung's family, comes from Shanghai. They're divided by language but, in the second part, they wind up getting to know one another. Unfortunately, I never filmed the second half of the script: the film came out at Christmas time and there were enormous expectations because of the stars in it. The public was convinced they were about to see another *As Tears Go By*, with lots of action. Well, now, *Days of Being Wild* had practically no action or plot, to speak of. It was a total failure. In Korea, viewers even threw stuff at the screen. The producer then refused to finance the second part. The aesthetics of the two films were very different. The first one had fast editing and lots of music. The second had a rather slow pace that corresponded to my idea of the 1960s. I tried to divide the film into four movements. The first was very Bressonian, with lots of close-ups. The second had the look of a B-grade film with very complicated camera movements and sequence shots. The third was filmed with depth of field. The fourth was more like the second with quite a bit of mobility. The story leaped from one character to another, which made the division into several movements more readable.

Have you evolved in the way you direct actors?

Since I'm constantly changing my scripts, I don't give them to my actors to read and I don't hold rehearsals. I've always got an overall idea of the scene and I come on the set three or four hours before filming starts. That's when I work out where everything is and the camera movements. Then I tell my actors the bits of dialogue they have to say. Of course, I've already gone over their characters a lot with them. What matters most to me is to know – and to communicate to them – the reasons for their moves and actions: why is he sitting over there, why does he take a cigarette, why is she sleeping there, why is she crying so hard? When you know a character in depth, the rest goes without saying; you can easily understand their motivations. At the start of the shoot, I take lots of shots, while my actors and I find a common rhythm. Then I'm much more economical with the number of shots.

For Ashes of Time, *you were inspired by the hero of a contemporary martial arts novel,* The Eagle Shooting, *by Jin Yong.*

Firstly, I was drawn to the two characters, Dongxie and Xidu, the first meaning 'East eccentric' and the second, 'West bad'. In the early 1980s, martial arts films became very popular again and a producer suggested I make one. I agreed since it's a genre I've always loved. I'd never made costume dramas and that attracted me. So I then took what I wanted very freely from the original novel, which is incredibly long. The two characters that appealed to me in it are sixty years old. I had to make up a past for them. Stories of chivalry – *wu xia* in Chinese – belong to Chinese literature, like *Romance of the Three Kingdoms* by Luo Guanzhong, a classic. But the contemporary tales of Jin Yong, who's very prolific – he's written a dozen of them- in fact belong to pulp fiction. They're extremely popular and everyone had it in for me! They didn't know I was going to do something different. My approach was different as far as the films I saw went.

Your consultant on the fighting, Sammo Hung, collaborated with King Hu on The Fate of Lee Khan (Yongchunge Zhi Fengbo) *(1973) and* The Valiant Ones (Zhong Lie Tu) *(1976). Have you seen the films of that great filmmaker?*

I discovered them when I was a child, but I didn't really follow them because of their philosophical content and their bearing on Zen Buddhism. Sammo Hung, apart from his skill in regulating the fights, is also the best director of action sequences that we've had in Hong Kong for twenty years. He was trained at the Peking Opera. He's the one who choreographs that kind of scene.

You tend to stylise your sequences, to elide, to the point where the action properly so-called becomes secondary in the general economy of the film.

The traditional martial arts film aims to stimulate the viewer's senses. I wanted it to be more a means of expressing the characters' emotions. When Brigitte Lin, for instance, plays with the sword, it's a dance. When I film the blind warrior, Tony Chiu-wai, in slow motion, it's to suggest his world-weariness, symbolised by the weight of his sword. Jacky Cheung is filmed at ten images a second to suggest that he's emerging, he's getting up, in contrast to Tony Leung Chiu-wai, who's heading for death. Certain sequences were shot just like that, others like the ones with Jacky Cheung, were essentially processed in the laboratory.

Tsui Hark put the tradition of martial arts back up on the screen, where they were so beautifully demonstrated before by King Hu's extraordinary ballets in the air, with actors hanging from wires. But so many people imitated him that the style has become sterile, it's reached a dead-end. When I decided to make *Ashes of Time,* I was determined not to mine that vein, which I felt had been exhausted. Except for Brigitte Lin, whose actions are exaggerated, I wanted the actors to fight on the ground, for their duels to give the impression they were real, not artifice.

The structure of the scripts, with their labyrinthine flashbacks and their commentary 'off', seems to suggest American film noir more than historical films!

In the days when I was writing scripts for other people, I was always asked for simple, direct stories, and that's what I came up with. My first film, *As Tears Go By*, was part of that trend. When I finished it, I read Gabriel Garcia Marquez's book, *Chronicle of a Death Foretold* and I was very impressed by his way of telling a story. I started reading lots of Latin American novelists and the one who most influenced me was Manuel Puig, the author of *Kiss of the Spider Woman,* with its tale chopped up into a series of fragments that don't obey chronological order. In the end, the emotions only reach us even more strongly in this form. This technique influenced *Days of Being Wild* and *Ashes of Time*.

The theme of betrayal dominates Ashes of Time.

For me, it's more the theme of rejection, of exclusion. That's what Leslie Cheung says in the narration, when he talks about himself as an orphan. So as not to be rejected, he rejects others first. Brigitte Lin, having been rejected by Tony Leung Kar-fai, creates an elder brother for herself. Betrayal is merely a consequence. Tony Leung Chiu-wai plays the role of a man who's rejected by his wife, who's cheated on him with his best friend. Since he still loves her, the only way out for him is self-destruction. Tony Leung Kar-fai's character loves Maggie Cheung, while she herself is in love with Leslie Cheung. Since he doesn't want to be rejected, he never admits his feelings and he compensates by making himself loved by others just to see how it feels. It's a way of living with the rejection he's a victim of that's different from Tony Leung Chiu-wai's way. There are two characters that are distinct: Jacky Cheung and Charlie Young. The former is afraid of being rejected. As for Charlie, she's sure someone will come along and help her, so she just waits patiently. Both of them will have a happy fate in the end and will influence Leslie Cheung in his decision to come out of the wilderness, in the film's final images.

I realise while I'm talking that it's a thread that runs through all my films, this idea of rejection. All the characters in *Days of Being Wild* have that feeling. I suppose there's an evolution in *Chungking Express* since, in the end, Tony Leung Chiu-wai and the girl aren't afraid of being rejected by the other.

How did you find the different locations for the action in Ashes of Time?

Due to budget constraints, the only place we could film was China. I combed the country looking for landscapes close to the ones in the book that inspired my film. After fruitless trips north and south, someone showed me a photo of the place Leslie Cheung retired to. I sent my artistic director, William Chang, to scout around and he came back telling me it was probably the right set for me.

How did you choose the actors?

I'd already worked with all the actors except Brigitte Lin and Tony Leung Kar-fai. I like to really know the people I'm going to direct. For me, the greatest challenge posed by the film was Brigitte, because you're used to seeing her in martial arts films, in drag. She really intrigued me and I thought she could play a schizophrenic personality. As for Tony Leung Kar-fai, he's on the small side. Now, our imagination prompts us to see these warriors of ancient times as tall and extremely virile. Tony Leung somehow manages to suggest that.

Is the period the action is set in imaginary, or are you referring to a specific period in Chinese history?

The original novel is set in the Song Dynasty, eight centuries ago. Jin Yong's talent is to create legendary fictions and to know how to integrate them into official history. When I approached the material, I decided I wouldn't do research like King Hu to achieve a historically authentic picture. My sole criterion was not to include elements from after the period in which the action occurs, but the objects, clothes and architectural features that preceded the Song period could be used. The other thing I didn't want was speech that was full of slang and too contemporary in the dialogue, but without consciously looking for a stylised old-fashioned language.

Why did you stop work on Ashes of Time *to make* Chungking Express?

We had a two-month break waiting for equipment to redo the sound: it had been recorded in the desert and it was really bad. Since I had nothing to do, I decided to make *Chungking Express,* just following my instinct.

The two policemen in Chungking Express, *with their parallel destinies, echo the characters of Ouyang and Huang in* Ashes of Time. *They are presented as though in a mirror, as two sides of the same coin: each of them is abandoned by his girlfriend.*

I chose two cops for *Chungking Express,* but I wanted the first one not to be in uniform. Brigitte Lin, with her frigid look and her blond wig, is also, in my view, in a sort of uniform. At first, I wanted to make a film in two parts. One would take place on Hong Kong Island, the other in Kowloon. The action of one would unfold in the daytime, the other, at night. And despite the differences, it would be the same story. After the more serious, more laboured treatment of *Ashes of Time,* I wanted to do a lighter contemporary film, but one where the characters would face the same problems.

What made you particularly interested in the area of Hong Kong around Chungking House?

It's a very famous building in Hong Kong. The statistics tell us that about 5,000 tourists visit it every day. With its 200 hostels, it's a mixture of very different cultures. Even for the people who live around it, it's a legendary spot where relationships between people are very complex. It's always fascinated and intrigued me. It's also a permanent worry for the Hong Kong police, with all the illicit trafficking that goes on there. The place is so overcrowded, so hyperactive, it's a great metaphor for the town itself.

Brigitte Lin and Tony Leung Chiu-wai also act in Ashes of Time. *Were you interested in the idea of exploring their personalities further?*

I was always fascinated by the other actress, Wang – the waitress in the second part of the film. In the scene where she bumps into Brigitte Lin, for me, it's the same woman with a gap of ten years. Tony Leung was perfect for the role as he really looks like a policeman.

In all your films, there is a very elliptical way of narrating, a manner of leaping rapidly from one shot to another.

That's the influence of Godard and Bresson, maybe. I decided to make *Chungking Express* in a very short time. For me, it was like a road movie. I'd thought up two short stories a few years back, but I didn't manage to turn them into a film. So then I got the idea of putting them together in a single script. When I started filming, I still hadn't completely finished writing it. I filmed in chronological order. The first part takes place at night. I wrote the sequel to the story in the daytime! Thanks to a brief interruption for the New Year festivities, I had a bit more time to finish the rest of the script.

Do the numbers you attribute to the two policemen to identify them have any particular significance?

I'm pretty lazy when it comes to finding names for my characters, so I thought of using figures, which gave it a certain flavour. After all, Kafka called all his heroes K! Whenever I read the nineteenth-century Russian novelists, I have such trouble finding myself among all those names and diminutives that I'm happy to go back to the simplicity of Kafka's names!

What's your relationship to the fifth generation Chinese filmmakers and to those of the new wave from Taiwan?

The filmmakers of popular China come from a long tradition, but one that's also very much closed to the outside world. In Hong Kong, there's a lot more mixing and we're influenced by the West. Since 1945, a number of mainland Chinese have become expats in Hong Kong. They used to speak Mandarin, not Cantonese, and they took part in the development of our industry, often dealing with the past in their films rather than the realities of the present. That was also the case in Taiwan. But for the last fifteen years, new filmmakers have become interested in the problems of today. They've broken with the propaganda films that were made by the bucketload in the 1950s and 1960s, like those of the continent, of course, even if their aims were opposed. In Hong Kong, we're more attuned to entertainment, and I imagine this will be the main concern of the three Chinese cinemas that will eventually come together as one!

From a cinematographic point of view, which Chinese films, whatever their origin, have most marked you in the last ten years?

Hou Hsiao-hsien's *A City of Sadness*.

14 AKI KAURISMÄKI

(1957–)

How to settle on a time for an interview with Aki Kaurismäki is an insoluble problem. Do you have to brave the wee hours when he's still nursing a hangover, or the end of the day when this legendary big drinker won't really have his wits about him anymore? Yet experience has shown that he can handle being habitually drunk. It gives him a cheerful lightness, a peculiar humour, chilled or on the rocks, you might say. At least that is what Noël Herpe and I felt on a hotel balcony in Cannes the day after the warm welcome *Drifting Clouds (Kauas pilvet karkaävat)* received in competition. The beauty of Kaurismäki's films is that they're devoted to the underprivileged, to the outcasts of society, without there being the least trace of miserabilism about them. Similarly, paradoxically, the muted emotion of each shot, like the acting, is subtly distanced. Through the play of colours, the stylised realism of the direction, he brings poetry into the quotidian.

Like the filmmakers of the new wave, Kaurismäki testifies to an ironic affection for American popular culture and a tender passion for the early cinema, as attested by the use of black and white in *Juha*, which is filmed like a silent movie or in *La Vie de bohème*, which aims at bringing the spirit of Mürger into the twentieth century. Like the climate of his country, it's an apparently cold world that Kaurismäki offers us, empty spaces, characters that seem frozen, feelings we would describe as glacial. But this unusual manner of capturing bodies and faces paradoxically restores emotions to us in all their freshness with a brutal acuity we weren't expecting.

ON *DRIFTING CLOUDS*

CANNES, MAY 1996

What is the literal translation of the Finnish title, Kauas Pilvet Karkaävat?

'Far Away the Clouds Escape.' The important, the symbolic, word is 'escape' – they're fleeing, running away. We managed to render the original in French, but English is such a poor language that we couldn't come up with anything better than *Drifting Clouds!* The film kicked off when we hit on the title. I wrote the script so that it'd end on that phrase. It's very personal. My characters and I, we're escaping far away with the clouds. But we don't know when or where.

After a very bleak, uncompromising, depiction of unemployment and dereliction, you seem to have felt the need to end on a note of optimism, almost à la Capra.

For me, the world we live in is hopeless and will come to an end in 2021. I didn't want to deliver a personal moral in the last shot. I didn't need to do propaganda for pessimism; we're surrounded by it everywhere we turn. I told myself that if I was going to deal with unemployment, I could allow myself to stick on a sort of Capra ending since, in reality, it'd more likely be a double suicide. In relation to the situation in Finland, this film is a fairytale since unemployment in our country has reached 26 per cent (officially 20 per cent). It's the worst rate in Europe, along with Spain. That's getting close to the Depression of the 1930s in the United States. The economy has spiralled out of control, banks have gone bankrupt, since the people who govern us are such amateurs they don't know how to control anything. There was too much money, it was like an upward spiral, then everything collapsed.

What's your relationship to neo-realism and to films like The Bicycle Thief (Ladri di biciclette)?

Actually, I wanted to do neo-realism in colour, with humour to cap it off since De Sica's style is pretty humourless. I also added a bit of Ozu in the manner of telling the story. After the event, I also saw the influence of Douglas Sirk and of Edward Hopper. It's the idealism of Technicolor films starring Jane Wyman and Rock Hudson that you see in *Drifting Clouds*. Thirty per cent Ozu, 30 per cent De Sica, 15 per cent Sirk, 20 per cent Hopper, 10 per cent Capra. That makes 105 per cent! Where am I in all that? I'm not a filmmaker; I'm a bloody cocktail shaker!

The 'Honolulu Winter' cocktail in your film is blue like the colour of the shirt, like the tablecloth, like the walls of the restaurant.

It's the Blue Hawaii of Elvis Presley's film! I don't decide on the choice of colours in advance. If I began to analyse it, it would take me hours. From one day to the next, I decide to have everything repainted blue, for example, according to my inspiration, and I get my actress to wear the shirts she normally wears and I choose the one that goes with the set. I didn't want to make a blue film like *I Hired a Contract Killer*, where it was deliberate. Today, you tell me that that's also the colour of this film. Maybe it's me who's 'blue' – like Billie Holiday!

Popular songs are important in this film as in all your previous films.

For me, in a film, the most important thing is the image. After that comes the dialogue, the sound effects and the music. But I'm particularly attentive to the choice of music because it can completely transform a scene. When I get to the mixing, I fill a plastic bag full of CDs and I do a heap of tests. I've always been hugely interested in music. After all, I've made seven or eight rock videos, a documentary on the group the Leningrad Cowboys and two feature films with them. But I stopped, as I was getting too old for those rhythms! With *Leningrad Cowboys Meet Moses,* I made a mistake: I thought everyone had read the Bible. As that is not the case, the film was incomprehensible.

Kati Outinen has acted in a number of your films. Did you write the character for her?

At the start, the main character was supposed to be played by another of my favourite actors, Matti Pellonpää, but he died two months before the shoot. So I then had to make Kati Outinen, who was supposed to play a housewife, the central protagonist and change the script. Matti and Kati are the actors I respect the most; I've worked with them for over fifteen years and we've always worked out their characters together. That's why no one could have put on Matti's clothes and played the role written for him. I had to switch around the main characters. Kati Outinen is very dear to me. No one, you know, has a perfectly symmetrical face and hers is particularly asymmetrical! She's also a very intelligent actress who knows how to create an inner life behind an impassive face. She's the opposite of those actors whose impassiveness hides emptiness. Right now, Kati is playing *West Side Story* on stage. She's been doing theatre for ten years now.

Do you talk about the role with your actors before shooting starts?

Not at all. My secret is to slip something into their ear before filming a shot, so as to create confusion in their minds. Then they forget to act! I find that nicer than Bresson's method since it leaves them their freedom. In general, I don't do more than two takes. The first one corresponds to the rehearsal and that's the one I most often keep. The second one is for safety's sake. It costs too much to do lots of takes. Working this way, I was able to shoot the film in twenty-six days.

Like Ozu, whom you mention, you don't move your camera most of the time. Sometimes, though, there is a camera movement when, for example, Lauri comes back with flowers or when Ilona's old boss offers her money for the restaurant. What do these choices correspond to?

To start with, I wanted to have more camera movements, but I was too lazy and too busy elsewhere to set them up! In my first film, *Crime and Punishment (Rikos ja rangaistus)*, the camera moved all the time, but I was twenty-six years old, I was young and full of beans. With time, I no longer see the reason for doing it; I can't manage to convince myself that it's valid. I must say it's a very old camera that I bought off Ingmar Bergman when he gave up making films. He shot *Fanny and Alexander* with it and a whole lot of other films. Myself, I've used it for over thirty films, my own and those I've produced. So it's an ancient machine. Like me, it's very tired and doesn't want to move. So, if I see no particular reason to shift it – and it's very heavy! – I content myself with fixed shots. After all, that's all Ozu did. In the films he made when he was young, he moved his camera, but in his last films, he only did for a single shot, in *Tokyo Story*, and it was totally pointless, to boot. What's more, during fixed shots, I can sit down on a chair, whereas in Japan the director is flat on the ground! You sometimes get that with Hitchcock – the camera moves in on the eyes of a character to get the viewer to see that he's in the process of thinking. Which seems redundant to me.

You prefer Ozu to Hitchcock.

Before making films, I read Hitchcock's interviews with Truffaut. Truffaut asked him if there was a subject he wouldn't dare touch, and Hitchcock replied that there was and it was *Crime and Punishment*, the book was too complicated. I was young and I told myself that I'd prove the old man wrong. And so I filmed *Crime and Punishment*, and I realised Hitchcock was right: it really is too complicated!

What interests you are the psychological and emotional effects unemployment has on people, and not the economic side of the problem.

It's too late as far as I can see to pit the nasty capitalist against the brave proletarian. Today, the enemy is invisible; technology has taken over. If you choose a company like Nestlé and you go to the parent company, in Zurich or somewhere, and you climb up to the top floor of the building and open the door of the biggest office, you find no one. In our day, the bosses are mere cogs in the wheel, semi-robots, who don't know where they're going or why. I told myself, too, that unemployment hadn't been dealt with enough by European filmmakers and that that was shameful. I needed to talk about the problem, otherwise I couldn't have gone on facing myself in the mirror.

When the female boss hits the cook, you don't show the scene, it takes place out of shot.

It would have taken too long to film; we'd have had to do several takes! More seriously, I wanted to say to you that I'm too old to show a weapon in a film, even as the object of a joke. I'm very hostile to violence in cinema. As 95 per cent of directors devote themselves to violence and sex, surely you can have a minority who don't make that the centre of their concerns.

Why did you film La Vie de bohème *in black and white?*

Out of a concern for realism. I wanted to make a 'historical' film in contemporary Paris. If I'd shot it in colour, it would look like a French film, which I didn't want. To get to the real Paris, I had to go to the suburbs, to Ivry and Malakoff. The Paris of my childhood has disappeared and even the one I knew on my honeymoon in 1982. Everything has changed.

We really like Take Care of Your Scarf, Tatiana *(Pida huivista kinnii, Tatjana).*

Like all my films, it's a sort of documentary about the cultural changes in our society. I only had a vague idea for the film and no script. It was totally improvised yet we actually managed to pull off a feature film. The film only lasts fifty-nine minutes, but don't tell anyone! The specification sheet says sixty-six minutes so as to meet administrative requirements.

You are very laconic in your films and in your interviews. Are you also laconic in life?

That's the only style I have. If I lose it, I'll have nothing left! I don't have much energy left and I have to pace myself so as not to lose it. I think that there are in the world too many sounds, too many images, too much movement, too many words.

One thinks in any case of silent movies, watching your films.

For years now I've been meaning to make a film without words, with just images and music. In the 1970s, I was a real cinephile. I knew three months in advance what I was going to see and I was a member of every cine club in Helsinki. I noted everything in my diary and I saw six films a day. I had a sports car and I'd go off to the country to see a particular film. That had a counter-effect. Today, I go to the movies once a year. I decided to become a film director while I was at a double bill of Robert Flaherty's *Nanook of the North* and *Moana: A Romance of the Golden Age* in a small-town cine club. I realised then that the cinema was not only entertainment, but also an art. At the time I'd run away from the army and, to earn my living, I'd taken a job as a postman for three months. After that I worked in the building trade. But the Post Office was nice because I only worked in the morning and in the afternoon I could go to the movies. One day, a friend gave me a book to read, Murger's *La Vie de bohème*. Since then I must have read it fifty times. I remember telling my friends that I was going to make a film of it. They all laughed and pointed out that I was only a postman, that I didn't have a cent to my name and that I was not a director. I told them they were right, but that I'd do it anyway. Which happened fifteen years later, after I made a few other films first to get into training.

You made two shorts at the beginning of the 1990s, Those Were the Days *and* These Boots.

Actually, they're rock videos five to six minutes long made with the Leningrad Cowboys. I call them shorts because then people take them seriously and show them at festivals. I use ideas that aren't enough for my fiction films but that I can't get out of my head and that I want to get rid of. On the other hand, I've never made an ad.

You have always used the cinematographer, Timo Salminen. How does your collaboration work?

We know each other so well that we don't even have to talk. We just whistle. Sometimes we add a lamp. For cameras, I use a 32 most of the time; for close-ups and close shots, a 40. Very exceptionally, when a room is tiny, I use a 24, but that happens once a shoot. In Finland, we don't have a studio, so I have to somehow build myself one every time, in real places. It's easy, since there are so many bankruptcies that you find empty spaces everywhere. That's how *Drifting Clouds* was filmed. The sets are non-temporary, but we've totally reorganised them, even rebuilt them.

You've just received the Ecumenical Prize at Cannes. That's pretty ironic, don't you think?

I'm used to it. I remember coming back from a festival once and finding myself in bed totally plastered. The phone rings. I'd received the Catholic Prize. Fifteen minutes later, second ring. It was the Protestant churches' one! It doesn't surprise me. They know that, deep down inside, I'm religious. I believe in forgiveness and in Saint Peter. God died a long time ago and Jesus was a drug addict. The only one living in the sky now is Saint Peter and he has the keys. That's the only thing that counts.

15 ABBAS KIAROSTAMI

(1940–)

Abbas Kiarostami had already been making films for fifteen years – his first feature-length film, *The Traveller,* dates from 1974 – when the West discovered him at the Locarno Festival with *Where Is The Friend's Home? (Khane-ye doust kodjast?)*, which was sneaked into the previous year's Festival des Trois Continents at Nantes. Reviewing the Locarno competition for *Le Monde*, I was able to salute the emergence of a great new filmmaker on the front page. With his inevitable dark glasses, Kiarostami was, in those days, extremely reserved, didn't give much away, was visibly on his guard, coming from Iran as he did and finding himself in the West, a part of the world that was hostile to his home country. In 1990, the following year, I found myself once more at Locarno, but this time as a member, alongside him, of a jury presided over by Nanni Moretti. I admired Kiarostami's rigour and his exactingness in discussing the films we were there to judge and, over the course of more relaxed conversations, he ended up accepting the idea of an interview in principle, and it turned out to be the first of a long series we did together. Until then Iranian cinema had been reduced, in the West, to a single name: Dariush Mehrjui *(The Cow, The Cycle)* and to a man in exile in Germany, Sohrab Shahid Saless. Very quickly Kiarostami became the leader of a prodigiously productive generation, with filmmakers like Mohsen Makhmalbaf, Bahram Beizai, Amir Naderi and Jafar Panahi. *Where is the Friend's Home?* turned out to be the first part in an unplanned trilogy when an earthquake in the region where the shoot had taken place drove Kiarostami to go back over the area looking for the protagonists. This produced *Life, and Nothing More (Zendegi va digar hich)*. He then performed a mise en abyme, providing a meditation on the relationship between reality and the way it is staged, with *Through The Olive Trees (Ziredarakhatan zeyton)*, in which he evokes the filming of the preceding film. *Close-Up* (1989) was already a dizzying investigation of truth and lies, cinema and the reality effect, an investigation that crops up again at the conclusion of *The Taste of Cherry (Ta'm-e gilass)*, which won the Palme d'Or at Cannes in 1997. The whole complexity of the cinema of Kiarostami, who is also a wonderful photographer, stems from this dialectic between respect for reality inherited from the great Italian neo-realist cinema of the post-war period and a sophisticated meditation on the meaning of the film image. His interest in new technologies and minimalist sets *(10 on Ten,* 2002) make him one of the most stimulating artists working today.

ON HIS FILMS UP TO *CLOSE-UP*

LOCARNO, AUGUST 1990

You started out studying art. What was your training and, more generally, what is your background?

I did painting, drawing and made advertising shorts as well as animated credits for features. Such credits were common in the 1960s, following the work of Saul Bass. My father was a house painter and I don't recall there being a trace of any cultural life in my family. I don't see any particular sign in my background that might have driven me towards art or cinema. When I was a child, my friends and I would go as a group to the theatre, but, there, too, my friends of those days have become doctors, scientists and so on, so there's no particular reason why I turned into a film director. The only thing I remember is that when I was young I was very strongly marked by the Italian neo-realist films.

There must be a reason, though, why you moved into the world of cinema…

It came from my first jobs: first as a graphic artist, then working in advertising and finally as an illustrator of children's books. Then someone suggested I make a film for children, since I knew their world and the world of images. The first short I made was the story of a boy who's just bought some bread and finds the door to his house barred by a dog he's frightened of. He waits for help but it doesn't come, so he has his first experience of danger as he walks past the dog. But nothing happens. Once he's inside the house, the dog wants to go in, too, but his little sister shuts the door on him. The dog then decides to lie down in front of the door, with his head on his paws, and, when he does that, he sees another boy pop up at the end of the lane… I recall that it was with this debut film that I had my first talk with a head cameraman, since I wanted to film the boy and the dog in a single shot. As that was hard to get, he suggested using inserts. I preferred to wait. After forty days, we managed to get everything into one shot and to do it in such a way that the dog's looking exactly where I wanted him to look. Now I know that my director of photography could also have been right, since cinema is also the art of editing. But I still believe in the long shot and that's the direction I've always gone.

Who financed forty days of a shoot just to get a single shot?

The Institute for the Intellectual Development of Children and Young Adults. I was their employee and they understood my demands. It was a twelve-minute film, which was bought by Channel Seven, to cap it off. I made it in 1969.

How do you think your training in drawing prepared you for directing?

I think drawing is the beginning of all the arts. One of the reasons why is that, when you produce a graphic work – a poster, an ad – you're working within strict limits. Someone has paid you, has given you a commission, and you know that all the data, all the information you've received, you have to fill a frame with it to get a message across. So you have to do your best. This apprenticeship in limits taught me to think and really groomed me for work in film. I think that the problems I've had to face, like the constraints, have helped me to thrive.

Have you worked a lot as a poster artist?

Yes. From 1960 to 1975, I drew a lot of posters, but only for Iranian films. I still do sometimes these days but especially for my own films.

Could you tell us a bit about this Institute for the Intellectual Development of Children and Young Adults?

It's an institute essentially devoted to children that was founded in 1965. It started out by setting up libraries for children throughout the country, then it extended its activities by creating painting workshops and theatre schools. Finally they got into publishing children's books and producing films for children, starting with shorts. Before the revolution, there were six or seven of us making children's films, but since then, my colleagues have left for Western Europe or America, and I've stayed here on my own. Of course, new people have arrived but nothing really serious has happened. For my part, I've made fourteen short features for children.

What strikes you, though, when you see Where is the Friend's Home? (Khane-ye doust kodjast?), *which is produced by the Institute, is that the film addresses a much wider public than an audience of children.*

I agree with you. I'm aware that most films made for children are comedies or animated films. In my country, we try to make films *about* children rather than just *for* children, which seems to me to be more serious, more interesting and more useful. This in fact allows you to create increased understanding between adults, particularly parents, and children. It's in that frame of mind that I made *Where is the Friend's Home?* to avoid misunderstandings between those two worlds. But when I think back to the film, I can see that it doesn't just deal with those particular misunderstandings, but also misunderstandings with old people and misunderstandings within the same person.

Do you do test screenings with children to see their reactions, given that it's even harder to gauge the feelings of a young audience?

Yes, we have done, but it doesn't always provide decent results. When children see a film together, they prefer adventure films, films that get them excited. When they arrived in school groups to take part in the screening of *Where is the Friend's Home?* no one liked the film! But when they returned separately to watch it in a movie theatre with their family, they loved it and it became a talking point. I remember once, in the middle of a screening of the film, a man of about fifty, who looked like an intellectual, walked out and shouted at the people queuing up outside that it was a lousy film and they shouldn't see it, while his wife tried to calm him down. At the same time, a little four-year-old girl had seen it three times and understood it very well. Which proves that the classification of the audience according to age brackets may be legitimate but it doesn't take account of the fact that the film communicates differently with each individual. You can't know in advance what kind of viewers are going to like the film or not. You can't make something that will communicate perfectly with everyone. The way a film is viewed is also the product of a synthesis: the film itself and the imagination of the filmgoer. Often I don't quite recognise the film I've made in the public's reactions, even when they're positive.

Are your short films all a similar length?

No. They go from twelve minutes to forty-five minutes. There are also medium-length features of over an hour.

Do you have collaborators working on your scripts?

Up till now I've always written on my own.

Of all your shorts, which ones do you particularly like?

One of them deals with brushing your teeth, since most of the films are connected to my personal experience. One night my young son asked me to give him permission not to brush his teeth just that once and to go straight to bed. I wondered why that was a problem for me, for, after all, it was really his problem! So I decided to make the film to explain to him why he had to clean his teeth. The film's forty-five minutes long and when it was shown on television, toothpaste sales went up considerably. Children were so influenced by it that they wanted to brush their teeth and it was never shown again because lots of parents rang the station to complain that they were getting really worried! So, although it deals with something very simple, it's one of my favourite films. In general I don't like any of my films as a whole, there are only certain parts that I'm happy with.

One of them has a strange title: Two Solutions for One Problem (Dah Rah-e Hal Baray-e Yek Masaleh).

There again the starting point was a problem one of my children came across going to school. A boy borrows a book from his friend and when the boy gives it back the next day, a page has been torn out. The owner of the book then decides to tear out a page of his friend's book and his friend responds by breaking the pen in his penholder, and on it goes. It's a spiral of revenge till one of them punches the other one in the face. That's the first solution to the problem. In the second part, the boy who's borrowed the book shows the other one what's happened and together they look for some glue to put the torn page back in place. I wanted children to see the choice they could make. Don't judge this very simple film by your criteria. In the country I live in, in the part of the world it finds itself in, there's a whole education to be gone through.

I made another film, for instance, about traffic circulation, *Orderly or Disorderly (Be tartib ya bedun-e tartib),* to explain to people why you should be careful when the lights change from red to green and not overtake and rush to be first. So I filmed two shots of a tunnel with cars getting ready to go through it and I stuck a stopwatch in. In the first shot, as soon as the lights change to green, everyone takes off together and in one minute flat sixteen cars go into the tunnel. In the second shot, where everyone's being mindful of their neighbour, eighty cars manage to go through in the same time frame. In another film that's one and a half hours long, called *The Wedding Suit (Lebassi Baraye Arossi),* I talk about little boys who want new suits for weddings and other ceremonies.

Do the children you get to play in the films have any experience of film?

Most of the time they have no experience of film, not even as viewers. In *Where is the Friend's Home?*, for example, the little boys had only seen a film of Charlie Chaplin's, one day, when they went into town. As there's no television in their village, they'd never seen anything else. So they acted perfectly naturally since they weren't influenced by the bad comedies you see on the small screen.

How do you prepare them before shooting the scenes they're in? Do you read them the story? Do you rehearse them?

I never tell them the whole story. For each shot, I tell the child a new story. In *Where is the Friend's Home?* there's a moment when the little boy thinks of his friend's book, which he took by mistake. I didn't say to him: 'You have to sit and think about the book'. I simply said to him: 'You have to be good at sums and now we have a bit of time for you to do some practice. I'm going to give you some numbers and you're going to add them up.' While he was doing the sum, I stopped talking, I put on the ambient sound and I filmed him while he was thinking. When you see the film you imagine he's thinking about the book. In fact, the children I use don't know what sort of story they're acting in while we're filming.

Given how spontaneous children are, do you try not to do too many takes so as not to lose the initial freshness?

For me, more often than not, the first take is the best. It's the one that captures people at their most natural and in general there's no reason to do it again. If we do do a second take, it's for safety reasons, in case the laboratory spoils the negative. For example, the kid's mother in *Where is the Friend's Home?*, Mrs Owtaari, never understood why we had to do a second take. My assistant nicknamed her Elizabeth Owtaari because, like Elizabeth Taylor, one take was enough for her! When she washed a shirt and hung it on the line, if you asked her to start again, she'd tell us the shirt was clean! I'd then tell my assistant to knock it to the ground when she wasn't looking, and when it was dirty again, she'd wash it, and we could redo the shot! It was the only way to get her to perform.

So for you, the editing generally happens in the camera.

Yes, that's how I work. Furthermore, I choose my lenses in terms of an actor's abilities. If an actor moves too much, I use long focal lengths. Certain directors tell their actors to approach, to stand over here or over there and then to say their lines. I can't do that with mine, they just wouldn't know why they had to go here or there. With long focal lengths, the actors can go on with their lives the way they want to and we can just follow their movements, recording the sound as we go. It's like playing golf. I give the ball an initial whack and then I run after it. In the end, I hope it falls in the hole I'm aiming for. One day I was asked: 'How do you choose your lenses?' and I answered: 'The only fair way.' For instance, this waitress who's just served us drinks on the terrace, I'd take a 35 mm lens to film her. If I decide to invite her for a coffee afterwards, I'd use a 50 mm lens, and if I were to get closer to her, I'd use an 85 or a 90 mm lens.

How did you go from short documentaries to your first full-length features, Mosafer (The Traveller) *and* Gozaresh (The Report)? *Did you feel the short film was too restrictive?*

In the beginning I had no intention of moving on to features. One day Professor Brousil, a Czech who regularly came to Tehran, encouraged me to shoot features, but I had to confess to him that they scared me. He said there was no problem; all it involved was putting a larger number of scenes together. So, in 1975 I came up with a subject that was suitable for a feature-length film and I made *Mosafer* and then *Gozaresh*. *Gozaresh* was once more inspired by my own experience, a husband's argument with his wife and the problems this man had at work. I was inspired by two families I knew and I put them together as one family for the requirements of fiction, but I used amateur actors. The film was a hit. I called it *The Report* because I wanted to do a sort of round-up of life in Tehran in the years before the revolution, the strange pressures people felt, their financial problems, moonlighting.

Your third feature, Avaliha (First Graders) *was made in 1985, nine years after* Gozaresh. *Why the long gap when the latter was a success?*

I'd never intended to keep making features, doing a film a year. Everything depends on the situation the country's in and how I feel personally. And, during the period you're talking about, the Islamic Revolution occurred and virtually no one was making films. *Avaliha* was about schoolchildren in their first year at school when they're six years old. It was a documentary but it had a continuous narrative thread from start to finish constituted by the relationship between the parents and the children. It's a mix of interviews and reporting, but we never leave the school.

For this kind of documentary, do you use lightweight cameras and hidden mikes?

My practical experience had taught me that children, once they're used to it, behave very normally; they carry on as usual. That's why we sit the camera where you can see it in the classroom from the very start of the school year. When the children turned up at school for the very first time, they saw the blackboard, the desk, the seats and also this camera, which they thought was part of the classroom. We never told them not to look at the camera, as that's the surest way to draw their attention to it. You'll notice that in *Where is the Friend's Home?* the children look at the camera but they don't stare at it, and then they look at something else. Very quickly in *Avaliha* the presence of the head cameraman was as natural for the children as that of the schoolmaster. If it's an important moment that people are going through in front of the camera, they end up forgetting it's there. When you're at the consulate filming people asking for a visa, you could stick ten cameras in front of them, they wouldn't see them, any more than two boxers in a ring would.

In your documentary films, what role does editing play for you?

You have to know first that in Iran, we don't work eight hours a day. When we're doing the editing, we're at the table twenty-four hours a day, seven days a week. We don't stop until the film is finished, which means the editing is usually over pretty quickly. The problem with *Avaliha* is that I'd filmed without a clapper-board so the children and even the adults wouldn't lose their concentration. But the upshot, of course, is that the editing and synchronisation were very hard because of the resultant confusion. That's the upshot of working with amateurs, but the compensation is that, when they perform, they really perform.

Do you have a team that regularly work with you?

In general I always work with the same collaborators since they're used to my way of doing things. I don't want some lighting cameraman always offering me the simplest solutions for filming a shot.

What led you to make your next film, Where is the Friend's Home?

The film has two sources. First a story written by a schoolmaster, then something that happened to my son when he was the same age as the protagonist. A woman friend was dining at our place and he'd gone out to buy her some cigarettes. We waited for him for a very long time. Finally, we discovered he'd covered six kilometres of Tehran at night, on foot, so as not to come back without the cigarettes. This sense of responsibility that he had touched me very deeply and I wanted to express it in the film. As for the teacher's tale, it was about a little girl who'd done her friend's homework.

Which part of Iran did you film in?

In the village of Mazandaran, four kilometres north of Tehran, by the Caspian Sea, which was the epicentre of a huge earthquake that occurred in the region. Most of my films are located outside Tehran and I'm not the only one in that category. I suppose that my colleagues and I are giving ourselves the chance to get away from the pollution, the traffic congestion, the lousy relationships between people that are characteristic of Tehran. It allows us to combine holidays and work! I chose this particular village because it was at the far end of a valley and for that reason, didn't have any television. Another reason is that the dialect of the peasants of this part of Iran is easy enough to understand for the rest of the population.

How did you choose the boy who takes up the screen for almost the entire film?

His character had to appear endlessly anxious and his anxiety had to be reflected in his eyes. I remember that while I was getting the film ready, I saw village people carrying a coffin, placed in a sort of display case, that they were going to put in the grave. It was very heavy and dozens of villagers joined forces to try and lay their burden properly in the ground. Children were playing alongside without paying the slightest attention, except for one little boy who looked so worried I realised he was the one I had to have. I signed him up that same day, together with his brother.

For your next film, Homework (Mashgh-e Shab), *you went back to documentary.*

The material there, too, was taken from personal experience. I've been separated from my wife now for several years and I live alone with my two sons. I have to do everything with my boys, and especially help them with their homework. It was getting harder and harder for me because of new teaching methods, especially with maths. I'd come home exhausted and I'd have trouble meeting their demands. I even hit them sometimes. I told myself it was a serious problem and I wanted to know how other people coped. I started doing a survey on homework with my camera. At the beginning, you see children going to school, and someone comes over to me and asks me why I'm making the film. I then portray the way children study at home, their relations with their parents, the way the parents help them. I think this film is a bitter and even tragic report, in particular about households where the parents have no education and don't know what to do, faced with their children's schooling. There aren't enough teachers, the number of students keeps going up and the premises are inadequate. The teachers don't manage to look after the children as much as they should and part of their task falls to the parents who, often, aren't up to the job. Among adults on either side of the divide – teachers and parents of schoolchildren – each one has a hundred difficulties to cope with, and it's the children who suffer from all this and who get punished at school and at home. Every adult dumps his or her problems on the kids. The film was shot following a method and style close to *Avaliha*. You can see the children are comfortable in front of the camera. At the same time they have a lot of honesty and dignity and you feel that they'll never betray their family secrets. Similarly, while I encouraged my son to say I hit him, he never wanted to.

Your last film, Close-Up (Nema-ye Nazdik), *is a blend of documentary and fiction.*

After *Homework* I was on the point of making another film, *Pocket Money*. Once again it was a theme dealing with children and it was set in the same school where I filmed *Homework*. After the revolution, children of different social classes found themselves in the same schools. Sometimes one kid's pocket money for the week was the same as another kid's for the whole year. That seemed to me to be an interesting theme, but just as the whole crew was ready to film, I read a story in the paper that gave rise to *Close-Up*. As Gabriel Garcia Marquez has already said: you don't choose the work, the work chooses you. I called my producer and told him I was going to change the project, that what I'd just discovered had taken hold of me, that the story was in the process of unfolding and that we had to film on the spot otherwise it'd be too late. I went and got my crew from the school and took them to the prison. I shot the opening sequence with an invisible camera. The trial scenes were also documentary in substance, but some things were changed because I wanted to be closer to the subject. There were thoughts going on inside this character that he wasn't aware of, and we needed to get them out and make him say them. Sometimes, to get the truth, you have to betray reality a bit. So during the breaks in the trial, I spoke to the judge and the accused to get them to express what I wanted. A trial of this kind generally lasts an hour whereas this one went on for ten.

You didn't have any trouble getting the law to cooperate like that with a film?

Something positive has happened in Iran recently, and that is that cinema's been rediscovered and even, quite simply discovered, by people who knew nothing about it, or didn't like it, or didn't go. For a long while movies were banned in the name of religious precepts. And today it's a bit like a return to the origins of the seventh art. So much so that when we declared that we were going to make a film about cinema, we got a more receptive ear on the part of officials, including the law, and they calmed down. So we were able to film wherever we wanted. I also remember that, during the trial, we'd talk about close-ups and wide-angle shots and the judge was right up with all this film talk we were butting in with!

What was it that interested you in the character of Sabzian, the impostor?

I'd read that after he was arrested, he said: 'I'm like a piece of meat and you can take me to the butcher's and do whatever you like with me.' I felt like he was talking to me, that I was the audience he was addressing and that I had to do something for him. I found out he wasn't a criminal and I wanted to know what he really was. There were some things I was sure about: that he was out of work, that he had no hope, no money. I wanted to get closer to him and find out more about him as a person. Every day of the shoot brought me new information. During the trial I realised that, of course, he'd lied to the family, but that, in a way, the family wanted to be lied to. That might perhaps lead us to the notion that in dictatorships, it's not only the dictator who wants to exercise his power, but also the people who want to be controlled. I've also observed something interesting about this relationship between reality and truth I was talking about. When I went into the rich family's house to re-enact the arrest, Sabzian told the son he'd never lied to them, that he'd definitely told them he'd come with his film crew and that that's what he'd done! That really moved me. What he said at that particular moment might seem like a lie, but at the same time it was true, the crew was there. After four days, we turned up with the camera, the lights, electricians, and in a way, we were at his service, this film was his.

With him I could measure the power of love. When someone loves something very much – and in this case it was love of cinema – they display amazing audacity and strength. *Close-Up* shows that, after oxygen, what a human being needs most is respect and dignity. This character knew he stood an 80 per cent chance of being arrested, and yet, thanks to his need for dignity, he clung to that 20 per cent and went to the house.

Are you a friend of Makhmalbaf, the filmmaker your protagonist claims to be?

No. I met him for the first time over this film. I asked him if he'd like to play his own role and he accepted. When Sabzian came out of jail, the scene was filmed by an invisible camera and he didn't know he was meeting Makhmalbaf.

Do you associate with other Iranian directors?

By temperament I'm rather an individualist, I live apart. That doesn't mean I don't want any contact with my colleagues. In reality, I'm friendly with them, and whenever I run into them at a party, I'm pleased to see them. But I believe artists are solitary beings. Furthermore, because of my specific family problems, I don't have much of a social life.

What are you working on at the moment?

A few days after the earthquake, I saw on a map on television that the epicentre was where I'd filmed *Where is the Friend's Home?* I also learned that 90 per cent of the inhabitants of the village were dead. I decided to go there to see if the children were still alive. All the roads were blocked but I managed to clear myself a path and look for them. The day I arrived, I got the feeling the village was just rubble and that no one had survived. I felt an immense sorrow, but at the same time, I noticed strange things. People were washing rugs and blankets and hanging them over trees to dry. I sensed an extraordinary survival instinct. An old woman was trying to pull a rug out from under four metres of debris all by herself. I asked her if there was no one who could help her and she told me that those who could help her, her husband and her son, were dead and buried, under the rubble. I went off to get help, and when I got back I saw that she'd made a fire with whatever was at hand and boiled water in a pot to make me some tea. I noticed a number of details of the sort that testify to the will to survive. I wanted to make a film in the form of a fictionalised version of this situation and, of course, use the earthquake as the basis. In the end, you see the olive trees, the river flowing, the mountains, the sun setting and the inhabitants who haven't given up.

Did you have censorship problems during the period of the Islamic Revolution?

I think you have to come to terms with censorship, accept it. We filmmakers, we're intellectuals and we ought to know what kind of government's governing us and the kind of audience we're working for. You can't make comparisons with your country. We're in the Middle East, in the Third World. Maybe in 500 years we'll be where you are now. We need time; we want to advance in stages. It's no use thinking you can change the world with a film, and it's mad to make a film knowing in advance that it'll be censored and will never be allowed to be shown. An artist should go as far as society will let him. Having made a film that's banned is the same as never having made it, so much so that you need to know what power the government has. That's why I believe in the simple films I make, for I think that, little by little, they're working towards a better future.

16 KRZYSZTOF KIESLOWSKI

(1941–1996)

There were a few of us at the end of the 1970s who, during Polish weeks at the Entrepôt or in a handful of other brave experimental art houses, discovered Krzysztof Kieslowski's *Camera Buff* and *The Scar* with the feeling that here was one of the two masters, the other being Krzysztof Zanussi, of a new wave of Polish filmmakers thought to be 'concerned with morality'. Zanussi, a cosmopolitan extravert, was much better known; Kieslowski, reserved and taciturn, always in the background, spoke virtually no foreign language and remained largely unknown. In 1988, the Cannes Festival finally decided to accept him into the competition with *A Short Film About Killing,* provoking a veritable thunderclap. The film was in fact only the long version, conceived for cinema, of Episode 5 of *The Decalogue,* a series produced for Polish television. The release of the latter ended up turning Kieslowski into a star and he became an indefatigable globetrotter, honouring symposiums, retrospectives, roundtables and international juries with his presence.

It took no fewer than three meetings for Hubert Niogret's and my curiosity about *The Decalogue* to be satisfied. The filmmaker is rather laconic by temperament, but he took the ritual of the interview no less seriously for all that, smoking cigarette after cigarette while he answered, with both gravity and humour, the questions provoked by an oeuvre among the most intelligent and complex of his time. The gambit of these ten films is indeed morality and Kieslowski thereby enlists in the tradition of Bresson and company. What he showed elsewhere in *The Decalogue*, as well as in *The Double Life of Véronique* and his *Three Colours* trilogy *(Blue, White, Red),* made in France, is to what extent our lives are connected with an infinite number of other lives. This dizzying reflection on chance and necessity, on coincidence and the ineluctable, with its metaphysical resonances, did not fail to touch a man of the calibre of Kubrick, who put him up there at the top among his contemporaries.

ON *THE DECALOGUE*

MONTREAL, VENICE, PARIS, SEPTEMBER 1985

No End (Bez konca), *your last film before* The Decalogue, *was doubtless the most political of all and the most pessimistic. After that, you didn't make another film for three years. Then you returned with ten films in which politics is absent. What's the relationship between these two facts?*

It's connected to the evolution of life. In Poland we have less and less faith in politics. We don't believe in it anymore. As for myself, it doesn't interest me at all. After the state of emergency declared in 1981, like all Poles I was in crisis. Anyway, I make a film every three years roughly so this silence is normal.

In Blind Chance (Przypadek) *there are three possible forms of engagement, communism, Solidarnosc and, finally, personal commitment. That perhaps heralds* The Decalogue, *in which politics is evacuated.*

It wasn't a conscious choice. In Poland in the 1980s only those three possibilities counted. I simply filmed those three stories, those three possible paths.

Is The Decalogue *an idea of yours or a Polish television commission?*

It was an idea of my collaborator's, the scriptwriter Krzysztof Piesiewicz, with whom I've been writing for some time now. He's not so good at writing but he has lots of ideas. To start with, I didn't think of doing it myself because it meant a lot of work. We thought of writing it for ten or more young filmmakers who didn't know how to get started in cinema. This was in the days when Krzysztof Zanussi wasn't around and I replaced him at the head of the production unit, TOR. But when we'd finished a few scripts, I felt remorse. I didn't want to give them to anyone else anymore, so I decided to make them myself. To be perfectly frank, I had no idea how long it would take me!

How did you go about writing together?

We'd chat together, then I'd write. Piesiewicz is a very well-known lawyer, outside the art scene. He's not a 'professional'. When I ask him, as an exercise, to knock me up some little thing at home, afterwards I have to redo everything. But he's fantastic to talk to and he's a friend who's full of interesting ideas. We wrote the episodes chronologically. And when they were all ready, I looked for the money. It took a year and a half to write them and four months to film them. They were each made in twenty days.

For The Decalogue *there were a number of economic rules that were built into the concept (a limited number of characters, a single neighbourhood). Were they voluntary constraints, to stay within a certain economic framework, or to unify the series?*

Both those reasons came into it. From the outset I knew I wouldn't have much money to make the films. On the other hand, even though it's not a real television series, I wanted to work for a television audience, which is a bit special. I wanted them to recognise the characters, for them to get used to them every Sunday afternoon. I was well aware that it wouldn't be the usual family serial that the audience looks forward to every week, with all the members of the tribe over, visiting. There would be different characters. But I still wanted it to be a bit like a series: to restrict ourselves to one neighbourhood, to a few apartment blocks. The characters knock on the door to borrow sugar, salt, they meet in the lift and, that way, they stick in the viewer's memory. But there was also a more important reason. If you look through any window there are people behind it. If you really want to look closely, there's something very interesting going on. I thought we could devote an hour to getting closer to them. In other words, inside everyone there's something interesting going on. You just have to lift the mask, peel off a few skins and then we can spend a moment together. Besides, if all the action is located in the same neighbourhood, it's because it's not as ugly as the new neighbourhoods of Warsaw. And it has the advantage of always suggesting enclosed spaces. The way the houses are built and laid out closes the field and that allows me interesting compositions with the camera.

What's also striking in these stories is the absence of material problems like food and lodging.

The problems that Polish people go through are so boring to me and to everyone else that I didn't want to touch them. What's more, I think the whole world is tired of seeing these poor old Poles on the screen! Of course there are things in the background – like the lack of water – in there, but they're signals we don't insist on.

How did the production get organised, since it was done in record time?

In all there are thirteen hours of film: ten films for television and two feature-length films for the movie houses. The production was the same. Obviously we changed the actors since they were ten completely different stories. Apart from Sobocinski, who did the photography on two episodes, the cinematographer is different for each film. That's the best idea I had for this *Decalogue*. The shooting is so boring that I looked for a way to remedy that. With a new cinematographer turning up each time, it changed everything. He'd have different ideas for the lighting and a thousand other things. A film means a crew of thirty to fifty people who earn very little money and who have no economic incentive to work. And I count myself among them! Getting new actors and new cinematographers allowed us to overcome that.

There were moments when we shot two or three sequences of different films on the same day because the work schedule required us to do so. For example, we were in the hallway in the block of flats and we shot the sequences of three films where the action partly took place there. So three times there were changes. The technicians were curious to know how it was going to work that particular day. Were we going to light with the hall light or with a pocket torch? It took a year and nine months from the first 'clapper' of the shoot to the last mix. But during the work there were interruptions, with the release of *A Short Film About Killing* and *A Short Flm About Love (Krotki film o milosci)*. Last year when I presented *A Short Film About Killing* at Cannes, I was still in the middle of filming.

Are all the actors professionals?

No. There are amateurs, like the father in *The Decalogue 1,* who's a theatre director living in Berlin. Most of the actors also work in theatre, as always in Poland, with the exception of Daniel Olbrychski. There was even a joke doing the rounds in Warsaw during the shoot whereby you divided Polish actors into two categories: the ones performing in *The Decalogue* and the rest!

How did you conceive the cinema and television versions of A Short Film About Killing *and of* A Short Film About Love *at the outset and what are the differences between them?*

When we got to *Decalogue 5* in the script-writing – we wrote them in order – it was clear the episode would have more or less the same form as *A Short Film About Killing* since it was a subject I'd had running through my mind for ages. To tell you the truth, I couldn't have done it before for a whole host of reasons. One of them being that my colleague, Grzegorz Krolikiewicz, an extremely active man who's always looking for something new (in 1972 he was the author of a film that was audacious for the time, *Through and Through (Na wylot)*, in which he worked out a theory about the out-of-shot, very often placing his hero outside the frame) – Krolikiewicz had done a screen adaptation of a book I myself was interested in. We'd both had the same idea almost at the same time but, without knowing my intentions, he'd got there a bit before me. Now, that film, *Killing Aunty (Zazbicie ciotki),* had a theme close to what would become *A Short Film About Killing (Krotki film o zabijaniu)*. Because of that I couldn't go anywhere near the subject for some years, it was like a mental block. Of course, it didn't deal with capital punishment, but there was a murder, the same cruelty, and the moment just didn't seem right for me to spend all that time doing a similar story in turn. On top of that, five years ago, I imagine I wouldn't have been allowed to make the film. It was the end of the state of siege, we were in a difficult period in relation to censorship and we didn't have the right to express ourselves in public on capital punishment. I can't say with any certainty if that's how it would have been because I confess I didn't even try. So when we got to *Decalogue 5*, I knew I wanted to tell that story. Naturally, it had changed in the meantime; there was no more Aunty, for instance. When Piesiewicz and I had finished the scripts we took them off to the television people who gave us the nod. I realised straight away that there wouldn't be enough money, I wanted more room for manoeuvre and I was really keen to make the fifth episode for cinema, to make a longer version. So I took that script and four others and I offered them to the Cultural Ministry, which is a second producer in Poland after television. They have the same government money at their disposal but the people who hold sway there are different and so are their requirements, since Polish television only produces for the small screen and the Cultural Ministry for cinemas. It sometimes happens that the two organisations pool their financial support, as happened initially with Andrzej Wajda's *The Birch Wood* and Krzysztof Zanussi's *Le Contrat*. The fact remains that this possibility existed and that I wanted to make use of it. So I went to the Cultural Ministry and I offered to film *A Short Film About Killing* for cinema with a budget half the size of normal costs. On top of that I promised them I'd do another feature-length film for the same price, so they'd get two films for the price of one. I also left them the freedom to choose out of the scripts I handed them and they decided it would be *A Short Film About Love*. So the movie version of the film is the result of a public servant's choice. It's not mine. Which doesn't mean they made a bad choice! On the other hand, *A Short Film About Killing* is a film I really wanted to make for the movie houses. That's the history of those two scripts.

Of course I later had to write longer versions as I had only hour-long scripts. I added scenes and at one point I had two versions of the same scenario. Each storyboard indicated the sequences that belonged to the movie version. And since we never filmed in 35 mm for television, I had to find a co-producer – channel SFB in East Germany – who gave me the 35 mm film to shoot the telefilm. We started by shooting the fifth film, *A Short Film About Killing*, and when I presented it at the Cannes Festival (at the same time that *A Short Film About Love* had its premiere in a Warsaw cinema), I was still in the process of filming *The Decalogue*, as I told you, editing all the episodes every night and on Sundays. The shoot was rough. You people in the West don't know what it means to tremble for every metre of film. When I film I never have a script in my hand. What I do have, on the other hand, always, is a bit of paper indicating how many metres of film I have a right to for each shot. And I never stopped calculating to figure out how much film I still had left. I had to think about that constantly, otherwise the film would have run out. On the whole I could hardly ever do more than two takes per scene, which is the minimum I needed since I was supposed to get two versions up! In Poland, not only do we have only a very short supply of negative stock, but there is no such thing as an internegative, for instance.

Yet the TV version and the cinema version are structured very differently. For example, in the TV version of A Short Film About Killing *(Decalogue 5)* we share the lawyer's point of view throughout the film.

I tried to build on the basis of the material I had at my disposal. There were two possible courses. Either to make a long version and then shorten it, but that's a boring job. Of course I could have given it to an editor but, since what I love most in making a film is the editing, I didn't want to deprive myself of that pleasure. So I chose the second course, to play around with various possibilities, and that's a lot more fun. And what is effectively characteristic in *Decalogue 5* is the change of perspective. I introduced the lawyer's monologue about the story from his point of view so at the end I can allow myself to have him cry out, 'I hate you! I hate you!', since we're ready for it then. I tried to put that ending in the movie version but it didn't go at all. In *A Short Film About Love*, the problem we had was with the last sequence. The two scenarios had different endings. When we began shooting scenes, the actress, Grazyna Szapolowska, who I'd hired at the last moment, had just finished reading the script on the beach where she was winding up her holidays and she told me we couldn't have such a sad conclusion because people preferred fairytales. She begged me to make one up. Which is what I did for the movie version. I shot another ending for the TV version and a third, which is the one in the script. For television, the ending is completely realistic: she doesn't come to his place. They run into each other at the post office where he works, his hands are bandaged, she tries to smile at him and he tells her, 'I don't watch you anymore.' And that's it. As for the third ending, the one in the script, I can't remember it anymore! All I remember is the extreme tension between the landlady and the young woman.

This idea of changing perspectives could have been a possible development for Decalogue. *In* The Human Comedy, *for example, Balzac introduces a hero from a previous novel as a secondary character in a new story. In* Decalogue 8, 'Thou shalt not bear false witness against thy neighbour', *a female student stands up and tells the tale about the pregnant woman from* Decalogue 2, 'I am the Lord they God; thou shalt have no other God but me'. *The old schoolteacher talks to a stamp-collecting neighbour who is of course a character from* Decalogue 10, 'Thou shalt not covet thy neighbour's goods'. *Were you tempted to set up further connections between the stories?*

It's only natural. In each episode someone appears who we already know or who we are about to get to know. In this precise case, what is exceptional is that the student narrates *Decalogue 2*. Let's say that I needed a clear and precise story as a prelude to that night in Warsaw in 1942. I thought of other tales I had in my notes and then I said to myself: 'Why not refer to something the viewers already know?' That gives the audience the possibility of saying to themselves: 'Right, I've already seen that story. They're my friends, my acquaintances, they're back.

Everything's OK.' An audience likes a puzzle like that; he feels cleverer than the director.

As for when the characters appear, I drew up a chart, which I love, where I indicated which character appeared when, and I tacked it up on the wall. But, naturally, I wasn't able to film everything I'd intended to. Sometimes an actor left for the United States or else the scene was buggered and I had to chuck it. In general I swung it so that a familiar face appeared in each episode.

At the most dramatic moment a secondary persona pops up who is always played by the same actor and who is only ever passing through.

He doesn't have any influence on the action but he drives the characters to think about what they are doing. He's a thought engine. When he turns his intense gaze upon the characters, it drives them to question themselves. In *Decalogue 2,* for instance, it's a male nurse who's there when the husband is dying.

We could imagine an eleventh film, which, like Grand Hotel, *would bring all the characters together in the same building.*

That's what the German co-producers wanted – a new episode in which all the heroes could meet up. But I'd had it up to the gills so I didn't feel capable of taking on such a film.

Are the tales fiction pure and simple or are they based on real events?

That depends. Certain events have inspired me but not directly. The stories we worked on are at some remove from news stories. For example, *Decalogue 7 (Thou shalt not steal)*, the story of a woman who's kidnapped her own child, is inspired by a case Piesiewicz came across in his professional life. A mother deprived her daughter of her right to maternity. In contrast, *Decalogue 10* is pure fiction. I've never met anyone who's mad about stamps except the film critic Jerzy Plazewski, a major collector, whom we consulted on the script.

Is there any difference for you when you film for television or for the cinema from the point of view of style?

As far as I can see, there's no difference for me. What's different is the way the film is seen, depending on whether it's in a movie theatre or on television. From that point of view, I think I've made a certain mistake that stems from the fact that I'm always thinking about the cinemagoer. I know very well what the difference consists of, but it doesn't worry me. The result, in my view, is that my films go too fast for a televiewer. There are too many references, too many associations that are obvious in cinema but are no longer obvious at all on the small screen where the viewer isn't as focused. They repeat the news three times on television. As you know, I've made quite a few documentaries for television and it's while I was working there that I realised that repetition was something totally natural in life. I spent a number of months in the editing room viewing documents, interviews, and I noticed that every human being – in 90 per cent of cases – repeats the same thing three times in conversation. Which means that the way people view things on television is completely normal; it reflects normal conversation. On the other hand, the documentary films I've made, which have generally been very short, only ten to twelve minutes long, have given me great discipline. I never had much time to express myself so I'd spend hours at a stretch editing very carefully so as to build my films on the basis of a single phrase instead of three. I probably transferred this habit of saving time to my feature films and now I can't help myself. But when they're shown on television it's a handicap, they're too elliptical.

Eric Rohmer made two series of six films, Contes moraux *and* Comédies et Proverbes, *in which he provides the moral of his story at the outset. You, on the contrary, just give a figure without any other information.*

I don't know all Rohmer's films, alas, but I really like what I've seen. They've had a strong influence on me, if only *Claire's Knee*. But I don't know about the approach he took in those two series. I've only just learned, actually, that he had such an idea. The difference is that I refused to call things by their name and so to give my films titles. That way, I set up a sort of game with the viewer. I tell him: *Decalogue 1*. He watches the film and afterwards he wants to know what it is. He starts searching for the commandment if he feels the urge. Whether he likes it or not, he does a certain amount of intellectual work. And I'd like him to do that since I take him seriously. He reaches certain conclusions, or not, under pressure from me. Everything isn't served up to him on a plate. But in Poland, which is a Catholic country, that got pretty complicated. Some of my actors who were believers didn't want to act in the films unless I told them which commandment was at issue. In fact it's not all that important. You could interchange the films, the sixth with the ninth, the fourth with the seventh.

Doesn't each film bear on the problem of choice?

Of course. I wanted to say that every day we find ourselves faced with a choice and that we are responsible for it. At the same time, we aren't conscious that these choices pull us in certain directions. In some way we're ignorant of this and it's only later when we examine our life that we realise the decisive nature of certain choices we've made.

What is striking in your films is the great intellectual rigour and at the same time the sense of life's vicissitudes, chance!!!

Chance is very important and so is fate. Chance has always struck me. Our ups and downs in life are often linked to chance. I see that in so many instances. I know the role chance has played in my own existence and I'm obliged to think about it when I write scripts. When you ask yourself why a person has had a certain fate, you have to look for the sources and you discover the importance of chance. Whatever has happened in the past has great significance for the present. If all four of us are here – you two, me and our interpreter – that's the result of something. Everything in our lives has led us to meet here today. All previous events heralded this meeting. It's the outcome of a thousand chances and that affects each and every human being. If you look at the scenarios for *Decalogue*, you realise they're constructed on the basis of such chances. We try to understand what's happened in the life of each of our characters for them to act the way they do today. In a sense the ultimate, total chance is my film, *The Decalogue*. Chance is also why I became a filmmaker. I also met Piesiewicz by chance and without him I might never have made *The Decalogue*. It might also be destiny. I *had to* meet Piesiewicz. I'd done documentaries and when war broke out in Poland, I wanted to make a film about a trial and I went looking for Piesiewicz, who was a barrister on the trial. It was fate or luck; the word doesn't matter.

In Decalogue 1, 'Thou shalt worship only one God', *the father and son venerate the computer which offers them a resistant barrier like ice. The son will die by drowning while skating on the frozen lake. Is that a religious interpretation?*

It's the problem of the definition of God. We're used to this handsome old man with a white beard who forgives everything. But there is also the God of the Old

Testament, who is very cruel. Maybe that's the real God. In the film, the father might well not be punished because he doesn't believe in God but because he's too rational. There's a conflict there between the rational and the spiritual that's very topical. By believing in rationality too much, our contemporaries have lost something. And this conflict is very pertinent for approaching the problem of God. *Decalogue 1* isn't about the other gods, like Buddha or Allah, but rather the negation of God by a substitute. Love, for example, can become a God, or else reason, or hate. Any strong feeling that possesses us, whether it's good or evil, takes us away from God. The best expression of the problem seems to me to be the conflict between the light of reason and the darkness of faith.

Would you describe yourself as an agnostic?

I believe there are mysteries, secret places in every individual.

Your films are at once X-rays of the soul that, precisely, reveal inner secrets and thrillers – in a way, Bergman meets Hitchcock.

If we always have to be compared to someone, it might as well be the best! What interests me above all is man. But after that I have to get the viewer interested. I don't think I can arouse his curiosity if I bore him rigid. So I have to captivate him while talking to him about what deeply concerns me.

In Decalogue 2, *for instance, we see a man in a tiny apartment. We think he is retired. Afterwards we discover a woman who is nervous and who is smoking. It turns out he's a doctor, that he's taking care of her husband and that she's worried about his health and wants to know if he's going to die for she's pregnant to somebody else. There are never-ending surprises but no sudden* coups de théâtre.

It's the psychological *evolution* of the character. In that film we really do see how the past influences the present. The doctor is what he is because his family died decades ago. I have to go back in time to explain his behaviour, otherwise you'd take him for a complete arsehole. You can't understand why he refuses to help this woman until knowledge about his past tells us why he *has to* behave like that. A man often does harm but his attitude has causes. I look for the explanation for everything. Maybe it's not fair, maybe we need to judge in terms of good and evil, but I can't do it because I don't believe in it.

In the Ten Commandments in the Bible, the one about adultery is the sixth. In your film it's the ninth.

They are completely different commandments. The sixth concerns the body, impure acts, the ninth, the purity of thoughts. Naturally, you could switch the films around but that's not the issue. The story isn't important. The fact that his wife cheats on the hero in the ninth episode isn't important. She could just as easily not cheat on him. The cheating bit is anecdote; it's what drives the story along. But the jealousy that the main character feels, that's the real subject, his impure thoughts. Not desiring the wife of another means you have to desire your own wife. Since he doesn't desire his own wife, he lets this terrible jealousy gnaw away at him. If she hadn't cheated on him, he wouldn't be any less jealous.

What occurs frequently in The Decalogue *is the role of the lie, betrayal, adultery that we also meet in* Decalogue 2.

I believe people are governed by feelings. The feeling of being scared, of dying, the feeling of hatred, the feeling of loneliness are more important than being a communist or a believer. I prefer to observe two people shut up in a room who are lying to each other than to watch two states or two cultures. The older I get, the more interested I am in what's to be found in a person's heart.

The theme of Decalogue 8 *tackles anti-Semitism in Poland, a subject that is hardly touched on in the cinema of your country.*

The eighth commandment is very important, maybe the most important. We wanted to tell a story that perfectly illustrates what we've just been talking about: one day a man does something that will mark him forever. This old woman, who used to be a teacher forty years earlier, asked a little Jewish girl to leave her apartment. Naturally she knew what she was doing and what might result and yet she couldn't foresee that this simple decision would weigh on her for the rest of her life, that remorse would hound her and that her existence would be totally different from what it would have been if she hadn't done what she did. She later tried to understand and tell others how to live so as not to constantly have this feeling of guilt. Everything she did later is nothing but the consequence of that single word. To tell this tale, we realised we'd have to refer back to a very distant past to show how huge the effects of that decision have been over time. The last war was perfect to set it in because the choices were very clear then. As chance would have it, one of my friends told me the story of a Jewish woman someone had promised help, but they hadn't in the end delivered. That's when I twigged that the subject was close to me and that it wasn't bad to talk perfectly openly about Polish–Jewish relations in the quotidian without Polishness or Jewishness playing overly prominent roles. They're just two people who meet, with one needing help and the other being able to give it or refuse it.

In Decalogue 10 *you adopt a completely different tone, black humour, with touches of the grotesque even. Since the series was written in chronological order, it's interesting that it ends on that note.*

It's very simple. We began in *Decalogue 1* with a tragedy, the death of a child. *Decalogue 2* concerns the possible death of a child who isn't yet born and the equally possible death of the husband. So death is present in the first episodes. We got to comedy in the end to lighten up this sombre set a bit. But the last film is pretty black, too; terrible things happen to these people but that just makes us laugh and regard them coldly because we aren't targeted. That's one of the elements that constitute humour: show a tragedy in a comic light.

Decalogue 7 *associates the mystery (the child's cry in the night at the beginning) and an almost melodramatic structure à la Griffith, with the mother finding refuge in the countryside with her child, pursued by her family.*

To tell you the truth, that's the film I'm least attached to. The story is a bit too complicated for me, too chatty, and I didn't tell it very well. I just wasn't on form. In any case, we obviously had to have the child crying in the night. I knew I had to start with that to create this anxiety but after that, the film crumbled. For every episode there's an image around which we began to think of the style, but I quite often ditch it after that because it feels too obvious to me.

Objects also play a very important role in your dramatic art.

That stems from minute observation. I think it's just as important to know what watch a character is wearing as the way they walk. It forms a whole. As a result, I frequently use objects to describe my heroes. Very often I go up to objects with my camera so that I can show them very clearly and then speak distinctly to the viewer. If a man has a battered briefcase, we are fully aware that he's been using it for countless years either because he doesn't have any money or because it doesn't matter to him. And if he's sewn it back together again, it's because he had the time and the energy to do so and because he thought it wasn't proper to have a briefcase that's coming apart. All these details explain his nature. So I look for objects that tell us something about their owner. In the vast majority of cases this is provided in the script. But, for instance, the bottle of milk at the start of *A Short Film About Love* was introduced during the filming.

In Decalogue 10 *we don't notice the dog until he's really used in the narrative, whereas, in fact, he's already there in the image.*

Yes. But only cinephiles like you notice that!

Unconsciously the viewer relies on such elements.

I hope so, because that's what cinema is…

One episode is particularly centred on an object and that is Decalogue 4, *'Thou shalt honour thy father and thy mother', with the letter that the young girl can only open on the death of her father. It's one of your most fascinating tales, one in which you play most on mystery and surprise.*

The story's totally made up. Naturally, like all the rest, it has a point of reference somewhere. How do you say today 'You shall honour your father and your mother'? You have to look for a different angle of approach. The simple illustration of such a commandment would be unacceptable. We wrote that script differently and it was a lot like *Blind Chance*. There were three stories. In the first, the man imagined what had happened. In the second, it was the girl. In the third, we said what really happened. But as it conjured up my earlier film too much I abandoned the script just before the shoot and tried to tell the story in a more linear manner. And I think it's better for it. I had a lot of luck with the actors, in particular Adrianna Biedrzynska, who sensed the problem clearly. Maybe because she'd been through something similar in her own life, doubtless not with her father but with an older man, she got the tone right. I'm happy about that because, even though she's known in Poland, she's always played really stereotyped roles of a sort of young cock-teaser or a drug-crazed rebel. As I know she's a good actress, I wanted her to change registers a bit and to be able to play a sensitive, delicate, quivering character.

Most of the time, the characters in Decalogue *have liberal professions – they're architects, teachers, surgeons, lawyers. Why did you mostly turn to that type of job?*

I wanted to remove my films from social problems, from the daily grind, which doesn't mean that simple people can't also break free of them. But if we tell the story of a worker, some small-time employee, you can't show his workplace and how he lives. On the other hand, when I say that someone's a surgeon or an artist, the audience understands that he earns a decent living and he doesn't have problems at the end of the month buying bread. So I don't show overcrowded apartments, people folding out their sofa beds at night to put their children to bed, others getting up at five in the morning and taking overcrowded buses or trains to work. In such daily ordeals, this painful determination to survive, in their extreme fatigue, average Poles have no time to think about other things anymore. Since I wanted to express myself in a different register, I just deliberately cut out the quotidian.

How did you work with the composer you used?

I'd met him when I was doing *No End*, which he wrote the music for. I was well aware that he didn't just think of the music but especially of its function within the framework of a film. We worked in a very straightforward way: towards the end of the editing, which is always a very long process for me since I mostly do five or six versions of a film, I gave him a cassette for him to work on. But he also came to see all the versions from the editing, and over five or six weeks we were able to get a pretty precise idea. But I never bound him to this idea. He discovered it bit by bit. Sometimes he succeeded; sometimes he failed – like me.

Are you a chess player? There's a rigour and, at the same time, an element of chance in that game that must seduce you.

I know how to play but I no longer do. I did get interested in it a while back but it's an activity you have to devote yourself to completely, since it's a passion that devours you and sweeps you away, and you can't just take it up from time to time once a week, so I preferred to give it up. When I'm doing something, I like it to immerse myself in it in very precise detail. With chess, I'd have had to dedicate my whole life to it. But of course there are connections to directing.

On the one hand, I'm playing solo and on the other, with the viewer. I make a move and I predict his reaction and I even predict several moves in advance. In that sense, the cinema is very close to chess.

Have your films been shown on Polish television?

Not yet. The only reactions have been from the West. There was of course a 'pilot', *Decalogue 10,* but at that precise moment there were a lot of interesting things happening in Poland. I don't remember now who was elected, the president or Miss Poland, but there were elections! I doubt anyone would have been interested in the film. With television, they normally have to programme them in December but they're dragging the chain. We can't manage to come to an understanding with them. It's such a vast government office that you never know who you're dealing with. Personally, I would like – and they've accepted – for us to begin on 10 December, a Sunday, and in that case, the third episode, which talks about Christmas Eve, would be programmed on 24 December. Apparently that has no importance, but it could have, there'd be a shared atmosphere between the film and ambient reality. Loneliness is felt more acutely during the festive season; people lash out a lot more; unhappiness goes deeper. Poles took the state of war particularly badly because it broke out just before Christmas. That was a huge political mistake. That was something people could never forgive them. Imagine, something like that, right before the Christmas holidays! It just wasn't elegant. Recently, the programme heads told me they'd changed their minds and that they'd broadcast *The Decalogue* in October. I'd really like to push the date back, for right now everyone's running round, ministers are being appointed, political affairs are blowing up all the time. I'd like things to slow down a bit.

17 TAKESHI KITANO

(1947–)

After the exceptional flourishing of new talent in the 1960s, Takeshi Kitano is the only Japanese filmmaker of the following generation who has really made his mark. Kitano started out as an actor doing manzaï, a form of verbal comedy, performing sketches with his accomplice, 'Beat' Kiyoshi, and going by the name of 'Beat' Kitano – a name he would keep for his appearances as a film actor. It was television that made him famous and he still presents a number of satirical shows on television. As an actor, he was selected by Nagisa Oshima to play Sergeant Hora, one of the lead roles in *Furyo/Merry Christmas, Mr. Lawrence* (1983). He is also the author of short stories and essays that display his iconoclastic verve. Kitano graduated to directing when he stepped in to replace an ailing director and put his signature to *Violent Cop,* which already advanced his signature themes and style: confrontations between gangsters, *yakuzas,* in which the violence is stylised and the images chilling. For several years he remained little known to Western audiences and films like *Violent Cop* and *Jugatsu (Boiling Point)* were released out of sequence after *Sonatine* (1994), which was presented at the Cannes Directors' Fortnight, revealed him to be a major artist. But Kitano refuses to let himself be boxed in any genre, even if he returned to the gangster film with *Brother,* a film partly shot in Los Angeles. We met him at the Lido in Venice, just before he took the Golden Lion for his film, *Hana-Bi,* which happens to mark a decisive turning point in his work, revealing new ambitions that would be confirmed by *The Summer of Kikujiro* (1999), *Dolls* (2002) and *Zatoichi* (2003), three films that are themselves very different from each other. Kitano is a wonderfully deadpan, gleefully mischievous interviewee, who likes nothing better than to catch the person opposite him off balance just as the filmmaker takes delight in surprising the cinemagoer. His composure during the following interview recalls the static state of his fixed shots. Kitano's world is dominated by death and despair and his style by rigorous composition. In *Hana-Bi* in particular he goes in for endless associations of images and ideas, alternating gunshots and fireworks and suggesting a connection with surrealism, as in the work of Oshima and of Imamura, beauty being for him, as for André Breton, a fixed explosion.

ON *HANA-BI*

VENICE, SEPTEMBER 1997

Your last film, Hana-Bi, *has a complex structure that can be read on several levels, from the role of the past to the use of visual works, from amorous relationships to scenes of violence. How did the material get organised when you came to write it?*

When I think about it, it seems to me that two things happened to me that had a big impact on my career as a showman and not just as a director. One of these was a motorbike accident three years ago, in which the right side of my face was seriously damaged. The other took place ten years ago, when I attacked a newspaper editor who'd sent out paparazzi to take sneak shots of my girlfriend. This made me even more furious because they assaulted her trying to get their shots. It's only very recently that I've thought of the possible impact of those two events on the genesis of *Hana-Bi*. For instance, when my girlfriend was reeling under the attack, both physical and moral, I wondered what I could do for her in such a moment of crisis. This might have inspired the sequence where Nishi takes his wife to the countryside for one last trip, without my being conscious of it.

I'd also like to add that a lot of critics and journalists describe my films as violent above all else. Now, for me, the relationship between gentleness and violence is like the swing of a pendulum. The more tender a man is, the more he's likely to turn extremely cruel and brutal. It's in that kind of man that the discrepancy between the two states of mind can be the most extreme since he has the capacity to feel the deepest emotions. That might seem like an exaggeration, but it seems to me that the ultimate act of love might be the murder of the person you love. What I'm saying to you might well be an echo of the stereotype from Japanese philosophy that prevailed before the Second World War. It's true, though, that before the contemporary period, when Japanese society has been excessively modernised and Americanised in this forced march, there was a time when the idea of finding romanticism and lyricism in death was dominant in Japan. Many of my compatriots, unconsciously, continue to associate love and death in spite of everything. It's been the reactions of certain Europeans at the Venice Festival that have brought the ideas of death and lyricism together for me and have led me to think about all that, and I'm surprised they're surprised, for it seems to me that there is a very strong romantic tradition among you Europeans that ought to lead you to understand this link between love and death, even more than the Japanese.

What were the different stages in writing the script?

To start with, the order of sequences was very different in the script. For this film, the most important part of my work has been the editing, which I took care of myself, and it totally threw the chronology. After I'd filmed all my sequences, I felt like I was standing in front of pieces of a puzzle I had to put back together again. I spent quite a lot of time shifting sequences around to give them the structure I needed and there were at least ten different versions before we arrived at the one you've seen.

The basis of the synopsis was the story of the friendship between Nishi and Horibe, who've been close for a long time. Then I had the idea of showing how much affection Horibe felt for his friend by getting him to ask him to go and visit his wife in hospital and leaving him on his own so he could undertake a police operation. It's because he's on his own that Horibe will be seriously injured and paralysed from the waist down. Nishi, of course, feels really guilty about it. The second idea I had from the start was Nishi's decision to do something for his dying wife, even though he'd neglected her in their married life together! Those two elements structured the tale and they were both connected to the emotional pressures Nishi feels. I wanted to show how he reacts, confronted by those two ordeals.

One of the most difficult tasks I faced was how to express the very close ties between Horibe and Nishi. It seemed to me that the best way was to use the pictures Horibe paints and connect them to Nishi's actions. And so Horibe's painting and the shot of the family watching the fireworks coincide, as happens at other points on their journey.

The drawings and paintings are yours. Have you been a visual artist for long?

Actually, I only started painting three years ago, after my motorbike accident. My injuries were so serious that I thought I wouldn't be able to go on making films or appearing on television as a presenter – which I do under the name of Beat Takeshi. Like Horibe, I had nothing to do, and I had a lot of spare time, and I said to myself: 'Why not try my hand at painting?' At first I thought of it as a distraction that helped me cope with the pain. Then painting and drawing became my favourite hobbies. In preparing *Hana-Bi,* I realised that Horibe, paralysed in his wheelchair, was a bit in the same situation I found myself in and that, like me, he could abandon himself to the activity of painting. I didn't think it would create embarrassment for the audience since they'd understand that Horibe, like me, was just an amateur, that he's only just starting to paint and has no claim to be a true artist. I know my technique is not terribly accomplished, but nevertheless, when I paint, I'm completely absorbed in my work and I get a lot of pleasure and satisfaction out of it.

What's striking is the opposition between your pictorial style and your cinemato-graphic style: your paintings are incredibly rich, full of animals and flowers, with a wealth of details, whereas your frames are practically empty, with one or two characters in barren places.

The contrast could well be due to my sense of balance. It's true that emptiness is one of my principles of filmmaking, in *Hana-Bi* as in my previous films. It's not the result of some deliberate intention – just the workings of my subconscious. No doubt I wanted to counterbalance that with the density of the canvases, which have an emotional impact on the audience, all the more so since they set up a contrast with the sobriety of the shots filmed.

Do you work with a storyboard or do you, on the contrary, improvise camera movements, as with certain camera crane shots? Similarly, did you intend at the outset to use video for the bank hold-up?

I don't usually sketch my shots in advance, since, even if I did, the places and angles would never coincide with my initial intentions. As for the bank hold-up, what bugs me is that most people's idea of this sort of action derives from the movies they've seen. Very few people have actually witnessed a hold-up and the image they have of it is just an illusion. I told myself that the best shape I could give it would be to use a camera concealed in the bank's surveillance equipment, and to juxtapose those video images with close-ups of people in the bank. That way I could shatter the stereotyped representation of hold-ups you see in movies. That's why some people will say the scene isn't realistic, since they won't judge it in relation to the reality of an actual hold-up but based on their memories of movies. As for the camera crane shots, that's purely accidental. My head cameraman, Katsumi Yanagishima, who's worked with me on my five previous films, had left for London on a scholarship to do an advanced course at a film school, just as I was about to shoot *Hana-Bi*. So I asked his assistant, Hideo Yamamoto, to do the photography on my film and I wanted him to distinguish himself from his predecessor. So we worked out the whole set of crane movements together for the sequence in the snow and the one at the scrap merchant's. That coincided with the phase in my work where I wanted to try new stylistic devices and bring out the movement more. The arrival of a new head cameraman eased the transition.

In your film you use visual stereotypes of Japan, such as cherry trees in flower, Mount Fuji, snow-covered landscapes. What's your relationship with this traditional imagery?

If I used those conventions for the journey Nishi and his wife Miyuki go on, that's because they're taking a trip together for the first – and last – time. And when a married couple undertakes this kind of visit, they generally choose typical tourist spots. Of course, if you live in that kind of environment, you don't choose it for your holidays! As far as I'm concerned, while I was born in Tokyo and have always lived there, I've never been to see the town's famous tower, which is obligatory for all tourists.

In your film there are also different mixes of tone and humour when things aren't going the way they're supposed to: fireworks don't go off; photos don't work out.

It's true that there's a fair bit of humour in *Hana-Bi,* but I'd like to stress that what the viewer sees as humour or as a comic situation is not experienced that way by the protagonists. It might even sometimes be tragic or sad for them, as is the case with the fireworks. It all depends on the eye that's turned on events. Another example is the episode with the broken kite. The public is, of course, going to laugh, but for the child, his most precious possession is destroyed. Similarly, what Nishi does for his wife in the end can be seen as a tragic situation, but it's also a mark of absolute love. His act may seem, for Westerners, the expression of age-old Japanese wisdom, but romantic lyricism remains present even if it's buried deep inside many Japanese people's heads.

But what Europeans have told you they see in the film is suggested by you yourself in the very title: Hana-Bi.

Yes. Without a hyphen, 'Hanabi' means 'fireworks'. The hyphen divides 'Hana', the flower of life, from 'Bi', fire, so destruction and death. They are complementary as well as opposing terms. And yet, as far as the title goes, I'm ashamed to say that the idea doesn't come from me. The producer suggested it to me and I didn't really understand what he was getting at. So he then explained, just as I've just done to you! I thought the idea was excellent and immediately adopted it.

What's so seductive about the film is the way it creates constant surprise in the viewer, its inventiveness, even if, in the end, the story reveals its logic. Similarly, the violence always occurs suddenly, in a way that's unpredictable and elliptical.

Cinema is a hundred years old and the audience tends to predict what's going to happen on screen. In the scenes of violence, for instance, I try to disappoint people's expectations. I don't like predictable films, and that's why I try to surprise by introducing bizarre elements into every sequence. I also wanted to set up an opposition between the scenes of impulsive violence and those where Nishi finds himself with his wife – the pace there is a lot slower and most of the time they unfold in silence. That allowed me to give the greatest possible weight to the last sentences uttered by Nishi's wife. I really liked the contrast between the action scenes and the ones where calm prevails.

How did you work with Joe Hisaishi who, for the third time, composed the music for a film of yours?

My collaboration with Hisaishi is very peculiar. We don't talk about the score much together. In the case of *Hana-Bi*, I showed him an initial very rough cut of the film and it was like a sudden punch in the face. It wasn't really a friendly consultation, more like a round of boxing. Metaphorically speaking, you could say that he came out from the screening knocked out. He didn't get up until after I counted to nine. And suddenly he thought up this music, which was a bit like a return punch on his part. In a way, it was his revenge, and I'm completely happy with it.

When we met previously, you didn't tell us about your tastes in film.

There are lots of film directors I like, but who I feel I can compete with. But, when, for instance, I see a film like Fellini's *Clowns*, I know I'm not capable of achieving a similar result. If I'd been in the ring, he'd have KO'd me. I also really like Godard's *Pierrot le fou*, but other films of his I've seen seem very hard to understand, to me. As for Tarkovsky's films, I don't have the necessary physical stamina to see them in their entirety. Among the Japanese, I particularly like Kurosawa, and especially *Rashomon* and *The Seven Samurai*. When I think he made them more than forty years ago, I'm fascinated by how polished they are.

18 IM KWON-TAEK

(1936–)

Korean cinematography is the last to have appeared on the world map of the seventh art and Im Kwon-taek is incontestably the leader of the pack, even if Sin Sang-ok has played the role of a precursor and young talents like Hong Sang-soo and Lee Chang-dong are ready to ensure the changing of the guard. Im's career is also a lesson in humility for international critics, since his name remained unknown for such a long time and *Chunhyang*, the first of his films to be accepted in competition at Cannes, in 2001, was actually his ninety-seventh film! Im became known mainly outside the circuit of the major festivals, even though Berlin offered *Mandala* in 1981 and Venice, *The Surrogate Woman (Sibaji)* in 1987, the year I first discovered his immense talent. In fact, as with a lot of Asian filmmakers, it was the Festival of the Three Continents at Nantes that revealed the scope and variety of his work at the end of the 1980s through a retrospective of thirteen films. I had the opportunity to get to know this man, who is both gentle and determined at once, during the Pusan Festival in Korea itself. For Im Kwon-taek's cinema, which often poses the question of identity and also of separation and reunion, can't be understood without some inkling of the history of his country and of its split into two opposing nations. If his filmography appears incredibly abundant, most of his first efforts were just to make ends meet and his personality only really emerges at the end of the 1970s, with the end of the military dictatorship. Im then reveals himself to be a demanding artist, alternating contemporary films and costume dramas, the latter revealing a profound knowledge of the history of his country and a magnificent ability to marshal other arts, from pansori – traditional Korean chant – to classical landscape painting. The wide-angle shots of his films, in which a character is lost in the distance, express, without the shadow of a doubt, the spiritual purity of Buddhism.

But Im is also a vigorous social critic and specifically a painter inspired by the suffering of his heroines. This alliance between the old and the new, realism and lyricism, dramatic intensity and contemplative outpourings, makes Im a worthy heir to Mizoguchi, with his sweeping, fluid shots. Hubert Niogret and I met Im to talk about *Drunk on Women and Poetry* (*Painted Fire* in the US), an oblique self-portrait. The man is the image of his films, solid and subtle. Behind his courtly manner one can't forget the citizen who shaved his head in public in defence of national film quotas on Korean screens.

ON *DRUNK ON WOMEN AND POETRY/PAINTED FIRE (CHIHWASEON)*

CANNES, MAY 2002

After Chunhyang, *you are once again making a period film,* Drunk on Women and Poetry (Chihwaseon), *this one set in the middle of the nineteenth century. What was the attraction of that particular time?*

The people in those days had things the Koreans of today have lost, and they're not interested in their beauty. They tend to forget them. I wanted to push them to the fore and show them to my contemporaries and to the whole world, too, to give them a certain universality.

When a film director makes a film about an artist, painter or musician, one naturally assumes there's a connection between him and this other creator. What connection do you see between yourself and this painter?

Cinema is not like painting, but no doubt they have one point in common to the extent that cinema is also a search for beauty. Maybe that's the connection between the two worlds.

But perhaps there are more personal elements in your relation to Ohwon. In the film the painter says: 'For an artist, to repeat oneself is to die.' The diversity of your cinema is perhaps proof that you think the way Ohwon does.

Obviously, a lot of my own experiences as a filmmaker have slipped into the film and into the life of Ohwon. I always have an urge to make myself over. I don't know if I succeeded in *Chihwaseon*, but in any case I always have this urge to go one better than what I've done till then. Without counting my first films, which are lemons, once I started making 'real' films, I've always had this urge.

That's also in the film: 'An artist shouldn't be a prisoner of his public.' What are your feelings about Ohwon's situation and your own in the cinema of Korea today?

I'll give you an example in relation to my film, *The General's Son (Chang-gun ui Adeul)*, which is an action film. It was a real hit, the public loved it and it made the producer quite a bit of money. Afterwards, the public and my producer wanted me to do the same kind of film again and it was tempting to accept. But I told myself that, if I tried to satisfy other people's wishes, I would never get anywhere. So I tried to get out of the situation.

Is Ohwon the first Korean painter to have abandoned writing in painting? Before that, writing and painting were integrated, as in Chinese painting.

Yes, he was the first. Today you can see paintings of Ohwon's that incorporate writing, poems, but they aren't paintings by Ohwon himself. They're by people who were given paintings of Ohwon's and decided to write a poem of their choice on them. Ohwon has never written a poem on or in a painting.

Why didn't Ohwon write poems in his paintings? To answer that, there are several hypotheses. It's been said that it was because he was born an orphan, and so was absolutely uneducated. I don't think that's an adequate explanation, as he was surrounded by patrons who were the intellectuals of the day. To have hung around with all those intellectuals, I don't think he can have been deprived of an education until the end of his life. I think he could write poems, after all, otherwise he wouldn't have had so many relationships with aristocrats and intellectuals.

So no doubt he could write, but not as well as the intellectuals around him, and as he was a very proud person, perhaps he didn't want to compete with them, knowing his poems weren't so high in quality. I also think he didn't like the idea of writing poems on paintings. He wanted to make paintings that stood on their own.

What does his surname mean?

Jang Seung-up took the name Ohwon, which is a transcription of two Chinese characters: *oh* (*wo*), which means 'me'; and *won*, 'garden'. It can mean 'my garden'. In fact, the story's more complicated. In his day, there were two great painters: Kim Won-do, nicknamed Danwon, and the second, a woman, Shin Hun-wok, nicknamed Hyewon. So Ohwon wanted to have a surname that included this second character, won, to say, 'me, too', me, too, I'm a great painter.

What kind of work is the one you've adapted? Is it a biography?

There are very few documents that exist about him. There are a few books, notably a critical essay on paintings of the period, though no biographies in the correct sense of the term. There are a few brief orally transmitted biographies of painters and anecdotes, as well. I didn't want to write a dramatic history of Ohwon's life, but I imagined all sorts of situations that a painter might find himself in. I also got interested in the lives of other painters, some of whom were very fond of alcohol, for instance. I read quite a few things on them. I interviewed an enormous number of contemporary painters to get to know their daily lives, in particular the great painters, who are pretty old today. In the last instance, there were also my own experiences.

Your film comprises both an individual story and a historical background. The situations in which the painter finds himself are contrasted with the chaotic situation Korea was in at the end of the nineteenth century. One thinks of Bertolt Brecht and Mother Courage and Her Children, the story of a woman in the Thirty Years War, as well as the history plays of William Shakespeare. What's the connection for you between the historical dimension and the individual dimension?

Ohwon's life did in fact occur within the framework of a certain history of Korea, but the books that I managed to find on him made absolutely no mention of the historical background. Unless you're a monk living in the back of beyond, you can't not know what's happening in society, especially as there was a lot of contact with intellectuals, notably the reformists. So he couldn't not have been aware of the course of history. As far as the peasants' movement goes, if he wasn't actively involved, he was inevitably caught up in the middle of it. He wasn't a politically active painter at all, though, even if he doubtless wanted to offer some sort of consolation to his suffering people. He was the kind of man who's essentially preoccupied by his own artistic world more than social reality.

In the past you've made films that were more directly historic. Recently, you've become more interested in individual destinies within the historical set. Does this mean you've evolved?

I don't know if I've evolved, but I think that with age I've come to reflect more and more about what a film can offer society. I could make more socially engaged films, but I myself have lived through a difficult time for Korea, with many dramatic events. With age, I feel like getting a bit of distance, I feel like making things that are lighter, healthier. I'm trying to make a film that brings a certain richness to life.

In your films, great importance is always given to the landscapes, as with Ohwon. How do you see the role of nature, which seems to bring a breath of fresh air into the interior of the narrative, like a sort of meditation before the more dramatic scenes?

What I don't like is a life where man and nature clash. I also don't like the Western spirit of exploiting nature. The idea that appeals to me is where man lives in harmony with nature. That's what I wanted to show.

That's a very religious idea, since the notion of conflict doesn't exist in Buddhism…

It's actually an idea that recalls Buddhism, but I'd say rather that it was an Eastern notion, with a vision of the world as it is. Christianity introduced a kind of duality between the life down below and paradise, God's world. In Buddhism and Taoism, everything circulates between nature and man, even at the time of death.

In Sopyonje, *when she finally attains perfection in song, she is staring out at a gigantic landscape…*

In my films there's always this idea of union between man and nature.

You took a very long time to make that film, from June 2001 to February 2002. What took so long? Was it filming nature at different seasons?

We had to wait for several seasons to show the evolution of Ohwon's life, that's why it took so long to film in continuity. What also took us a lot of time to do was to represent the life of the times faithfully, with the right costumes and accessories. I didn't notice the time passing.

How do you explain the success of Ohwon, who wasn't a court painter responding to commissions, or an educated painter making works within a closed circle. He was a commoner, extremely lowly?

Because he painted so well. According to the documents, it seems he became famous at the age of twenty as he was considered a genius. But I'm not totally convinced. I think that in painting, you have to have acquired solid basic skills. That's why I've slipped in scenes where you see Ohwon at aristocrats' homes in the process of learning the basics of painting.

In Eastern painting, there's a very physical side. The painter starts at the top of the page and finishes at the bottom, an hour or a day later. There's a real physical relationship in the act of painting, like in the action painting of Jackson Pollock.

The big difference between Eastern painting and Western painting is doubtless that Western painting works on several layers. Eastern painting is like writing. You use the nature of ink, which spreads, with one or two strokes of the brush to achieve the painting. There aren't several layers. That's the big difference.

Isn't it more interesting for a filmmaker to film this kind of act of painting than the act of the Western artist before his canvas? Have you asked yourself that question? It's a body in movement, action.

Filming a painting was a real problem. If you film an Eastern painting too closely, you can't tell what it is. You get the impression it's not finished, whereas at a distance, the painting looks like a success. I couldn't not use close-ups or close shots because of the size of the paper the painter works on. In close-ups, I wanted to show the force of the act of painting. If you got the idea that Korean painting was something very physical, that reassures me precisely because I wanted to show that force.

You used a technical double for the painting. Are there painters today who paint like Ohwon?

We called on over ten painters between forty and fifty years old, who are all university teachers and fairly famous as artists. They had a hand in all the paintings you see in the film, including the ones on the screens. Several painters worked on the scene where Ohwon and his colleagues take turns painting. For Ohwon, it was a painter and teacher, Kim Sôn-du, a great master, who did the paintings. The actor who plays Ohwon, Choi Min-sik, had basic lessons to get the gestures right. He worked well, even the specialists can't fault him.

There are still painters today who practise this kind of painting, but they're no longer all that young. Young painters are trying rather to revive the genre by attempting a kind of fusion with Western painting, but for the moment, despite their efforts, this hasn't yielded any great results.

Were those scenes difficult to film? How did it work with the cinematographer? Was everything extremely precise or was there some improvisation? Was the cameraman free to some extent in relation to the painting being done?

The cinematographer wasn't entirely free because he himself didn't know the whole process of elaboration, and I didn't either. So we asked the painter how the act of painting would develop and we got him to do an initial canvas. After that we decided on the shooting script. The picture was painted several times, because the first time was fine for the long shot but not for the close-up, so the painting had to be done again for the close-up.

Did Ohwon have his drunkenness sufficiently under control to be able to create?

There were other painters who lived like Ohwon. I don't think Ohwon was really a drunk. He drank to get himself in the mood, but I don't think he really painted in a state of drunkenness, especially since he made such an effort to achieve beautiful things.

What's the exact translation of the Korean title of the film, Chihwaseon?

Chihwaseon is the transcription of three Chinese characters, since at the time people basically used Chinese characters. These characters are: drunkenness, painting, sage. He was a great painter, drunk, but so great that he was almost a sage and he attained perfection.

Women are not in the title?

No, but I have nothing against their being in the title. When you think of alcohol, of wine, you necessarily think of women, too.

Would you accept being defined as drunk on wine, women and film?

I was in fact drunk on wine when I was young, but today my health doesn't permit me to drink so much. As for women, it's a bit the same, since I'm not as strong as I was. And film? Why not.

The female characters in the film are very interesting and pose a social problem. They are of modest, common origin, and there's also an aristocrat. Did you have research material or did you make these characters up?

Ohwon adored women; the documents show that. He got married at around forty – like me – but he left one night soon after his wedding, which was inconceivable at the time. In such a case, the abandoned spouse disappeared socially. He sought out women he could get along with, otherwise he rejected them. You have to understand that at the time, a painter was sent for, but he wasn't asked to paint straight away. First he was offered all possible distractions, courtesans were wheeled in, he was offered food, he'd have a bit of a break. Sometimes a painter would spend a month in these conditions, sometimes several months, before getting down to painting.

There was also collective painting, with musicians and singers. Often governors and aristocrats would bring in several painters to celebrate a birthday or a particular event. Painting then included symbols of power, like the symbol of the rooster. Painters who turned up at this kind of invitation didn't just go to make masterpieces, but also to have fun.

How did you write the script and who did you write it with?

Actually, Kim Youn-oak, the co-scriptwriter on the film, is one of the great intellectuals of Korea today. He's a professor of philosophy at university and he has also taught in Taiwan and at Harvard, in the United States. He's very famous, very much loved, and hated because he doesn't hesitate to speak badly of the great savants, the great intellectuals. I worked with him on the script of *The General's Son*, and on another script devoted to the student movement, but I couldn't get the finance up for that one. For *Chihwaseon*, he didn't get involved in the story, just the dialogue. I wrote the rest. He wrote the dialogue on a canvas I gave him, as he's very familiar with Eastern painting, having written a book on Chinese art.

Do you think cinematic beauty also goes beyond form? That is said in Chihwaseon *in relation to painting. It was already said in* The Pansori Singer *about singing. Is there a moment when you surpass the form to attain the truth of creation?*

I think that with cinema you don't film a logic but a spirit, feeling. If you attach too much importance to form you spoil the freedom.

19 MIKE LEIGH

(1943–)

After the revelation of his first film, *Bleak Moments*, in 1972, recognition for Mike Leigh was long in coming and it was really only twenty years later that his cardinal presence in world cinema became obvious, with the presentation of *Naked* at the Cannes Festival, where it took out two prizes. This was because Leigh's oeuvre was essentially underground, most of his productions up until the 1980s *(Abigail's Party, Nuts in May, Meantime,* etc.) being made for television and not being visible outside England. *High Hopes* and *Life is Sweet* allowed me to pick up the thread of an oeuvre of rare coherence. A mania for labels tried to see Mike Leigh packed away with other talented filmmakers of the same generation who were also concerned with social issues. But Stephen Frears's eclecticism, like Ken Loach's strictly realist and ideological vision, are far from the world of Mike Leigh, marked as it is by an existential despair, black humour, the dereliction of his characters and a feel for caricature that we might liken to Dickens. Leigh also has a unique way of working with his actors, making them partners in the shooting of each of his films, which are truly works in progress.

Along with Cassavetes and Altman, he is one of the directors who have brought the most to 'directing' actors according to a process of improvisation and research. A man of the theatre to top it off and the author of numerous plays (one of which, *Bleak Moments*, was behind his start in film), he has a genuine love of language and his characters enjoy a linguistic kinship like those of Rohmer, without ceasing to be themselves. Mike Leigh has remained an angry 'young' man, caustic and sharp in the face of social injustice, but also in his likes and distastes. In debates and press conferences, as well as in interviews, where he reveals himself to be lively and profound, he doesn't hesitate to provoke the interlocutor, to sandblast sham, to get at the naked truth. His cinema, which cuts down to the bone, has no other goal.

ON *NAKED*

CANNES, MAY 1993

Your previous feature films were more centred on a group. In Naked, *you've opted for a main character.*

Until now, it's true, my concern has been to depict families or at the every least individuals in a family context. On the whole, the characters lived in a static domestic environment. And so I inevitably dealt with groups. In *Naked*, we also go through a temporarily static situation, but in an incidental way. Another of my concerns is the relationship between form and content, between the concept and my methods of working. In the final analysis, I have to take into account what is going to allow me to get the maximum out of my actors. Obviously, it's easier – to put it crudely – to work on a group of actors than on a central protagonist. With *Naked*, in the beginning, I wanted to get away from the family group and come out onto the street. I also wanted to talk about the lack of a home, the homeless, but I wasn't attracted by the idea of doing that based on a group, especially as I'd been toying with the idea of concentrating on a main character for quite a while. Furthermore, in most of my films, the accent had always been on the strength of the female characters. I wanted to explore a male protagonist a bit further. All these considerations explain the genesis of *Naked*, where the linear is preferred to the circular.

In the beginning, Naked *wasn't going to be the film that succeeded* Life Is Sweet.

It all depends on when you have to take seriously the idea of a film project, which always more or less belongs to the 'twilight of hypotheses'. It's true that, at the start of 1992, I was supposed to do another film. It was provisionally entitled *Flight Attendance*. I'd intended to work in a bigger format. But my problem has always been that I never want to say what my project will be, or read it to some star. The result is that I can never find more than a modicum of money. I had the idea, with my producer Simon Channing-Williams, of doing a 'broader' subject, giving it a title and offering it to some company. For a long while there were two film ideas I couldn't get out of my head. The first was called *Whingeing Poms*, 'pom' being the nickname Australians give to the English who, according to them, are always complaining (whingeing). The idea was to do a film about English people who emigrate to Australia and who, very quickly, get fed up with the place because it doesn't correspond to the utopia they'd imagined. They decide to go home. It's a recurring phenomenon and it's very interesting. The second project, *Flight Attendance*, came out of my reflections, every time I step into a plane, on the work of hostesses and stewards. These were both projects we could have put forward to backers. One company, Mayfair – which shut up its Cannes office even as we mounted the steps of the palais to present *Naked* there! – claimed to be ready to invest two million pounds in *Flight Attendance*, which would have topped up the usual contribution from Channel 4 and one from British Screen and a small sum advanced by the distributor. They had two demands: the film had to be finished for the Cannes Festival this year and part of the action had to take place in the United States. I ended up giving in to their pressure, we started on pre-production, but they still hadn't signed anything. So we withdrew. Channel 4 suggested using the money they'd already given us on another project of our choice and that's how *Naked* came about. I can't imagine how the other film would have turned out, but I don't think it would have been as good as *Naked*, so luck played in our favour.

Does the idea for Naked *go back to a precise moment?*

Honestly, that's a question without an answer. A subject like the one in *Naked* can only be a constant concern, it can't just suddenly spring to mind. There are lots of ideas in the film that I'd wanted to tackle for a long time in film. And at the same time, I could say that, as with my other films, I started from scratch with *Naked*. To start with, there's the casting. David Thewlis had played in my short, *The Short and Curlies,* in 1987, then he'd had a small role in *Life Is Sweet.* I'd have liked to have expanded it, but there was nothing to be done, I couldn't manage to get him back in the story. So then I said to him that one day I'd give him the starring role. And I thought of *Naked*. I've worked with brilliant actors, but David is exceptionally talented. It's incredible what he's capable of doing. To start with, he has the ability to read his part, to immerse himself in it, which is crucial for this kind of role. He is emotionally and intellectually inside things.

What were the stages in the development of the script? The film is built around a wandering life but its structure is made up of symmetries: he meets three men and three women, there are three other women in the house and a parallel between Johnny and Jeremy.

Most of my films are reasonably structured without it being too apparent on the surface. That comes from months of work with the actors before shooting, and this structure is more or less implicit in the development of the characters and the relationships between them. I think the structure has to be talked about at two levels. First at the conceptual level, where the dynamics of the story are established. When I develop a film, I work six days a week with the actors. On Sundays, I rest, that is, I go up into my office, I shut myself away and, as I think in fundamentally graphic terms, I draw the relationships between the characters on paper. For *Life Is Sweet*, I laid out Wendy and Andy, Nathalie and Nicholas, then Audrey. In my view, that's the structure, the seeds of the future narration. But it's important to remain open, not to commit yourself formally too prematurely. Later, as late as possible, even after the choice of the shoot locations, comes the second stage, the second level of the structure, where I write the script and divide it into scenes. Scene 1: Johnny and the woman in Manchester. Scene 2: Johnny steals the car. Scene 3: Johnny drives to London, etc. Scene 10: Johnny meets Brian. Office block. For each scene, there is, then, a minimum of information. You don't know just reading the script if the scene will last fifteen minutes or three. Myself, I have an idea, but I don't know exactly where I'm going; it's only later on, during the filming and the rehearsals with the actors, which have never stopped, that the dialogue is worked out, scene by scene. I have to test my own presuppositions constantly. The ending of my films is always open to discussion. It's never established in advance and it's only when I get there, that I make up my mind. It's like writing a novel: you only know the conclusion when you reach it; it's a progressive distillation. I'm very happy, for instance, with the final image in *Naked*, where Johnny goes off limping. But we were lucky enough to have a house – which is almost never the case – that we could still get in the shot by moving the camera back in the street. This shot occurred to me when I came every morning to film at that spot. Of course, a set-designer suggests possibilities to the head camera, but often the elements make their contribution, places influence the action. When the actors live on a set and react to the surrounds, the whole thing becomes an organic whole.

Did you ever doubt that Johnny would leave in the end?

That was subject to discussion. For myself, there was no doubt. But I have to constantly test my ideas in relation to the psychological and emotional motivations of the character and so of the actor. And it's obvious that he mustn't go back to Louise, as that would mean reducing the film to a magazine romance.

In Naked, *as in your other films, we have the clash of two social classes in the opposition between Johnny and Jeremy. But unlike in your trilogy,* Meantime, Four Days in July *and* High Hopes, *you don't directly refer to political issues.*

No, it's implicit. There's not a lot to say about social classes in the film. It's obvious. With Jeremy, we're dealing with power and money, in a typical representative of the Thatcher era. At another level, he's there to help make certain of Johnny's character traits less ugly. For that reason, I conceived these two characters together. The viewer goes through varied feelings in relation to Johnny's behaviour. At the beginning, you could very easily hate him. At the end, you end up loving him and respecting him. I'd have trouble rationalising that but it seemed to me that, in making Jeremy such an odious character, I'd help get Johnny accepted. As always, some people have attacked me for making Jeremy a caricature. But I don't agree. There are men like him in our society, he's entirely plausible, he reeks of the mustiness of Sloane Square. From the point of view of the narrative's structure, one of the hardest problems to resolve was the problem of his disappearance from the story. I tried numerous solutions. The only one that seemed acceptable was threatening Louise with his knife and Jeremy's departure, leaving the money behind. Every other conclusion to his visit seemed melodramatic. There's nothing to be done with a bloke like that. He goes off, will find someone else to fuck, but in no case can he be destroyed by these people he's met.

Why did you choose Manchester as the starting point for the action?

It could have been another town. But there are several reasons. First, I come from Manchester. I also wanted an industrial town in the country. Then, Lesley Sharp, who plays Louise, and David, come from that area – she comes from Liverpool, he comes from Blackpool, on the coast. Finally, Manchester is a very alive town for young people with a lot of rock music.

What is striking in Naked *in particular is the linguistic inventiveness, especially with Johnny. Not since Alex in* A Clockwork Orange, *perhaps, have we heard such a verbally creative character.*

Speaking prosaically and technically, the work wasn't much different from the work on the characters of my other films. It's Johnny who's different, more complex perhaps. But all I did with him was to extend research done elsewhere – for example, with the character of Aubrey, a director on tour, played by Timothy Spall in my play *Smelling a Rat*. We'd developed a kind of Dickensian language – I must say that Dickens has always had a great influence on me. You know, you meet people in life who talk like that. I remember that one day, when I was going off to rehearsals for *Naked*, at the entry to my tube station in North London, there was a man out of work on the pavement, gesticulating and yelling away, ranting about the end of the world. It's an image I shared with David and it's something you see every day in the great metropolises. At one point, while we were developing his character, I thought of ending with that, but it didn't feel right. Without the privilege of turning into artists or writers, loads of people are extraordinarily creative in their handling of words. David was brave enough to take the plunge, to go off and research the language he uses, whereas my role was to discuss the style and nature of it, to assess the ideas and objectives behind it. Basically, that came down to studying people's behaviour, the way people conduct themselves on a daily basis. And from that, if you use your imagination, you can always build a more complex character. There are, of course, specific influences lurking in the background. In *Naked*, there's a bit of Joyce, a bit of Beckett and a bit of Flann O'Brien, another Irishman whose book, *At Swim Two Birds,* is one I particularly love – it's a very funny novel full of imagination. I've also been marked by writers like Garcia Marquez, with *A Hundred Years of Solitude,* and Céline. I remember that, a long time ago, people would ask me why so many of my characters were catatonic when I had such a zest for language. I suppose that, since then, I've felt a growing need for words for my characters and Johnny allowed me to push the envelope in that direction.

How did the film's central scene develop – the philosophy discussion with the night watchman?

As always, it starts with the character. I like rehearsing in old buildings. That particular day we were in a decrepit office block in the centre of London. I'd started working with David Thewlis on the character of Johnny and Peter Wight joined us. I realised that I needed another character, on the same wavelength as Johnny. In *Meantime*, which is set partly in an unemployment office east of London, Peter Wight played a sort of hippy who, after falling from a window on the fifth floor, began delivering a speech on space, openings, termite mounds and all that nonsense, sitting on the ground. That was like an antecedent for *Naked*. So I thought about the character of Brian with Peter, about this man lost in thought, introverted, lost in his cogitations on space and time, marked by the failure of his marriage. Then I compared him with David and, using our method of improvisation, we worked out their dialogue. Later, on the advice of Alison Chitty, my brilliant set-designer, we filmed in an empty modern office block, which evoked the recession. During rehearsals, I also introduced the character of the woman at the window. I got her to come only of an evening. All she had to do was stay in her room for two hours; she didn't know that during that time the two men were also in rehearsal and were watching her through the window.

Do you equip your actors with an imaginary biography of their character?

Absolutely. We build it up together and sometimes we go back as far as the great-grandparents. But that depends on the character. Not many people know their great-grandmothers or great-grandfathers – outside the Irish and the upper classes. In any case, we discuss the members of their family, we give them names, jobs, everything you can think of. In a way, I go as far as making them relive certain experiences prior to the action of the film.

Yet some characters are more mysterious than others, like Sophie?

There are plenty of clues. We know that her father left her when she was little, whence her need for affection from men, that she's been through two abortions, one of them when she was just fifteen years old, that she's spent time in Paris, etc. What I never do, on the other hand, when I'm rehearsing with the actors is give them information about the other characters.

David Thewlis, for example, never knew why the barmaid (Gina McKee) suddenly chased him out of her place.

No, of course not. But, on the other hand, we understand that she's a loner who won't let anyone get near her, and doubtless the only really 'beautiful' face in the film. For me, she was someone inaccessible. You've noticed how a good number of the characters aren't from London. Her accent is from the north-east, near Newcastle. I imagine she must have had a job on the south coast, not far from Jersey or Guernsey, working in hotels, having been mistreated by guides, having taken drugs and drunk a lot in a sort of downward spiral. But I won't say anymore to you than to David about why she throws him out! In any case, when I work with the actors, and particularly with those who, like this girl, meet the character at a certain moment in the film, I force myself not only to invent details, but I push them to go out and discover their character, to find out what makes them tick. You can talk to an actor till you're blue in the face without him being any the wiser about how to play it, because performing is a practical, physical, psychological, emotional activity. All this preparatory work is aimed at getting them to explore their identity on their own.

Anglo-Saxon cinema, like literature, attests to a taste for excess, for the poetic imagination, which stems perhaps from the fact that you've been brought up from an early age on two sources: Shakespeare and the Bible.

Actually – but you mustn't take this too seriously – while we were filming, we told ourselves that our next film ought to be *Hamlet,* with Thewlis in the title role, a sort of Johnny Hamlet! When I was talking about influences a moment ago, I didn't mention Shakespeare because for an Englishman, as you say, that goes without saying, you always live with it. One of the happiest things that's ever happened to me is having worked at Stratford-on-Avon as an assistant director, in the 1960s. It was fruitful for me to work on productions of Shakespeare – good, bad or indifferent. I don't know if it's influenced the way I direct, but it's certainly influenced the way I write my scripts and dialogues – unconsciously.

The idea of the end of the world connected to the end of the millennium – does that spring from your pessimism faced with the British situation?

To be honest, it's a more global observation! Of course, at a certain level, you can analyse the film as a reflection on post-Thatcherism. But you only have to compare it to *High Hopes*, made only five years ago, to see the difference. In *High Hopes,* things are clear; you know who the goodies and baddies are, the rich and the poor. That reflected the Thatcher era, for Thatcher was a black and white institution, you knew where you stood, with her. From that point of view, things have changed, but not only in terms of power. After all, in *High*

Hopes, people still talked about socialism, they went to visit Karl Marx's grave. I remember going to Cracow with the film a bit before the collapse of the Soviet Union and, at one in the morning in the middle of winter; Polish viewers were still booing a film that they found obscene because the characters were clinging to the revolution! What's happened in five years is colossal; and we have *Naked,* an ambivalent film, in which the distinctions are no longer so clear. The film translates this 'grey' that's taken over from black and white and that you get in France, too, I suppose.

The palette of the film comes from reality, but there's nothing realistic about it. You play with black on black as with the black posters on black walls. It's very stylised.

Firstly, I'm assisted by a brilliant cinematographer, Dick Pope, who already photographed *Life Is Sweet*, and by my set-designer, Alison Chitty. *Life Is Sweet* was her first film. She'd achieved a lot of notoriety for her work in opera and theatre. She has an acute sense of colour and of characterisation and is a real team player. This film is unique for me, as I've started discussing the photography and sets with my collaborators well before the start of filming. I knew it had to have a very particular visual look and texture and that we needed to plan it. We did a bleach bypass in order to get denser blacks, a process that had been used by Tarkovsky in *Solaris* and Michael Radford in *1984,* as well as by Terence Davies. We wanted a nocturnal tonality, absolute control over the colours, but without it looking artificial. For myself, one of the jokes of the 1960s was Antonioni's abominable film, *Red Desert,* with its trails of red scattered more or less all over the place, which I find incredibly silly. I remember one shot – we did about twenty takes of it using methods from documentary cinema – where Johnny and Sophie are walking along the street. In the best take, a woman goes by in a red coat. Alison Chitty doesn't like that shot because we did everything we could to see that there was no red in the film!

Dick Pope does both the framing and the photography.

I've only once used two separate people, for a television film, *The Kiss of Death.* I don't like it; for me, the framing and the photography form a whole. Otherwise it's really schizophrenic. Dick Pope and Roger Pratt, who worked on *High Hopes*, are both really excellent and both like doing either. If they're happy just to take care of the lighting, they're not really in the film with the actors.

Obviously, that makes the filming more difficult since there are sequences where the lighting problems were very complex. You need to take your time and find locations that offer lots of possibilities. The house we filmed in had more angles for shots than we used. It had a 'gothic' resonance with *Psycho* and I enjoyed giving Hitchcock a wink and a nod in the shower scene. I really love that kind of Victorian architecture.

It's rather rich that you're so hostile to Antonioni when your films, like his, deal with lack of communication.

I'd resent him less if from time to time he gave me an opportunity to laugh. How can you make films about non-communication without a bare minimum of humour?! Really, Antonioni's films of the 1960s, along with *Last Year at Marienbad*, used to be my 'bêtes noires'! Resnais' film was a weird experience: I admired it and at the same time it bored me to death.

Andrew Dickson's music is also particularly remarkable.

I'd already worked with him on *Meantime* and *High Hopes*. I've been well served by three composers: Rachel Portman on *Life Is Sweet* and *Four Days In July*, Carl Davis on my earlier films and finally Andrew Dickson. I work very closely and intensely with musicians. I detest all forms of synthesised music and never wanted a synthesiser or any electronic device. All the sounds have to be organic. Music, in my view, can only serve a film if it works independently, if you can listen to it for itself. That comes specifically from the influence French films have had on me. People like Jaubert are the opposite of Hollywood music, which is too illustrative for me. I've kept my forty-five of the music from *Jules and Jim,* written by Delarue, and when I listen to it, it makes me regret my lost youth! The music is written once the film is in the can. For *Naked*, I wanted a continual, obsessional movement, one that could carry the film, a real 'riff'. It was really hard; it had to be varied and at the same time very coherent. We found a harpist, Skaila Kanga, who writes classical music and jazz, and we had to experiment because Andrew Dickson has never composed for the harp. He's a very interesting man; he lives in the back of beyond in Dorset and doesn't write much film music because nobody knows how to find him! Recently, he earned his living by going into prisons and teaching the cons how to make music. He lives in osmosis with the landscape, which is straight out of Thomas Hardy. It's a real expedition to go and work with him, whether you go by car along the most impossible roads or you take a train that stops at every station. Then, you have to factor in pauses while he goes and walks his dog or feeds his chickens or drives his two kids to school! But it's worth the trouble as his music has an integrity and a purity that are exceptional. In general, at the end of my work with the musicians, I've always got too much music, and I start taking some out, a bit more each time. Now I work with the video placed just above the piano, which allows you to compose directly as you watch the film.

Naturally you work just as closely with the editor.

The editing is vital for me, I spend a lot of time on it and we're very meticulous. For *High Hopes, Life Is Sweet* and *Naked*, my last three films, I was lucky enough to have the perfect editor, Jon Gregory. He's able to take the film we've shot that day and put it together so perfectly that, often, what he's done won't shift right to the end. He's exactly on my wavelength, he works very fast and we've never had words. We can spend the whole day until late at night at the Steenbeck, establish the editing of a sequence and when I come back the next morning, he's already there suggesting another possibility, which I accept or not. It's an ideal partnership because I absolutely do not want to be the editor. It's not healthy; I'm too close to the material. I prefer having to react when a solution is put to me. At every stage of a film, I get a maximum of benefit, personally and creatively, out of the process of collaboration. It stimulates me. In general, I don't shoot much more than I use in the edit, unlike Ken Loach, for instance, and I keep the scenes I've shot. In that sense, you could say that my editing is 'classic'. I do an average of eight to ten takes per shot and essentially what I look for are the nuances and the variations in the actors' performances. In the editing, it's the same thing: it's a matter of finding a subtle, internal balance between all these psychological and emotional states.

How did your partnership with your producer, Simon Channing-Williams, come about?

Simon was my first assistant on *Grown-Ups*, in 1980. I called him in as co-producer on *High Hopes* when I realised that the production company was particularly slack. Then we decided to set up our own company, an idea I'd always resisted as I didn't want to add another family to my own. It turned out to be very positive because Simon is brilliant and knows how to come up with the financing. He's an ideal producer, his activity is essentially practical and not caught up with the rest of it, he doesn't have any ambitions to become a director. His goal is for me to be able to do what I want. In the past, I've had good partnerships, but sometimes with producers who wanted me to accept them as co-authors on my films. With me that doesn't work. Wrongly, Simon sees himself as a philistine, which he isn't.

The film has more exteriors. Was the budget higher than for your previous films?

Yes. The film cost 1.6 million pounds sterling as opposed to 1.4 million for *Life Is Sweet*. At one point, towards the end of the shoot, I thought we wouldn't finish it. We went to see our financers, Channel 4 and British Screen, and told them we needed six more weeks, two for rehearsals and four to film the ending. After seeing the rushes they really loved it and they gave us the green light. They gave us amazing support and the film cost £200,000 more than estimated. There were two reasons why we were late. The first is that the photographic process we were using demanded more time for the lighting. The second is that writing the scenes during rehearsals took longer than usual. But, given our artistic requirements, 1.6 million pounds is not a lot of money; people worked enormously hard for very little gain so that the film would get done. For a long time I'd wanted to work on a bigger scale and by cheating I managed to do just that.

Do you think your scripts are more condensed, more compact today than your first films?

It might seem a bit academic, but I tend to divide my films into two groups: before and after 1980. The second lot are much more rigorous in their narrative structures. It's a constant concern in my work and it pursues me right into the editing room. I don't have any training in documentary; my background is in dramatic art. I have an architectural view of film.

What has stimulated you in recent cinema?

Chen Kaige, Zhang Yimou, Kieslowski. Very little coming out of the United States, with the exception of Robert Altman, I continue to be a fan of his. I like

Miller's Crossing, but I really didn't think much of *Barton Fink,* which felt to me like a pretty thin stylistic exercise.

The British presence at the Cannes Festival was spectacular, with four films in competition.

That's a fifth of our annual production. You can't talk about a Renaissance! Yesterday, they sent a minister from the Tory government to Cannes. Simon Perry from British Screen invited him to lunch. His visit was pretty brave since he must know that the British delegation was not particularly a bastion of conservatism, that just about everyone was in fact Labour. I don't think he'll do anything major, in any case not in the form of a direct idea as in France. They don't believe in it. I think the situation is dire. There are good films getting made, here and there, but the infrastructure is appalling. So little is made that the day will come when you won't find a dubbing room, a camera. It's very alarming. On the other hand, cinema going is on the upswing, but only in favour of American films. *Life Is Sweet* played to full houses across the United States. *High Hopes,* against all expectation, was a box office hit in Austin, Dallas and Houston. But over that same period, a great number of British houses refused to show it on the pretext that the public didn't want to see it. Now, I don't see why they wouldn't want to see my wife, Alison Steadman, in *Life Is Sweet,* when she played on stage in the West End for seven months to sell-out audiences and she's extremely popular. We are victims of Hollywood propaganda and it brainwashes our exhibitors into believing that only American films interest viewers. That's the war we have to fight.

20 MANOEL DE OLIVEIRA

(1908–)

The only active filmmaker alive to have kicked off in the silent era – he finished *Douro, Faina Fluvial* in 1931 – Manoel de Oliveira has had an exceptionally fertile career, churning out one film after another, even in his eighties and then in his nineties. It is likely that his long years of inactivity (he made only two feature-length films in forty years) and the frustration they engendered explain this creative explosion after 1970. Luis Buñuel, at once close to him and very different from him, also enjoyed an old age particularly rich in works inspired after a prolonged silence.

An artist fuelled by culture and in particular by literature (Claudel and Madame de Lafayette, but especially by his compatriots José Regio, Camil Castelo Branco and Agustina Bessa-Luís), Oliveira is also an inventor of cinematographic forms. As a true baroque artist, he loves mirror effects, reflexive irony, the *mis en abyme* of his subjects and parody, but he doesn't deprive himself of devastating flights of lyricism, either. Following the career path of this inspired filmmaker over the last thirty years has been one of the most intoxicating experiences of my life as a critic and being part of the celebration of his ninetieth birthday in his hometown of Porto was very emotional. Oliveira loves words and films his dialogues with the same delectation as a Rohmer, but he is also a highly visual man who refreshes his palette as he does his scenography. Witness his tetralogy of frustrated Loves, *O Passado e o Presente, Benilde ou a Virgem Mae, Amor de Perdiçao*, and *Francisca*. His oeuvre is a vast cultural and psychological fresco of his country, Portugal, though it later shifts towards more intimate works, like *Viagem ao Principio do Mundo* and *Je rentre à la maison*, in which Marcello Mastroianni and Michel Piccoli show themselves to be his alter egos. To meet Oliveira is always a moment of jubilation, of the sort procured by a deep but impish spirit, sufficiently wise not to take himself too seriously. Noël Herpe and I enjoyed the time we talked about *La Lettre*, a very free adaptation of *La Princesse de Clèves*.

ON *LA LETTRE*

CANNES, MAY 1999

The first question that springs to mind is to do with the great liberty you've taken (as in the case of Vale Abraao) *with a seventeenth-century novel that is itself set in the sixteenth century...*

For *Vale Abraao,* I asked Agustina Bessa-Luís to write a book about Madame Bovary that would be set in the Portuguese countryside of today... She was immediately interested and phoned me a few days later to get me to tell her a bit of a story. I said, 'I don't want you to write on demand: what I love about you is your spontaneity... What would be ideal is if you were to write the book how you liked – and then, I'd make the film of it!' And so that's how I adapted an adaptation. What's curious is that Flaubert said, 'Madame Bovary, that's me'; and then the book was rewritten today by a woman, with another point of view on the feminine condition. Then, lastly, I made a film of the book, which is written beautifully but is very literary, so it needed a lot of readjustment – and this brings us back once more to a man! But, when Flaubert uttered that phrase, he wasn't talking so much about Madame Bovary herself as his own work and of the social status of women at the time... With *La Princesse de Clèves*, the question posed itself very differently because we were dealing with an intimate drama: the novel is set in an old-world society, but it has to be transposed to today. Yet there is still a gap, even so, since the problem of freedom in love no longer presents itself as it once did; and what interests me precisely is maintaining some sort of status quo, with the same conflict as always... It's always the same heart beating!

But we are no longer governed by the moral rules that applied in the seventeenth century: how did you manage to get these accepted?

I felt that, and I tried to weigh up two ethical positions. We are seeing so-called freedom, but other cases still exist: I know of some that no one knows anything about because you don't see it, it's hidden... You might get, say, naked women at the beach, packaged and presented for show, or even the sex act itself, which is often reproduced in cinema, and not in a very loving way (see 'hydraulics', as someone in Portugal said to me…). That's what we see, that's what the press and the media reveal. But the other side of things remains hidden; we know nothing about it; you might say it doesn't exist! At such a point in time, we have to wonder what constitutes identity and dignity, how any connection might be established, whether it's a matter of an individual or of a nation: when a king loses a battle, he reminds us that he has not lost honour – which is more important than the battle… In the film, I never opt for either one of these points of view, I leave it up to the viewer to judge, which only leaves the problems unanswered: it's interesting to see how behaviour that seemed normal in the seventeenth century today seems shocking to some people! But it doesn't shock me at all: there is, there, a higher state, a stop on the way to sainthood: any commentator on Camoen's *Lusiades* sees different heroes in it: the sailor, the captain, Vasco de Gama, the mythological gods, etc. And man's physical and psychological constitution is made up of crisscrossing vertical and horizontal lines that rise or fall according to the circumstances.

While shifting the plot to the contemporary world and playing with the anachronisms (with the duc de Nemours morphing into a rock singer), you accentuate the religious dimension which is not overtly present in the book, you make it Jansenist and thereby take it back to the seventeenth century…

It's not the framework of Port-Royal that interests me, it's the representation of Jansenism, in the sense of a fate that governs beings: when Madame de Clèves regards the portrait of Angélique Arnaud, she feels doomed to her fate. What commands souls are impulses that inspire certain acts that are sometimes against our will, or very difficult for us… Orson Welles once said: 'That's my nature': it's the old story of the scorpion and the frog! As for the nun, she declares herself in favour of the marriage, which would be the simplest solution… If I've invented a nun who doesn't exist in the novel, it's because the princesse de Clèves is going to seek refuge in a convent where she has a childhood friend – which allows her to give in to intimacy, to find a confidante.

Did the idea of having a rock singer come to you straight away or was it inspired by Pedro Abrunhosa?

I wanted the film to be based on strong contrasts: in the seventeenth century, women didn't cheat on their husbands or leave them like they do today. But it's also a contrast between cultures: today, in the rock singer, you find an equivalent character, but one belonging to an entirely different milieu: this creates a feeling of strangeness that didn't exist in the seventeenth century – as do the allusions to the actual situation in Africa, in the final letter, or to the political context... These are questions that are extremely important, but, when a serious event occurs (an illness, a woman who is about to die), you forget the social side and return to a more intimate register.

Did you know Pedro Abrunhosa before and is the character close to him?

No, I didn't know him, I only had a few notions about his career... It was only after the event that I learned he was my grandson's music teacher! I thought of him when I saw him on stage; and as he'd acquired an international reputation that suits the role, I offered him the part. As for his dark glasses, they add to the originality of the character, to his special nature, which is neither common nor vulgar. That's why I asked him to keep the glasses; he simply toned down the density of the darkness.

On the other hand, you have accentuated the intensity of the darkness by filming the concert as the final scene...

Yes, it's like a clown performing the day his wife dies!

Did the adaptation go through several versions, notably in relation to the concert at the beginning and at the end?

I cut out a lot of things, always aiming for the essential and eliminating the rest, substituting inserts, which are faster and which offer a kind of pause. As far as the beginning goes, I substituted the Foundation for the couture house, where the film was first supposed to start, to evoke the concentration of a court where everyone knows everyone else and to establish the relationships between the characters.

Why alternate very long scenes (like the death of Madame de Chartres, which is played straight out of the book) and the breaks in rhythm or use of ellipses? For example, you don't film the final explanation between the two protagonists...

I preferred to maintain the mystery by avoiding having them meet. If they find each other, there's a risk of a loss of resistance, a decline into weakness or the danger of a 'brief encounter'... That passion is made for distance: if you diminish the distance, the passion is lost. In truth, material realisation undoes the dream.

Speaking of inserts, Kubrick used to say that, in silent film, they let you economise on whole scenes...

Yes, I understand this view of Kubrick's: there's no point wasting time with images to say So-and-So's not here, he's gone somewhere else, if that's not really part of the drama... Here, we stay within the drama. In most American films where they want to do action, we see the character get out of the car, walk along the footpath, go into the lobby, take the lift, walk through the office building until he gets to his office, sit down at his desk and get busy with his affairs... All that is nothing just so you can begin to say something. And after, it's only his words that count! Such images are only interesting as archives: 200 years later on, they'll remain as testimony to daily life, which is fine... But, to economise on the dramatic art, it's much better to slap in an insert.

At the end of the film, Madame de Clèves is going to devote herself to others, whereas all through the story, she has stayed in the background... From the social 'world' she moves to the world outside, she broadens her vision.

Yes, she has crossed a hurdle: it's her way of fleeing; she needs a very strong object, something that really focuses her attention, to stop her remaining on her own, thinking about that man... Having known sisters who left like that when they were very young, I used what they told me about the desire to teach religion to people who are hungry and sick... It's a situation that touches me greatly, I'm the one who wrote the text of the letter – but in words that I'd heard before! And even Madame de Chartres' reply, about the thief and the criminal, who haven't changed in 500 years, that's a phrase that I heard and liked... Things change and don't change, evil goes on, it simply shifts ground from love to vice: we're not at the beginning of the twenty-first century, we're at the real end of the twentieth century!

Do you know The Ladies of the Bois de Boulogne, *in which Bresson transposed a novel from the eighteenth century to the Paris of the Occupation?*

That's the first film of Bresson's that I ever saw: the image of the car coming into the garden has stayed with me... But, even with Bresson, there's a huge evolution, from *A Man Escaped* to *Money*! That's a film with an impressive structure, since all the different elements occupy different places without any communication or connection between them; they're all scattered facts, without any link... And, at the end, it all only goes deeper.

How did you come upon La Princesse de Clèves *and what made you decide to turn it into a film?*

Jacques Parsi told me about it when I was in pre-production on *Amor de Perdição*; it's a subject that fits into the long line of frustrated loves. That really touches me, just as lost wars do: the loss of a war invites meditation, and victory, futility!

And The Satin Slipper *was also the story of an impossible love...*

Yes, magnificent! Prouhèze, too, keeps her passion at a distance. But the character that interests me the most is don Pélage, her husband: he's a man who conducts himself in keeping with his sense of dignity and duty. For the good of the country, he sends his wife to Africa, to Camille, who is passionately in love with her: he sends her into danger, but only because of his confidence in her and in something higher. That's where the man's incredible dignity lies – if it exists at all, which I'm not too sure about...

For the costumes, how did you manage to strike this balance between the old and the new that suggests some indeterminate time?

I always give this question a great deal of attention: this time, I asked each actress to choose her couturier; but for Anny Romand, we hardly had to look, because she dresses in a way that always suits me... Françoise Fabian, too, chose her models and jewels without too much trouble, and we quickly agreed. For Chiara Mastroianni, it took longer, because of the time spent changing clothes, hats, etc. But we got there in the end, with the help of the costume supervisor, who I asked to add a few missing touches to the whole thing.

Did you direct the actors very precisely to obtain such neutral performances, stripped of any psychology?

I don't talk much to the actors. I give very precise directions as to positions and movements so that one actor doesn't hide another and passes behind him, or, on the contrary, hides him if that's intended... I've read interviews with Chiara

Mastroianni where she says I even spell out which foot should take the weight of the body ... and it's true! All that is very important, because it determines the arrangement of the figures in the tableau. As for directions about diction, they're few and far between, because I prefer what the artist gives me to what I can tell them, even if it's right: it's like sticking a hat on your neighbour's head!

To what extent is it necessary for you to build a film around a written text?

It's necessary to the simple extent that I don't want to get away from human behaviour. People behave in the strangest ways, but this has its limits and it can't be false or abnormal... For instance, in *Inquiétude*, I directed the characters from *Immortelles*, not without telling myself that it was fairly extraordinary, even if only for the murder of the old son by the old father: because they're famous scientists, they don't want to leave behind an image of decadence. So they have to kill to remain at their peak... But afterwards, it's like Deleuze throwing himself out the window and leaving a letter to say he didn't want to remain so diminished: we're brought back to reality, to the real world, it's no longer some fantasy... That's why I made the film. What I look for in a story is what's human – curiously, oddly human, but human nonetheless.

But is the work very different if it's a baroque play like The Satin Slipper *or a classic novel like* La Princesse de Clèves?

The Satin Slipper was a very particular experience: I made a cut-out by buying two of Claudel's books to have two pages; on one of them, I glued a sheet where I wrote down notes concerning the text... That's how I conceived of the film. Why do otherwise? Claudel's family asked to see the cut-out: I replied by saying, 'You've already got it: it's your father's play.' Luckily, they loved the film and I was happy to have worked that way. But there is, on the one hand, what is written and, on the other, the imagined notion of what you're going to film: that's why I've done a lot of drawings with artisans working on the sets and indicated the angles of the shots so we could calculate the distance in advance... It was a very long, very expensive film, and we had to be pretty precise. On that basis, we could vary the point of view along with the actors' performances... For *La Princesse de Clèves,* I first thought of doing a fairly faithful adaptation, but it would have been very hard to do and very expensive, because of the palace, the court, the costumes, the carriages, the horses... We would have had to provide the ambiance of the era and its mentality, too. After that, I got passionate about transposing this rigidity of behaviour to our day, when the current has absolutely reversed: it sets up a very nice contrast.

But don't you give any political or religious weight to the sacrifice of your princess?

No, neither of the above. Like she says, she doesn't have a religious vocation… It's a sacrifice in favour of other sacrifices, something that can't be explained. I think that what best explains humanity works through things that can't be explained! Marx made a mistake when he forgot this side of man: his system is magnificent, but utopian; the motive that drives a man to seize power, whether Stalin or Hitler, a king or a dictator, is the dream of transforming himself into God.

You get the impression somewhat that Madame de Clèves is trying to recover the real meaning of words, while all around her everyone is talking a superficial language, notably when it comes to politics…

She's indifferent to the whole of that conversation, because she's only thinking of one man! And the words of others, which are far removed from serious personal problems, allow us to observe how society is reflected in her own story… It's the framework that awaits her, the echo of global politics that is going to have an impact on her own personal fate. And the immediate echo is the announcement of Abrunhosa's death, which provokes the scandal and forces her to acknowledge her infatuation; it's the equivalent of falling off the horse in the novel, something we also find in *Anna Karenina* – something that television offers a more 'modern' substitute for!

Do you see a connection between the Emma of Vale Abraao *and Madame de Clèves, in this sort of love of the impossible?*

No, it's the opposite: where Madame Bovary, from the point of view of social reprobation, falls into the vice of infidelity, Madame de Clèves rules that out, even in a setting that's open and permissive, due to the strength of her ethics and her love for her husband. It's another way of loving that implies respect unto the death, and even after death… And she flees the vulgar mundanity whereby you give yourself, following your heart's desire: she prefers to keep an imaginary passion intact.

One gets the impression that the man she loves is a shadow, that he exists in another world...

He is from another world! That's what passions are made of – not material reality or egotism... I remember seeing a film of sketches from Argentina, in which a character always passes the same place at the same time on his way to work. And a woman appears to watch him go by, at the window on the fourth floor. When he comes back, there she is, and he waits for her to come down, he's fallen in love and his passion for this pretty woman is extremely violent, irresistible... One day, he makes up his mind, he goes up to the fourth floor and there, he's greeted by a dressmaker and discovers that the woman at the window is a dummy. You see how passion is made up of strange sensations, it's an area we have no control over.

Often in the film there are effects of displacement that modify the structure of the book...

I kept what was essential in the dialogue at the mother's death, of the confession in the garden and of Monsieur de Guise's monologue before he kills himself. But when she comes back to the garden where she has confessed her sin, it's in honour of her husband, who has died for love of her, and also because something leads her to this spot; and she meets the man she loves on the very bench where she made her confession... Here it was a matter of very subtly, very roughly, showing her in the process of discovering that he has overheard her admission of love for him, and of running away because she's running away from herself! And the fauna represent the sexual arousal that's been triggered inside her since she's not an angel or some supernatural being, but a woman attracted to a man.

Did you thinking of keeping an episode that's important in the book, the one about the lost letter?

That made me think especially of *my* letter. Doubtless I told myself that the title would create confusion, that people would think of the letter in the book... But I'm fond of *The Letter*: it suggests a difference and a bridging of the gap from one century to the next. In fact, the letter represents a secret that's never revealed: it's not what is said, it's what is not seen. There's something in humanity that escapes us: that's what I call 'the letter'. I'd also written a script for a short film that was already called *The Letter*. I was asked for material, but I had to abandon it because it wasn't sufficiently developed to make a film out of and I didn't want to see it up on the screen with my name on it. I preferred to do another *Letter*, even if it's an adaptation! The story was about a woman who writes a letter we know nothing about and she goes off to post it with a satanic smile on her face… The woman who receives the letter goes mad and throws herself out the window. Someone saves her, retrieves the letter, puts it in another envelope and addresses it to another person. We see wildly different reactions until we come to Provence. There, we see a young woman who is delighted and she dances round and then collapses, dropping the letter. At that point, one of her two old aunts grabs the letter and the other one follows her, the first one is running all over the place … but, when she sees that she can't hide the secret in the letter from her sister, she throws it in the fire that's burning in the fireplace. We'll never know what the letter says!

21 SATYAJIT RAY

(1921–1992)

The man was a lord. Imposing by his height, by the beauty of his English, by his physical presence, by his intellectual radiance. I'd published the first overall study of his work in France just as *The World of Apu* was released, very late in the day, in 1964. This was the third film in the trilogy that began with *Pather Panchali* and that brought him fame in the mid 1950s. Ray had been touched by my interest, especially as France had turned away from him, curiously, shortly after he made his debut, leaving the Venice Festival the honour of awarding him the Golden Lion for *Aparajito*, then the Berlin Festival of programming his great works of the 1960s. On several trips to India, where I got to know other creators of importance who venerated him, such as Mrinal Sen in Bengal, Shyam Benegal in Bombay, Adoor Gopalakrishnan and Aravindan in Kerala, I was able to meet Ray several times and visit him at his home in Calcutta, the city of intellectuals and artists. He was Calcutta incarnate, simultaneously a cartoonist, draughtsman, pen and ink illustrator (he published numerous illustrated children's books), musician (he wrote the music for all his films from 1961 on), writer, filmmaker, of course – and one of the best. Later, I sat in on the filming of *Agantuk*, his last film, where he showed remarkable stoicism, given that he was already very weak. The long interview published here is a complete transcript of a show put together by French television station Antenne 2, when Ray was finally recognised in France, in the 1970s, before being glorified for his weakest films in the 1980s.

Ray's cinema is a reflection, in occasionally Chekhovian tones, on the old and the new, the necessary abandonment of the past despite its real lures. But Ray is nonetheless closer to Renoir than to Visconti. For him, a dewdrop holds the world and his aesthetic is more one of contemplation than action. He doesn't leave out modern India, though – an accusation that has sometimes been levelled at him, unjustly – and he knows how to evoke the emergence of a new social class and the problems linked to a great town. From adaptations of Tagore (*Charulata, The Three Sisters*), to the depiction of the obsessional love of a landowner for music (*The Music Room*, perhaps his masterwork), from the famine of *Distant Thunder* to the tender lyricism of *Days and Nights in the Forest*, Ray's world is a vast fresco painted in humanist colours. One single regret: that he cast his equal, the immense Bengali filmmaker, Ritwak Ghatak, unknown in the West until after his death in 1976, in the shade. One word of praise for the foreigner from Ray would have done the trick. He never uttered it.

ON HIS FILMS

PARIS, JUNE 1978

Since your first film, the one that made you famous overnight, Pather Panchali (Song of the Little Road), *is a film about childhood, I won't ask you if the film is autobiographical but what your own childhood was like.*

It was completely different from the one shown in the film as I was born in a town, I was completely unfamiliar with the country; I was a real little city dweller. I was born in the north of Calcutta. I never knew my grandfather, but he owned one of the most beautiful printing presses in India. He was also an inventor, a painter, a musician, a writer – he wrote beautifully for children. He died roughly six years before I was born and my father took over his business, the printer's. He was also full of talent. He was also a painter and a writer, and he'd studied etching and lithography in England. So I was born into this atmosphere of various artistic activities. But I lost my father when I was very young. I was only two when he died.

So you lived with your mother?

Yes. The business was put into liquidation, we moved, we had a very great struggle. I never realised because I was brought up at my maternal uncle's where I received a good education. My mother worked to bring me up. And so that's what my childhood was like. I grew up in my uncle's house, I went to school, to 'College', I got my diploma, a degree in economics, then I went to Tagore's university to study painting.

Was there a connection between Tagore and your family?

Yes, they were very close. He was roughly the same age as my grandfather; he used to come to our house, as they had a lot in common. But everyone, all the intellectuals, knew Tagore, respected him. In fact he influenced all the writers and musicians of the time. We were very close to him.

And you yourself, when you were at his school or later, did you have a lot of contact with Tagore?

Actually, when I left 'College', I didn't have much of an idea what to do, but my mother was extremely keen for me to go to Tagore's university. I was already ... I had a natural gift for drawing, and I wanted to become a graphic artist, to work in advertising, because you could earn your living that way. But my mother asked me, 'Why wouldn't you go there?' Tagore was still alive, this was in 1940, and she'd then say, 'Why don't you spend some time at Shantiniketan University? I think it would do you good.' And I think it was a very wise decision, because when I was at Shantiniketan, I found myself in contact with some wonderful people. We had extraordinary art teachers; I studied painting and I immersed myself in Indian traditions; we went on trips to all the art centres of the country, two or three friends and I. And Tagore was there. But he was a most venerable character, one you rarely approached. We might have gone to see him once every six months, since he lived some distance away. He was already eighty years old and he died while I was studying there. So, Tagore was there and we felt his influence, even if you couldn't get near him because he was a bit withdrawn.

I read somewhere that one day you went through his papers and archives and you found traces of a sort of 'séance' during which he spoke to your father.

Yes, but that was later. That was in 1960 and I was already a filmmaker. In 1960, we were celebrating the centenary of his birth and the government asked me to make a film as a tribute to him. So I went back to his university and I had access to all his manuscripts and all his papers, everything, down to the last little scrap of paper preserved in his bedroom. I spent a month going through all that. And it was extraordinary because I found notes recording the séances he'd conducted with a medium who was a young woman poet, a young poet who died at the age of twenty-seven and who was apparently a very good medium. So there were transcriptions of conversations with the dead, with Tagore's relatives, and with my father. I found three notes relating to a conversation with the spirit, with the presumed spirit, of my father.

When you lived in Calcutta, did you often go to the country?

I became interested in *Pather Panchali* when I was illustrating a special edition of the book. I was a commercial artist at that point and I was working in a British agency as a designer, working on layout and typography, and I was also in touch with a very good publishing company that was quite revolutionary in that it published Bengali books with very good typography and illustrations. So I was working for this publisher and the advertising agency at the same time. And the publisher decided to bring out a slightly abridged edition of *Pather Panchali* for young people and asked me to illustrate it. We'd already founded the Calcutta Film Club by that time. Cinema interested me more and more and advertising less and less as I didn't find the job very absorbing. So, we used to talk about films – and I was naturally very familiar with American movies, since I'd been a film buff from childhood or at least since my schooldays: I knew all the American movie directors.

So that was my attitude to cinema in the beginning: I was a film buff. But at Tagore's university there was a library where I started to read serious books on film, the rare books available in English at the time, those by Poudovkine, Raymond Spottiswood. Eisenstein was much later. *Film Sense* was published in 1947, the year our film club was launched. I was then already what you call a film buff and we decided we needed to do something in that direction and we founded our film club. That was in 1947, the year of Independence. And in 1949, I illustrated *Pather Panchali* and I realised that there was a film to be made out of it; but there was no question of leaving my job since I was an artistic director on a good salary – it was what you call a position with 'an assured future'. But in 1950, my British advertising agency sent me to work in the parent company in London. So I spent four and a half months or five months in London, and I devoted them especially to going to see films.

And what did you find in London?

The first thing I did was to get my card to the British Film Institute and the first thing I saw was *The Bicycle Thief*, in a double with a Marx brothers' film. And

The Bicycle Thief was a great, a very great film. It was a revelation to me, since I'd already brought up the possibility of filming *Pather Panchali* in Calcutta with professionals who'd told me, 'You can't work with amateurs, you can't work in exteriors, you can't film in the rain, you can't do this, you can't do that. You have to build a village at the studio.' I'd said, 'Certainly not, I'm sure you can do what I say.' And I see De Sica's film: he'd filmed with non-professionals, in exteriors, in all weathers, rain or shine. And that gave me courage again. In the boat that brought me back to India, I wrote the first film treatment – I mean, it was just a few pages, the general idea for the film.

And on your return you met Renoir?

No, I'd met him before I left, because he'd originally come to Calcutta looking for locations and to audition local actors. My office was right next to his hotel, hardly more than three minutes on foot. A notice in the *Statesman*, a major Calcutta newspaper, said that Monsieur Jean Renoir would like to meet actors for a film he was hoping to shoot in Calcutta or surrounds. I knew his American films, but not the French ones. I'd seen *The Southerner* and a few others.

The Southerner *also deals with country life and is notably realistic.*

Exactly. In fact, *The Southerner* and *Pather Panchali* are very much alike to the extent that there's an old woman, two children and their parents, poverty and the struggle to survive. So I went and saw him and I introduced myself as movie mad: 'I know your films, and I'm also a painter, and so I know your father's work.' He showed a lot of interest and surprise when he discovered that a Bengali knew so much about his work and his father's. So I got into the habit of visiting him at his hotel, then accompanying him as he looked for locations around Calcutta, because I know the countryside well. I suggested some of the locations he filmed. It was especially at times like those that I had time to talk to him about all sorts of things. I think I swamped him with questions, but he was very obliging, and he loved talking about his father's work and his own.

So when Renoir first came to India I was still in Calcutta, then I left for England and he came back and made *The River*. I came back before the end of the shoot and I'd have liked to watch him working more often, but, as you'll understand, I had my own work and I actually only went to watch him filming twice. Then he took off.

Was that useful for you?

Oh yes, very much so. And the conversations with him were wonderful, extraordinary. He was a great man and I don't know that I admire anyone more.

Speaking of encouragement that visitors lavished on you, I also heard that John Huston...

The Museum of Modern Art in New York decided to do a major exhibition of Indian art and one of its representatives, Monroe Wheeler, came to Calcutta to examine the works. He knew me as a publicist – I had a name in advertising – and he came to see me. I told him I was working on a film project and he replied, 'If you finish in time, I'd like to show it at MoMA.' Then he left and maybe three or four months later, John Huston turned up as he hoped to film *The Man Who Would Be King* with Humphrey Bogart and someone else. And our meeting took place as usual: he stayed in the same hotel as Jean Renoir, I went to see him and I said, 'I have about 2,500 metres of rushes and I'd like to show them to you.' And I showed them to him. It was an initial cut, really very rudimentary. And it so happened that he was a friend of Mr Wheeler's. When he returned to New York Wheeler said to him: 'I think this film is going to be interesting, so show me.' That's how John Huston recommended my film to Monroe Wheeler who had already more or less made his decision. But it was cutting things short as far as timing went. The film was shown at MoMA in New York even before it was shown in Calcutta. The last of the work on the film was done in mad haste – my editor and I did the final cut in ten days and ten nights without sleeping. And after the mixing I couldn't manage to see a copy. It came out of the laboratory only to be carted off immediately to Pan American, where I feel asleep with my arms on the counter. The person on the desk woke me up. The film left for New York, was screened at the Museum and came out in Calcutta two months later.

And the Cannes Festival, where did that fit into these events?

A year later. Someone was going to Cannes – one of my Indian friends ... and it all happened before the official selection process began. It was a bit easier then, because you could just turn up with a film and show it. That's what my friend did. I later learned that at the screening, which was at the end of the day, there was hardly anyone there, apart from half a dozen viewers!

André Bazin.

Yes, André Bazin was there, and Lindsay Anderson, Lotte Eisner.

Then the film gained an international reputation.

Yes, but not all the members of the jury saw it, as you can imagine, and a second screening had to be organised. Then it won a prize, which was incredible.

And after that you made all these great films…

I'll tell you something. I hadn't left my job to make *Pather Panchali.* It took us two and a half years to finish it, partly because we didn't have any money for long stretches of time. We'd started off with our small personal resources and part of my salary went into the film. So those were the conditions in which my first film was made. But after it came out and after its success – it was a success in Bengal, already, before Cannes; it has sometimes been said that Satyajit Ray only became a film director after the Cannes Festival but that's not true: people here loved the film and it played for a long time – after that, then, I decided to leave advertising and make films. I had the idea of doing a second part. Originally it wasn't conceived as a trilogy.

I'd like to talk about your relationship to India, but let's first get the outside influences, neo-realism, Renoir and so on, out of the way. What is your relationship to Great Britain and British culture? It must be ambivalent.

It is, since, after all, we learned English, we went to schools where they taught English. You could go to an English school, a religious school run by the Jesuits, but that's not what I did. I went to a Bengali school, but there, too, we learned English, we read English books, English literature, and even popular English novels, cartoons and all that. I was in contact with all that. But I think I'd define myself as a product of the East and the West – not necessarily of Great Britain and India, but of Western culture and Indian culture because, since my school years, I've been interested in Western music, which is not British music but classical Western music.

Beethoven, Mozart?

Beethoven, Mozart, Bach. I'm talking about when I was fourteen, fifteen. It's incredible, because ever since I was a child we had a gramophone in the house. I don't know who it belonged to. But there was a Beethoven violin concerto movement, the rondo, in an old recording made by Kreisler at the Berlin Opera. It had been reissued as an old classic, but we had, I had, this single movement from one of Beethoven's works, and I used to read the *Book of Knowledge* and Beethoven was one of my childhood heroes: this deaf composer, with this strong personality. His character interested me, naturally, and so I wanted to hear other pieces by him and I started a record collection. But in the beginning I had so little money that I could only buy one movement a month. But I saved my pocket money to buy a movement of his works every month and later Mozart.

During my 'College' years, at the same time as my interest in cinema, my interest in Western music grew, and I read everything I could on the subject, I'd buy records, I'd listen to the radio. So, there you have it, as far as Western culture goes. Later, I started to get interested in classical Indian music. I was born into a musical atmosphere, because everyone, on my mother's side, was a born singer: my aunt, my mother... And they'd sing Tagore's songs – he was also a composer. I told you it was at Shantiniketan that I became interested in Indian traditions, in Indian art, but also in Western art. There we learned all about impressionism, the Renaissance, Japanese art, Chinese art. We were taught calligraphy and how the Chinese held the brush this particular way – calligraphy was part of our curriculum. Later, I did Bigmali calligraphy using Japanese brushes. And so I was in contact with the art and music of the whole world.

That's what The Music Room *is about.*

That's what it's about. I'll tell you how it started. The second part of the trilogy had been a financial disaster and I decided ... I had somewhat confused ideas after the success of *Pather Panchali* and this unexpected failure – a commercial failure, since it was a critical success. So I decided to make a film about music. I thought the Indian public liked bit of song and dance and so I'd make a film about music and dance. I read this story and...

The story of an old man…

Yes, but in writing the script, you know it's the story of a feudal lord who's reached the end of… It's the symbolic end of the feudal world and the birth of the…

New class.

Of the new class. But while I was writing the script, I was no longer thinking about the public and it turned into a very serious, very grave study of feudalism and the music I used was classical, not at all the music of popular films. So in the end that film, too, turned out not to be made for a big audience but for a much smaller audience. From a commercial point of view, that was doubtless a mistake, but even though I enjoyed making the film and I find it interesting as a study of feudalism, I next did a comedy.

The Philosopher's Stone (Parash Pathar).

That's right, since for various reasons I wanted to change, I don't like repeating myself. And so I'd made *Pather Panchali*, and *Aparajito,* which is more or less about the same thing. But then I wanted a complete contrast, so I did *The Music Room.* Then I wanted a fresh contrast and so I did *The Philosopher's Stone.* I wanted to use an actor who'd only ever had small roles and who I felt was capable of much more. I wanted to give him a major role in a big film; I wanted him to be the film. And so I made *The Philosopher's Stone. Aparajito* was then shown at Venice, won the Golden Lion there and, in the course of a press conference, I was asked if I planned to make a trilogy and I heard myself say: Yes. I still don't know why I gave that reply. When I came home I reread the book and I found there was a third film in it. So I made a trilogy. And I was very proud of it!

How useful press conferences can be!

Yes.

To get back to England, you spoke, in your ambivalent attitude, about the positive side. But what was your feeling about England and the English presence? Did you have the impression they were dispossessing you of your culture?

By that time we were already independent.

But earlier, I mean before 1947. As an adolescent, then as a young man from India, how did you feel about the presence of the British?

The thing is that I didn't much feel it directly and as a student, not at all: we had teachers from England teaching us English, which was not a bad thing, which was even a good thing. There was of course the political aspect. I was very young, I think I was nine or ten when Gandhi began his first civil uprising in India: so we were too young.

I remember we were spinning cotton, even as young children. Everyone was supposed to spin their own cotton, wear homespun cotton. So we did. I was very good at it. Then another phase began, in 1942 actually, when I was a student at Tagore's university, the first great anti-British movement, the 'Quit India' movement of 1942, launched by Gandhi, which I wasn't personally active in. I was abreast of things, but I was perhaps too preoccupied by the discovery of Indian art and Indian tradition to be directly attracted to politics. I didn't have that kind of personality.

Then came Independence… And it was a good thing, but I have the feeling that I owe a lot, not to British culture in particular but to Western culture.

How do you regard Bengali culture? I mean that for us it's difficult to see the main differences between Bengali culture and the other great Indian cultures.

It so happened that the capital of British India was Calcutta and that what we called the Renaissance in the nineteenth century occurred in Bengal. It was a whole group of intellectuals who'd studied English culture – Mill, Bentham, those were the philosophers they read. And the two great influences of the day were Mazzini and Garibaldi, you see, for all the people on the left at the time. Their contacts with Western ideas were ironic in that this Western education was responsible for the development of an anti-imperialist attitude on the intellectuals' part. It's very interesting: one read Mill, Bentham and Locke, and Hume, then one read the history of Garibaldi and Mazzini and what they did in Italy, and then one felt that the British… This attitude of questioning British power only began in the nineteenth century in India, and it began in Bengal. The signal was given by a few major intellectuals who knew what the British were but who were ready to oppose the bad that imperialism did. That was the start. And from that movement, gradually, the most enlightened people found themselves drifting to the left, and communism continued to undermine imperialism, relentlessly. But that is ironic.

Yes, but it's interesting because we can feel in what you've said the same contradictions one finds in your work: things are never simple; revolt was brought about by the very people who were oppressing you, and in your films one finds this kind of contradiction again. You don't give pat answers.

That's because I don't think there are any and, if they do exist, I don't know what they are. What I try to do is to present certain problems, and the situation, in as much depth as possible and to leave people to think, to leave them to become aware of certain things and draw their own conclusions from them. I don't think there's a ready-made answer to any question.

In Pather Panchali *and the whole trilogy, you show poverty, misery, the countryside, but you also show the unity of the family.*

Yes.

Then you go to the city, where there is more wealth, but also more loneliness. It's a contradiction.

Yes, loneliness. And the second part deals with this interesting moment when the mother lives in the village while the young boy has to grow up far from his mother because he's dragged away by education and by the thirst for knowledge, which takes him to the city. That's one of life's contradictions.

In The Music Room, *too, there's a sort of nostalgia for this culture that's disappearing.*

Yes. Certain circles, let's say very much to the left, certain among them only, have attacked me, claiming that I showed sympathy for feudalism, that I defended it, which is not true. It's just that everything that dies has something pathetic about it and I don't think it's right to leave out that aspect. So this feudal lord is wrong to cling to those values and yet history wipes out feudalism and the other class appears. So there's a conflict. He doesn't know what has caused his downfall and I find that there is pathos in that.

And each culture has its own values.

Each culture has its own values, because they were, after all, the protectors of music and after the death of feudalism, the musicians experienced dire poverty because no one gave them work anymore. That's also a historical fact that must be taken into account, to be authentic.

We also see in you, as in the Russian filmmakers and in the American filmmakers, too, in fact, a preoccupation with life's transformations. For instance, the image of the train…

Yes, Chekhov.

The image of the train taking people to another civilisation.

Yes, I think the train is used symbolically in the trilogy. In the first film you get the first sight of the train: the young boy has never seen or heard one. In the second, the train comes to symbolise what takes the son away from his mother, so much so that the mother has to wait and see the train to understand that her son might well be on this train, that he's coming back to her. And in the third, it's the most sordid aspect of the train and the city, since the train travels alongside the young man's house, with blasts of the whistle, steam, smoke and the grit associated with it.

One thing that allows us to judge the social attitude of a filmmaker and his openness to social issues is the problem of women. What struck me is the way you got interested very early in the piece in the problem of the emancipation of women, as you do in Mahanagar (The Big City).

Mahanagar is indeed directly about this subject. It's the story of a young woman who has to go off to work, braving the opposition of her in-laws. Her husband doesn't make enough and she has to maintain her family. She becomes a shop assistant. A psychological problem emerges from this situation because her husband, even though he encouraged her to take the job, doesn't cope all that well with the fact that she earns more than he does.

The subject must have been a first in Indian cinema and it no doubt provoked strong reactions.

It may have been a first, but the problem existed.

Did the conservatives attack you?

No, not really, they attacked me more when I made *The Goddess (Devi)*. That was about a young girl, and they thought I was attacking the Hindu religion whereas I was only attacking dogmatism.

And superstition.

Yes, and superstition. Her father-in-law is there. And she's in a situation where she doesn't know what to think; she's trapped by circumstances. Her young son is there, too, and he's been brought up in a Western school and put in touch with modern ideas. So he questions his father and it's from that situation that the tragedy arises.

And her father-in-law thinks she's the reincarnation of the goddess Kali.

Yes, that's right.

Charulata (The Lonely Wife) *is also a story about a woman.*

She's in love with her husband's young cousin. She's a very sensitive and cultivated woman but at that time (in the nineteenth century) women didn't have the freedom they have today. Faced with this conflict, she tries to express herself by writing and also by questioning her husband, who doesn't devote enough time or attention to her. So she falls in love with the young cousin, who's closer to her intellectually and has the same kinds of aspirations.

So the film's a defence of women's emotional and economic rights.

Most of these films are taken from stories written by other people. Many of our writers have been interested in this side of things, Tagore himself dealt with it in numerous novels. As for me, I merely reflected their ideas, by sharing them of course, and by putting a lot of myself in my films.

I suppose you're very conscious of this yourself: in the 60s a social current can be seen more and more in your work.

Certainly, yes, yes. Since the end of the 60s, Calcutta has become a city that's increasingly interesting for all the political movements that have been cropping up there all over the place and I felt the overwhelming need to put that in my films. Up until 1970, I'd made films that interested me a lot, but that were set in the nineteenth century and in the country. I think only one of them, *Mahanagar,* was directly connected to the social problems of Calcutta. But from 1970 onwards, Calcutta has become a very lively city, full of political movements, with the Naxalites, and the far left. I decided to explore Calcutta and its many aspects for a change, especially in regard to the problem of unemployment. First I did *Days and Nights in the Forest (Aranyer din ratri),* about young people in Calcutta, once they're cut off from their normal urban environment and transplanted into a rustic setting. My feeling was that, with a city dweller, if you cut him off from his daily routine and he finds himself in a setting that has nothing to do with him, he would then reveal his personality in a most interesting light. So that film showed these people, with their psychological and other conflicts, in an agrarian setting. It was followed by *The Adversary (Pratidwandi)* – my first film to deal directly with contemporary social problems in Calcutta – about a young man who doesn't have a job and who has to struggle to get one. Then there was *Company Limited (Seemabaddha),* about a young man who has a job and a few problems: he wants to climb up the hierarchy and he has to encounter corruption and so on to get to the top.

The Middleman (Jana Aranya) *is like the fourth part of a tetralogy.*

Yes, it is a tetralogy. That's exactly what it is. But before that film, I made something else, a story I wanted to do for a long time, from the same author as *Pather Panchali,* on the Bengal famine of 1943 that I'd gone through, not dying of hunger or even suffering from hunger, but, as a city dweller, seeing people from the country taking refuge in the towns and dying there of starvation.

That's Distant Thunder (Ashani Sanket).

Yes, it's *Distant Thunder.* Banerjee, the author of *Pather Panchali,* had written a very beautiful book on the subject, just dealing with one small village and one small group of people over a very short period of time. I wasn't able to make it straight away because I couldn't find the right actors and also doubtless because I had other things to do. And in any case I got the impression, I think, that I needed a bit of distance to deal with it objectively. So it was only in 1972 or 1973 that I decided to make *Distant Thunder.* I signed up a young girl from Bangladesh. I didn't see anyone in Calcutta who could play the wife of the Brahmin. Relations had already been set up after the independence of Bangladesh. I also signed up one of my favourite actors for the role of the husband and I filmed in a village very close to Shantiniketan, Tagore's university where I'd been a student. That's where we stayed, five kilometres from the village where we shot the film on the famine. It was after that that I made *The Middleman.*

To get back to The Middleman *and the other three films on economic and social problems, irony would have it that it was only when the Westerners left that India really fell victim to the economy, from a political and military standpoint. You are very critical of this situation. For example, in* The Music Room, *the loan shark confronting the aristocrat. You criticise the way money and social ambition destroy human beings.*

It's true, that's one of the themes that always returns, no doubt because it's there. Corruption exists and it's very widespread.

In The Middleman, *love itself...*

Yes, and that's also very true of Calcutta today. It's one of the aspects of this society, whose equivalents are doubtless to be found the world over, it's a global phenomenon and in this, India is in line with the rest of the world.

To get back to The Goddess, *are you religious?*

No, but religion interests me intellectually in all its aspects. I myself don't practise any religion, but all of them fascinate me because in India you can't be unaware of religion. I've just been filming in Benares and there you can see that India hasn't changed in a thousand years. Down by the river and in the temples, you can see that nothing's changed and you ask yourself about the movements of the left and all that....

So you haven't changed. I read something you said ten years ago: you said that when you thought about India you were a bit fatalistic. In this sense, you haven't changed?

I think *The Middleman* demonstrates that to some extent. There's a note of cynicism in there that my other films didn't have, but that's only one aspect of the film. Yet I feel as though there's a certain hope, but it's up to the political parties to keep their promises...

Your films aren't pessimistic. You show a lust for life but also a certain scepticism.

That represents my feelings at a given moment. But a person can change.

You haven't changed in the last ten years. Are your observations from the beginning of the 1960s still valid?

Yes.

You've taken many of your films from novels or short stories. Is that because you see them as a sort of trampoline or a necessary structure, or is it because literature draws you in?

We have such a rich fund of literature that we can dip in and help ourselves. That's one of the features of Bengal, the vast number of novelists or short story writers who are very interesting. To start with, obviously, I didn't know if I'd be capable of writing myself. I just wanted to make films of other people's work. It was of course an opportunity to read a lot of Bengali literature. I got a lot of projects out of it and I took the time to bring all of them to the screen eventually. But as I went along, around about 1960, I decided that a person should write his own stories from time to time and *Kanchanjungha* was my first original subject. I wanted a certain genre of film about a certain genre of people and I couldn't find a book on the subject. Later, I wrote other original material, such as *The Hero (Nayak)*. I wanted two things: to make a film about a train trip, which is a subject that fascinates me, and a film about cinema. So I combined the two. It's the trip an actor does from Calcutta to Delhi where he's about to receive a prize. So I had my train story and my cinema story. But there are so many good books, old and new, that very often I don't need to write my material. Obviously, lots of these original sources undergo considerable adaptation. Very few tales, in fact, with the exception of some of Tagore's short stories and of other earlier writers, are ready-made scripts. So I just use them as sources. In my treatment I keep certain details that please me, I add others, and that becomes my own material. That's how it goes.

Before you made Pather Panchali, *had you written scripts that didn't get turned into films?*

Dozens and dozens, but that was my favourite pastime. Whenever I heard someone was making a film based on a story, I'd write my own film treatment and I'd compare it with the finished film. It turned out I could often predict what the film would be like and I'd note the differences between my adaptation and the film. It was a pastime. I've written heaps of them. Sometimes I'd hit on something, write a scenario and, before I'd even finished, someone had bought the rights to the book and made a film. I did all that in the hopes of one day being able to make a film myself.

Are your scripts very precisely written? For instance, for your first film?

Yes, but it was never really written. I wouldn't say I improvised, but I think I had a pretty clear idea of the shape of the film. And I hadn't yet learned how to write dialogue. That's only true of my first films. After *Aparajito* I started writing complete scripts. In fact, in Bengal you have to be very economical and you can be if you write a very precise script. And from the beginning my scripts have had a very visual form. I don't see the point of writing descriptions. It's a waste of time and a waste of words. After all, it will end up just as images and dialogue. Since I learned to draw, I do little sketches of different sets and frames with notes on the side giving the dialogue and the camera movements. This really helps me in my discussions with the director of photography since he's used to my way of working. So, nothing like a typed script that you hand out to everybody.

So yours is illustrated?

I do little frames and when I open the notebook I see exactly how to edit it: close-ups, middle shots, distant shots and all sorts of things like that. That's the way I work.

And is that what you've always done?

For all my films, and now with even more details, drawings of sets, costumes, the lot. I've become more and more precise over the years, partly for reasons of economy and partly because I can't do it any other way. I think it's important to save money since I shoot three or four times the footage I keep. It's impossible to do more, so it has to not cost a lot. And if you have a fairly precise project, you can cut down the cost. But, of course, when you're shooting natural exteriors, you have to allow for a margin of improvisation because new ideas often crop up that you have to incorporate. But the first take, the basic framework of the film, rarely changes. I only improvise the details.

And what's the backbone of the film? Is it the character who drives the story?

When I write a script, the characters are obviously very important because a character can sometimes pull the story in a certain direction. But I think it's the combination of various elements. I mean, I think a lot about the atmosphere, so that includes the landscapes, their aspects, the moment of the day that we've chosen to shoot. I also have a very keen sense of time: I want to know how many days a tale takes. Is it four, or seven? Does it take place in the morning, at night, at what pace? Because the rhythm changes. If you edit in a night scene after a day scene, the whole context changes, and that's something I feel very strongly. So, the characters, the milieu, the set, the visual aspect – everything's important. I think it's a harmonious combination of all these elements that each of us has in our mind.

The editing, according to what you're saying, seems to play a very important role in your work, and yet you don't give yourself much room to manoeuvre, by not shooting much.

I've forced myself to have the edit in mind as I'm filming. So not much ends up on the cutting room floor. As I myself look after the camera, I know in advance where I'll cut. That's not the method used by certain Hollywood film directors and others who cover a scene from every possible angle and leave the editor to work as he sees fit. We don't have the means for that. Even the filming… For instance, on my last but one film, *The Chess Players (Shatranj ke kilhari)*, Richard Attenborough was one of the actors and he was very surprised that I didn't cover every scene from every angle. He asked me: 'What are you going to do in the cutting room?' I answered: 'I know what I'm going to do, I know in advance; it's already in my head. So, I'm already using it.' So, there you go, that's my method. And one of the reasons why I've been my own cameraman since 1963 – we'd been using an Arriflex and, as I also employed non-professionals, amateur actors, I discovered they were more at ease when they couldn't see me and I was hidden behind the camera. And what happens with professional cameramen, even the best, is that sometimes after a take they want another one and if you ask them why exactly, they can't tell you. They content themselves with saying: 'It's just that I'm not happy with this one.' So I ended up taking the decision to let my cameraman take care of the lighting, and to be director of photography and take care of the camera myself.

The unions don't force you to have a cameraman, then?

We don't have that sort of thing. I mean that the unions don't get involved. I look after the camera myself.

But during the first rehearsal, you're on the set, not behind the camera?

Yes, of course, but I don't do much rehearsing. I can only rehearse if I'm filming in the studio, when all the props are in place, the set all ready. So we only rehearse the day we shoot. It's not like a reading of a play, where you're comfortably seated in a room. No one does that. The actors know their lines in advance; they know the script. So you do a first reading with all the actors, at least, the leading ones; I read myself. This reading also implies a certain degree of performance, of acting: I read each character differently. My actors know, then, more or less, what I've got in mind. Then we do a rehearsal on the set, with the set finished and everything in place. They then rehearse their movements with the technicians. Then we set the lighting, then we shoot. Sometimes the first take is the best, and I don't ask for any other. If I'm happy with the first take, there is no second.

And the mix of professional and amateur actors…

I think it's really good, because in the beginning I only used non-professionals; I'm talking about the first two parts of the trilogy. I wanted to work with professionals after that. In *The Music Room* and *The Philosopher's Stone*, there are only professionals. Then it became a habit. When you write a script, you think of a character and his physical attributes to which no professional actor corresponds. I can go to the theatre and get a theatre actor. I'm open to any eventuality. And anyone can come and see me. I'm in the phone book. If an actor wants to work with me, he comes and sees me at home and while we're talking, I sometimes do a little sketch of him – often they don't bring photos – then I note his name and address. It often happens that someone I saw in 1960 springs to mind in 1965 and I offer him a role. That's often happened. And the mix of professionals and non-professionals is very interesting.

But doesn't the number of takes then become an issue? A professional can be ready from the first take and an amateur might lose a bit of their expressive force…

If a role involves long tirades in a single shot with complicated movements, it's very hard to work with amateurs unless the amateur is very gifted – in which case, he's not an amateur. In *The Adversary*, I used a man who'd never performed in a film before, but he turned out to be a first-class actor, and he's now a professional. That sometimes happens. But at other times, a few interviews with an amateur tells me what he's capable of. And I discover he has the face required, and the gait, and the voice; and I don't need anything more. And if he isn't a born actor, I give him a lot of help. I use all sorts of tricks to get the reaction I want. If I want him to look surprised or to express a strong reaction, I get someone to make a loud noise on the set. Once it looks good on screen, it doesn't matter what means were used to get there.

What about the old woman, the grandmother in Pather Panchali?

She was a professional theatre actress and we gave her a new lease of life, since she hadn't done any theatre for thirty years. We were looking for old women in the streets, in rice paddies, but we discovered that old women usually have very defective memories...

A shoot like the one for Pather Panchali, *which took two and a half years, must pose problems of continuity with the actors, especially the children?*

Naturally, but as luck would have it, the two children didn't grow as much as they should have and you can't tell the difference. Sometimes we had to stop in the middle of a scene. For example, we'd be filming the scene at a certain angle and the takes for another angle of the same scene had been filmed six months or even a year earlier. Imagine the continuity of movement we had to keep in our heads! Here's a concrete example: there was a scene with a dog in the film. One shot shows the dog approaching the camera and the following shot shows the dog moving away. We'd taken the shot from a certain angle and when we had a bit of money to go on with the filming, the dog was dead. They're just strays, there's no difference between dog A and dog B. So dog A approaches and dog B moves away and no one can tell the difference.

There's a very important scene in the film that turns on sweets. A man is carrying sweets on his shoulder and the two children follow him with the dog behind them. And the confectioner died. We'd filmed three shots, when he died. So for the fourth shot we got a stand-in who we filmed from behind. It was a completely different man. But when the rhythm of the film is carrying you along, you don't even notice that it's a different man.

We had more trouble with the trees and the surrounding countryside because spring is very different from autumn... But we were shooting in black and white. It would have been a lot more complicated in colour.

So you write, you draw, you direct and you work the camera. But you also compose your music. What place do you give film music? Do you use it after the editing or do you think about it before you edit?

Musical ideas sometimes crop up while I'm writing the script. I started out working with other musicians, such as Ravi Shankar and Billard Khan, who are professionals, virtuosos. And it's not easy working with virtuosos because they don't really know about film music. What I wanted to use, rather, was their interpretation and their instruments, more than their ideas. In any case, Ravi Shankar was very good in the trilogy. But I later decided to write my own music. Musical ideas sometimes crop up during filming. The moment I get one – I have a little notebook that sometimes has its place in the script – I jot it down immediately. I taught myself how to write music using staffs and I also know Indian notation. But now that I'm making more and more films about contemporary life in cities, I use less and less music. We're calling film music into question and I try to use natural sounds, and to use these fortuitous sounds in a creative, thematic way, a bit like leitmotifs.

Do you only write music for films or also concert pieces?

Only for my films. It's just music with a job to do. I don't record it on discs!

Do you play an instrument?

Not really. I use a piano to compose. I have a piano and I play it after a fashion. I mean, I don't play in a very orthodox way. It's just a base to compose with. And I whistle.

You've made a film that's actually all about music, The Music Room. *Do you have any other projects?*

I've made an adventure film for children called *The Adventures of Goopy and Bagha (Goupi Gyn, Bagha Byne)*, which is in a way a musical comedy. There's a lot of music in it, songs that I composed with words I wrote. I really enjoyed making it; I may well do another film in the same genre.

Do you have a project dealing directly with music?

Yes, for French television. I'd like it to be a film that somehow involves a certain aspect of Indian music. I've made two films in Rajasthan, in the desert, a region very rich in popular music. It's extraordinary, because the countryside is so arid and the people there are so poor, but there's a great fund of music that I didn't know anything about beforehand and I'm going to make a film about it.

About traditional music?

About the music of a particular part of West Rajasthan. There's even a village where everyone is a musician. There are only musicians there. I hope to do that.

To go back to the way you prepare your films, you say you attach a lot of import-ance to the atmosphere and the light. Do you spend a lot of time choosing your locations?

Yes. But it depends on the film. For example, my second-last film, *The Chess Players*, is set in Lucknow, but that place has changed a lot and the interiors, too, because there was an uprising there in 1857 during which everything was destroyed. So we filmed the rare sets at Lucknow but we had to reconstruct all the interiors in the studio. Whereas for *Pather Panchali* we spent days and nights in the village studying the light, the seasons, the vegetation and choosing the most propitious moments.

What struck me at my first viewing of Pather Panchali, *twenty years ago, is the way very small details, a flower or a jar of seeds, merge into a cosmic conception that recalls Tagore's dewdrop.*

Yes, he wrote a poem on the subject in my autograph album. I was only seven or eight years old when I met him for the first time. I gave him my autograph book and he wrote this poem for me and he said: 'You'll understand what it means when you're older.'

How did it go?

The idea was that I'd travelled the whole world, I'd seen mountains and seas, all there is. The only thing I'd missed was stepping outside my front door to see a drop of dew on a blade of grass. That's what it said. It's obviously at the heart of all the arts. I think Indian painting expresses it very well: there's a great concentration of details that nonetheless suggests vastness. The macrocosm and the microcosm. That's one of the keys. In my films, there's obviously a story, a theme, but also, as much as possible, a concentration of small details to do with human behaviour, the details of life, of objects.

Thank you very much, Mr Ray.

Thank you.

22 MARTIN SCORSESE

(1942–)

There weren't many of us milling around the door of the Cannes hotel where Martin Scorsese was staying when he came to present his first great film, *Mean Streets*, at Directors' Fortnight. The director was for the most part unknown, the parallel sections, though so rich in discoveries at the time, could not match the attraction of the official competition and young American cinema was not that popular – *idéologie oblige* – with hip critics. So Michael Henry and myself had all the time in the world for an initial interview that was extended in Paris and then in Los Angeles in which we evoked his following films, *Alice Doesn't Live Here Anymore* and *Italianamerican*.

If Scorsese is now less directly accessible, to put it mildly, he's hardly changed in thirty years: same torrential outpouring, same piercing look, same breathtaking movie buff's erudition, same passion for his art. At the time, we were familiar with *The Big Shave*, his gory short feature, and *Boxcar Bertha*, produced by Corman, but then we discovered his impressive filmography (the director was barely thirty years old) and the tireless activity of a man living at breakneck speed. With the interview that follows, he generously delivered himself to two strangers, performing a sort of autobiographical confession improvised while he shed light on the genesis of his films. Scorsese would scarcely deviate from the two main lines he traced before us: the importance of the ethnic crucible and of the Italian community of the Lower East Side, the role of religion and of its liturgy, the ever-present violence in his environment and finally salvation through the movies. His passion is expressed every bit as much in his documentaries, such as *A Personal Journey With Martin Scorsese Through American Movies*, as in the restoration of films or their distribution. But above all in his virtuoso style in which the shimmer of the colours and the variety of the palette vie with the feverish movements of the camera. How his energy has remained intact over the course of the years, from *Mean Streets* to *Gangs of New York*, is Martin Scorsese's secret.

ON *MEAN STREETS* AND *ALICE DOESN'T LIVE HERE ANYMORE*
CANNES, MAY 1974 — LOS ANGELES, MARCH 1975

We know almost nothing about your first two shorts.

What's A Nice Girl Like You Doing In A Place Like This? was made in a summer workshop at the University of New York. At the time, I was twenty years old; we were stunned to discover the new American humour in shows that Mel Brooks and Sid Caesar were writing for television. Brooks had just done *The Violinist* and *The Critic* with Ernst Pintoff. With Carl Reiner he recorded *The Two Thousand Year Old Man*, the story of an old Jew two thousand years old, who'd lived through all human history, chatted with Shakespeare, etc. We hadn't heard anything like it before and it's that nonsensical comic sense that I tried to get in my first film. No real shots, just fixed images, animation, special effects, lots of rigging. Nine minutes of visual nonsense with the voice of a narrator from end to end. I nicked the first two minutes of *Jules et Jim* from Truffaut! It was a shaggy-dog of a story, pure paranoia: a man buys a painting that represents another man on a boat,[1] and he winds up finding himself inside the painting, floating on the water…

I filmed *It's Not Just You, Murray* two months later. That's a buddy movie and also a kind of an introduction to, a draft of *Mean Streets*, I now realise. The two characters, Murray and Joe, are close friends, but of the kind that never stop stealing from each other, nicking each other's drinks or girls. They live the way I used to live, with my gang. Relationships where there's just as much hate as love. That was the starting point, but then it turned into the biography of a gangster between 1922 and 1965, a bit inspired by the life of my uncles. Murray is in his office, facing the camera. Behind him is the American flag. And he introduces himself: 'You see this tie? Twenty dollars! This car? Ten thousand dollars, etc. What d'ya say about that?' That's how they behave; they are America. I especially didn't want to present him at the outset as a gangster: it could have been any CEO, any university president. I was brought up in Little Italy, I saw corruption up close, I saw it at work everyday. After that, you can't take the Establishment seriously anymore. Everything's rigged. For me, *Murray* is also valuable as testimony, since we filmed in the cellars and bars and dives of Little Italy. Now, we noticed while we were location spotting for *Mean Streets*, that nearly all those sets had been demolished. So the vignettes in *Murray* immortalised a world that's disappeared. The story was very free, studded with sudden skits. There was even some choreography à la Busby Berkeley – well before he came back into fashion!

With The Big Shave, *did you want to send up 'commercials' and advertising in general?*

The Big Shave has a lot of points in common with *Mean Streets* but it's more surreal. Even though *Mean Streets* is not 'realistic' except in inverted commas. At times, you leave reality completely behind, you enter something else. When Harvey Keitel talks about his dreams, when he lets himself go dancing around the black woman, when he staggers around with his face stuck to the camera in the middle of the party given in honour of the veteran, it's like he was taking off, floating in space. It's very physical, but at the same time we're on the edge of something mysterious. The panthers in the room out the back of the bar – I didn't invent them, but you mustn't take them literally, either.

Rather like a metaphor of the male characters?

Exactly. But it wasn't really deliberate. I'm very sensitive to the madness that surrounds us, to all these absurd, incongruous incidents that I stumble across in the street. And I incorporate that unreality into my films. *The Big Shave* is an incident of the kind, a dare pushed to its most absurd consequences. It's also what I felt at the time. I was broke. My feature film couldn't find a distributor,[2] and after separating from my wife, I was camping in sinister, empty apartments ... and I always had trouble shaving! When I wrote the script, it was very serious, but during the shoot we couldn't stop laughing. In the rushes, we were buckled up. It was only afterwards that I tried to rationalise what I'd done. I'd almost convinced myself that it was an anti-Vietnam film, that this bloke who shaves himself so meticulously and who winds up cutting his throat was a symbol of the average American of the day. It was for its political implications that I used Bunny Berigan's original 1939 version of 'I Can't Get Started' as background sound. I even wanted to end with stock-shots of Vietnam, but they were pointless. In fact, *The Big Shave* was a fantasy, a strictly personal vision of death.

Religion held a major place in your youth. Is that still the case today?

Neither more nor less than what you see in *Mean Streets*. A feeling of guilt, yes. Lots of superstitions, too. I surround myself with a whole series of rituals, I hate certain numbers, there are certain bits of paper that I wouldn't throw away for all the world, but I don't set foot in church anymore, I don't talk to priests anymore...

Yet you entered the Seminary?

I only followed a preparatory seminary on Eighty-sixth Street. I wanted to become a priest. This was around 1956. But then the rock 'n' roll revolution broke out... Music, that particular music, was very important to me. In my neighbourhood, the kids imitated Brando, wore leather jackets, hung around bars and 'candy stores'. *Blackboard Jungle* is what we lived on a daily basis. And then, there were the girls... Impossible to concentrate on my studies under such conditions! I was expelled. For them I was a lout, a gangster in the making. I went to a Catholic college with the intention of going back to the seminary one day, but later I couldn't get in to the Jesuit University, my grades were lousy. So then I made do with New York University, where I very quickly headed for the course on cinema history.

So, in a way, you escaped your environment, but wasn't that exceptional?

When you've been brought up in Little Italy, what can you become, if not a gangster or a priest? Well, I couldn't be one or the other. Physically I couldn't cut it as a gangster. I always got beaten up. You remember *Manhattan Melodrama*, Clark Gable turned into a bad boy while his pal William Powell gets elected governor and has him sentenced to death? Well, my friends are still there; they still dress the same way; they've hardly changed. I have a lot of affection for them, but myself, I had to take another path to survive. I survived by talking very fast, by flowing over with crazy talk, by making other people laugh through my buffoonery. And whenever there was a brawl, as though by chance, I always missed it by a few minutes. Without too many regrets... There are so many who got smashed up, wrecked, in these stupid scuffles.

If cinema was for you a way of distancing yourself, how did your gang react to such a 'betrayal'?

They were fascinated at first, they helped me make *Murray*, they were closely involved in finding the locations and the costumes. But two years later, when I undertook my first feature length film,[3] a dramatic story this time, I used their real names and they felt offended by the film. The only well-drawn character was J.R. And J.R. was me! They were perfectly right. It was far too narcissistic and smug. I only showed a tiny fraction of what they were like and they thought I'd painted them in the worst possible light. In reality, I'd wanted to compare a boy brought up as a Catholic and a girl who he wants to see now as a madonna, now as a whore. A problem as old as Sicily! When I screened the film for my teacher, he put it to me that that was all very old hat, that you needed to move with the times, talk about drugs and free love. But those who grew up in the ghettos, the Poles, the Jews, the Irish, the Italians, they understood. And the sadness of those lives, I see it everywhere, in all the minorities. Robert Redford, for me, that's another planet, a foreign America that I watch from a long way off.

How do you position yourself now in relation to your origins?

Still between two stools! We're the third generation. My grandparents emigrated in about 1910. They spoke only Italian and never took out American nationality. My parents, on the other hand, got married and have almost always lived in Manhattan. The background to their life was the Great Depression and in many ways they represent the electorate of George Wallace. They've always lived in other people's apartments. Whence the endless disputes, the family differences, with their complicated ramifications. I was born on Long Island, but in 1950 they came back to Little Italy, to Elizabeth Street, right where they were born. They took their first trip to Sicily last year. When they're talking among themselves, they constantly jump from Sicilian to English and vice versa. Me, I can only just read Italian, but I can't speak it, I'm 'blocked'. And today the third generation is leaving Little Italy to set up in Queens and especially Staten Island. Mardik Martin and I want to provide a sequel to *Mean Streets* one day and that's where we'll find our characters again, only older.

How did Who's That Knocking At My Door? *evolve up to its definitive version?*

It took me three years to finish. The first version, *Bring On The Dancing Girls*, is the first film in 35 mm to have been made in a university framework. The subject, the encounter between J.R. and the girl, wasn't really dealt with. What I mainly shot in Little Italy were the scenes between J.R. and his gang, the brawls, the drinking binges, the orgies. A disaster: everyone hated it. Then, in 1967, my old teacher, Haig Manoogian, who was setting himself up as an independent producer along with Joseph Weill (he's the one who published *Cahiers du Cinéma* in English), pushed me into writing new episodes with the girl, and developing J.R.'s inner conflict. Zina Bethune replaced the previous actress, I got Harvey Keitel back and we shot both of their scenes over four weeks, with Michael Wadleigh behind the camera. The difference between the scenes photographed in 35 mm by Richard Coll and those shot in 16 mm by Wadleigh two years later leaps out at you. You never see Zina and the gang all together in one shot! The film was presented at the New York Festival but didn't find a distributor. After having made *The Big Shave*, as I was fairly discouraged, I let myself be persuaded by Richard Coll, who was living in Amsterdam, to join him in Europe and make advertising films with him. I spent six months there. I quickly discovered I hated ads. At the Cinématèque in Brussels, I met Jacques Ledoux. He told me I was crazy to waste my time on Flemish 'commercials'! Luckily, Manoogian phoned me from the States and told me that Joseph Brenner, a distributor of erotic films who was trying to break into more 'respectable' circuits, was happy to take my feature film as long as I added a nude scene. But I couldn't go back to New York; I was stuck over there in an incredible mess. So we had Harvey Keitel come over to Amsterdam. The scene was finished in two days with Anne Colette, the actress in *Tous les garçons s'appellent Patrick*, and it was shot by Max Fisher, since Richard Coll had fallen ill meanwhile. There's no connection to the rest of the film. Without any transition, in the middle of a dialogue about girls, good and bad, virgins and sluts – bang! – it fades into this masturbation scene, deliberately overexposed, and with the music of the Doors which I stuck over it. It's so insane that the audience thinks the projector's gone off the rails every time! Jonas Mekas wanted me to cut it out at any cost so he could screen it as a film on its own!

Who's That Knocking ... is a bit like the first instalment of your autobiography.

Every incident is autobiographical. Even more than in *Mean Streets.* There isn't really a plot: J.R. falls in love with a young girl but is always with his buddies, who are jealous of her. He feels guilty and he refuses to make love to her on his mother's bed (I shot that scene in my own mother's bedroom, with holy statues everywhere...). She doesn't understand, so he takes her to see *Rio Bravo* and *Scaramouche* and he points out Angie Dickinson and tells her that she's his type of woman... The scenes with the gang are barely structured. You see them, dressed in black, playing with weapons, then you find them in the mountains, completely out of place and clumsy, scared of snakes, sniping at each other. At the summit, J.R. gets them to admire the twilight. Then – bang! – it fades into the girl saying she isn't a virgin anymore. J.R. refuses to accept this, wants to believe she's been raped, joins his buddies again at a party that's actually an orgy. The next day, this guy who loves Percy Sledge and Ray Baretta, finds her reading *Tender Is The Night* and listening to a record of Sinatra's! He kisses her, apologises, forgives her, then calls her a 'whore' again and wrecks the joint. He leaves to get back to the gang, but he actually leaves them too. Everything falls apart around him. That's what happened to me at the time, and I think it's the reason I didn't manage to make an intelligible film. I didn't have any distance. It's a patchwork, but here and there, even so, there are some good sequences, like the one where the gang is watching Charlie Chan on television and the one, in slow motion, where Baretta sings 'El Watusi'.

What happened on the set of The Honeymoon Killers?

I was in charge of all of the pre-production work and I shot it in a week, before being fired and replaced by Leonard Kastle. I haven't seen the film, so I don't know if any of my shots are still in it, notably the suicide on the beach. I doubt it, since they re-shot almost everything. They didn't like very complicated crane movements, the stunning sequence shots I'd perfected. I cost them too much. They were tearing their hair out. Especially, I didn't manage to explain to them what I was trying to do, no doubt because I wasn't mature enough for such an experience. In any case, Kastle should have been in charge of the directing in the first place since it was his script. I was mortified nevertheless. I went back to the film course at New York University. I wound up getting expelled from there, too, as I was hardly ever there. In those days, to survive, I edited documentaries for Michael Wadleigh, as well as Jim McBride. While I was editing *Who's That Knocking*, Jim would be editing *David Holzman's Diary* in the next room. We'd give each other suggestions, with him trying to persuade me to cut as little as possible and me, on the contrary, urging him to cut more! In 1969, I also got a pretty mad project off the ground, a story about soldiers that was supposed to end with the opening speech from *Patton* – only, this time, the whole speech, uncensored. Oliver Wood, who I'd got onto *The Honeymoon Killers*, was supposed to be the cinematographer. It would all have been in 16 mm except for one big erotic flashback in 35 mm, which we would have decked out in colours from the 1940s. I had to wait for *Alice Doesn't Live Here Anymore* to make it! The film was cancelled two days before the shoot for lack of money.

We are curious to know how you feel about the militant film experiment that Street Scenes 1970 *represented. What was your role in the 'Cinetracts' collective?*

At the time of the invasion of Cambodia, I was teaching at New York University. The student movement was in full swing. I then had the idea of using the very advanced equipment in the film department to organise squads of students who'd go and film or record the demonstrations. Several of them were beaten up by the counter-demonstrators of Wall Street; cameras got destroyed. The only scene I 'directed' is the very violent discussion at the end, in the Washington chamber where we ended up on the final day, after a week of exhausting filming. We were like cut off from the rest of the world, most of us had been seriously roughed up or gassed, and I myself was as sick as a dog... Harvey Keitel was there, he'd brought us photos. Like the rest of us, he was absolutely beside himself with rage; he couldn't stand the waiting and the fact of being powerless. Then, as it was the end of the academic year, everyone scattered. There was no one left to edit our kilometres of film. The dean of the University bawled me out as we'd lost $16,000 worth of equipment. He gave me notice to get this mass of material into shape. The best documents were brought in by Don Lenzer, who'd worked on Woodstock: I was able to use his shots just as they were. I edited all night for ten days in a row, trying to give a formal structure to the whole – and also swearing to myself that I'd never again let myself embark on a political film if I couldn't make it from end to end. When I showed it to the people in it, they hated it: they didn't find it confrontational enough. They felt let down, didn't recognise what they'd gone through. Yet, I believe it was fairly honest as a picture: I showed the sad reality, the anger, the frustration, the irresponsibility, the general feeling of powerlessness. We weren't dealing with the Weathermen, with true radicals, here, but with average students, well-heeled young men, weekend lefties. And that's what they couldn't admit. I was pretty bitter and the film ends on a very pessimistic note, in the middle of a sentence, with a fade-out to sudden black. Every time we screened it, viewers, even students who weren't politically engaged, spontaneously pursued the debate in the auditorium, taking up the arguments from the Washington debate. That was the sole merit of *Street Scenes*.

You had worked till then in the most complete independence, so how did you fit into the stable of American International? Going on the outcome, Corman seems to have left you complete freedom to improvise and innovate on Boxcar Bertha.

I'd come to Hollywood to edit *The Medicine Ball Caravan*. Soon after I got there, I ran into Corman. He'd seen *J.R.* and liked it,[4] but more to the point he knew that I'd worked on *Woodstock*. His idea was to provide a sequel to *Bloody Mama*, which I hadn't even seen. I don't regret having accepted as I had a lot of fun. It was Julie Corman who'd come across the autobiography of Bertha Thompson, but the script has very little connection to the book. American International bought the title and we only used a few of the characters. Me, I wanted to make a spectacular film, a film for the boys on Forty-Second Street. With a budget of $600,000, that was impossible. We had to shorten the script, cut all the epic scenes, rewrite some of the others, give up going as far as Baton Rouge, Texacana, etc. The whole thing was shot in twenty-four days in a corner of Arkansas, and you get the impression that the rails of the railway line describe a complete circle! The characters keep popping up at the same place, like in a dream. It's very strange, that circularity...

The strangeness of the film also stems from the fairytale quality that shows through under the violence, don't you think?

You noticed all the allusions to the *Wizard of Oz*? There are some at every turn in the film! In the opening scene, Barbara Hershey wears Dorothy's hairdo; in the brothel scene, there's the line, 'Pay no attention to that man behind the curtain!' On the set, it became a bit of a game between the actors and me. David Carradine was the bogeyman, Bernie Casey the tin lumberjack and Barry Primus the fearful lion! The character of Rake Brown, which Barry plays, I completely rewrote so that it represents me in the film. He dresses like me; you'd say he was straight out of *Mean Streets*. He keeps saying, 'What you gonna do in Arkansas? Let's get out of here!' Exactly what I said over and over again on the set! I commented on the action through him. He thought, as I did, that when you find yourself face to face with someone holding a revolver of a bigger calibre than yours, the only thing left to do is skedaddle... And also that you shouldn't draw unless you've decided to pull the trigger! The moment he forgets this principle, the move he makes is fatal to him!

Those four 'drop-outs' of the Depression have a lot in common, each in their own way being a minority, with the four young Italo-Americans of Mean Streets. *Are you targeting American youth of today?*

They're kids who are having a ball. They only kill towards the end. Morton then becomes a Black Panther and Bertha doesn't recognise him anymore. To start with, the script ended with Bertha dancing in the middle of blacks at a funeral in New Orleans. These Uncle Toms – she could accept them. You know, in America, the blacks adored the film. Me, I like it for the small details, like having made Rake Brown a Jew. I also like the interview improvised in the brothel, the old man eating glass, the whore at the back of the room who is in reality a transvestite, the door gag (I stole it, like the interview, from *Vivre sa vie*), the fantastical climate that permeates the whole episode. Everything's bizarre in this film. And Barbara Hershey and David Carradine had a whale of a time! They were so madly in love they didn't even need to 'play' their love scenes. It was quite different on *Mean Streets*. Amy Robinson and Harvey Keitel didn't get on much at all and so I used their animosity.

Is the crucifixion of Big Bill Shelley inspired by your own obsessions? Charlie, in Mean Streets, *precisely, also seeks martyrdom.*

The crucifixion was in the script. Even though Big Bill was killed differently, that happened to trade unionists in those days. I approached the scene frankly, without cheating. I was thinking of *Duel in the Sun*, of Jennifer Jones crawling over the rocks... The strangest thing is that I shot it on my birthday and, the following year, the same coincidence occurred again with *Mean Streets*. It was on my birthday that I killed off Johnny Boy and my friends.[5]

And, like the brawls in Mean Streets, *the final bloodbath by the railway embankment is more choreographed than acted.*

For *Boxcar Bertha*, I drew every shot beforehand, for *Mean Streets* half the shots and for *Alice* a third. You notice that every character has *his very own* death. The camera movements are different every time. Corman left me perfectly free. He only intervenes when you're sabotaging the work. He always tells you: 'Your turn.' Luckily, he didn't show the film to Arkoff until it was finished. Before the screening, he'd warned him: 'Sam, it's not quite *Bloody Mama*'... But Arkoff walked out, appalled, cursing the digressions, the hermetic jokes, in a word, the new wave aspect. Afterwards, all the filmmakers in A.I.P. came to see me to ask me how I'd found the nerve to treat a house project so cavalierly! The only actor Corman foisted on me was Barrry Primus. We got on so well together that I planned to give him the role of Charlie in *Mean Streets,* with Harvey Keitel lined up to play Johnny Boy.

Who had the idea of exchanging quotes from the Bible when the Carradines, father and son, are face to face for the first time?

I did! The relationship between John and David is very strange. John was delighted to take his son back – he still calls him by his nickname, 'Pooky'. I think he wanted to steal the scene from him. The dialogue was improvised and written in front of the cameras. What I wanted to say is that in politics, like everywhere else, you have to chuck out the wimps. I don't like wimps. Von Morton sees his radicalism through to the end.

In Mean Streets, *the behaviourist approach, the chronicle mode, free you from concerns about the plot. To tell the truth, it's hard to see when the 'story' in the traditional sense of the term really kicks off.*

The story starts without your realising it. I could, of course, have tightened the narrative, but as it unfolds, I add further scenes, for instance the one with the two boys from Riverdale, to establish the relationship between Michael and Tony, and so on. These sequences are just as important, if not more so, than the storyline itself.

You obviously had problems introducing the female character, Teresa.

By adding scenes at the start, I kept putting off her entrance! I finally convinced myself that it would be wonderful to introduce her only in the sixth reel. You couldn't show more clearly that it's a society dominated by the males. Teresa has no right to a vignette in the beginning; she had to be the last person to be introduced if we wanted to describe a lifestyle – and describe it once and for all. Too bad about the structures!

Why make Teresa an epileptic?

Epilepsy fascinates me. Charlie is so obsessed by his feeling of guilt, he hates himself so profoundly, even though the only thing he has to reproach himself with in reality is 'bad thoughts', that the only woman he can have has to be 'marked', debased. She's not a virgin, that's why he wants to be with her. He thinks he doesn't deserve better. In his heart of hearts, he considers epilepsy to be a holy malediction. Sleeping with Teresa is like a punishment he inflicts on himself.

Several characters are close to madness: Teresa, Johnny Boy, the Vietnam veteran…

Johnny Boy isn't mad. He feels enormous rage and frustration at his environment. The code of honour, the rituals, the signs, all that comprises that way of life, he refuses to accept. He's the buffoon who's seen through things but is powerless to change their course. He torpedoes the rules of the game, but without being able to liberate himself. He doesn't even destroy himself; someone else has to take care of that. When he defies Michael with a revolver that isn't loaded, he mocks the very foundations of that society. And then again his parents are divorced, which is really rare down there. The real-life Johnny Boy, Sally Gaga, had a nervous breakdown after accidentally killing a drunk woman by throwing a bottle from a rooftop. He was so offended by *Who's That Knocking …* that he walked out of the screening. The neighbour at the window, in *Mean Streets*, is his mother. She never realised that Johnny Boy was her son.

The 'party' where the veteran throws himself on a young girl and suddenly rapes her introduces a madness of another order, this one political.

That scene was dreamed up, in the first script that I wrote around 1966, as a costumed ball. Charlie turned up to it disguised as Christ, blessing everybody.

The symbol was too obvious. Moreover, we couldn't afford the costumes and we were short on time so there was no question of transporting the crew to a new set. We had to stay in the bar. There, too, the dialogue is improvised. It's not a political commentary. The important thing is all this repressed violence that suddenly bursts through the surface.

Compared to Charlie and Johnny Boy, Tony and Michael represent normality. They're going to fit in.

For Tony, who's the least developed of the four characters, I should have specified a few things: Tony got his bar thanks to his father, a gangster who owns all the nightclubs on the East Side. Detached, objective, pragmatic, he'll be the first to enter the world of organised crime. In a sense, he's Charlie's best friend, the one who understands him best. Michael is from another block. In Little Italy, each 'block' has its own gang. No two are alike. We, ourselves, we were the nice ones; we didn't play with firearms, or only rarely. Michael belongs to the hardest gang, the Hester Street gang, six blocks from ours – real gangsters, tough guys, nasty. Yet Michael won't go too far, he doesn't have the brains, the guts, to be the big shot gang leader he'd like to be. He dresses up, he tries to acquire the style, without being able to gain the others' respect. Do you remember the guy in the car, on the docks? He's the real thing. He's not the only one in the film. I had others, serious guys...

We get the feeling that you wrote a veritable biography for each one of the characters before the shoot.

I even specified the books each one of them was reading! In the editing, I cut, because it was a bit pretentious, too deep and meaningful, a whole discussion between Charlie, his 'godfather' and Mario about Hemingway's short story, 'The Short Happy Life of Francis Macomber'. It posed the whole problem of cowardice. Physically, Charlie is a coward. When I lived down there, that was my constant problem. How to avoid getting hit... Having fifteen hulks fall upon you ... allowing yourself to be trapped by a 'macho' attitude. Being a hero for one minute is fine, but you get whipped! You can even get killed. Every time I walk into a bar, I can feel that violence. Every time I'm in the thick of a crowd, even here at the Festival. But maybe you end up knowing what matters and what doesn't.

There's a relationship of cause and effect between the characters' religious upbringing and their neuroses.

That's not peculiar to Italo-Americans. The Jews know all about that. The Irish? No, they know how to enjoy the pleasures of the table, they have fun at funerals, they see the good side of life. That's a different Catholicism. Us, when we sit down to table, we enter into a battlefield. At wakes, we cry, we weep. The old women try and rip the body out of the casket. If you don't behave that way, people conclude that you didn't love the deceased. That's what I'll show in the sequel to *Mean Streets*, that hysteria, that guilt, this legacy of the old generation.

Charlie is torn between the Mafia and religion. Are those two forces complementary, in your view, at the heart of the Italo-American community?

The Mafia is stronger. There is to start with the Family, that is, yours plus the Mafia, and then there's the Church. Material aid, then spiritual aid. In the hierarchy of respect, the priest comes after the 'godfather'. On Mulberry Street, the priest of my precinct often told me that his parishioners only greeted him after the 'godfather' set the example.

Tony says to Charlie, 'Religion is a racket like any other'…

The story about the retreat happened to me personally. I believed doggedly in what the priest told me. You know: fiancés who can't restrain themselves from making love in the backseat of a car before marriage and who are crushed at that very instant by a truck… The last night of the retreat, I had a vision: Christ was watching me through the window. I ran in the dark as fast as I could go… The next day, I related it all to a pal and he tells me that he'd been spun the same story, too. It was a standard number! After all, they've got a job to do. It's an organisation.

Why did you take Harvey Keitel's place to deliver the first line of the film?

It was a way of getting involved. When Charlie's standing in front of the candles, I'm the one who recites the prayer. I've always been fascinated by the cannibalistic ritual of the Eucharist. And I said it myself because I wrote it and I find it tremendous. It's as though I was taking Charlie by the hand to present him to the viewer and to say to them, 'Here's what we're going to do.' My feeling about the Church is that it shouldn't have been run like a business. Charlie tells himself that the Church should be out on the street, so he goes down into the street, he becomes the Church, but in spite of everything, he, too, tries to turn it into a business.

Because he's a 'politician'?

Exactly. The more you go in for politics, the more corrupt and dangerous to others you become. In my heart of hearts, I've always wanted to be a saint. But how do you become one? Start off as a missionary? At eight years old, I wanted to look after lepers in the islands. But that wasn't convenient: leaving your family, going far way, looking after lepers... I told myself there must surely be another way. I was brought up close to a priest I admired, who I tried to imitate, but who scoffed at my vocation. And then, he was a snob: he only went to European films, adaptations of Shakespeare. He despised our movies. On top of that, he only listened to classical music, not rock 'n' roll. He was always encouraging us to do sport, and he'd add: 'Stay away from girls, above all!' I hated sport, that's one of the reasons he insisted. For me, he was religion. His influence was enormous. He called us retards because we responded to any provocation in the street. He'd say: 'You're idiots. Holding up a bank, for you, consists of bursting in and shooting in all directions.' I used that in *Boxcar Bertha*. He was right; we would have burst in, shooting in all directions. Thanks to him, I started to think about things. He came close to my ideal, but when I really needed spiritual aid, he wasn't there, he didn't understand me, he didn't want to take me seriously. The priests were all the same, functionaries of the confessional. To be a priest, you have to be close to people, in the street. The habit's not enough. That idea is incarnated in Charlie, who takes himself for a saint. There's something else: the snobbery of that man, his pride. He wasn't aware of it. I wanted to make a film where the priest would discover, after wanting to save others, that he's the one who most needs saving. At the end, Charlie understands that maybe he wasn't helping others, that he was ruining their lives, that he was only helping himself.

Like the heroes once played by John Garfield?

Harvey Keitel adores Garfield. 'Shoot at the white of the eyes': he's the one who slipped that in when he improvises his little speech. He was in the Marines; he takes the army very seriously, even though his ideas are the opposite. *Force of Evil* is one of my favourite films, which is clear, I think, in *Mean Streets*. I'd love to do a film with Polanski one day.

I suspect you and Samuel Fuller would have got on like a house on fire!

I'm crazy about Fuller! One of my very first memories of the movies is of my father taking me to see *I Shot Jesse Kames*. I'll never forget the shock of *Forty Guns, Park Row, Pickup on South Street,* which I saw as soon as they came out when I was eighteen. I only met him once, but we talked for a long while about emotional violence, which is not to be confused with physical violence. That's what Fuller's films taught me, and also that such emotional violence should be created not only through the actor but especially by the camera.

Speaking of that, why did you use slow motion for the travelling shots along the bar at Johnny Boy's entrance?

I love that! It's most often used for fights, but me, I wanted to isolate, to analyse very simple gestures: a girl lights a cigarette, a guy grabs a glass, another guy observes the scene, etc. As for Johnny Boy's entrance, I wanted to set off his first appearance, which is explosive. We needed a special effect. From time to time, the film 'takes off', sends you 'reeling'...

The music also contributes to that! When did you select the musical numbers?

Most of them before the shoot. The piece at the end, for example, ends all Italian celebrations. The one for the initial sequence, 'Be My Baby', by the Ronettes, is very important, as it evokes the music coming up from the street, in summer, when the juke-boxes are outside and the kids dance on the road... 'Rubber Biscuit', on the other hand, wasn't provided in the script. It's a song that'll send you flying if you listen to it at the wheel! I hope the audience lose their heads at that moment! I remembered that rock 'n' roll was always the background noise to our barhops and our brawls. William Wellmann's *The Public Enemy*, which I've seen at least ten times, influenced me a lot in the use of music as counterpoint.

Are the film extracts in Mean Streets *only there as a tribute to their directors? They also constitute a counterpoint...*

Those films were part of our lives. We'd talk about them for hours on end. Ford, for instance, my favourite director, we kept going back to see his films, we learned the lines by heart. We defined ourselves in relation to his characters, in relation to John Wayne, Jeffrey Hunter or Ken Curtis. In *Who's That Knocking*, Harvey Keitel is waiting for a ferry and he sees his girlfriend reading an article on The Searchers in *Paris-Match* and he starts raving about it like a lunatic for nine minutes! Here, I wanted to take *Donovan's Reef*, but John Wayne didn't want to find himself in an R-rated film.[6]

You got your revenge by having Johnny Boy *quote* Back to Bataan!

The problem is that the other Fords from Warner such as *The Rising of the Moon* or *Sergeant Rutledge* weren't among the ones we saw on Forty-Second Street. I had to be very careful choosing these films in terms of the fifteen-cent movie theatres that we used to frequent. Like Corman's, for example. In the first script, the 1966 one, there were more references, collages, 'private jokes' for the 'lucky few' – as many as in *Who's That Knocking*.

Robert de Niro and Harvey Keitel have worked with Lee Strasberg but, in Mean Streets, *their performance does not bear the mark of the Actor's Studio. What's your approach with the actors?*

I don't know anything about the Method. I've never set foot in a drama course. I have to love my actors personally; we have to go out together, to be very close to each other. I need their trust. I expect a lot from rehearsals. On *Mean Streets,* we rehearsed for ten days, untangling together the web of relationships between the four male characters and Teresa, giving them the impression that they could invent whatever they liked. When they were relaxed enough, they no longer deprived themselves of introducing gags into their lines. The scene between Harvey Keitel and Robert de Niro in the backroom was written based on improvisations recorded during the rehearsals. Harvey and Bob played it again in front of the cameras, but at the end, Harvey forgot his lines and had to improvise again and Bob played along. The brawl around the billiard table was entirely sketched out but I'd only written the dialogue at the beginning. I was too lazy to go on. When we got there, there was only an hour left. So then George Memmoli had an idea for a gag and everything got under way. On that score, the exchange of blows is only just simulated... In the days of *Who's That*

Knocking, I didn't know how to improvise, and the film registers that. I learned on *Boxcar Bertha*.

But, on Mean Streets, *to what extent was the improvisation compatible with the extreme complexity of the lighting?*

I never lost sight of the storyline. The improvisation never undermined the script. We couldn't allow it to. The bar was lit in such a way that we had to go really fast. No question of trying to be clever. On top of our light projectors, we had to move the bar lights as we went. Our lighting man was deaf, he was seventy-two years old, but he worked at a phenomenal speed, and to stimulate ourselves, we kept telling ourselves he'd managed to get *Return of the Fly* in the can in three days, in 1959! *Mean Streets* was shot in twenty-seven days.

Is the 'home movie' in the credits listed chronologically?

No. It's a miniature film. It's self-sufficient. It says that it's the film. In our community, violence is integrated into social, family and conjugal activities, into all those rituals that give the impression of one big united family. Some of the shots were filmed by my brother in 1965 when I became the godfather of the baby you see on the screen. The others I took all on my own in Super 8, in amateur fashion, without a zoom or lighting, without trying to interpret what I was recording, either.

What technical problems did the final sequence pose?

It was shot in a night. For want of time, I had to accept three compromises. I'd have liked: (1) for Teresa to smash the windscreen; (2) for the car to be a convertible (Johnny Boy would have been standing, shouting, pissing blood); (3) for it to smash into a shop window. Corman's stuntmen lost a whole night setting up their act. It was a balls-up every time. I was furious. Just as the car was supposed to knock over the fire hydrant, it was five o'clock in the morning, the sun was about to come up and I still didn't have an overall shot. We had twenty minutes to wrap it up. I could carry on like a madman all I liked; I never got exactly what I wanted.

You gave yourself the role of a killer. Why?

First reason: I wanted a role in the film, especially if I could handle a firearm. Second reason: our budget, which was $350,000 at the outset, $500,000 in all.

In order to save money, most of the interior scenes were shot in Los Angeles, the rest in New York. Now, the final sequence was supposed to be shot in Los Angeles. We didn't have enough money left to get all the actors back there. You'll see, besides, that certain actors never appear in exteriors, others never in interiors. I was the only extra who could be in both towns! The third reason, you know: I had my birthday to celebrate.

What prompted you to make Alice Doesn't Live Here Anymore, *which is such a different project from your two preceding films that talked about gangsters or the Mafia?*

Several reasons. One is practical: after *Mean Streets*, I was offered scripts about gangsters but none of them came near the quality of *Mean Streets*. Even though I had similar projects, I wanted to tackle something else. Ellen Burstyn asked Coppola which young director he'd recommend for a script she'd read. He mentioned my name, she saw *Mean Streets* and offered me the script.

John Calley, from Warner, told me it could be filmed on the cheap. The script has faults, but the characters and their relationships interested me. And I also liked this idea of responsibility and this situation where a woman finds herself on her own with a child after thirteen or fourteen years of marriage. She's faced with several choices and she doesn't know what she wants. What are her responsibilities to herself and to her son? In terms of emotions it was 'a work in progress' for me. And Ellen's emotions also came through in her character and those of the boy, who's a brilliant kid, full of energy. I also wanted to start exploring relationships and feelings between men and women, to see how you could ruin a relationship with somebody, then fall in love again and make the same mistakes all over again. That's what happens between Ellen and Kris Kristofferson. They don't have any ready-made solution, but at least they realise they're falling back into the same old traps that they'd fallen into with their respective exes. The only permanent relationship in the film is between Alice and her son. That's why we end with them, like in a Chaplin film. But, as in *Mean Streets*, the emotions are always on the surface.

Did you tweak the script much?

Enormously. There's also more improvisation than in *Mean Streets*. During the three months of pre-production, Getchell was involved in the revisions. Ellen

Burstyn worked with me. She'd say her monologues on video, do improvisations with the other actors. Larry Cohen and Sandy Weintraub, who were physically the producers of the film, in being at the shoot, in doing the casting, also took part in the rewriting sessions.

Getchell would be brought the results of our work, since he'd gone off to rest, and he'd give his opinion, approve our proposals or not. Then he'd take up our scenes, listen to the suggestions, make others, rework the script and hand it back to us. We'd improvise again. That went on forever, these mutual exchanges, until the shoot and even during the shoot. So the scene in the toilets between Ellen Burstyn and Diane Ladd was improvised from an idea of Getchell's and four pages of his script. I filmed ten minutes of it, simply shot-for-shot, which allowed me to get it down to three minutes. Similarly for the scene between Ellen and Kris Kristofferson in the kitchen after they've made love for the first time: same mix of written lines, improvisation and condensation in the edit.

Things between us all were breezy, crazy, open and very funny. The first edit of *Alice* was three hours sixteen minutes long. It was a real odyssey. And it was fantastic. What I especially don't like, in the actual version, is that I had to cut so much out at the beginning, to the point of reducing the role of the husband to practically nothing. He's an excellent actor, but what we now see of his character is that he behaves like an animal, with the only moment of humanity being where he kisses her in bed because he can't speak anymore. That's it. You could just as easily start the film after his death. In the primitive version, there were scenes where he was right, where he refused, for instance, to go to Monterey in the car for the weekend because he'd been driving a truck all week and he wanted to rest. He was much more human. The couple's life together went on for an hour on screen and the scenes alternated, with the differences in behaviour.

The opening of the film is brilliant.

In the script, it read: 'Flashback 1948 – Monterey – California'. We've seen all sorts of flashbacks in cinema, black and white, slow motion, with soft-focus all around the screen, etc. At first I thought of filming it like the rest with a simple subtitle, then I got the idea that, since she lived a lot in relation to certain films (for example, *Coney Island*, with Betty Grable, which she watches on television), I'd film this scene like a film of the times, and it became a tribute to William Cameron Menzies and also to *Tobacco Road* with the dam, to the *Wizard of*

Oz and finally to *East of Eden* when the mother comes out of the house and calls him. As for the credits, they're like Ross Hunter's. And since I had money – $1,700,000 – why not spend it? We built a set for $85,000 and we filmed the sequence in a day at the end of the shoot on the back-lot at Columbia, which has since been turned into a tennis court. It's the last set ever built there and it's the work of the set-designer for *Citizen Kane*.

Why did you choose to again employ, for Alice, the principle of the hand-held camera, which is very mobile, as in Mean Streets?

I wanted to start *Alice* like a Douglas Sirk melodrama, of the genre of *All That Heaven Allows*, then – bang! – move on to something else, reflect what was happening in this woman's head. She no longer has any security. But, actually, up until her husband's death, there's no hand-held camera filming. There are circular travelling shots that express her imprisonment.

After the accident, the danger looming is evoked by the hand-held camera in the scenes with Harvey Keitel. He's an interesting character. He drives like a maniac. But he's not a maniac. He has a certain intelligence, he's a bit of a psychopath and very quickly regrets what he's done. He knows he's losing her, but he can't do anything about it. In the film, all the emotions are very strong since the characters don't know what they've decided to do, they're in a state of transition. At the end, when they kiss in the café, it's like in an old Frank Capra film, but we get back to reality straight away.

But the ending in the café contradicts the meaning of the film. Once again we find the female character depending on a man and this dependence is not seen in a critical fashion by the staging. The viewer is back with his stereotypes.

For us, that was in keeping with the character. She's the kind of woman who needs someone else. In the same way that I've never been able to live alone, that I've always needed to live with a woman. That's my way of identifying with her. The most important moment in that scene is the one where Kristofferson sits down, looks at her and says to her, 'I think I understand you', and she nods. At that moment, both of them agree to try a new experience with mutual respect. It didn't feel right to me to let her go off alone with her son at the end. The applause is 'off' and it's a bit like the audience clapping. I like the scene up to the point they kiss, but I don't like the discussion that follows: I directed it badly.

In any case, the film ends on a note of uncertainty. Maybe they won't get on, but what I think is that you always learn something when you live with someone. I don't think, on the other hand, that the audience is going to think she's found Prince Charming. But I wanted her to really have a moment of happiness, so I laid it on, like in a good old-fashioned movie. It's absolutely not realistic given the context; it's deliberately overdone, for there are moments in life when you believe that this is it. And the feminists liked the film since Alice is like most of the women they try to get along to their meetings.

When she sings in the bar at her audition, the camera turns around her in a lyrical movement that's different from the style of the film.

It's both lyrical and satirical at once. Lyrical firstly in the sense that the more she sings, the more confidence she has in herself, the more the camera turns around her without showing the people listening to her. But when she sings 'Where or When', it becomes ironic because Alice is really like Ida Lupino in *The Man I Love*, she's right down there at the sentimental level, a 'torch-singer', as we say in America and, although she's totally sincere, we, the viewers, we smile. And when she sings 'I've Got a Crush On You' and meets Harvey Keitel, she also has confidence in herself and the camera turns around her and sticks with her. But neither Ellen nor I wanted to patronise the character. Ellen was keen for her to answer her son that there's nothing wrong with being a waitress. And in my own family, some women were waitresses.

How did Ellen Burstyn work with the boy?

The scene where he tells her a story is representative of their relationship! The boy had never acted before. And she, being trained in Lee Strasberg's Method School, needed concentration. And while she was concentrating, he kept watching her and asking her questions: 'How do you manage to cry like that?' And she kept asking him to leave her alone. He was a real nightmare but he played beautifully!

It's Ellen who recommended Lelia Goldoni to me – she was in Cassavetes's *Shadows* – and also Diane Ladd. She'd known them for years and I could play with everything that had happened between them all that time. I knew there'd been a long-standing rivalry between Ellen and Diane and that Ellen had always had better roles but it was only after the shoot that I found out they hadn't spoken to each other for ages. To the point where, in the toilet scene, things happen between them that stem from experiences they shared.

After Alice *you made a film about your parents.*

It's called *Italianamerican*. The film was made for the National Endowment of the Humanities in Washington and is part of a series of films for the bicentennial of the United States, each one being devoted to a group of immigrants – Jews, Italians, Irish, Greeks, Armenians, etc. Saul Rubin asked me to do the film for the government. Instead of the usual documentary with a commentary 'off', I had the idea of going to my place, in New York, to the Lower East Side, of dining as a family and asking my father and mother to talk about my grandparents. That way they could tell stories they'd already been telling me for years, only, this time in front of the camera, with the aid of family photographs.

It's an unaffected documentary, essentially made up of dialogue, that started out with immigration as its subject and that wound up being a film about two people who've lived together for forty years, about their relationship with each other and with me. It's a strange film and very funny. It lasts for forty-five minutes. It doesn't belong to me and I can't release it commercially. We filmed it in six hours and we edited it at the same time as *Alice*. Alec Hirschfeld, who worked in the second crew on *Mean Streets* and who is the son of Gerald Hirschfeld, the cinematographer on *Young Frankenstein*, did the 16 mm photography. After the presentation at the New York Film Festival, Don Rugoff wanted to buy the film but the government holds it and wants to reduce it to a half-hour film for television, which will empty it of its meaning.

What are you working on?

With a script of Paul Schrader's, I'm going to film *Taxi Driver* in June in thirty-four days, whereas I shot *Alice* in forty days. The character resembles Arthur Bremer, the man who tried to assassinate George Wallace. He's someone from the Midwest who arrives in New York and drives a taxi at night because he can't get to sleep.

New York is surreal; it's like Hell. There'll be lots of commentaries 'off'. It'll be a mixture of *Pickpocket*, Fuller and *Mean Streets*. I don't know how we'll get this mixture to work, but that's how I see the film. He falls in love with a girl who works for a candidate in the primary elections and who rejects him. The violence of the town and his experience with the girl drive him to kill the politician, but he won't do it and at the same time he'll start to want to save a thirteen-year-old prostitute who doesn't want to be saved and who's in with gangsters. He kills a few of them and becomes a hero in the papers. I hope Bernard Herrmann will do the music. After that, I'd like to do a musical comedy, *New York, New York,* which would be set in the 1940s with Robert de Niro, who'll have been the taxi-driver, and Liza Minelli. Later on we have another boxing project. If all goes well, I'll be booked up for years to come!

NOTES

1 Who is none other than Martin Scorsese himself!
2 This is *Who's That Knocking At My Door?*, which was presented at the Chicago Festival in 1967 under the title, *I Call First* and at Los Angeles in 1970 under the title, *J.R.*
3 See Note 2.
4 See Note 2.
5 In *Mean Streets,* Scorsese plays the role of Shorty, the killer in the backseat of the car driven by Richard Romanus.
6 'R' for 'Restricted', following the MPAA code (unaccompanied children are prohibited).

23 ANDREI TARKOVSKY

(1932–1986)

During the Moscow Film Festival of 1969, Andrei Tarkovsky made himself rather scarce. The resounding splash made by his second film, *Andrei Rublev*, when it was presented at Cannes two months earlier under the auspices of the French distributor, to the great displeasure of the Soviet authorities, couldn't fail to impose such intelligent reserve on him. Any publicity surrounding his name could only lead to dubious ambiguities or to fairly unscrupulous exploitation. This interview, conducted in the company of Luda and Jean Schnitzler, who also served as interpreters, is the only one he granted a foreign critic at the time and, as his film wasn't mentioned in the Soviet press, we can even claim that the following comments had an absolute value as unpublished material. It only took a few calls to Moscow to measure the importance that *Andrei Rublev* assumed in enlightened circles and the prestige that Tarkovsky enjoyed among the filmmakers of his generation as well as certain elders. His intellectual honesty, his gravity, the breadth of his inspiration, the patient labour that had taken up almost seven years of his life, earned him the respect of all. His oeuvre was like the standard for filmmakers who were trying to open up new paths and if it addressed itself to all, it is no less true that it expressed above all the difficulties and aspirations of the intelligentsia. I saw Tarkovsky again during his exile in Europe after the shooting of *Nostalgia (Nostalghia)* in Italy and before the shooting of *The Sacrifice (Offret)* in Sweden, the two last films in an oeuvre that, tragically, amounts to only seven titles. It felt to me as though he could not be consoled for having left his mother country, Russia. He was bound to his native land by all the fibres of his being and *Andrei Rublev*, the portrait of a painter, is to Russian cinema what Pialat's *Van Gogh* is to French cinema and Im Kwon-taek's *Drunk on Women and Poetry* (or *Painted Fire*) is to Korean cinema.

ON *ANDREI RUBLEV*

MOSCOW, JUNE 1969

How did you become a filmmaker?

I was born in 1932 in my grandfather's house on the banks of the Volga, where my parents had gone for a rest. Afterwards … a mass of details of no interest. I finished music school; I did some painting for three years – all this while I was a high school student.

Then the war broke out. We left for the place where I was born. When the war ended, I finished high school. In 1952, I went to the Moscow Institute of Oriental Languages where I learned Arabic. I left the Institute after two years because I realised it wasn't right for me… Do you know the Arab language? It's a mathematical language – everything obeys laws whereby root-words are introduced to achieve a new quality: a declension, or a new grammatical state. It was not for me. Then I worked for two years in Siberia doing geological prospecting, after which, in 1954, I went to the VGIK, Moscow film school, to Mikhail Ilyich Romm's atelier. In 1960, I finished the VGIK. My graduation work was the short, *The Steamroller and the Violin (Katok I skripka),* which is important to me because it's when I got to know my cameraman, Vadim Yusov and the composer Vyacheslav Ovchinnikov with whom I continue to work.

Did they, too, come out of the VGIK with you?

No, Yusov had finished his studies well before me and Ovchinnikov was winding up his studies at the Moscow Conservatorium. In 1962, I finished *Ivan's Childhood (Ivanovno detstvo)* and I began to think about the scenario for *Rublev (Andréj Rublev)* in collaboration with Andrei Konchalovsky. So we wrote it and the shoots were finished over summer, 1966. Right now I've just finished a script based on a novel by a Polish author, Stanislaw Lem, a science fiction novel whose title is *Solaris (Solaris);* I gave it to the Conseil Artistique who will deliberate over it. I'm counting on directing this film soon.

To specify the type of science fiction in question, is it a sort of social futurism?

No, this film doesn't include any social problem; it deals more with the problem of the relationship between morality and knowledge.

We know that Rublev *stirred up a fierce polemical debate that used as an excuse the historical inaccuracies that supposedly crept into your film. Among other things, it was said that Rublev and Theophanes the Greek could not have worked together because in reality there was a century between them. Now, specialist research seems to prove you right. But it is certain that we know very little about Rublev's life. Did you amass historical material on Rublev and extrapolate from it?*

As far as historical accuracies and inaccuracies go, I hesitate to talk about them. We moved a mountain of documents in a bid to be as close as possible to the historic truth. And we had a lot of advisers who saw what we were doing and accepted our point of view without reservations. On the other hand, I can tell you what I think about the whole thing: it's not a matter of historical inaccuracies here; it's about the fact that in making this film we have, to a certain extent, changed tack regarding our intentions. We didn't set out to meticulously reveal all the events of the era. What counted for us was to trace the path Rublev had taken throughout the terrible years he lived through and to show the way he overcame his era. That's why a certain condensation of events or, better still, the emphasis we introduced was indispensable in bringing out the difficulties Rublev had to overcome, moral difficulties in the first instance. Without that, you wouldn't get this feeling of triumph at the end, which is the film's whole *raison d'être*.

One other thing: Engels expressed a marvellous idea when he said a work of art soars to an even higher plane the more profoundly buried – better still, hidden – the idea behind it is. And that's the course we chose to take. We forced ourselves to submerge the idea in the ambiance, in the characters, in the conflicts between different characters. And that's why, perhaps, pure, direct history, without shifting to a secondary plane, is diluted in our film in the atmosphere of the times. It might well be an unusual approach to historical material, and that's what led certain people to talk about historical inaccuracy. I think that's the basis of the misunderstanding.

There is, in Rublev, *an almost systematic use of sequence shots, sweeping camera movements, that is the very opposite of the Eisenstein manner that people often cite, wrongly, in relation to your film.*

What can I say on the subject? I deeply respect S. M. Eisenstein, but it seems to me that his aesthetic is foreign to me and frankly counter-indicated. In *Battleship*

Potemkin and Eisenstein's earliest works, what's close to me is his attachment to detail and the 'realist pathos' of his shots, but not his principles of editing, his 'editing pathos', not at all. In his last films, like *Alexander Nevsky* and *Ivan the Terrible*, which are studio films, all he does is get down on film sketches drawn in advance – and that doesn't suit me at all as I have a quite different view of editing.

I consider cinema to be the most realistic art, in the sense that its principles rest on identification with reality, on the fixing of reality in each shot taken separately – something we found with Eisenstein in his very first films. As for the parallel people draw between me and Eisenstein, that's the business of critics. It's hard for me, myself, to judge my film from that perspective. In terms of the two principles, of the realism of the image on the one hand, and of the editing on the other, it seems to me that we're obliged to go our separate ways, here, Eisenstein and I... The specificity of film consists in fixing time, and film works with this captured time, as with a unit of aesthetic measure that you can repeat indefinitely. No other art has such a tool at its disposal. And the more realistic an image is, the closer it is to life, the more time becomes authentic, that is, not fabricated, not recreated... Obviously, it's both fabricated and recreated, but it comes so close to reality that it merges with it.

For the editing, my principle is the following: a film is like a river, the editing must be infinitely spontaneous, like nature itself, and what forces me to move from one shot to the next by means of editing is not the desire to see things up closer or to rush the viewer by introducing very short sequences. It seems to me that we are always in the riverbed of time, which means that to see more closely you don't have to see more close up. That's my opinion anyhow. And speeding up the rhythm does not mean making sequences shorter. For the very movement of the event can speed up and create a new sort of rhythm, just as a long shot can give the impression of being detailed – it depends on the way you compose it. That's why I'm in no way close to Eisenstein in these two precise cases. Furthermore, I don't consider the essence of cinematography to be a clash between two sequences that is supposed to give rise to a third notion, according to Eisenstein. On the contrary, the nth shot appears to me to be the sum of the first, the second, the third ... the fifth, the tenth ... plus $n-1$ shots – meaning, the sum of all the shots that preceded the nth one. And this is the way the sense of a shot takes shape – in relation to all those that have preceded it. That's the way I edit.

For me, the isolated shot in its unadulterated state makes no sense. It only derives its fullness from the fact that it's part of a whole. Better still – it already contains what will happen after. It's often incomplete – that's how it's shot – because you take into account what will happen after. I know that in one of his last letters, if not the last (Professor Svortzov from the VGIK told me about it), Eisenstein renounced his principle of montage and his way of fixing scenes of a theatrical nature on film, and he did so in the name of new ideas that are very close to mine. But he didn't have the time to apply them; death prevented him from doing so.

With Eisenstein, in Ivan *or even in* Nevsky, *the character is at the centre of the film. It seems that in* Rublev *the world looks as if it's being watched by the painter and that in the end the society in which Rublev lives plays a part at least equal to that of Rublev himself. That seems fundamentally different from the conception, let's say 'heroic', of Eisenstein's characters.*

The world as seen through the eyes of the hero is exactly what we wanted to achieve in our film. But, to have done once and for all with the vexed issue of my relationship to Eisenstein, let me just add that I read in the French press – and it gave me more pleasure than anything else I've read – that it was clear that I was working without turning my back on tradition. I'd go even further: I'm convinced that nothing serious can bear fruit without the bedrock of tradition and this for two reasons. The first is that you can't climb out of your Russian skin, the ties that bind you to your native land, to what you love, to what has been done in our past cinema history and our art, and therefore, in the end, to your own land. You can't free yourself from all that. That's the main reason I consider myself a traditionalist, a traditional director. The second reason is that the so-called 'new' cinema, which, in its search for the new, tries in principle to break with tradition, is in its essence experimental. It appears like a starting point of a future development of the art. Myself, I don't feel I have a right to experiment because I have a fundamentally serious attitude about what I do; I want to get a result first go. In an experiment, you never manage that.

Eisenstein was comfortable experimenting for, at the time, cinema was in its early days and for him it was the only course possible. Today, taking into account the established traditions in the art of film, we shouldn't be doing that anymore. In any case, as far as I'm concerned, I wouldn't want to experiment. It takes a lot of time and energy, and, well, I consider you should only work when you're certain of the outcome. An artist shouldn't do rough sketches anymore, shouldn't try putting down vague sketches anymore – he should only make films that matter.

Lastly, I'd like to say that if you must, at all costs, compare me with someone, let it be to Dovjenko. He was the first director for whom the problem of atmosphere was paramount, and he loved his land passionately. I share his love for my land, and for that reason I feel he's very close to me. Also, he made his films like vegetable plots, like gardens. He watered them himself, made everything grow with his own hands... His love of the land and of people made his characters grow, so to speak, from the land itself, they were organic, perfectly complete... And I'd love to be like him in that sense. If I haven't brought it off, that would upset me greatly.

We felt, watching Rublev, *that its true subject is the difficulty of being an artist, not only in relation to the surrounding milieu, but also in the quest for oneself. For me, it is a film about the responsibilities and the fate of the artist.*

It's possible that what you see as the main subject of the film is, in fact, in there. But that's more the result of the main aim that I set myself when we were shooting the film. For us, what mattered was to prove (why did we choose the character of Rublev?) that this difficulty is the essence of any artist of genius. What interested us was to ask the question: why is he a genius? And the result provided answers to the questions that you formulate after seeing the film. It's no accident if, alongside Rublev, the figure of Theophanes the Greek figures in the film. It's hard not to call him a genius since he was, in actual fact, a very great painter. And yet, when I think 'Rublev', I say 'genius' and when it's Theophanes, I no longer know... I can't say without hesitation that he too was a genius because I have my own criterion of genius. And this is what it consists of: an artist like Theophanes the Greek (who was indispensable to us in our film as a way of really bringing out our ideas) reflects the world, his work is a mirror of the world that surrounds him, his immediate reaction is to think that the world is badly put together, that men are perfidious and cruel, that they deserve to be punished even after their death, after the Last Judgement, if only because they're useless, depraved and guilty. All that is a normal reaction to the atmosphere of his day. When I'm frightened, that's how I react. I immediately condemn, not this force that is crushing me, but the defects that I attribute to people, to each and every person. Here, the analogy would be with Kafka.

But Rublev is opposed to Theophanes the Greek in our film. In what sense? Rublev, exactly like Theophanes, goes through the hardships of his day, the internecine struggles just prior to centralisation, when the civil war redoubled in intensity. The incursions of the Tartar hordes and all the difficulties that surged around him, he endured these at the same time as Theophanes the Greek, only, more intensely. Theophanes the Greek was able to adopt a more casual, a more philosophical attitude than Rublev, because he was a painter covered in glory, he wasn't a monk, he was generally more cynical, because he behaved like a foreigner, a traveller from Byzantium, who had more experience. His view of life benefited by a distancing Rublev was incapable of. Rublev sees and perceives this world with a lot of pain, but in spite of this he refrains from reacting the way Theophanes does. He goes further. He doesn't express the unbearable weight of the life that is his, of the world that surrounds him. He seeks a moral ideal that he carries within, and in that alone he expresses the hope of the people, their aspirations due to their living conditions, the attraction of unity, fraternity, love – all that the people are lacking and that Rublev feels is indispensable to those around him. This is how they anticipate both the unification of Russia and a certain progress, and sustain hope in a future that alone can sweep people along by opening up perspectives for them. That's what Rublev's genius consists in. His character, his image, are secondary. He's very complex, he suffers, and that's where his nobility lies; he expresses the hope and the moral ideal of a whole people and not only the subjective reactions of the artist faced with the world that surrounds him. There you have what mattered most to us.

It's precisely because of this that we contrasted Theophanes the Greek with Rublev; it's precisely because of this that we put Rublev through the temptations that weigh on his destiny; it's precisely for this reason that the finale for us is creation, the only possible way out for Rublev, the creation of the trends of a whole people symbolised by the street kid who melts down the bell. That was the important thing. All the rest is a mere consequence of what I've tried to explain to you: Andrei Rublev is obviously a man who knew how to express himself, express his ideal, and his genius is to have made this ideal coincide with the ideal of his people, whereas Theophanes the Greek is a man who, as we say in the East, 'sings what he sees'.

I felt you also wanted to say that there is no master in art, that art can't be taught, something that is especially marked at the end of the film.

In a certain sense what you say is right. But it's secondary because the essential thing for us was to say that experience is irreversible, that every man has his own experience. And I just can't believe that a man can refuse to take his experience into account. Individual experience is acquired with trouble, with effort, with a certain amount of suffering. It's only after being fertilised by such difficulties that experience can bear fruit. Your interpretation of the film in the sense that no one knows how to teach art is only one explanation of a symbol. For us, what mattered most was to show that experience is irreversible. For the whole history of Rublev's personal experience as an ideal character who knew how to hang on to his idea of morality throughout all the crises he went through, along with his love for the people and his faith in their future, culminates in the moment of his victory, a victory that is the result of his suffering. By the side of his people, he was able to go through all the hardships that, finally, forced him to believe what he believed from the beginning. But at the outset, his belief was purely intellectual. It was the ideal he'd been taught in his monastery, the teaching of Sergius of Radonezh, the founder and ideologue of the Trinity Monastery of St Sergius. He came out of there equipped with this science but without knowing how to put it to work. In real life, everything was different; everything was upside down. Towards the end he believed even more in this ideal, the ideal of love and of the union of men, solely because he'd suffered for this ideal, alongside his people. And it's then – at the end of the film – that his ideal becomes unshakeable to him and you know he'll stick to it come what may. This idea, besides, finds its symbol in the kid who says, in the last scene, that no one has taught him anything and that he was forced to do everything on his own. In this scene the kid is in a way Rublev's double as far as ideas go, he actually expresses the conclusion, the result of Rublev's life.

What's the meaning for you of the shift at the end of the film from black and white to colour?

The appearance of colour at the end of a film in black and white allowed us to set up a relationship, a correlation, between two different notions. Basically, what we wanted to say was this: black and white film is the most realistic for, in my view, colour film hasn't yet reached the realism stage, it still looks like a photo and, in any case, it's exotic. Man is physiologically incapable of being struck by colour in real life unless he's a painter, unless he's deliberately looking for relationships between colours, unless he's especially attracted by colour. Now, what mattered to us was real life, to tell it like it is. For me, real life is translated in film in black and white images. All the more so as we had to provide a relationship between art and painting, on the one hand, and art and life on the other. The relationship between the colour finale and the black and white stock was for us an expression of the relationship between Rublev's art and his life. Roughly speaking, it can be summed up like this: on the one hand, daily life, realist, rational, on the other, the convention for expressing this life artistically, a stage following a logical progression. We enlarged the details because you can't possibly translate painting, which has its own laws of composition that are as dynamic as they are static, into film, by making the viewer see in short sequences what you would normally only see by standing for hours on end contemplating the icons of Andrei Rublev. Here, no possible analogies. And it's exclusively by introducing details that we tried to create an impression of his painting as a whole.

Apart from that, we intended to lead the viewer through a succession of details to an overall view of the *Trinity*, as the highest point of Rublev's oeuvre, to take the viewer to this oeuvre, done with a sort of coloured theatricality, by having him wend his way from fragments to a whole, by creating a sort of flow of impressions. In the third place, this colour ending, roughly 250 metres of film, was indispensable to us in getting the viewer's attention, in stopping him from leaving the movie theatre straight after the last black and white images, and giving him time to detach himself from Rublev's life, to reflect, so that in looking at the colour and listening to the music we've imposed on him, a few general notions about the film as a whole can go through his head, and then he can fix, retrospectively, on certain moments of the story, the most important ones. In a word, it stops him shutting the book straight away. I think that if the film ended straight after the chapter, 'The Bell', it would have been a failure. We had to keep the viewer in the theatre at any cost. This is the purely theatrical function of that last colour sequence. We also had to provide an extension to the tale about Rublev's life, make people think about the fact that he was a painter, that he went in for precisely that sort of painting, that he bore what he lived through so that it could be expressed in certain colours... So we had to suggest all these thoughts to the viewer.

I'd like to add this: the film ends on the image of horses in the rain. Here we wanted to go back to the symbol of life because for me the horse symbolises life. That is perhaps my inner, subjective vision, but the fact is that when I see a horse, it feels to me like I have life itself before me. Because a horse is both very beautiful, very familiar and very suggestive of Russian life. Besides, lots of horses go by in our film. One example: in the balloon scene, there's a horse and it's the horse that looks pained by the death of the man who stole. Another horse perishes during the sack of Vladimir and so symbolises all the horror of violence. Everywhere in the film the horse is, so to speak, a witness to and a symbol of life. In reverting to the image of horses in those last shots, we wanted to emphasise that the source of all Rublev's art is life itself.

Is it intentional that the sky is missing in your film? You never see the sky, there's nothing but the land. There isn't even any wind...

That's completely subconscious. What interests me, always and above all, is precisely the land, I'm fascinated by the process of growth of all that comes from the soil, grows on it, trees, grass... All that reaches up for the sky. Which means that at home the sky only figures as the space that all that is born and grows in the soil stretches towards. The sky doesn't have any symbolic significance for me on its own. For me the sky is empty. There are only its reflections on the land, in the river, in pools of water, which interest me and are important to me. When the man is flying in the first scene of the film, you only see the reflection of the sky on the ground and for us that was a provisional visual solution. The relationship between the flying man and the ground was the only one that mattered to us; there was no relationship between him and the sky. Directing, moreover, in my view, is also a way of making events grow, the way in documentary films you can see the stems of plants shoot up out of the ground and grow before your very eyes – images that I can look at for hours on end. Similarly with directing... In general, I love the land. I never see mud; I only see soil mixed with water, the clay in which things are born. I love the land; I love *my* land.

I got the impression that there had been pictorial influences in certain scenes, in their visual design, in particular the way the crucifixion is seen in the distance like in a Bruegel painting. Were you actually inspired or is that a coincidence?

For that episode, you're right. That was in fact inspired by Bruegel, who I really love. We chose it, my cameraman and I, because Bruegel is close to Russians and makes a lot of sense to us. There's something very Russian about the way the planes are arranged in tiers, the way his pictures always have parallel action, with numerous characters each busily going about their own business. If Bruegel's manner didn't reverberate in the Russian soul, we would never have used him in our film – it just wouldn't have occurred to us ... But I think it's something of a defect in that scene because, the way we filmed it, it incites the intellectual viewer to make the analogy, which is pointless when all's said and done.

How did you get the idea of starting the film with the sequence featuring the flying man, a sequence that took everyone by surprise?

For us it was a symbol of boldness, in the sense that creativity requires you to give yourself completely. The fact that the man wants to fly before it became possible, or to melt down a bell without having learnt how to do it, or to paint an icon – all these acts demand that a man die as the price for his work of creation, that he dissolve into his work, give himself entirely to it. That's the meaning of the prologue – the man tried to fly and sacrificed his life in the attempt.

What was the nature of your collaboration with Konchalovsky while you were working on the script?

To start with we talked and agreed on the general outline of the film. Then we looked into how we'd structure the film. It was plain to us that it had to include a succession of 'short stories'. We wanted to get in an enormous cross-section of life. So we decided on the number of short stories we had to write, and their sum was to yield the film. Besides, for us these short stories are equally important in value. The general impression of the film is provided by the contrasts between the short stories, by the interference between their subjects and their visual resolution. Then ... well, then we wrote. We discussed the contents, the dialogue, the situations in great detail and one of us – which one, it didn't matter, we took it in turns – wrote it all down initially. Whoever did it passed it to the other one who added comments and this was repeated several times. In the end we'd really hit our stride so we worked together – one of us dictated to the other one who typed the text on the typewriter. Towards the end, the work process flowed on from the thinking process, which followed its course unobstructed, in perfect understanding between the two authors.

Why isn't the first prologue, which figures in the initial script (in place of the flying man, who opened the second part of the film in that version) and which was 'the fight in Koulikovo's field', in the film?

I took that scene out because it cost a lot and the studio wasn't in a position to grant me all the money needed.

There are numerous scenes of violence in your film and some of them were almost unbearable, for me; besides, at the 'Art of Old Russia' exhibition currently being held at the Hermitage, I found one of your shots in the icon of St George. What are the reasons for this use of violence?

There are three. The first is that, if you study any account of the times, by any historian whatever, you'll see that every page of the history of Russia before centralisation is literally dripping with blood. Literally! We re-enacted this to such a minimal extent that it sometimes felt like we were betraying the historic truth, in that sense. Later we realised that it was enough to see all this blood appear on screen, even in a small way, for us not to need to go any further. That is the first reason: the desire to be historically accurate. The second is that it was indispensable to our subject: the horrors that Andrei Rublev sees. And to the extent that our tale was very realistic, we couldn't limit Rublev's suffering to the moral plane alone and only show the reflection in his mind of the ordeals he underwent: that would have taken us somewhere else stylistically. Thirdly, as a director, I always count on the shock produced on the viewer: a break with prevaricating, with long explanations of the horrors of war, since all you need is a short naturalistic sequence to send the viewer into a state of traumatisation after which he'll believe absolutely what we show him later.

I consider film to be a realist art and I don't think it should be afraid of the direct impact it has on the viewer. On the other hand, it seems to me that 'literature', in the pejorative sense of the term, the principles of theatricality, weigh too heavily on film and force it to avoid realism as a mode of expression. Now the good Lord himself didn't want cinema to do that! So there you have my three reasons...

How did you recruit your actors? Were they big names or were there other criteria as well?

The main character had to be a man who'd never been seen before on film. Everyone imagines the role of Rublev in their own way, so we couldn't introduce someone who'd remind them, by association, of other characters he might have played previously. That's why we took a small-time actor from the Sverdlovsk Theatre who'd only ever played minor roles. Besides, after reading our script, which was published in the *Iskustvo Kino* review, he came, at his own expense, and tracked us down at Mosfilm and declared that he was the only one who'd know how to play Rublev. And after doing tests we were convinced that he was, in fact, the only one right for the role.

With the other actors, we chose them in terms of our aversion to all theatricality. My actors for me are divided into two categories: those who play a role essential to the story-line established by the script, and those who play the moods of the characters – in a way, they're the roles that don't get written because they're impossible to write. These include Rublev himself, the simple-minded woman my wife plays, Danila the Black (who you see in the first part of the film) played by Grinko and finally the Khan played by Bolot Bechenaleev (who played the first master in Konchalovsky's film). Those are my favourite characters because they're not conceived in terms of the plot but are created by the actors, by the moods, by the milieu they come from.

Can you tell us what sequences were cut from your film?

Firstly, no one cut anything from my film. I myself made the cuts. The first version of the film was three hours and twenty minutes long. The second, three hours and fifteen minutes. The very last version was reduced – by me – to three hours, six minutes. And I have to say – and I insist on this point, it's my most sincere opinion – that the last version is the best, the most successful, the 'right' one. And anyway, I only cut the tedious bits that viewers don't even notice. These cuts don't change the subject in any way, or the tones we were keen to keep, or the important lines in the film. In a word, we cut the stuff that was too long, which was something we hadn't calculated properly at the outset. We did effectively shorten certain scenes of violence, but only to create a psychological shock instead of a painful impression that would have gone against what we were aiming for. And all my comrades and colleagues, who, over long discussions, advised me to make my cuts, were right in the end. It took me a while to see it, but afterwards I could see that the rest of the film was more than enough to do the job I wanted the film to do. And I don't have any regrets about having brought the film down to its current length and shape.

You've been attacked for showing the Mongols to be handsome and exuberant in contrast with the miserable, depressed Russians. What was your intention?

It was important to give an exact idea of the Tartar occupation. That was translated like this: the Tartars were so sure of their strength – their domination lasted more than three centuries – that they conducted themselves like masters on this earth. And it was this that was so galling for the Russians. When people told me stories about the last war, the most frightening thing was seeing the Germans calmly walking around, without fear, on Russian roads; their calmness, their ordinary everyday behaviour was what frightened people the most.

And the crisis in the Tartar occupation, which was heralded in 1380, after the Battle of Kulikovo Field, consisted in the decline of a whole institution of enslavement. For 300 years, the Tartars had pillaged Russia in a perfectly systematic fashion; they'd invented a process that allowed Russians to re-amass their goods and chattels between two Mongol incursions so as to better profit from the pillage and sackings. The beauty of the Tartars in the film is intended to express their calm assurance, their confidence in their supremacy, for that's where the tragedy of the Russians' predicament lies. These people's task, after all, was to block the successive waves of barbarians with a dam that was fragile but indispensable to the safeguarding of Western civilisation. Besides, I don't think you can humiliate the enemy by showing him to be physically repulsive. You have to show the moral superiority of those fighting against him instead.

What do you like in cinema? Who do you like in cinema?

When I was making *Rublev*, I forced myself to be very hard and very no-nonsense. I tried for a sort of Olympian calm that, for me, is the most important quality of the art of directing. That might tell you how much I love Bresson. But the one I love most is Dovjenko. It seems to me that, if he'd lived longer, he would have been able to do many more interesting things still. There are several directors I love, but their place changes according to the moment: Dovjenko, Buñuel, Kurosawa, Antonioni, Bergman and that's it. Oh, and Vigo, of course, he's the father of contemporary French cinema. It's even annoying to see to what extent people plagiarise him, though it's true that they haven't yet managed to pinch everything from him.

And among the young Soviet filmmakers?

I really like Khutsiev, who has great potential. He's getting ready to do a film on Pushkin. I really like Alov and Naoumov – in parts. You say the young ones? You see, for me, with cinema, it's not the potential that counts; it's the result. That's why it's hard for me to answer. Our young directors are so young they haven't yet had time to make their best films. As for gazing into a crystal ball and telling the future... I'm not a critic. I don't know how to.

Is there any connection between Rublev *and the script you've just finished?*

It's a funny thing. Everything I've made and that I intend to make is always tied up with characters who have something to overcome, who have to struggle for the sake of this optimism that I cling to and that I'm always going on about. In other words, a man sustained by an idea passionately seeks the answer to a question and goes as far as you can go to understand reality. And he understands this reality thanks to his experience.

24 LARS VON TRIER

(1956–)

There was immense arrogance and at the same time staggering virtuosity in *The Element of Crime (Forbrydelsens Element)*, Lars von Trier's first film. It was selected right away for the Cannes competition of 1984, when its author was not yet thirty. Interviewed at the time by Hubert Niogret and myself, the filmmaker showed himself to be curiously less provocative than on screen and answered concisely. This would not always be the case later, when he would happily indulge in political or philosophical generalisations. He had a shaved skull, played at being a punk and asserted that he was a child of cinema. He claimed his film referred to the past, to film noir in particular, and its thematic was already in place: the presence of water, the morbid atmosphere, the sense of sin. The darling of the biggest film festival in the world, all his films (apart from *Epidemic*, which was programmed in a parallel selection) were entered in the competition until he took out the Palme d'Or for his most dubious film, *Dancer in the Dark,* a film that didn't stint on the showiest effects to catch the viewer's eye. At each stage of his career, von Trier has tried 'to shock the bourgeoisie', and he has succeeded without any difficulty, from *Europa*, a questionable reconstruction of post-Nazi Europe, through *The Idiots* – for which he invented the 'Dogma', a theory of directing (no static camera, no artificial lighting, no locating a film in the past) that was as arbitrary as it was ephemeral – to *Breaking the Waves*, with its undeniable physicality and attenuated lyricism but also sheer indulgence, making the woman a willing victim and a staging a truly perverse finale. With *Dogville*, the director changes register, resorts to a Brechtian aesthetic, but the pseudo-distancing reveals itself to be just another form of manipulation. There is cynicism in the nihilism of von Trier, who is well aware of the fact, a deliberate dazzling in his directing, but also the talent of a true magician and illusionist. Whatever reservations I may have about his later trajectory, I don't regret gambling on a gifted child who has left his mark on his era.

ON *THE ELEMENT OF CRIME*

CANNES, MAY 1984

You began with short films?

First I made two short films in 16 mm. I got together the money I needed working in the building trade, building houses. The first, *The Orchid Gardener*, which was thirty minutes long, was a strange film. The second, *Nantes la bienheureuse,* was filmed in French and very much influenced by Marguerite Duras. I showed my films at the Film School and they accepted me as a student. That was in 1978, and then I did three years there. I also made three shorts while I was there, with two students I'd met, the editor and the cameraman who then did *The Element of Crime* with me. The first of those shorts was called *Nocturne,* and it was an eight-minute film that was shown at the Biennale des Jeunes Artistes in Paris, but I don't know if anyone actually saw it. After that we made *The Last Detail*, a pastiche of gangster films, which was really terrible. The third film was *Images of The Liberation (Befrielsesbilleter)*, which won a prize at the Munich Film Schools Competition. It was an hour-long film about the final days of the Occupation of Copenhagen, seen from the Germans' side.

Wasn't your terrible pastiche of gangster films good training, though?

Absolutely. We made a lot of mistakes that stood us in good stead. The three last shorts were fiction films with actors. In the last one, there were colour experiments. The beginning was monochrome, and little by little colours entered the film. It was a technique that I was starting to work on with the cameraman, Tom Elling, and the editor, Thomas Gislason. We collaborated very closely as we wanted the film to be completely thought-out, 'edited', even before we got to the film location. We made a very precise storyboard, which already included the editing. Everything was written down. And *The Element of Crime* was filmed the same way. There were sixty sequences in the film, which meant a lot more than sixty drawings. It's an economical way of filming, but you can also have some nasty surprises. Let's say we filmed one on one, without a safety net. What you see in the film is what we filmed, no more, no less. But when you take that kind of risk, if it doesn't work, you have problems trying to get out of it in the final edit.

Where did the idea of the film come from, since it's not based on a pre-existing story?

There were several sources of inspiration, taken from different literary elements. I was telling Niels Vorsel, the scriptwriter, about three images, and I said to him: let's try and build a story starting from that... It was one scene at the start, one in the middle, one at the end. The first was the one of the harbour with the lake behind, and the cross, and the body of the first little girl. The second scene was the body of the second little girl and the dead animals. The third scene was the one with the boys diving with a rope tied round their foot. It was based on those elements that we developed the story. Those three scenes, which were very exciting in themselves, didn't actually add up to much in relation to the whole story. But that's how we worked.

Did you start developing the storyboard at the same time as the writing?

We wrote the script first, tackled the location finding, rewrote the script so that it would closely follow the sets we'd come up with. For instance, we found the sewer they travel along in a boat. In the script, there was just one scene between them in a bedroom. We told ourselves that we absolutely had to use that set, and so we stuck in the bedroom scene. I think that's a good method: first you make up the story, then you go out scouting for locations. I love natural sets outdoors. The studio doesn't interest me much, or only on condition of using it in a much more stylised manner, because it's very hard to combine the reality of the studio and a beautiful set.

It's curious that you like filming exteriors, because your film comes out of an expressionist style that favours the studio. Is money also an issue?

Yes, in a way, but I don't think you can do the same thing in a studio. I think there's a clash between the stylisation and the characters. There's a patina in a natural set that is very important to me.

Did you transform the sets you found?

Not much, and everything was shot in Copenhagen. And also because we didn't have enough money to go anywhere else. If you scout around for the right places, it's easy to find them.

What was your budget?

Eight hundred thousand dollars in 1983; roughly five million francs in 1984. Which is not much.

Why did you begin the story in Egypt? Because thrillers often begin in the Orient?

It's a 'cliché'. If you want to show a country, Europe, which is more than one country, it's good to have a guide for the film, someone who's come back from a far-off, non-European country. That way he sees Europe with the viewers, and it's good visually.

You speak of 'clichés'. But the whole film is a reworking of clichés.

I think that's one way of working. I don't know if a person is allowed to do it, but it's my way of doing it, to take this enormous material of films that have already been made, and use them in my own way.

Because films can no longer be innocent...

I think that's always been impossible.

The problem is using references without simply creating duplicates. The problem with American cinema today is that it makes imitations of films.

I agree with you, but reproduction doesn't seem interesting to me.

What is your cultural context: comics, the visual arts, film...?

As far as comics go, it's my cameraman who's really interested in them. My tastes lean more towards old masters, Hieronymus Bosch. People like him have something fundamental that plunges you into dream. They're the ones who try to show the beauty of chaos and catastrophe, nightmares, and so on. That's sort of what they attack in Denmark. Some say that it's a 'nasty film'. Why? I personally think it's the opposite. If such things exist in people's minds, as in reality, they ought to be shown. It's an obligation.

In film, you like Welles...

In some way my film is also a tribute to Orson Welles, since I really worked hard on the way each scene evolves to get information through and let the story unfold.

But all black and white cinema, too: the old German films, Fritz Lang. The greatest for me, though, is Carl Theodor Dreyer. I was 'brought up' on him.

It's pretty original for a Dane to like Dreyer...

I know. I've spoken to lots of people, journalists, who ask me if I'm bound by the Danish tradition. There is no Danish tradition. Dreyer was never bound by it. He's hated in Denmark. I spoke with the whole crew who made *Gertrud* and they couldn't care less. They've never taken him seriously. They made bad puns about him, which made me furious because I think that film is a masterpiece.

It's very different from your manner of filming. Dreyer is very composed, contemplative. He plays on theatricality.

I know what you mean, but strangely, I feel very close, for example, to what he wrote about film. He had very curious theories about colours, even if he only ever made films in black and white.

Why sepia?

Our aim was to make a 'noir' film such as we'd like to see today, but using colour stock. For me, very few people have managed to make 'noir' films in colour. Beforehand we did experiments with colours and we hit on the sodium lighting used on highways. We could have made a monochrome film and added a few white lights, and other sources of light like blue. I'd like to go further down that path but it's very expensive. You'd have to manufacture lamps ad hoc to get such a reduced colour spectrum. There is no film equipment adapted to this kind of lamp. Not everything was lit up in colour. For certain very wide shots, we didn't have enough coloured light, and we needed lots. So we sometimes filmed in black and white, and then we shifted to colour, but I wasn't too happy with this last method. I prefer the sequences where we were able to use coloured light in a stylised way. We had an ideal vision of the way the film needed to look, and we tried to achieve it.

In your press conference, you were rather polemical in relation to your contemporaries or the preceding generation, like Godard...

I really liked Godard's films when I saw them a few years back, but today they're hard to watch, whereas other films, like Dreyer's, you can watch over and over again, endlessly. Different films age in different ways.

And today's filmmakers…

Obviously I like Tarkovsky enormously. I'm starting to see what I like in him and what I don't like. That's the way one should work with one's ancestors. I think I'd like to make tougher films, sometimes I find that his films are too soft. But *Mirror (Zerkalo)* is an admirable film, truly revolutionary.

I like Wim Wenders a lot. I've just seen Syberberg's *Parsifal,* which I like, even if it's not what I'd like to make as a film. In the United States, I like Coppola.

Is the use of English an additional reference to film noir?

I think it's important to be loyal to your ancestors. With lots of films today, there's no loyalty; people don't think they have ancestors. They don't want to be connected to any film culture whatever. You have to bear in mind what went before, use what's good in all that. The use of Danish would have been too concrete and would have removed the European aspect. On top of that, in Denmark the film would have had a fairly limited audience, not big enough to finance a film like this. We had no choice but to try to get out of this overly narrow niche market and get a foot in the international market.

How did you choose the actors: Michael Elphick for Fisher, Esmond Knight for Osborne, Jerold Wells for Kramer?

We looked at lots of photos. I love it when the characters resemble the sets, when you can see that they're worn. Behind the ones I chose, you can sense a whole film culture in addition, a whole history. Esmond Knight has done such a lot of films, from Hitchcock to Renoir (*The River*). We knew he was blind and that the performance he'd give us would be unique. He has a fantastic face.

With Michael Elphick, I'd seen him on television somewhere. He's done a lot of theatre, often comic stuff. He's a very successful actor, pretty costly, which was not without posing money problems for us, but as it fitted into his schedule, he agreed to do it for very little.

These kinds of actors lend more weight to your characters than if you just took new faces out of context.

How did you work with them?

We didn't have any rehearsals. Everything was dubbed. We filmed with a guide track, while playing music, lots of Wagner, during the takes. In the beginning, they were surprised, then they really liked it. 'Ambient' music is also really good for the crew. A certain kind of music, a certain kind of ambiance of colours, produces a certain kind of work, with or against the elements.

The guide track allowed me to give indications for the actors' movements during takes. Sometimes I didn't rehearse the shots. 'Here are your lines, you move from here to there. Off you go.' You can get away with that with very professional actors. They like the 'challenge' of being directed as you're shooting.

Did you improvise much in the space?

Not at all, every movement was drawn on the storyboard. I like working within a very planned framework. One good thing about using a guide track, post-synch, is that you can work at two different tempos. In the filming, what we were looking for was control of the colours, the visual elements, which you can achieve if everything is well thought out. And at the post-synch stage, you can control the sound. You can get two different performances from the actors, one based on the filmed image and one based on the post-synch sound. You can balance one with the other. If an actor has 'overacted' in a take, you can contain the effects of his performance at the post-synch stage, and vice versa.

But for Edmond Knight, that must have been a problem?

It was a very big problem and we didn't always manage to do what we were trying to do. At the post-synch stage we counted: one, two, three, four, five, over to you. During the shoot, we had other problems. We placed guides on the ground or someone guided him. That's why there are very few full-length shots of him.

Do you think that because of the prevalence of television, people are always looking at realistic images, whereas cinema is more creative, less realist?

Yes, and also we don't need to be so concerned with the story. I see more and more films that are solely concerned with the narrative and, looking at it that way, I think that in the end there will soon be nothing but narratives.

It's more the plot than the narrative.

Yes, the plot.

What is the narrative of your film, as opposed to its plot?

When I was at the Film School, I had a drama teacher who had a very interesting theory about the filmic form of funny films. He made a distinction between the 'dramatic' Anglo-Saxons and epics. Here we have a form somewhere between the two, the characteristic feature being that the main character always has the time to stop and look at things, like Chaplin, to be fascinated by the world. Through him the audience is going to feel the same thing. I don't know if it's the narrative, but I think it's a 'funny' film.

In your shorts, were you just as interested in this very visual writing that is a modern feature of film?

I'd like to look at this film as a supermarket where you take the things you need from what's on the shelves, but there's a lot more there. You can take other things. There are many ways of making films. The ones that look like they're made for television have no future as far as I'm concerned.

When you wrote the script, did you have all the characters in your head or did you add some afterwards?

That's perhaps the weakest part of the film, when you start running all over the place and you leave psychology a bit too far behind. That's a defect of the script. I think one of the most interesting scenes is the one where Fisher and Osborne meet for the second time, because there's a tension, thanks to a good mix of images and the actors' performances. The four main characters were in the first version of the script.

Were the young men jumping with the rope also part of it?

Yes, because that was one of the three images that served as a starting point for the script. And I really loved filming that scene. It took ten days for two minutes of film, in a shoot that lasted ten weeks. In that sequence there were a lot of travelling shots, camera movements, rain and things that are hard to carry out.

Do you have a project going at the moment?

With the same scriptwriter and the same technicians, a project on the Second World War, very freely adapted from *The Divine Comedy*. That's a period where there's an enormous amount of material to explore. It's a subject so serious that people are frightened of tackling it. I think my generation has the freedom to approach the Second World War and to make a real film about it and I'd like to do it. One part would take place in a concentration camp, which, in my opinion, no one has ever really shown in a feature film. The view of the concentration camps in *Sophie's Choice* is completely crazy, because in fact they didn't give a toss about showing a concentration camp in an emotional manner.

Is it possible to show that? It's exactly what Resnais tried to do in Nuit et Brouillard (Night and Fog).

That was a very good film. Maybe it's not possible but we ought to try. There shouldn't be any limits such as this 'this shouldn't be told.'

You might create a sort of fascination. Don't you think that that type of image is so strong that it can betray the motive for undertaking this kind of film?

To betray means leaving things in the dark, because that's an insult to the pain and suffering. For thousands of years, art has shown pain, always. Today in our Western world, maybe we're so civilised we don't want to do that. We want to escape things by forgetting about them. To me it's insulting not to use the things that matter. That became clear to me a few years ago. I went to Dachau. It's impressive. My parents were Jewish. They fled to Sweden. They were public servants. I didn't go through that. But I feel it intimately. We shouldn't have such limits. Even if I make a film that causes a sensation, due to such suffering, one that exploits it, the film is there, in your mind. You work with these things present in your mind, and that's better than not seeing them, than forgetting them. It's dangerous to say: this can't be shown in a film.

25 ZHANG YIMOU

(1950–)

The most important film director of the Fifth Generation of Chinese cinema, along with Chen Kaige, whose cinematographer he was on Kaige's first two films, *Yellow Earth (Huang tu di)* (1983) and *The Big Parade (Da yue bing)* (1986), Zhang Yimou suffered, as Kaige did, during the Cultural Revolution, doing three years' labour in the country followed by seven in a factory. He enrolled in the Beijing Film Institute rather late in the day as a result. Camera work was thus his first job (though he is also an excellent actor, as he shows in his performance in Wu Tianming's *Old Well*) and this has had a considerable influence on his directing, which emphasises visual values and always has done, from his first film, *Red Sorghum (Hong gaoliang)*, which took the Golden Bear at the Berlin Festival of 1987. That was the film that revealed Gong Li, whom he discovered and who was to become his wife, and who starred in most of his following films, such as *Judou* (1990) and *Raise the Red Lantern (Dahong denglong gaogao gua)* (1991), whose sets, a dry cleaner's in the former film, an aristocrat's mansion in the latter, allowed Zhang Yimou to give his full measure as a colourist and as an orchestrator of light and shadow. My meeting with him took place at a turning point in his work, the amazing *The Story of Qiu Ju (Qiu Ju da guansi)*, which took the Golden Lion at Venice. In this film, for the first time, Zhang tackles a contemporary subject, displaying an unexpected realism and exalting the struggle of a peasant woman who fights to defend her husband's honour, which has been trampled underfoot by the authorities. Not as political as Chen Kaige, in his subsequent films, Zhang was to evoke, often ambiguously, certain defects in the Chinese system that are all too easily corrected in his optimistic fictions. Today he seems to accept to accept the role of well-behaved film director, as proved by *Hero* (2002), otherwise brilliantly made, where the sacrifice of a rebel and the death sentence meted out to him are shown as a necessary step in maintaining the greatness and unity of the state. *Qiu Ju* now looks in retrospect to have been a peak in his oeuvre and a fresh demonstration of the privileged relations between a filmmaker and his beloved wife, in the tradition of Griffith and Gish, Sternberg and Marlene, Rossellini and Bergman, Antonioni and Vitti, Godard and Karina.

ON *THE STORY OF QIU JU*

VENICE, SEPTEMBER 1992

You've often claimed that your films started off with an image. Is this also true of Qiu Ju?

As always, I started with a novel, but this time I wanted to do something different. I wanted to change styles and, to start with, I focused my attention more on the story than on the images. After reading the book, which I loved, I tried to figure out what the best way of telling it on screen would be and I realised that the camera had to be at man height, that it had to be itself a character among the rest. So almost half the film was shot with a hidden camera to get the greatest possible spontaneity. The easiest solution for the actors not to be conscious of its presence would have been to film using high angle shots, but I didn't want to do that. The camera had to be on the same level as the characters. It was extremely hard since amateurs then tend to look into the lens. The film's opening shot gets the atmosphere I wanted pretty well. You see people walking, coming towards us, and, little by little, you see Qiu Ju. I wanted to tell a simple ordinary story about simple ordinary people by avoiding any emphasis.

For Raise the Red Lantern (Dahong denglong gaogao gua) *you had Zhao Fei as cinematographer. This time did you choose your two cinematographers, Chi Xiaoning and Yu Xiaoqun, in terms of the new method of filming?*

Actually, there's a third man, Liu Hong Yi, who isn't listed in the credits. First, I needed several directors of photography because I was filming with several cameras. I also wanted people who had experience on documentaries. Chi Xiaoning had also done loads of advertising films.

Yet you still give just as much importance to colours, with red dominating in particular, as so often, repeated as it is in capsicums, corn, Qiu Ju's red dress.

I can't say I controlled the colours deliberately as much as in the past. I shot the film in north China where red is a dominant colour. And, on the other hand, the film was made over the two months before and after the New Year. It was in January and February this year. And during that period, red is used a lot for festivities. So it was very realistic. The people who belong to this northern culture, which is known as the culture of the Yellow River, really like strong vibrant tones for reasons that escape me.

What appealed to you in Chen Yuanbin's novel and how did you work with Liu Heng, your scriptwriter?

Chen Yuanbin is a young writer who'd already had things published before, but this work is his first real novel, and it won this year's prize for the best Chinese fiction, as well. What I like most in him is the naturalness, the fluidity of his style. He's a born storyteller. The literary critics seem to think the novel kicks off a new way of writing in China. As I myself wanted to change my approach radically, it seemed to me that his material would suit me particularly well. The first change we made with Liu Heng was to shift the action from the south (the novel is set in the Anhui region) to the north. I thought in fact that to bring off this kind of film, I needed to know the setting extremely well. So I located it in the province I was born in and where I grew up, so I could find my way around and have a real rapport with the people, knowing their language, their dialect. The issue was not just to tell a story but to know how the people move, how they eat, how they talk. We had to be very precise. I worked easily with Liu Heng. First he did an adaptation, then I changed a certain number of things, and then he worked up a third version of the script. That's the way we'd already collaborated together on *Judou*.

The title of the novel, Wanjia susong, *is different from the title of the film,* Qiu Ju da guansi.

The book's title means 'the lawsuit filed by a family', which is very literary, whereas the film's title literally means 'Qiu Ju lodges a complaint', which is taken more from the spoken language. It also puts the emphasis on the character of the woman, whose first name is very common in the countryside throughout northern China. In the novel her name is Qiu He Peng.

During the Cultural Revolution, you were forced to go and work in the country for three years. In what way did this forced activity allow you, the son of a doctor, to get to know the peasant world?

I learned a lot during that period. I sowed, I planted seeds, pruned branches off trees, brought in the harvest, turned the fruit of the soil into food, learned how to cook. I also looked after cows, horses, donkeys. In the film, there are lots of things that were part of my experience in the country. In fact, I was sent to a place very close to the one where I shot the film, about an hour away.

Are you Qiu Ju, to the extent that you weren't allowed to go to film school because you were past the age limit and that, for a long while, you fought to the point of calling on the Minister of Culture to get justice, your lateness being due to the Cultural Revolution?

It's not important to know whether I'm Qiu Ju or if her story recalls my own since this story is perfectly banal, it happens constantly in China. You never know who you should speak to, what you should do, where you should go. To start with, most problems aren't important, they only become important because of how the bureaucracy works and the ordeals you have to go through. I wanted to depict this very banal situation with humour. Before coming to Venice, I'd already found myself asked that question in my own country. I answered that what Qiu Ju wants – and she uses the word in the film – is *shuafa*, a Chinese word that means, not an excuse, but an answer, an explanation, some clarification. With *Judou* and *Raise the Red Lantern*, I had the same experience. The films were never distributed and no one ever provided any *shuafa* as to why they were banned. It's the same thing, in the novel and in the film: the lawyer helped her a lot, he worked for her, and, in the end, he managed to get the village chief put in jail, but no one took the trouble to find out exactly what Qiu Ju wanted.

She doesn't react to what the public scribe tells her, whereas his words announce the conclusion of the story since he informs her that he's managed to send a certain number of people to their deaths.

In China, this character is everywhere, since many people are still illiterate. But there's also quite a bit of black humour in the presentation of that scene. In China, at the end, the audience is doubled up laughing, when they learn that the village chief has been incarcerated, since they'd read the scene with the public scribe as a bad sign.

The film shows that the idea of justice is relative, as the nature of a verdict changes over time; Qiu Ju no longer has the same relationship with the village chief after she has her baby. Is absolute justice impossible?

There is a huge discrepancy between the family justice she's clamouring for, the village being one big family, and the justice meted out by the court. She just wanted the village chief to conduct himself properly with her, which he winds up doing by helping her give birth – and when, at the end, he's arrested and taken away, it's the whole administrative machine that spirals out of control and heads off in the wrong direction. The comedy stems from the discrepancy inherent in the situation. You have to understand that this type of Chinese village, as I've already said, is one big family. Qiu Ju wanted justice at a particular moment, later she's got nothing to do with it.

Do you mean to say both that the authorities wind up doing justice but that the individual must fight anyway, otherwise he'll never get anything?

Yes. If you don't ask questions, no one will give you an answer, ever. You have to fight endlessly for something to happen. In China, for the smallest problems to be fixed up, you have to go at it twenty times, spend years at it. Among officials, it's not that anyone really makes a mistake, but at the end of the day, there's never any answer. Making demands is the beginning of democracy. With this film, I wanted to say that every Chinese person – and not only the peasants – has to do the same thing: fight to win the case and find himself by filing a lawsuit in order to obtain his aims.

Even if they regret, in the end, as Qiu Ju does, ever having taken all that on?

It's true she's unhappy at the end, but that's only because she didn't get what she wanted: an explanation. The sense of the last shot – a freeze frame – is to ask yourself what the law can really bring people. Is this justice? If someone wrongs you, should you wrong them back? Is that really an answer?

How many professional actors play in the film and how did you integrate the amateurs?

Gong Li and the actors playing the husband, the policeman and the village chief. I got them to live in the village for the two months prior to filming, so they could live with the people, learn their dialect, read the same things, dress like them. That was the best way of integrating them: getting them to share the daily life of the inhabitants of the village. The latter had never seen a camera or a microphone, which posed problems. So I decided to familiarise them with the equipment by walking around with it in front of them for a few weeks. This was necessary since not all the sequences were going to be filmed with an invisible camera. As I couldn't ask the locals to act, I got the professional actors to behave like peasants. It was up to them to make the compromise, and by reversing the roles I was completely free to get on with the job. For the scenes we rehearsed, I avoided projectors, used natural light as much as possible and made sure the technical crew was reduced to a minimum.

Did you have to do lots of takes because of the many non-professionals involved?

I did have to go through a lot of film, in fact. For ten takes, there was maybe only one that was usable. For a single shot we sometimes worked all night, the following day and part of the day after that.

For the scenes shot with a hidden camera, we'd set up a wooden partition in the street. Then, the night before the shoot, the cinematographer would set himself up behind this partition and stay there without moving, without even going to the toilet, until midday, when the animation was at its peak. Through a hole we'd made in the wood, he'd watch what was going on. Then, suddenly, we'd take away the board and he'd photograph the scene. Of course, sometimes, someone would look into the lens, and we'd have to find another camera and start all over again in another spot!

Did the fact that you shot a lot of film draw out the editing?

Not really, since I edited the film while we were filming. I like working that way. I film during the day and I edit till three o'clock in the morning.

The character of Meizi, Qiu Ju's sister-in-law, emphasises, through her amazement, Qiu Ju's energy and determination. Not being an actress, in what way was her experience new for her?

It was the first time she'd been into town. She lived in the village and had never had enough money to make the trip. Indeed, from the narrative point of view, she serves to bring out Qiu Ju's strength. And since Qiu Ju is pregnant, she needs to have someone with her. So there's a logical reason for her to be there. Similarly, her silence expresses the astonishment she feels faced with her sister-in-law's conduct, but it's also typical of country people, who don't talk much.

The film is a co-production between China and Hong Kong. The previous film was produced in Taiwan by Hou Hsiao-hsien. How do these productions get up between Chinese companies?

I'm not involved in finding the finance and I don't know what part the different producers play. I get paid a salary, that's all.

What made you choose a contemporary subject for the first time?

The same reason I gave at the beginning. I wanted to go down a different road, adopt a different style. One of the most obvious decisions to express this need for change was to choose a contemporary subject since all my other films are set in the past.

You acted in Wu Tianming's film, Old Well (Lao jing). *How did that experience count in your work with the actors?*

It was important to me to perform before I crossed over to directing, because it's only when you've been an actor that you can understand what the work represents. It was very useful to me afterwards in directing my performers to know what they were feeling inside. In China, when we're filming, the actors don't always feel comfortable because of the lack of organisation on set. Having felt that myself allowed me to make up for their deficiencies and to improve their performance through the editing or by being better organised. I think the most important part of a film is the actor: everything should contribute to them being the best they can be, from the music to the photography and editing. The whole crew should be at their service, because at the end of the day, it's through the actor that the film says something to the audience. There are several ways to shoot a film, different styles that can date over time, but what allows a film to last – or not – is the performance of the actors. The actor alone allows us to find out what human beings are really like.

By training you were a cinematographer and nothing pertaining to the visual realm was foreign to you. Your work as an actor gave you access to another dimension of cinema: life, characters.

Of course, having been a director of photography was important in my training as a director, but having acted was the decisive experience for me. The cinematographer also has to work in relation to the actor and not the other way round. That's why I'm a director today; I like collaborating with my head cameraman to get him to speed up so the actor's not made to wait. I use my past experience to avoid those long periods between shots that spoil an actor's performance. Having myself been both an actor and a cinematographer helps me create a convivial atmosphere where we can film without dead time.

You also performed alongside Gong Li in Ching Siu Tung's A Terracotta Warrior. *Could you tell us about your work with your favourite actress?*

I acted with her just before directing *Judou,* and she was the main actress in four of my films. I work the same way with her as with all my actors. I like to leave a month free before the start of the shoot to discuss the script in detail with them, so they can ask questions and also make suggestions. I like to hear what they have to say. During those few weeks of preparation, I also get them to wear the clothes they'll be wearing in the film so they can get used to them, to do their hair the way they'll be doing it during the shoot. That way they become more familiar with their characters. About ten days before the camera starts rolling, we do rehearsals that I record and then I show them to them on cassettes. Once the filming has started, I put the script aside and I don't talk about it with them anymore, unless it's about important and complex scenes that we might need to discuss the evening before. At the end of the day, I want them to relax and to hang out among themselves because I don't want to impose my point of view too much on them. There are two sorts of actors: the cerebral ones, who think a lot before tackling a role and prepare every scene in detail, and the emotional ones, who enter into their characters and act instinctively. Gong Li is one of the latter. That's why, once she's gone over her preparation with me and I've explained to her clearly what I want, I leave her alone and let her go with whatever she comes up with.

Even though the four films of yours that we've seen are very different, the female lead is often strong and takes her destiny in hand.

Even though men and women have more equal relationships in China today, feudalism ruled my country for thousands of years and men have always held a dominant position. That has stayed imprinted on people's minds, particularly in the countryside. My films are always based on novels that have a strong female character at the centre, and I think that from a narrative point of view, that's necessary to set up a contrast with this feudal mentality. And since I'm faithful to the books I adapt, as well...

But you chose the books!

The best way of highlighting a protagonist is to place him in a difficult situation, in a complex environment. External pressure brings out his personality, which has to be strong if he's to control his destiny. The new Chinese literature that describes an oppressive context proceeds in this fashion, in any case. The female characters who are in an inferior social position, but who have more intelligence and sensitivity than the males, are particularly good at moving the audience. It's also important and new for Chinese filmgoers to see in action a woman who's her own mistress. This is a recent phenomenon in Chinese culture.

There is also in your films the presence of a superior authority, the husband in Judou, *the master we never see in* Raise the Red Lantern *and in* Qiu Ju, *a Chinese woman, the judicial authority figure.*

One relationship has always interested me and it's the one that exists between a fragile personality, who is nonetheless strong, and a powerful force, such as is exercised in these three films. Women in China have always had to listen to what others say to them or do what they're ordered to do. Women who don't knuckle under are rare. But I think there are more and more women today who have the strength and the courage to stand up to the powers that be. It seemed like a good moment to show this at a time when quite a few women are taking stock.

Does Su Tong, the novelist in Raise the Red Lantern, *belong to the same generation as the author of* Qiu Ju?

All the writers I've adapted are more or less the same age. The author of *Red Sorghum* was thirty-two or -three when he wrote the novel, the author of *Qiu Ju* was thirty-four, Su Tong twenty-eight and Chen Yuanbin thirty-six. They form a new generation, different from the preceding ones in style and themes.

They look at society from a modern angle, even if they're talking about the past. They've abandoned propaganda and adopted a human standpoint in observing society from the inside. They all started in the 1980s.

Are they movie fans?

There are about ten of them in all and they're extremely flexible culturally. They're particularly interested in cinema and take part in roundtables on films. Every time I wrap up one of my films, I organise a screening where the writer is invited to come along and discuss it in public. We Chinese filmmakers have very close relationships with these new writers. They're even friends and they've helped me a lot. I also think that the cinema has influenced their literary output. Then again, you have to take into account the fact that the films based on their works have brought them to the attention of a wider audience, not only in China but also in Taiwan, Hong Kong, Japan and the West. That's stimulating for an artist. What's also interesting is that since these films have been such a success abroad, novelists are just as keen to see their books adapted to the screen as filmmakers are to acquire the rights to a new high-quality novel.

Exactly when were Judou *and* Raise the Red Lantern *finally allowed to be shown in China?*

Judou is now showing and *Raise the Red Lantern* will be released in October. I think both films will be very successful, especially as we made 200 copies of each of them, which is pretty unusual. *Red Sorghum*, for instance, only had 100. There was a première of *Judou* in Shanghai, with Gong Li there, for several thousand viewers held in check by fifty or so police. I have to say everyone's curiosity was aroused by the Oscar nomination in Hollywood, by the waves it made abroad and by the fact that the film was held back for so long. That's the way it always is in China: if you tell people they can't see something, they want to see it even more.

How do you explain the authorities' change of attitude?

No one has ever really explained it to me. In China, particularly with co-productions with Hong Kong or overseas in general, the process is like this: you have to submit the script for the censors' approval, then once the film's finished, you have to go before the censor once again to get his approval. The scenario of *Judou* had been passed, but the censors found that the film was different, without, however, telling me how. That's really the story of Qiu Ju! I think it has a lot to do with the speech Deng Xiaoping delivered recently, which relaxed the atmosphere in China. But no member of the censorship board wanted to take responsibility for giving me an answer. All that happened, I think, is that the distribution office submitted a request document to bring out the two films and the board just contented itself with putting its stamp on it without any other form of process. It was a purely formal procedure. We just had to wait! That's the reason why *The Story of Qiu Ju* makes people in China laugh so much: everyone has had the same experience. At least, that was the reaction of the public at the first festival of Chinese films, where it won the Grand Prix, and also at the previews and the press screenings. Around 200 copies will be distributed in October.

What relations do you have with the Chinese filmmakers of Taiwan, like Hou Hsiao-hsien and Edward Yang, and do you see any differences in your approach to cinema?

The first time I met those two was in Hong Kong in 1985. It was also there that I discovered their films, and I immediately thought they were great. I also found out they liked Chen Kaige's *Yellow Earth (Huang tu di)*. We're close even though we don't see each other often, sometimes not for over a year at a stretch. Generally we meet up at film festivals. To see your respective films is a discovery because for a long while we had no idea what was happening on screen, just across the water. I don't think there are mutual influences and when we meet, it's more like a gathering of friends than a discussion between film directors. But naturally everyone wants to see what the others have been doing.

The films of Taiwan deal more with contemporary subjects, use fewer metaphors (with the exception of Qiu Ju *of course), than the films of China, and stylistically they use more sequence shots and depth of field.*

The films of mainland China are influenced by the literary tradition, which puts stories together using history and metaphor. So more often than not, our films are set in the past. Taiwan is a relatively new country, less weighed down by history. As far as their style goes, I think that's linked to their relationship with Japanese cinema. They were occupied by Japan for fifty years and the

Japanese influence has permeated their way of thinking. Our cinema, on the other hand, has been subject to two influences, first the Chinese literary and artistic tradition, then Western cinema. For my part, I'd have trouble pointing to precise influences, but for my generation, who were at film school between 1979 and 1982, we were very much exposed to the new wave and to Italian neo-realism. And also to American movies. But when we left school, we went to the country, to places most representative of our culture, and we tried to find sources of inspiration there that were ours while at the same time holding in our minds these images from the Western films that we saw while we were at film school.

INDEX